**Tell no lies; claim no easy victories.**
*Amilcar Cabral*
*Party Directives, 1965*

Demonstration organized by Stop the Apartheid Rugby Tour, New York City, 1981. *Photo by David Vita.*

# No
# Easy
# Victories

## African Liberation and American Activists
## Over a Half Century, 1950–2000

Edited by

**William Minter, Gail Hovey, and Charles Cobb Jr.**

**AFRICA WORLD PRESS**
Trenton | London | Cape Town | Nairobi | Addis Ababa | Asmara | Ibadan | New Delhi

## AFRICA WORLD PRESS
541 West Ingham Avenue | Suite B
Trenton, New Jersey 08638

Book and cover design:    Saverance Publishing Services
                          (www.saverancepublishing.com)

Front cover photos: top, David Vita; center, courtesy of Stephanie Urdang; bottom, Rick Reinhard. Back cover photo: David Vita.

Library of Congress Cataloging-in-Publication Data

No easy victories : African liberation and American activists over a half century, 1950-2000 / edited by William Minter, Gail Hovey, and Charles Cobb Jr.
      p. cm.
   Includes bibliographical references and index.
   ISBN 1-59221-574-2 (hardback) -- ISBN 1-59221-575-0 (pbk.)
   1. Africa--Relations--United States. 2. United States--Relations--Africa. 3. Political activists--United States--History--20th century. 4. Political activists--Africa--History--20th century. 5. African American political activists--History--20th century. 6. Africa--History--Autonomy and independence movements. 7. National liberation movements--Africa--History--20th century. 8. Civil rights movements--United States--History--20th century. I. Minter, William, 1942- II. Hovey, Gail, 1940- III. Cobb, Charles E., Jr., 1943-

DT38.N58 2007
303.48'2730609045--dc22

                        2007020577

The mythical Sankofa bird, from the Akan people of West Africa, always flies forward while looking back. It holds an egg symbolizing future generations in its mouth. The Sankofa bird reminds us that we need to understand the past in order to move forward to build the future.

Paul Stookey and Mary Travers of Peter, Paul, and Mary sing in front of the South African embassy as Randall Robinson and Desmond Tutu look on, January 8, 1986. *Photo © Rick Reinhard.*

# Contents

# Foreword
## by Nelson Mandela

The title of this book, *No Easy Victories*, is well chosen. Taken from the great West African leader Amilcar Cabral, it reminds us that the people of Africa, struggling to end colonialism and gain majority rule, paid, and continue to pay, a heavy price. Some, like Cabral himself, were killed before achieving the prize of victory and they are too little remembered. Others, like me, were able to complete our long walk to freedom and have remained in the public eye. Despite the best efforts of the apartheid regime to make me invisible, I walked out of prison after 27 years into the glaring light of television cameras that projected my release around the globe. This was proper, for my release was the result of developments in South Africa, strengthened by the demand for my freedom from a worldwide anti-apartheid movement.

The editors and authors of this book have undertaken to tell the story of the American involvement not just in the anti-apartheid movement, but also in the broader anticolonial movement that is decidedly less well known. As it recounts five decades of activism, it explores the relationships between anticolonial and anti-apartheid movements in Africa and struggles for justice within the United States.

The Americans we trusted most were those who understood that their civil rights movement and the anti–Vietnam War movement, for example, were part of the same battle we waged in Africa. We were all working to free ourselves from the bondage of race-based oppression, whether in the form of apartheid in South Africa or the legacy of slavery and racism in the United States. We were part of a worldwide movement that continues today to redress the economic and social injustices that kill body, mind, and spirit. Just as we watched and learned from the continuing struggle within the United States, so too did activists there gain strength from our struggles.

On occasion the work of our American colleagues was indispensable. The economic sanctions bill passed by the U.S. Congress in 1986 is a case in point. Without the decades-long divestment campaign undertaken by university students, churches, civil rights organizations, trade unions, and state and local governments to cut economic ties to South Africa, the U.S. Congress would not have acted, even to the extent of overriding a presidential veto. International sanctions were a key factor in the eventual victory of the African National Congress over South Africa's white minority regime.

This successful campaign demonstrated what can be accomplished when citizens take up their responsibility to help shape U.S. political and economic policy for Africa. This work remains urgent. The post–September 11 world has witnessed an alarming rise in U.S. unilateralism, proliferating areas of instability and armed conflict, a growing gap between the world's rich and poor, and a shocking failure to adequately respond to the HIV/AIDS crisis, which will kill more people in Africa than all the wars for national liberation put together. *No Easy Victories* makes clear that our lives and fortunes around the globe are indeed linked. My hope and belief is that it will inspire a new generation to take up today's challenges.

# Preface and Acknowledgments

At the midpoint of the twentieth century, colonial powers still ruled almost the entire African continent. Apartheid prevailed in South Africa, and segregation in the United States. Within two decades, most African states gained their independence. But both white minority rule in Southern Africa and racial inequality in the United States continued, confirming W. E. B. Du Bois's famous 1903 prophecy that "the problem of the twentieth century is the problem of the color line."

The second half of the twentieth century was the era of the Cold War, featuring the bipolar confrontation between the United States and the Soviet Union. For most political leaders and the wider public in North America and Europe, this conflict was the primary reality defining global politics. Yet the movement for freedom from colonialism and racism grew around the globe, developing into an unprecedented transnational social movement.

At its height, focused on South Africa, it became known as the anti-apartheid movement, and it achieved its most dramatic victory with the fall of apartheid. Yet the movement against colonialism and racism was never concerned only with South Africa. Around the world, anti-apartheid activists saw apartheid as tied to their own particular experiences of injustice. In every country—the United States, Cuba, the Netherlands, India, and elsewhere—activists saw their commitment to abolish apartheid as linked to their vision for the future of their own country.

Of course, the most decisive role in achieving South Africa's freedom was played by the people of South Africa and those of neighboring countries. But the process involved the entire continent and engaged activists outside Africa as well. International institutions provided support to the global anti-apartheid cause, and sympathetic governments, most notably the Nordic countries, offered resources. Cuban troops and military support from the Soviet Union were crucial in checking apartheid South Africa's military power in the region.

American activists also played a significant role, working to halt U.S. support for the apartheid regime. The movement eventually was able to force changes in Washington and on Wall Street that sent a definitive signal to Pretoria that apartheid was doomed. At the height of the conservative Reagan era, in 1986, popular pressure compelled the U.S. Congress to override a presidential veto and impose sanctions on South Africa. At the same time, U.S. corporations withdrew their investments, so that private sanctions reinforced the official ones. Both were the result of decades of political work in the United States involving African exiles and a diverse set of American activists and organizations.

The sanctions signaled an end to international confidence in the apartheid regime. Events then moved swiftly: Nelson Mandela was released from prison in 1990, and democratic elections were held in South Africa in 1994.

The U.S. anti-apartheid movement is commonly seen as having emerged suddenly, with demonstrations at the South African embassy in the 1980s, and as having retired from the scene after Mandela's release in 1990. But that is a misleading picture. There is a long, largely untold history of connections between African liberation and U.S. activism. These links, intimately related to the history of race in the United States itself, preceded and shaped the anti-apartheid movement, and they continue today.

❧

Drawing on the voices of activists of several generations, *No Easy Victories* explores the history of connections between African liberation and activism in the United States. The story includes solidarity with African struggles for independence in the 1950s, the reciprocal connections between the civil rights struggle in the United States and African liberation, the initiatives of African exiles and visitors, and the complex networks that linked international institutions and activists across both national and ideological boundaries.

The book presents a range of voices and insights that reflect the diversity of the movement itself. While the book includes the better-known narrative of national policy, national organizations, and events covered by the media, our primary focus is on the networks of individuals and groups—local, national, and international—that made the public movement possible.

We have taken the title for the book, and our mandate in exploring this history, from the saying by Amilcar Cabral: "Tell no lies; claim no easy victories." Cabral, who was assassinated in 1973, led the people of two small West African countries in their fight against Portuguese colonialism. His thinking and his example reached across borders, inspiring a generation of activists not only around the African continent but also across the Atlantic.

Like the anticolonial struggles, the movement in solidarity with African liberation can look to hard-won victories that are worth celebrating. Yet understanding the significance of that history and its lessons for today's activists requires us to take an approach that is neither celebratory nor cynical, and that recognizes failure as well as success. Although the movement won sanctions against South Africa, for example, it was unable to block U.S. support for South Africa's destructive regional wars. And in 1994, the same year that South Africa gained freedom, activists in the United States shared in the broad international failure to respond to the genocide in Rwanda. More generally, the movement built opposition to the most blatant racially defined denial of political rights—colonialism and apartheid—but proved unable to carry that momentum into broader campaigns for the achievement of full political and economic rights.

The victories won by Cabral and others of his generation were real, as was the international convergence that helped bring the downfall of political apartheid. But Cabral also counseled us that "the people are not fighting for ideas, for the things in anyone's head. They are fighting to win material benefits, to live better and in peace, to see their lives go forward, to guarantee the future of their children." These benefits have been slow to come. The post-independence era has seen a wide range of experiences around the continent. Great contrasts are evident even between countries closely linked by history, such as Cabral's own Cape Verde and Guinea-Bissau. The image of uniform failures since independence in African countries is clearly wrong. But for the majority of Africans, the economic and social victories that would fulfill the promise of political independence are still to be achieved.

In this book, therefore, our goal is not only to recall a history but also to spur reflection on how that history can contribute to renewed international solidarity with Africa. As in the decades of the fight against colonialism and apartheid, the primary responsibility for addressing today's challenges lies with people and groups in Africa. But the success or failure of their initiatives will, as before, also be determined by global structures of oppression and by countervailing forces of solidarity.

❧❧

Work on this book began in 2003, coinciding with the 50th anniversary of the American Committee on Africa (ACOA). ACOA, now a part of Africa Action, is a central component of the story. But the book is not a history of this or any other single group. The networks that built the solidarity movement in the United States were linked to several organizations with national constituencies, including the Council on African Affairs in the 1940s, ACOA beginning in the 1950s, and the American Friends Service Committee, the Washington Office on Africa, and TransAfrica, which took on greater prominence in subsequent decades. These networks also included a host of local and shorter-lived groups around the country and in many different sectors of society. It was the cumulative impact that was essential to the victories that were achieved.

The editors and writers of *No Easy Victories* are activists who have been participants in various aspects of this history over several decades. When we began working on this project, we were motivated in large part by our dissatisfaction with existing accounts of the period, which relied largely on images promoted by the media. Entire chunks of history that we knew to be important, and especially the work of behind-the-scenes activists and local organizations that never gained media prominence, seemed to be entirely invisible, even to the few scholars who had begun to chronicle the history.

Of the decades in question, only the 1950s has so far received significant attention from scholars. Other critical areas have hardly been touched by researchers, much less explored in depth. They include U.S. connections to Tanzania and the liberation struggles against Portuguese colonialism in the late 1960s and 1970s, as well as the role of American activists in the anti-apartheid campaign that reached a high point in the 1980s. Existing treatments of the period from the 1960s through the 1990s tap few archival sources and have included only a handful of interviews with activists.

Focusing on the movement itself, we have not attempted to document the broader history of the struggles in Africa, nor to analyze the evolution of U.S. government policies toward Africa. Our aim, rather, is to illustrate the main features of the solidarity networks that played a critical role in this history from the 1950s through the 1990s.

From the 1980s through the current period, right-wing forces have consolidated hegemony over the national agenda in the United States. In this context, the achievement of sanctions against apartheid in the mid-1980s stands out as a singular victory. But it cannot be understood without seeing its origins in an earlier history. Yet that broader context risks being oversimplified or even forgotten. The historical sources are slipping away as activists die or forget the details of campaigns. Most written and photographic records kept by smaller organizations and individual activists, if they are preserved at all, are consigned to moldy basements rather than placed in archives where they can later be found by scholars.

As we approached the writing of this book, the need to preserve this record and tell the stories was obvious. How to accomplish the task was less certain. Given the limitations of time and resources, we knew that the project would have to be a modest one, a mere beginning point, to whet the appetite of readers to know more. We hope it will spur others who were involved to revisit their own files and memories, confirming or challenging what is presented here. Related materials will be available on a Web site (http://www. noeasyvictories.org).

Our process has relied on interviews with a diverse set of activists, many of whom feature prominently in the narrative we present. But it was not our goal simply to substitute a new set of names for those that are highlighted in other accounts. Such an interpretation would miss the point. Rather, we hope to demonstrate the richness and diversity of the history and to encourage future researchers to dig more deeply, both within the networks we cite and beyond them.

As our research proceeded, we were reminded of the fallibility of memory and the limitations of available records. The recollections of direct participants, including ourselves, frequently varied, even on such basic questions as the year specific events occurred. We have done our best to verify and cross-check statements of fact, but we fully expect some details to be corrected by participants or by researchers with access to additional archival material.

⬦⬦⬦

The organization of the volume is designed to highlight a range of voices and sectors of the movement and to show an evolution that was multidimensional rather than linear. Following an overview chapter, chapters 2 through 6 focus on specific decades. A series of shorter vignettes at the end of each decade chapter highlight the role of particular individuals and groups. Both the overview and the decade chapters conclude with the end of the 1990s. A brief afterword looks at what lies ahead in the dramatically changed context for solidarity in the new millennium.

The chapter headings reflect our thinking about the connections between African liberation and American activism. The division of history into 10-year segments is of course arbitrary, and the great majority of the people profiled were engaged for more than a single decade. Nevertheless, there were clear shifts in context that roughly correspond to the decades. Our five writers were asked to portray key features of the decades, drawing on their own experiences and on interviews with other activists.

It is a measure of the scope of the movement that after an overview, five decade chapters, and more than two dozen vignettes, many relevant names and organizations are still left out of these pages or mentioned only in passing. For every person whose role is discussed there are five more, or 10 more, who should be profiled as well. The innumerable local activist groups, church committees, caucuses in professional and academic organizations, student groups, and ad-hoc coalitions of community activists form a web far too complex to document in a single volume. To all the individuals and organizations who are not mentioned in this story but should be, we can only say that we hope you see this book as also reflecting your own experience, and as a catalyst for documenting other threads of the movement for African liberation.

In the radically changed context of a new millennium, the work goes on. There are no formulas for twenty-first-century activism. But there is new thinking and new energy, as movement veterans offer the lessons of experience and younger activists bring their own ideas and motivations for struggle. *No Easy Victories* opens and closes with the voices of six people whose work on Africa has focused on post-apartheid issues. Their brief reflections affirm that the passion for Africa activism lives on, and that a new generation will find the strength and creativity to meet the challenges that lie ahead.

The editors and writers of *No Easy Victories* are indebted to all from whom we have learned over the course of our involvement with African liberation struggles—a host of friends, colleagues, and comrades past and present, scattered across several continents. We are especially grateful to those who agreed to be interviewed for the book, many but not all of them quoted by name.

For financial support of the research and writing, we especially wish to thank the Stanley and Marion Bergman Family Fund, Betsy Landis, Sue Wootton Minter, and the Samuel Rubin Foundation. The Aluka project provided assistance for obtaining and transcribing interviews. Anthony Bogues, chair of the Africana Studies Department at Brown University, hosted two crucial meetings of the writers and editors, whose locations spanned the approximately 5,000 miles from Hawai'i to California to Washington, DC. Imani Countess, of the American Friends Service Committee, provided support for a video interview with veteran activist Bill Sutherland, as well as consistent encouragement along the way. Others who gave financial support include Marylee Crofts, Margaret De Rivera, Robert Grant, Margaret Holt, Janet Hooper, Carmen and Bruce Johnson, Donna Katzin, Deborah Knight, Haaheo Mansfield, Miracle Corners of the World, Thomas Moore, Linda Moyer, Nancy Myers, Chris Root and David Wiley, Jim Weikart, and Irving Wolfe. The Center for Democratic Renewal in Atlanta provided fiscal sponsorship for the project. Our thanks to all.

The book also benefited from contact with related projects, particularly the African Activist Archive project at Michigan State University (http://www.africanactivist.msu.edu), directed by Richard Knight, and the Aluka digital library project (http://www.aluka.org). The African Activist Archive seeks to identify and encourage the preservation of archives of American activists, both individuals and groups. The Aluka project includes among its initial content areas the history of freedom struggles in Southern Africa, and the project is collaborating with institutions in Southern Africa and elsewhere to compile a digital library. Selected interviews for this book will be included as part of the international component of that library.

In the process of collecting photos within very difficult constraints of time and money, we have benefited from the generosity of dozens of photographers, archivists, and friends. We are particularly grateful to Richard Knight for assistance in locating photographs and to photographer Rick Reinhard for serving as our lead photo consultant as well as contributing a number of his own photographs. The list of others who have helped is far too long to include here. We have provided credits, obtained permissions from photographers, and identified those shown in photos in all cases for which the information was available.

We thank all those who provided invaluable support through their advice and encouragement. Adwoa Dunn-Mouton and Prexy Nesbitt were consistent and indispensable guides. Others who read drafts and provided feedback included Jennifer Davis, Sylvia Hill, George Houser, Nunu Kidane, Chris Saunders, Betsy

Schmidt, Cathy Sunshine, Evalyn Tennant, Cherri Waters, and readers for the Human Sciences Research Council Press in South Africa and for Ohio University Press.

At Africa World Press, publisher Kassahun Checole and editor Damola Ifaturoti believed in the project, kept us moving, and fitted the book smoothly into their production process. Copyeditor Cathy Sunshine brought consistency and readability to the manuscript. Designer Sam Saverance made the history come alive with his creative book design. Our thanks to all. The views expressed in this book are those of the writers and editors, and the editors are responsible for any errors that may remain.

*William Minter*
*Gail Hovey*
*Charles Cobb Jr.*

Marching to the South African embassy, December 1984. Front row, from left: Roger Wilkins, Andrew McBride, Rev. Rollins Lambert, Walter Fauntroy, Gloria Steinem, Randall Robinson, Eleanor Holmes Norton. Joseph Jordan is in second row on left. *Photo © Rick Reinhard.*

# Map of Africa

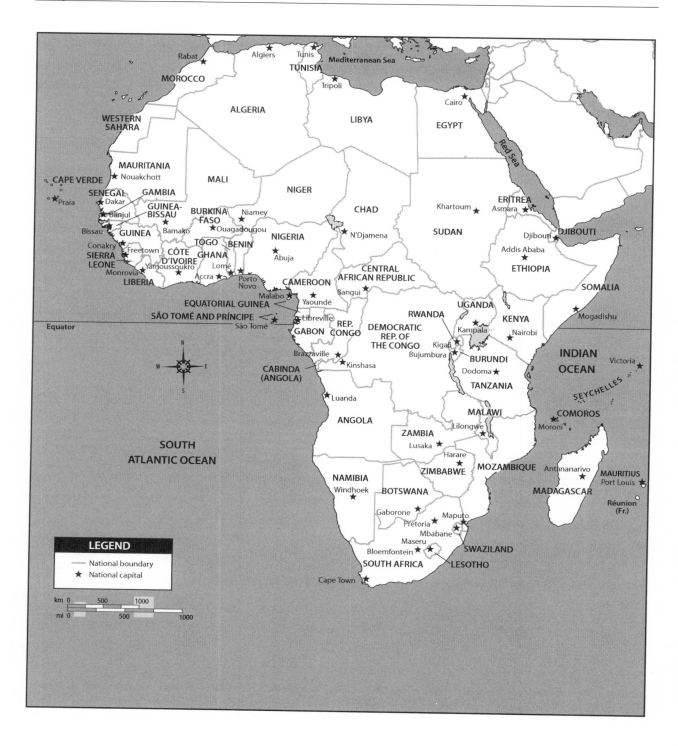

# Map of Southern Africa, with Dates of Independence

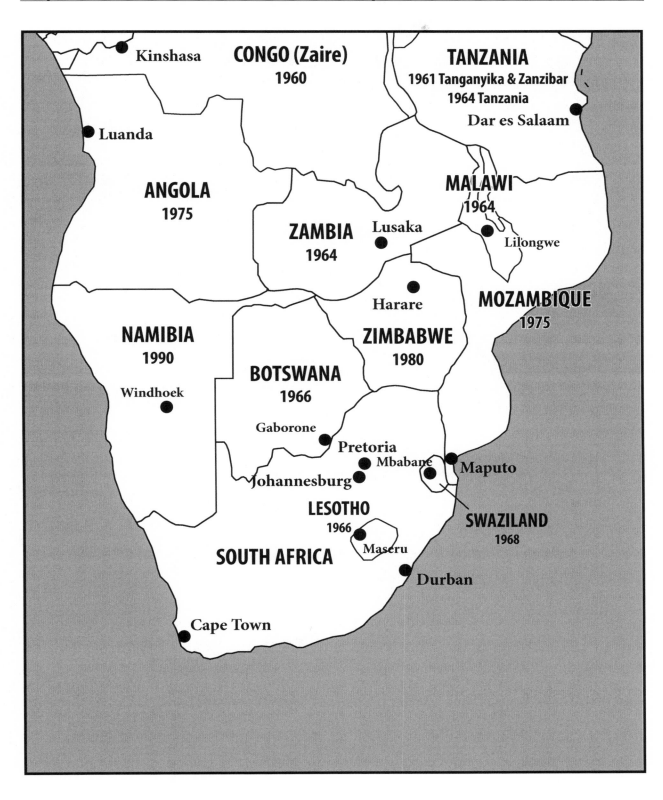

# Abbreviations

| | |
|---|---|
| AASFU | All-African Student and Faculty Union |
| ACOA | American Committee on Africa |
| ACTWU | Amalgamated Clothing and Textile Workers Union |
| AFSAR | Americans for South African Resistance |
| AFSC | American Friends Service Committee |
| AIS | Africa Information Service |
| ALD | African Liberation Day |
| ALSC | African Liberation Support Committee |
| ANC | African National Congress |
| ANLCA | American Negro Leadership Conference on Africa |
| APIC | Africa Policy Information Center |
| BCLSA | Boston Coalition for the Liberation of Southern Africa |
| CAA | Council on African Affairs |
| CBC | Congressional Black Caucus |
| CCISSA | Chicago Committee in Solidarity with Southern Africa |
| CIA | Central Intelligence Agency |
| CIDSA | Coalition for Illinois Divestment in South Africa |
| CORE | Congress of Racial Equality |
| COSATU | Congress of South African Trade Unions |
| FBI | Federal Bureau of Investigation |
| FLN | National Liberation Front |
| FNLA | National Front for the Liberation of Angola |
| FOR | Fellowship of Reconciliation |
| Frelimo | Mozambique Liberation Front |
| FSAM | Free South Africa Movement |
| HIV/AIDS | human immunodeficiency virus/acquired immune deficiency syndrome |
| ICCR | Interfaith Center on Corporate Responsibility |
| ICFTU | International Confederation of Free Trade Unions |
| IFP | Inkatha Freedom Party |
| MPLA | Popular Movement for the Liberation of Angola |
| MSU | Michigan State University |
| NAACP | National Association for the Advancement of Colored People |
| NATO | North Atlantic Treaty Organization |
| NSC | National Security Council |
| NSCF | National Student Christian Federation |
| OAU | Organization of African Unity |
| OSU | Ohio State University |
| PAC | Pan Africanist Congress |

| | |
|---|---|
| PAIGC | African Party for the Independence of Guinea-Bissau and Cape Verde |
| PAN | Priority Africa Network |
| PATAM | Pan African Treatment Access Movement |
| R | rands |
| Renamo | Mozambican National Resistance |
| SAC | Southern Africa Committee |
| SALC | Southern Africa Liberation Committee |
| SASO | South African Students Organization |
| SASP | Southern Africa Support Project |
| SCLC | Southern Christian Leadership Conference |
| SDS | Students for a Democratic Society |
| Six PAC | Sixth Pan-African Congress |
| SMU | Southern Methodist University |
| SNCC | Student Nonviolent Coordinating Committee |
| SWAPO | South West Africa People's Organisation |
| TAC | Treatment Action Campaign |
| TANU | Tanganyika African National Union |
| U.N. | United Nations |
| UCC | United Church of Christ |
| UCLA | University of California at Los Angeles |
| Unita | National Union for Total Independence of Angola |
| WOA | Washington Office on Africa |
| WTO | World Trade Organization |
| ZANU | Zimbabwe African National Union |
| ZAPU | Zimbabwe African People's Union |

Children demonstrate in support of the people of Namibia at Freedom Plaza, Washington, DC, 1983. *Photo courtesy of Joseph Jordan.*

Local folk singers from the Washington area accompany demonstrators at the South African embassy in 1984. From left: Ron Wallace, Luci Murphy, Mike Honey, Steve Jones.
*Photo © Rick Reinhard.*

# VOICES

# Keith Lewis

Keith Lewis
*Photo by Langston Maynor.*

I was born in Muskegon, Michigan, a small, working-class town. Muskegon Heights, where most of my extended family lived, was almost entirely African American. North Muskegon was almost entirely white. But I went to racially mixed schools, and I played drums and saxophone in the band. So I ended up having experiences that some members of my family had not had.

Growing up, I wasn't especially conscious of Africa. But I knew first-hand about the harsh realities of poverty and the class divide. My mother was a single mother and she worked in a factory, making auto parts. It was the era of Reaganomics, and she struggled to provide the bare essentials for my sister and me. At this point in my life I wasn't yet "political." I didn't think about how our situation related to the wider world, to the long history of racial oppression and resistance.

That began to change during my junior year at Michigan State University. I met other black students—African Americans, a brother from Jamaica—who had Pan-Africanist and black nationalist views. I didn't yet embrace all of it, but they got me thinking. I began to see that years of miseducation and lack of knowledge of our history had contributed to my own lack of self-knowledge. Studying the teachings of Naim Akbar, Marcus Garvey, and Assata Shakur, I began to see the connections between struggles in black America and struggles in Africa. I got involved with the Black Student Alliance and went to Black Power rallies on campus.

After graduating in 1996, I moved to Chicago. I'd been in the business school at Michigan State, being groomed for the corporate route. But by this time I had decided that wasn't for me. I worked first with a program called Public Allies, which trained young adults as community leaders. This was another new experience, because I met young activists from many different backgrounds who were fighting for social change.

At Michigan State, a mainly white institution, there were many non-black students, but I hadn't necessarily interacted much with them. It was when I went to Public Allies that I had a chance to dialogue with folks from all different walks of life, talking about race, class, gender, sexual orientation. That expanded my world view. I learned about the issues that other people, beyond my own black community, were facing. Connecting with them, I joined a social justice struggle that cut across racial, geographic, and gender lines.

Now, in 2007, I'm an educator, an activist, and a father. I work as a counselor at Little Village Lawndale High School in Chicago, helping create a multicultural learning environment. The students at the school are about 70 percent Latino, mostly of Mexican origin, and about 30 percent African American. They come from racially homogeneous neighborhoods and elementary schools, so it's a challenge for them to come together.

I'm part of a group called Solidarity not Charity, which is contributing to the rebuilding of New Orleans after Katrina. We facilitate dialogue among young people of color from Chicago, New Orleans, and the Bronx. African American and Latino youth come together to discuss their common problems of displacement, criminalization, and lack of education, and to understand each other's histories and struggles.

For me and for many other black Americans, there's so much about our own past that we just don't know. We have a lot of history that's been stolen, history that we never were taught. I've been fortunate—I've had people who've challenged me to look beyond the surface, to seek out more about our connections to Africa and Africans in the diaspora. I've studied ancient Egypt, learned about the struggles in South Africa, about what happened in Liberia, the genocide in Rwanda.

I visited Senegal and Gambia for a month in 2004. There was no particular mission—I went to observe, learn, and make connections. And I had some rich dialogue with folks there about relationships between African Americans and Africans on the continent, about our perceptions of each other and where those perceptions come from. I'm planning a trip to Ghana soon.

So many people in this country, including black Americans, have an image of Africa as a distant, alien continent, a place of famine, disease, and despair. Those issues exist, of course, but having gone to Africa, I know that many other things are happening there too. I saw that as black Americans, we can contribute to the development of Africa from an economic and social standpoint. But I also realized that historically, culturally, socially, there's much that we don't know. There are many opportunities for us to learn and connect.

In my work with youth, I try to dispel some of the untruths. About famine in Africa—a land rich in resources—I ask: Why does it exist? Where does it come from? Those are the kinds of questions I raise.

When I think about the issues facing black communities in the U.S. and abroad, I realize that "there's nothing new underneath the sun." We have to connect with the history of struggles that have preceded our own. Though apartheid has been dismantled in South Africa, it provides a historical context of racial segregation and struggle. Racial and class isolation exist within many American communities today, leading to disunity and hatred. If the lessons of the past go unlearned, history will continue to repeat itself right before our eyes.

# Erin Polley

Erin Polley
*Photo by Mario Quezada.*

In the spring of 2003 I'd been living in Chicago two years, working as a cocktail waitress. I wasn't sure what I wanted to do with my life next. Then President Bush invaded Iraq. As the bombs fell over Baghdad, I went downtown to join the march against the war and was arrested along with several hundred others. In jail I met all these amazing people, and we went to court together and stayed in touch. I found myself a part of a community that was actively working for change around the world. Soon I found a job doing antiwar work at the American Friends Service Committee office in Chicago. So, you might say I fell into activism.

That fall I enrolled at Columbia College Chicago, where Prexy Nesbitt and Lisa Brock were teaching. I had gotten to know Prexy through AFSC, and he encouraged me to take his African history course. I worked with Lisa in an independent study on Cuba, but it turned into an independent study on the world.

Both of them encouraged my interest in Africa, and they gave me opportunities to become part of their work. Over long lunches and tireless meetings at school, they taught me to use history as a way to understand racism, colonialism, and culture today. I learned about Ella Baker and Helen Joseph. And I learned about Prexy's and Lisa's own lives as activists. Their commitment to the anti-apartheid movement and to teaching people about Africa inspired a new kind of activism in me, a 22-year-old white girl from the Midwest.

I became more aware of the racism happening around me every day. I grew up in Indianapolis, but my family was originally from rural Indiana and Oklahoma. They were pretty apolitical, involved in the Southern Baptist Church. Growing up, I wasn't particularly conscious of racism. And I think that's one of the big things Prexy taught me. We were talking about our families one day, and I commented that I really didn't see much racism when I was growing up. He asked me pointed questions about the diversity of people who lived on my street, the diversity of people who were in my classrooms. I started to realize that even though there were not overtly racist things being said at my dinner table, I was experiencing a different kind of racism, in a white, exclusive, suburban world.

By my second year at Columbia, I was filling my schedule with classes on African art, literature, and history. Most of my free time was spent hunting for South African music, watching films about Africa, and reading the histories of people like Nelson Mandela and Albie Sachs. I became fascinated by postcolonial Africa and the liberation struggles.

In August 2006 I joined a group that visited South Africa, Namibia, Zimbabwe, and Mozambique. I met activists in all four countries. Even though I'd done a lot of preparation for the trip, my experiences completely changed my view of Africa. I met young Zimbabwean men my age who'd been banned from studying at the public university after they protested tuition hikes. I met descendants of the Herero in Namibia who have been struggling for the world to recognize the genocide their people suffered under German occupation. I visited the Hatcliffe informal settlement in Harare, where 6,000 people settled after their homes were bulldozed by the government. In each new place, we started an incredible cross-continental dialogue.

I'm now working full-time at AFSC as an antiwar activist and attending Columbia College with a full-time load. I don't sleep much! I hope to finish my degree next year, with a major in cultural studies and a minor in black world studies. I don't know yet what I want to do. I'm thinking about graduate school, but I also plan to continue my work as an activist. I do know that Africa has changed who I am and how I view the world. My interest is in being an ally of people who are working for change in their countries, rather than being somebody who is there to save them.

# Dara Cooper

Dara Cooper
*Photo courtesy of Dara Cooper.*

Who am I? We grow our entire lives trying to answer that question! What I know so far: I am an activist, organizer, student, educator, writer, and passionate priestess of Shango, the Yoruba deity guiding social justice, among many other things.

Activism is my life. I worked with the Treatment Action Campaign (TAC) and the Pan African Treatment Access Movement (PATAM) in Johannesburg, South Africa, while I was completing my graduate studies in community development. In 2006 I became the national organizer for a campaign to defend political exile Assata Shakur, who's now in Cuba, against unjust charges of terrorism.

The spirit of activism comes from my mother, a beautiful black nationalist and Yoruba priestess. It also comes from my grandmother, a savvy teacher and union organizer who was once the target of McCarthyism. From both of them I learned the lesson that every injustice can be fought, and the people can win.

My introduction to liberation movements was through the anti-apartheid movement in the 1980s. I remember going to rallies as a child and hearing about the parallels between Jim Crow and apartheid. I remember boycotting international corporations—I still refuse to use Shell gas or purchase Liz Claiborne to this day. I remember meetings with Africans born on the continent, African descendants, and supporters, all working in solidarity. The movement wasn't based on pity or charity but on justice. We understand that our individual freedom only lies within our collective liberation.

As an undergraduate at Ohio State University, I was an organizer with the African Student Union. I was a spokesperson for a successful eight-day sit-in protesting racist administrative policies and demanding support for OSU's Black Cultural Center and Office of Minority Affairs. I also worked to support the Communication Workers of America's campaign to secure living wages and improve health benefits for custodial and health care workers at OSU. Later I worked with groups in Chicago, especially Incite! Women of Color Against Violence. I attended the World Social Forum in Mumbai in 2004 as one of their representatives.

My work in South Africa with the Treatment Action Campaign involved research and reporting on HIV treatment rollouts across the continent and assessing their treatment literacy program. TAC has successfully combined research, advocacy, and organization of HIV-positive people to take action for themselves. It has protested against big pharmaceutical companies and taken on the South African government itself, demanding that antiretroviral and other treatments be available to all who need them. With PATAM, a continent-wide coalition in which TAC is a leading participant, I helped with research and with coordinating an eight-day training on HIV virology and treatment.

During my time at TAC I was fortunate to participate in a TAC-sponsored protest. After the long and successful battle to have the South African government commit itself to an HIV treatment rollout plan, TAC focused on monitoring the government's progress. But the government was withholding information, so TAC filed another lawsuit against the government for denying information to the public.

The morning of the case, TAC led a rally down the street from the courtroom and held a press conference. Members spoke about living with HIV and their struggles to access treatment and information. They danced and sang their legendary South African *toyi-toyi*. I could never capture in words the camaraderie I felt in the midst of this demonstration. TAC eventually won the suit and the government was ordered to pay a settlement and commit to making information more accessible and transparent. It would be difficult to imagine such a victory for a community organization here in the U.S.

After returning to the United States, I worked with an aid agency to improve laboratory testing and monitoring of HIV/AIDS in Southern and Eastern Africa. Visiting and working in Ethiopia, I learned that it isn't enough to try to help; you also have to confront the paternalistic structures that often undermine the goals of helping communities.

In my current job I focus on one particular instance of injustice, the injustice against Assata Shakur. She was shot by police on the New Jersey turnpike in 1973 and convicted of murder despite evidence that she had never fired a gun and was wounded while holding her hands above her head. The U.S. government has offered a million dollars for her capture. In working on Assata's case, I also try to educate people about the broader, intersecting issues, such as the position of women and the role of the prison-industrial complex.

For me, all these issues are connected. While over 39 million people are living with HIV, Third World governments are being forced to cut social services, including health care. The devastation and death that result deserve to be called genocide.

One of the problems with much of the activism and discourse around Africa is disregard for history. If we're serious about debt cancellation, we have to recognize the exploitation that helped create the debt in the first place. How can we understand the disparities of resources available to Africans without understanding colonization? How can we call U.S. and European countries "donors" when much of the wealth they possess was created by exploiting the labor and resources of the very continent they are claiming to help? How can we not acknowledge this? Does history have a cutoff point where we no longer have to consider previous injustices?

As we fight today's battles, we need to understand where those injustices come from. We need to see ourselves as part of a long lineage of freedom fighters and draw inspiration from battles won.

# Chapter 1

# An Unfinished Journey

## William Minter

The early morning phone call came on February 4, 1969, the day after I arrived back from Tanzania to my parents' house in Tucson, Arizona. "Eduardo has been assassinated."

The caller was Gail Hovey, one of the co-editors of this book. She was then working with the Southern Africa Committee in New York, a group supporting liberation movements in Mozambique and other Southern African countries. Eduardo, as he was known to hundreds of friends around the world, was Eduardo Mondlane. At the time of his death by a letter bomb, he was president of the Mozambique Liberation Front, known as Frelimo. Had he lived to see the freedom of his country, he would likely have joined his contemporary and friend Nelson Mandela as one of Africa's most respected leaders.

It's hard to say what factors build lasting connections between people, but surely the deaths of those engaged in a common struggle must count among the most powerful. I had just said goodbye to Mondlane at the airport in Dar es Salaam, Tanzania, on New Year's Day 1969, after two years of teaching in Frelimo's secondary school. I was one of many inspired by his leadership, and his sacrifice reinforced our commitments. The deaths of Mondlane and others involved in freedom movements had profound impact not only on their own countries but around the world. The list is long: Amilcar Cabral, whose words provide our title, was killed in

1973; Patrice Lumumba in 1961; Malcolm X in 1965; Martin Luther King Jr. in 1968; Steve Biko in 1977; Ruth First in 1982; and Samora Machel in 1986—to name only a few.

Memories of those who gave their lives can bind together and inspire those who carry on their legacies. So can highly visible public victories, such as the dramatic release of Nelson Mandela from prison in February 1990 and the first democratic election in South Africa in April 1994. The worldwide anti-apartheid movement, which helped win those victories, was arguably the most successful transnational social movement of the last half century. All of us engaged in this book project were minor actors in that movement, and our roles will become clear as the story unfolds.

In February 1969, when Hovey and I spoke of Mondlane's assassination in Tanzania, I had not yet met Charlie Cobb, also a co-editor of this book. But he and his comrades at the Center for Black Education in Washington had already made connections to liberation circles in Dar es Salaam after years of civil rights organizing in the U.S. South. Later that year he moved to Tanzania, determined to live in an African country "long enough to really learn something about it." "What looks simple turns out to be complex," Cobb told an interviewer in 1981, after returning to the United States to continue his career as a journalist. "If you want to write about it, as I did

Eduardo Mondlane's funeral, in Dar es Salaam, Tanzania, February 1969. Janet Mondlane stands with the couple's children, Chude, Nyeleti, and Eddie. President Julius Nyerere of Tanzania is at left with arms crossed. *Photo reproduced from Manghezi 1999.*

when I got to Africa, or if you want to organize it, which is what I did in Mississippi, then you have to learn to deal with these complexities."

Dar es Salaam was indeed a gathering place in the 1960s. The city welcomed both the liberation movements of Southern Africa and veterans of the U.S. civil rights movement who looked to independent Africa for answers that were not forthcoming in the United States. Exiles from apartheid South Africa, its colony South West Africa (Namibia), white-ruled Rhodesia (Zimbabwe), and the Portuguese colonies of Angola and Mozambique all found their way to Tanzania. Liberation movement leaders regularly visited, even from distant West Africa, where Guinea-Bissau and Cape Verde remained under Portuguese rule.

It was in Dar es Salaam in 1968 that I first met Prexy Nesbitt, who was still there in 1969 when Mondlane was assassinated. Over the decades Nesbitt, who has been an indispensable adviser to this book project, traveled from Chicago to Mozambique and South Africa and around the United

States, making connections between African and American activists on many fronts.

Nesbitt and I became involved with groups working on Africa in the mid-1960s. Even earlier, however, we felt the influence of Eduardo Mondlane and other Africans who came to the United States as students or visitors and spoke out eloquently for the freedom of their countries. Nesbitt, growing up in a progressive African American family in Chicago, had already met Mondlane at his family's Warren Avenue Congregational Church. Mondlane was exceptional in his range of contacts and his powerful presence, winning the respect of hundreds of Americans who would become involved with African liberation.

In a still-segregated United States, Africans speaking of freedom for their homelands found eager listeners among those engaged in organizing for equal rights in the United States. George Houser, for example, became the first executive secretary of the Congress of Racial Equality (CORE) in Chicago in 1943 and helped organize a "freedom ride" to the

South in 1947. Later he moved to New York and headed the American Committee on Africa, which was founded to support the civil disobedience campaigns of South Africa's African National Congress (ANC) against the apartheid system.

Both the African and African American movements entered a new stage in that decade. The year 1955 marked a turning point for both. In June, the ANC and its allies convened the Congress of the People in Kliptown, near Johannesburg. The Freedom Charter adopted there, just before police moved in to disperse the assembly, declared that "South Africa belongs to all who live in it, black and white." Two months later, a 15-year-old from Chicago named Emmett Till was kidnapped, killed, and dumped in the Tallahatchie River in Mississippi, accused of provocative remarks to a white woman. That killing was one of the decisive catalysts for the U.S. civil rights movement of the next 10 years.

Prexy Nesbitt and I were only a few years younger than Emmett Till. For both of us, there is a direct line from his death to our engagement with support for African liberation. Nesbitt was in Chicago when Till's body was brought back and viewed by thousands at an open-casket funeral. I, a white American growing up on an interracial cooperative farm in Mississippi, spent my childhood just 35 miles from where Till was killed. Our cooperative, a legacy of the Southern Tenant Farmers Union of the 1930s, served the local black community with a clinic and a cooperative store that were more successful than our limited farming operations. In the charged atmosphere of the mid-1950s, white plantation owners targeted the co-op with a boycott, threatening their black workers with expulsion if they continued to associate with it. Within a year of Till's murder, the co-op residents had dispersed, most leaving Mississippi.

For both Nesbitt and me, our memories of the 1950s and our understandings of racism in the United States are linked to our later involvement with Africa. Similar links are common to many other activists we have spoken to. But diverse connections between Americans and Africans, embedded in the history of race on both sides of the Atlantic, are not unique to this period. They predate the 1950s by decades and even centuries, going back to the earliest years of the slave trade. To cite only one prominent example, in 1839 captive West Africans rebelled and took over the Spanish slave ship *Amistad*. Afterwards the ship was captured by a U.S. Navy ship; the Africans were charged with the murder of the captain and jailed in New Haven, Connecticut. After a long legal battle, in which they were supported by abolitionists and represented in court by former president John Quincy Adams, the Supreme Court freed the "mutineers" in 1841, and they returned to Africa.

Historians are beginning to trace far earlier connections as well, such as the contacts between black American and Caribbean sailors and the black populations in Cape Town, South Africa before the nineteenth century (Atkins 1996; Linebaugh and Rediker 2000). In the nineteenth century, the complex interaction among the Americas, the Caribbean, and Africa featured influences in many different directions. In the first half of the twentieth century, the links between resistance leaders in South Africa and African Americans were particularly close, as shown most recently in David Anthony's (2005) richly textured biography of the complex figure of Max Yergan.

Nonetheless, the last half of the twentieth century stands out as a distinct period. In Africa, a remarkable march to freedom produced more than 50 independent states. In the United States, organizing, protest, and legislative changes resulted in the passage of the Civil Rights Act of 1964 and the Voting Rights Act of 1965, the most important advances for African Americans since the Emancipation Proclamation. Throughout this period, there was a constant interplay between how activists in the United States understood their own country and how they made connections with others in Africa and around the world.

These reciprocal connections—and in particular the influence of Africa on Americans—hardly appear in conventional historical accounts. When a journalist from *Ebony* magazine asked Mandela about how the American civil rights movement had influenced South Africans, Mandela replied, "You are correct, there are many similarities between us. We have learned a great deal from each other" (May 1990). While the reporter's question implied one-way influence, Mandela's tactful correction stressed that the learning process was two-way, and that the struggles on both continents shared much in common.

The journalist's facile assumption is part of a larger pattern of narrowing the historical narrative.

Thus Martin Luther King Jr.'s nonviolent civil rights leadership is celebrated in classrooms, while his opposition to the Vietnam War goes unmentioned. As Lisa Brock notes in chapter 2, despite the internationalist perspective of almost all the principal civil rights figures, the standard narrative focuses exclusively on civil rights at home. There is little consciousness of that stream of American internationalism that identifies not with American preeminence but with the demand for full human rights both at home and abroad.

## A Half Century of Connections

World War II provided Africans, African Americans, and other colonized people the opportunity to make their commonalities visible, especially in the black press. Paul Robeson and W. E. B. Du Bois linked the fight against Jim Crow with the war against fascism and the anticolonial campaigns. Many whites as well as blacks applauded them. The two outspoken leaders exposed doctrines of white supremacy that the then-segregated U.S. army shared with European colonial powers and the white settler outposts in Africa, even during the battle against Nazi racism.

President Franklin D. Roosevelt had hinted that the promise of freedom for oppressed peoples might apply not only to those conquered by the Nazis but also to those ruled by Western powers. But the United States and its allies did not expect that day to come for generations. As the United States mobilized for the Cold War in the late 1940s and early 1950s, even most groups working for social justice at home downplayed the connections between anticolonial and domestic antiracist movements. The dominant civil rights forces, in an effort to prove their American loyalty, dropped the language of identification with oppressed peoples.

As a result, during the second half of the twentieth century there was little public awareness of the connections between movements in the United States and Africa. None of the organizations engaged in making these connections gained a sustained mass following or political influence. Yet in each decade these ties, both organizational and personal, had powerful if unseen effects on how wider sectors of American society saw the world and their country's global role.

In the 1950s, nonviolent resistance in South Africa as well as the success of India's independence

Daily protests at the South African embassy on Massachusetts Avenue NW in Washington began on November 21, 1984. Organized by the Free South Africa Movement, they were scheduled to last for a week but continued for well over a year. The coordinator, Cecelie Counts, was a staff member of TransAfrica from 1983 to 1988 and a member of the local Southern Africa Support Project. Here she holds a sign from the National Education Association, the largest national teachers' union, whose members participated frequently in the embassy demonstrations. *Photo of embassy © Rick Reinhard. Photo of Counts courtesy of Clarity Films and TransAfrica Forum.*

William Minter

movement in the previous decade inspired Martin Luther King Jr. and other U.S. civil rights leaders to adopt the strategy for themselves. In doing so, they ventured beyond the cautious approaches of the National Association for the Advancement of Colored People (NAACP) and the Urban League. Ghana's independence in 1957 provided visible evidence that freedom was possible, energizing a generation of African and American activists.

In the 1960s, despite legislative victories, the pace of civil rights advance was painfully slow. The battle-weary movement was visibly fractured after the assassination of Martin Luther King. As the Vietnam War dragged on, disillusionment grew; the New Left expanded rapidly, but fell apart into factions. At the same time, however, new opportunities for personal contacts between Americans and Africans left their mark on a growing number of individuals and institutions. Large numbers of African students and exiles came to the United States. Peace Corps workers and other Americans went to Africa; many, if not most, returned with changed perspectives and new commitments.

In the 1970s hundreds of U.S. groups organized on behalf of African freedom. Tens of thousands of individuals established strong personal ties and identified with liberation movements in Southern Africa. While most organized groups were short-lived, their outreach extended in many directions. Those involved included African Americans, other Americans, and African students and exiles. Organized groups and informal caucuses on African issues emerged in universities, churches, communities, and unions, among artists and athletes, and in almost every profession. Densely interconnected but not centrally coordinated, these groups spread the message of African liberation around the United States.

This organizing laid the groundwork for the final push for sanctions against South Africa in the 1980s. Both domestic and international policy veered to the right under President Ronald Reagan. But after Reagan was elected to a second term, activists began demonstrations at the South African embassy in Washington and around the country. Congress overrode Reagan's veto of anti-apartheid sanctions in 1986.

The sanctions imposed on South Africa by Congress represent perhaps the high point of official U.S. support for majority rule in Africa. The U.S. solidarity movement celebrates the sanctions victory as its greatest achievement. Yet a closer look at the circumstances reveals that the anti-apartheid movement was in fact sharply limited in its ability to influence U.S. policy toward Africa.

Congressional support for sanctions was narrowly focused and went hand in hand with backing for South Africa's regional war against Angola and other neighboring countries. In the late 1970s and particularly in the 1980s, South Africa, both directly and through covert intervention, mounted attacks that caused hundreds of thousands or even millions of deaths. The South African government rationalized its "total strategy" as defense against a communist "total assault." U.S. senators and representatives could see that it was time to end support for apartheid in South Africa. But they continued to view Angola and Mozambique through Cold War blinders, allowing them to embrace South Africa as an ally in the global conflict with the Soviet Union.

The decade of the 1990s started out with jubilation. Mandela walked free in 1990, and even U.S. politicians who had dismissed the imprisoned ANC leader as a communist terrorist were eager to be seen applauding his address to the U.S. Congress. In April 1994, hundreds of activists from around the world, many of them with decades of solidarity work behind them, traveled to South Africa to serve as observers for the historic first election. But at the very moment that celebrations in South Africa were marking the end of white minority rule on the continent, in Central Africa the Rwandan regime launched its genocidal attack on the Tutsi population and moderate Hutus. The outside world, which could have stepped in to stop the slaughter, did virtually nothing. More than 800,000 people were dead by the time the Rwandan Patriotic Front ousted the regime and brought the mass killings to an end.

Despite the end of the Cold War, official Washington continued to assume that economic prescriptions from the West were the appropriate solutions for African problems. Efforts such as the Jubilee 2000 campaign to cancel the debt of African and other developing countries initially won only token concessions from rich countries and international financial institutions. And Africa was marginalized even within the new wave of global justice protests that started in 1999 with the World Trade Organization summit in Seattle.

We undertook this book project because we believe that lessons from the last half century are relevant to the debate on how to confront today's global inequality and the marginalization of Africa. Amilcar Cabral's mandate to "tell no lies, claim no easy victories" is as relevant today as it was decades ago. It is our guide as we tell this story of 50 years of solidarity between Africans and Americans.

The connections run deep. They were shaped, of course, by public figures and public events, but they were also influenced to a remarkable degree by a host of less visible actors and influences. Many public records are available in centralized archives, but the history of solidarity is not so neatly preserved. Even when historians explore news accounts and the written archives, many pieces are still missing. This book starts from networks in which we have been involved and from recent interviews with a diverse set of activists. We have also consulted secondary sources when available, but we are particularly conscious of our obligation to point to realities that we know to be obscured or distorted in the public record. We see our work of recovering and weaving together threads from this history as part of an ongoing process.

The 1950s, along with the 1930s and 1940s, have attracted significant attention from historians exploring the connections between U.S. Africa policy and U.S. race relations. Brenda Gayle Plummer (1996) has painted a broad canvas of black American engagement with foreign affairs from 1936 to 1960. Penny Von Eschen (1997) covers much the same ground, highlighting in particular the "decline of a radical anti-colonial politics" (155) resulting from the marginalization of Du Bois and Robeson. Thomas Borstelmann (2001) and Azza Sadama Layton (2000) have shown how Cold War interests shaped changes in domestic race policy as well as Africa policy. James H. Meriwether (2002), also reviewing the period from the mid-1930s to 1960, brings out the critical roles of South Africa, Kenya, and Ghana in shaping black American consciousness that "proudly we can be Africans."

This literature makes little use of oral history, and almost all the people who could tell stories of this period are no longer alive. Nevertheless, works such as the dissertation by Charles Johnson (2004) as well as the book by Anthony (2005) mentioned earlier show that there is rich archival material still to be explored on these themes.

Very little has been written about the decades after the 1950s. The three most prominent overview volumes, by Massie (1997), Culverson (1999), and F. N. Nesbitt (2004), cover the main features of the national anti-apartheid narrative, and Massie adds some detail on the divestment campaign in the northeastern states. But none gives attention even to solidarity with Namibia, much less to other countries in the region. Each spends a few pages on the year-long demonstrations at the South African embassy in 1984–85, noting the media impact of the events and the prominent figures arrested there. But not one of the three mentions the Southern Africa Support Project, which worked for years to educate the local community in Washington, DC about apartheid and provided the core of the organizing work for the daily demonstrations. These overview volumes and media accounts of the period do capture the broad picture, but the number of missing pieces makes these portrayals seem seriously misleading to those of us who were involved.

Only a few published works to date, such as those by Love (1985), W. Johnson (1999), and Gastrow (2005), provide detailed case studies of action at the state or local level. A recent dissertation (Hostetter 2004) looks more closely at the role of three organizations: the American Committee on Africa, the American Friends Service Committee, and TransAfrica. In general, however, historians have hardly begun to explore the varied aspects of the movement in these decades.

The stories we tell in this book are, in our view, just a beginning of the history that needs to be written. As noted in the preface, for every activist mentioned in these pages, any of us could name many more who should also have been included, and an even larger number surely remain unknown to us. And while we concentrate on tracing the links between Africa and the United States, we are well aware that these fit within a context of wider links between the Americas, Europe, and other parts of the world. It would be simpler, perhaps, to tell the story of one or two organizations or a few individuals, or to limit our investigation to a careful examination of a few critical years or specific campaigns. Indeed, if the book is successful, future historians will take up such tasks. When they do, we hope that they will realize that to understand a movement it is not enough to look at the individuals and organizations that appear on stage at high points of the drama. One must also trace the often invisible networks and supporting cast offstage, and the threads linking struggles across decades and even generations.

## The 1950s

At mid-century, the broad internationalism emerging from World War II was still influential if not dominant in U.S. public life. "Let's Join the Human Race" exhorted a widely distributed pamphlet published in 1950 by Stringfellow Barr, a prominent white American educator. Barr's internationalism, which inspired one of the predecessor organizations of the Peace Corps, paralleled the vision being eloquently expressed by Paul Robeson. Son of a former slave, Robeson was an athlete, lawyer, activist, and star of stage, screen, and concert hall, and was at the time one of the most famous Americans of any race, inside the country and around the world.

Yet in that same year, 1950, the United States went to war in Korea, and the U.S. Congress passed the McCarran Act to defend "internal security" against subversives. Traveling to Moscow and other European cities as an artist, Robeson had been warmly welcomed and had encountered little of the racism and prejudice he experienced at home. He began to protest the growing Cold War hostility between the Soviet Union and the United States, questioning why he should support his own government when it did not treat him as an equal citizen. The U.S. government could not tolerate the fact that he had been "for years extremely active in behalf of the independence for the colonial people of Africa," and in 1950 the State Department seized his passport to prevent him from traveling abroad (Von Eschen 1997, 124). Robeson's virtual disappearance from public view meant the loss of a powerful voice speaking out for international understanding and African freedom.

In 1952 South Africa's ANC and its allies launched the Defiance Campaign Against Unjust Laws, sending more than 8,500 volunteers to be arrested in protests against racial discrimination. The NAACP, the largest U.S. civil rights organization, passed resolutions

George Houser with Walter and Albertina Sisulu at ANC headquarters in Johannesburg, 1999. Houser traveled to South Africa to present the Sisulus with the book *I Will Go Singing: Walter Sisulu Speaks of His Life and the Struggle for Freedom in South Africa.* The book is based on conversations Sisulu had with Houser and Herbert Shore. *Photo courtesy of George Houser.*

condemning World Bank loans to South Africa and calling for a more active role against colonialism at its July 1952 convention (Meriwether 2002, 117–18). But it also joined official Washington in denouncing Robeson for his communist ties. Subsequently, NAACP leaders chose to focus almost exclusively on domestic issues and sought support from the Harry Truman administration, turning away from active involvement with African causes.

For the ANC and for many activists in the United States as well, common opposition to racial injustice took priority over the U.S.-Soviet rivalry. Yet over the next decades the Cold War continued to define the context of solidarity work in the United States.

The ANC's Walter Sisulu appealed for international support of the Defiance Campaign. Those who responded included Robeson's weakened Council on African Affairs (CAA) and the newly formed Americans for South African Resistance (AFSAR). AFSAR was organized by radicals and liberals wary of the Communist Party for its Soviet ties but, unlike the NAACP, committed to direct action based on strong anticolonial convictions. It was part of the organizational nexus that included CORE, the Fellowship of Reconciliation, and the Socialist Party.

The CAA and AFSAR each organized meetings and demonstrations in support of the ANC, and each raised a few thousand dollars to send to South Africa. The CAA, weakened by government harassment, dissolved in 1955. In 1953 AFSAR gave birth to the American Committee on Africa (ACOA), which would soon establish itself as a small but critical link between African movements and American activists.

The negative impact of the Cold War dominates this period. There is little question that U.S.-Soviet rivalry fostered division among progressive groups and reduced popular identification with anticolonialism and with Africa. Even so, the drama of Africa rising had a powerful impact on organizations and individuals in the United States. And despite the removal from public view of the influential bridge-building figure of Paul Robeson, the African cause continued to draw in white as well as black Americans who saw anticolonialism and opposition to domestic racism as interrelated. The Council on African Affairs and the American Committee on Africa drew on overlapping networks and on similar repertoires of action, with a focus on combating ignorance about

E. S. Reddy protesting apartheid in 1946, soon after his arrival in New York. When African National Congress president Dr. A. B. Xuma visited the United Nations, the Council on African Affairs picketed the South African consulate in support of the ANC. Reddy brought a group of Indian students to join the rally. *Photo reproduced from Hunton 1946.*

Africa with information about liberation struggles against colonialism and apartheid.

In the 1950s, the efforts of this small contingent of Africa activists had little or no direct influence in Washington policy circles. Outreach around the United States was modest at best. As Lisa Brock notes in chapter 2, both the CAA and the ACOA succeeded in disseminating information about Africa and in helping African nationalists make connections in the United States. But without broader media support, the active involvement of large organizations such as the NAACP, or any strong advocates for Africa within the State Department or Congress, the scope for influence was decidedly limited.

Both the CAA and ACOA found ways to be effective, however, within the small but potentially influential context of the "international community" taking shape around United Nations headquarters in Manhattan. Retired U.N. anti-apartheid official E. S. Reddy (2004) recalls that as early as 1946, Alphaeus Hunton of the CAA provided delegates with critical information they needed to stop South African annexation of South West Africa (later Namibia). The ACOA made a significant contribution in the 1950s by supporting African petitioners who came to make their case, helping them with office space, networking, and day-to-day survival in New York City. The list of visitors includes famous names such as Julius Nyerere of Tanganyika, but also less prominent figures such as representatives of Algeria's National Liberation Front and opponents of South African rule in South West Africa.

Around the country, first the CAA and then the ACOA reached thousands of supporters who subscribed to their publications. Still, public opinion about Africa, among both black and white Americans, was shaped primarily by how the mainstream media reported events. The visibility of Africa in the press grew significantly over the decade. Liberal journalist John Gunther published the 950-page *Inside Africa*, one of his widely read "Inside" series, in 1955. Raising its own profile, the ACOA was able to attract the Reverend Martin Luther King Jr., as well as white liberals such as Gunther and Eleanor Roosevelt, to serve on a committee of sponsors.

Though there may be a common impression that the United States at least nudged Europe toward faster decolonization, the historical record shows otherwise. It is true that by the end of the decade, with the advance of decolonization on the continent, activists were in a stronger position to facilitate contacts in Washington. Democratic politicians in the opposition began to refer to Africa. In 1957, for example, Senator John F. Kennedy spoke out against the French colonial war in Algeria and the Dwight Eisenhower administration's support of French policy. Nevertheless, "the overall thrust of U.S. policy toward Africa in the 1950s was the same as the administration's policy toward civil rights at home: to avoid it as much as possible" (Borstelmann 2001, 116).

Both the Truman and Eisenhower administrations focused on keeping the Soviet Union out of Africa. But their strategy for doing so continued to depend on the subordination of Africa to Europe rather than on forging alliances with new African leaders. There were voices within the U.S. Congress and the public demanding that more attention be paid to African aspirations, but those voices were virtually inaudible to policy makers. African nationalists who had hoped that U.S. involvement might provide new negotiating space were disappointed (Nwaubani 2001, 232–34).

If U.S. policy was to develop in support of African freedom, far more Americans would have to know and care about the continent. It was during the 1950s that this began to happen, in part as a result of influence in the other direction—from Africa to the United States. African freedom movements reached out to Americans, through the ACOA as well as through many other connections. American activists were also learning about African freedom movements and asking questions about what the African example might mean for freedom at home. The example of Ghana was foremost, followed by that of Kenya.

At the beginning of the decade the strategies of the leading civil rights organizations were focused on appeals to dominant white institutions—the courts and the political establishment, most often the president. These appeals made the argument that racial discrimination at home handicapped U.S. global leadership by giving ammunition to Soviet propaganda.

Progressive American activists were divided about the Soviet Union. Some, notably those linked to the Communist Party, saw the Soviet Union as an ally against racism and injustice around the world, building on the World War II common front against fascism. Others disagreed, citing internal repression in the Soviet Union as well as the Communist Party's history of manipulation of its allies. But whatever their disagreements about the Soviet Union, activists who looked to the CAA or the ACOA agreed with the African National Congress in South Africa: action against racism and colonialism took priority over Cold War disputes. The national leadership of the NAACP, in contrast, feared offending those in power by staging demonstrations at home or supporting liberation abroad.

Restaurant sit-in, 1945. Bayard Rustin, left, and George Houser led interracial workshops sponsored by the Fellowship of Reconciliation and CORE. When a restaurant in Toledo, Ohio refused to serve them, they decided to sit in. *Photo courtesy of George Houser.*

When Rosa Parks famously refused to give up her seat to a white man on December 1, 1955, the bus boycott in Montgomery, Alabama launched a new phase of the civil rights movement. This was just a few months after the death of Emmett Till. Her act and the boycott that followed were part of a tradition of protest that included Paul Robeson as well as Mahatma Gandhi. Looking back through the prism of the debates about nonviolence in the 1960s and 1970s, it is easy to forget that when activists in the 1950s—in South Africa or the United States—turned to Gandhi, the lesson most embraced was the need to resist rather than the aspect of nonviolence as such. And the perspective, even in the United States, was international. Civil rights activists were influenced not only by Gandhi's ideas but by India's achievement of independence. Many also looked to the examples of resistance in South Africa and in Ghana, which in turn drew inspiration from India's example.

ACOA founder George Houser already had some experience with direct action. In 1947 he had been one of the organizers of the "Journey of Reconciliation" that took a handful of black and white activists through the South, defying bus segregation and courting arrests and beatings but gaining little national attention. He was ready to do more. During the ANC's Defiance Campaign, he recalled, the newly organized Americans for South African Resistance got information from Z. K. Matthews, who was at Union Theological Seminary as a visiting professor for the 1952–53 school year. Matthews was one of the top leaders of the ANC, and his son Joe headed up the Defiance Campaign in the Cape province. While the Defiance Campaign was finally suppressed by the apartheid regime, American activists were impressed to see some 8,500 South Africans going to jail to fight for their rights.

William Minter

In contrast to South Africa, Ghana became a story not only of resistance but also of victory. Returning to Montgomery after Ghana's independence celebration in 1957, Martin Luther King Jr. told his congregation that Ghana taught the lesson that "the oppressor never voluntarily gives freedom to the oppressed. . . . Freedom only comes through persistent revolt" (Carson 2001, chap. 11). The *Amsterdam News* heralded Ghana's independence in March 1957 as "the first robin of spring" for "millions of colored people around the world" (Meriwether 2002, 163).

Kwame Nkrumah himself was one of the interpreters of Africa to Americans. As a student at Lincoln University and the University of Pennsylvania in the 1930s and 1940s, the future Ghanaian leader built ties to U.S. civil rights activists. In July 1958, as president of newly independent Ghana, he made a triumphant visit to the United States. There he not only addressed the House and Senate in Washington but also spoke to enthusiastic thousands gathered to receive him in New York and Chicago.

Pioneer West African nationalist Nnamdi Azikiwe, Nigeria's first president, also counted Lincoln as his alma mater. Like Nkrumah, he established contacts around the United States in his student years that prefigured later ties between Nigerians and Americans. Yet it was also less-known interpreters like Z. K. Matthews and Eduardo Mondlane who made personal connections and friendships behind the scenes. Mondlane, who studied at Oberlin College and Northwestern University, reached out to Americans much as Nkrumah had done two decades earlier. Such relationships helped shape these African leaders, but equally important, they had profound influence on the Americans who came to know them.

In a country as vast as the United States, however, neither these contacts nor the network being built by the ACOA was powerful enough to counter the pervasive ignorance and stereotypes concerning Africa. A 1957 survey found that only 1 percent of African Americans and scarcely 6 percent of white Americans could name as many as five countries in Africa (Nwaubani 2001, 233).

Some of the most pernicious stereotypes stemmed from coverage of the 1952–55 Mau Mau insurrection in Kenya. Robert Ruark's 1955 bestseller *Something of Value*, with its graphic descriptions of African "savagery," helped shape public perception of the uprising, as did biased media accounts. In fact, Mau Mau was a revolt by people in Kikuyu-speaking areas that had suffered mass expropriation of land by white settlers. It was brutally suppressed by the British. While both sides committed atrocities, less than 100 whites and some 2,000 Africans were killed by insurgents; the British killed, by official count, 11,500 insurgents and executed 1,015 captives (Minter 1986, 118–24). Two new studies by historians David Anderson (2005) and Caroline Elkins (2005) provide detailed documentation of the horrific violations of human rights perpetrated by the British authorities, settlers, and loyalists, including torture, displacement, imprisonment of civilians, and summary execution of prisoners and suspects.

In Britain, criticism of the war by opposition Labour party politicians eventually gained some attention. But in the United States, with the exception of a 1954 conference organized in New York by the Council on African Affairs (Meriwether 2002, 124–49), there was virtually no analysis or criticism of the war. Among many black Americans, the term "Mau Mau" signified resistance. But few Americans, black or white, were in direct communication with Kenyans who could have provided a more complete picture of the revolt and the events that led up to it.

In the early 1960s, following the independence of many African countries, an influx of African students arrived to pursue higher education in the United States. As Americans came into contact with these students, opportunities to know Africans and learn about Africa increased substantially. The receptions for Kwame Nkrumah and for Kenyan nationalist leader Tom Mboya in the 1950s had illustrated the eagerness of Americans for direct contact with African spokespersons. Most young Africans who came to study in the United States were not destined for high political office, of course, nor were all inclined to political activism. But with their numbers growing from only a few hundred in the early 1950s to several thousand a decade later, their influence was greater than is generally recognized.

Beginning in 1959, the students included those brought by the ACOA-linked African-American Students Foundation, as well as those who found their way to the United States on other programs.

Jackie Robinson

Ida Wood of the Phelps Stokes Fund, left, and Eunice Kennedy Shriver.

## Welcoming African Students

The African-American Students Foundation chartered planes in 1959 and 1960 to bring more than 300 East African students to New York to take up scholarships around the United States. The welcome programs for their arrival, organized by Cora Weiss, included meetings with prominent Americans, from baseball pioneer Jackie Robinson, who headed the fundraising campaign for the 1959 airlift, to Malcolm X, Eunice Kennedy Shriver, Ida Wood of the Phelps Stokes Fund, and Rep. Charles Diggs. The second airlift, in 1960, was financed with a grant from a Kennedy family foundation.
*Photos courtesy of Cora Weiss.*

William Minter

*Clockwise from top left:*
Lorraine Hansberry
Malcolm X
Cora Weiss, left, and Ida Wood
Representative Charles Diggs

They were dispersed to colleges and universities around the country, some to Southern white colleges where they were the first blacks admitted, some to historically black institutions and large universities (C. Weiss 2003). At the end of the decade, African students were enrolled at almost all of the historically black colleges in the United States. Repeatedly, in interviews or in conversations about this book, activists who grew up in the 1960s mentioned that their families had hosted African students or that they had met African students on campus.

These students brought with them not only an understanding of their home countries but also a growing consciousness of the unfinished freedom march down the continent, a march that was blocked by white minority regimes across the southern third of Africa. A 1960 study of black youth in the United States reported that African students often challenged their African American colleagues to be more aggressive in seeking freedom (*Washington Post*, March 6, 1960, A17). At an ecumenical student conference in Athens, Ohio at the end of the 1950s, which was attended by hundreds of Southern black students, the Africans present reportedly "stole the show" (Carson 1981,16).

## The 1960s

For me, the 1960s began with the Athens conference over the 1959–60 winter break. A college freshman, I was one of some 3,500 people gathered at the University of Ohio in Athens. Sponsored by the Protestant ecumenical National Student Christian Federation (NSCF), the conference included more than 100 Africans and at least 900 students from other countries. We were guided through an intensive program that emphasized the Christian responsibility to take action for social justice at home and abroad. Conference co-chair Bola Ige, who went on to become a highly respected Nigerian lawyer and was attorney general at the time of his assassination in 1998, eloquently denounced imperialism as well as racism. Martin Luther King Jr. and Nashville-based James Lawson, soon to be one of the leading sit-in leaders, called for action, not words, against racial injustice.

Less than a month after they returned to their campuses, in early 1960, many students who had been at Athens joined the wave of sit-ins against segregated restaurants across the South. Our small

Eduardo Mondlane in his senior class picture at Oberlin College, 1953. *Photo courtesy of Oberlin College Archives.*

student group in Tucson, Arizona, took on a less dramatic campaign to ban landlords who discriminated from the university registry of off-campus housing.

That same year, 17 African countries gained their independence. British prime minister Harold Macmillan declared at a widely heralded speech in Cape Town, South Africa, that the colonial powers had to adapt to the "wind of change" that was sweeping the continent. John F. Kennedy narrowly won election over Richard Nixon after a well-publicized intervention to help gain the release of Martin Luther King Jr. from jail. Just as Africans expected Britain to respond to peaceful protests by accelerating progress toward independence, so civil rights demonstrators hoped to arouse Washington to support their campaign against segregation.

Already, however, there were signs that the journey would be dangerous and prolonged. On March 21, 1960, South African police killed 69 demonstrators at Sharpeville. And just after Kennedy's election in November, Congo's elected prime minister, Patrice Lumumba, was captured by the forces of Joseph Mobutu at the instigation of the U.S. Central Intelligence Agency (CIA). They turned him over to be executed by Belgian-backed rebels only days before Kennedy's inauguration in January 1961.

By the end of the 1960s, few African liberation leaders or U.S. Africa activists retained any illusions that Washington would respond to moral appeals to act against white minority rule in Africa. Africa activists were part of a generation radicalized by their experiences in the domestic civil rights movement and their opposition to the Vietnam War. This radicalization was reinforced by the realities they saw in Southern Africa. African movements were forced to take up arms, while the United States continued its ties with the white regimes. Activists in turn identified with the African movements. The activists targeted not only U.S. government policy but also corporate interests that were seen as bolstering oppression at home and abroad.

This shift in perspective was propelled in part by events in Africa, but it also reflected the changes in American life associated with the 1960s. The narratives of this period are as diverse as the decade itself. For some, whether they applaud or deplore the results, the emergence of a counterculture is the central story. For others, the political evolution from Kennedy to Johnson to Nixon takes center stage. For historians of the period, and probably for the majority of activists, Africa was hardly visible. Indeed, most volumes recounting "the 1960s" hardly mention the continent. For many of us, however, African connections and experiences were closely interwoven with engagement in the civil rights movement and the movement against the Vietnam War. By the end of the decade, as Mimi Edmunds describes in chapter 3, a much larger and diverse array of political forces on the left was becoming aware of Africa and other parts of what was then called the Third World.

Developments in the civil rights movement at home were fundamental to this evolution. The commonly repeated civil rights narrative centers on moments such as Martin Luther King's "I Have a Dream" speech at the 1963 March on Washington. Historians also often cite President Lyndon Johnson's appropriation of the anthem "We Shall Overcome" in pressing for a new civil rights act after the nationally televised white violence at Selma, Alabama in 1965. The summary lesson is that Washington and the mainstream white majority joined protesters in rejecting the explicit racism of Southern whites. In this celebratory version, the victory over segregation was won in the 1960s. The meaning of Martin Luther

King's opposition to the Vietnam War, his assassination, and demands for economic justice as well as political inclusion have no place in this story.

Bill Sutherland and George Houser at Zambian independence celebration in Lusaka, October 1964. *Photo courtesy of George Houser.*

For most civil rights activists, white as well as black, the story was more complex and the outcome far more ambiguous. Despite the laws passed, the restaurants integrated, and the voters registered, we also saw the Federal Bureau of Investigation (FBI) target protesters more enthusiastically than they investigated white racist violence. It was no secret that liberal white politicians, from the White House on down, were more interested in urging protesters to be patient than they were in addressing racial and economic inequality. In 1964 the Democratic Party refused to seat the elected delegates from the Mississippi Freedom Democratic Party, giving preference to the racially exclusive delegation of the Mississippi white establishment. Murders of civil rights workers—Medgar Evers in 1963, James Chaney, Andrew Goodman, and Mickey Schwerner in 1964, and many others less known—went unpunished or unsolved. In August 1965 violence in the Watts section of Los Angeles led to the killings of 34 people, most by police or national guardsmen. Watts marked the beginning of years of urban unrest that exposed the fact that racial inequality was entrenched nationwide rather than confined to the Southern states.

As the war in Vietnam escalated, student and civil rights activists joined traditional peace groups in mobilizing against the war. In April 1965 over 20,000 demonstrators showed up in Washington for an antiwar demonstration spearheaded by Students for a Democratic Society (SDS). Speakers at the gathering included Bob Moses of the Student Nonviolent Coordinating Committee (SNCC), the civil rights group that was most active in speaking out against the war. By 1967 Martin Luther King Jr. had overcome resistance from his more cautious advisers to denounce the U.S. government as "the greatest purveyor of violence in the world today" (King 1967). The speech brought down on King a barrage of condemnation from "mainstream" liberals and civil rights leaders, reminiscent of that unleashed against Robeson and Du Bois in the 1950s.

After an exhilarating beginning, the 1960s witnessed a slowing of the momentum of liberation that had brought so many countries to independence. The decade that opened with the Sharpeville massacre and Lumumba's assassination continued with South Africa's arrest of Nelson Mandela in 1962, allegedly with the help of a tip-off from the CIA. There were civil wars in the Congo (1960–65) and in Nigeria (1967–70). A military coup ousted Kwame Nkrumah in Ghana (1966). Portuguese colonialists and white settlers prevailed in the southern third of the continent. The Nixon administration that took office in 1969 based its Africa policy on the stated assumption that the white minority regimes were "here to stay." Activists' hopes to the contrary were based as much on the conviction that justice must eventually triumph as on any evidence then available.

While the 1950s provided the hopeful image of independent Ghana, it is the specter of the Congo that haunts and still obscures the 1960s. Because of the preoccupation with the Cold War, what little

attention presidents Kennedy and Johnson gave to Africa was centered on the Congo. The United States aided white mercenaries who were slaughtering thousands of Africans in the eastern Congo in 1964, yet U.S. officials and media focused almost exclusively on the fate of white hostages. By mid-decade the CIA had installed Joseph Mobutu as the country's dictator, sealing Congo's fate for the remainder of the century.

In the United States, meanwhile, white racist groups mobilized to influence U.S. Africa policy, including the Friends of Rhodesia and a lobby for secessionist Katanga in the Congo. Their clout significantly outweighed the impact of those of us campaigning for African freedom. Neither the ACOA, which had supported Lumumba, nor black nationalists from Harlem, who had demonstrated at the United Nations after his death, had the capacity to project alternative policies for the Congo into the U.S. political debate. More than 40 years later, an official U.S. apology or investigation of U.S. complicity in Lumumba's assassination remains hardly conceivable.

In retrospect, one might think that repression by South Africa's apartheid regime in the early 1960s would attract more attention in the United States, given the dramatic rise of the civil rights movement at home during the same period. President Kennedy's inauguration led to expectations that Washington would take action against apartheid and colonialism. But his administration was driven by Cold War concerns. Apart from a vote for a voluntary U.N. arms embargo against South Africa in 1963, it gave little more than lip service to anti-apartheid ideas. Senator Robert Kennedy's June 1966 visit to South Africa—one of the few signs of awakening concern—failed to lead to any ongoing engagement. Nor, apart from the symbolic identification with the anti-apartheid cause, did Robert Kennedy himself follow up his speeches with proposals for a changed U.S. policy.

The emerging New Left, for its part, paid no more than passing attention to Africa. In March 1965, five years after the Sharpeville massacre, a demonstration called by SDS, with the support of smaller groups such as the National Student Christian Federation, brought more than 400 demonstrators to the New York headquarters of Chase Manhattan Bank to protest the bank's loans to South Africa. SNCC organized a sit-in at the South African consulate. Yet Africa dropped from the SDS agenda after the demonstration. Although Todd Gitlin was one of the organizers of the demonstration for SDS, for example, there is no entry for Africa in his book on the 1960s (Gitlin 1987). In SNCC also, there was little follow-up to the demonstration despite growing consciousness of Africa. As conflict escalated both in Vietnam and in U.S. cities, only a few U.S. activists—most with recent personal connections to the continent—saw Africa as a primary focus for their work.

Throughout the decade, the American Committee on Africa continued as the principal contact point in the United States for African liberation movement leaders. Shortly after Sharpeville, Oliver Tambo of South Africa's ANC toured the country at ACOA's invitation, as did other liberation movement leaders in later years. The Lawyers' Committee for Civil Rights Under Law created its Southern Africa Project in 1967, providing a way for progressive U.S. lawyers to support political prisoners in South Africa and Namibia. Groups of younger activists also emerged, including the Southern Africa Com-

mittee of the NSCF in New York in 1964, the Liberation Support Movement among U.S. draft resisters in Vancouver, Canada, in 1968, and the Africa Research Group in Boston the same year. Also in 1968, SNCC veterans founded the Center for Black Education and the Drum and Spear Bookstore in Washington, DC.

The ACOA already shared a common agenda with the younger activists. Despite the pacifist roots of some of its leaders, the organization supported the African liberation movements as they turned from nonviolent protest to armed struggle in the 1960s. The 1960 Emergency Action Conference against Apartheid that was convened in response to Sharpeville fully endorsed African demands for a boycott against South Africa. And the ACOA pioneered in exposing U.S. corporate ties that reinforced apartheid, an effort that would grow over the next three decades into a multiplicity of actions targeting such companies as well as institutions investing in them.

By the end of the decade, there was broad agreement among activists on the twin objectives of

The World Conference for Action Against Apartheid held in Lagos, Nigeria, in August 1977 brought together liberation movement leaders with representatives of more than 100 governments and the United Nations. Theo-Ben Gurirab, right, the SWAPO representative in New York, was very well known to U.S. activists. At his left is SWAPO president Sam Nujoma. *UN Photo.*

direct support for liberation movements and action against U.S. companies linked to South Africa. On both fronts, the movement had its most consistent congressional ally in Representative Charles Diggs of Detroit, who took over as chair of the House Subcommittee on Africa in 1969. Diggs, who also helped launch the Congressional Black Caucus that year, had been outspoken on civil rights at home and abroad since he was first elected to Congress in 1954. He traveled to Mississippi to witness the sham trial of Emmett Till's killers in 1955 and was an active supporter of the African-American Students Foundation from its inception in 1959.

David Sibeko, who represented the Pan Africanist Congress in New York from 1975 until his death in 1979, was an active campaigner who was well received by groups around the United States. *UN Photo.*

More than any organization or politician, however, South African exiles in the United States helped raise awareness of South Africa among Americans through their personal ties to universities and communities around the country. Ben Magubane, profiled in chapter 3, was one of many. The 1969 conference in North Carolina mentioned in that chapter included organizer Rev. Gladstone Ntlabati, Magubane's university colleagues Martin Legassick and Anthony Ngubo from California, as well as Rev. Chris Nteta and Rev. Ken Carstens from Boston. Magubane himself, who did not attend the conference because he was in Zambia at the time, maintained a broad range of contacts that included PAC supporter Peter

Molotsi; Liberal Party member Leo Kuper, who was his academic adviser; and Dr. A. C. Jordan, a prominent member of the Unity Movement, a small but intellectually significant liberation group.

Among the exiles, perhaps the voices most widely heard by Americans were those of musicians—Miriam Makeba, Hugh Masekela, Abdullah Ibrahim (Dollar Brand), and others. Like American singer-activist Harry Belafonte, who took the initiative to open doors for them in the United States, these musicians were deeply engaged with the fight for freedom. They lent their talents to freedom concerts hosted by the ACOA and sent a powerful message through their music.

Miriam Makeba was banned from South Africa in 1960 and lived in the United States for most of the decade. She sang at President Kennedy's birthday celebration in Madison Square Garden in 1962. In 1963 she testified before the United Nations Special Committee Against Apartheid, calling for a complete boycott of South Africa. Her songs were banned in South Africa, but in the United States she sang to overflow crowds around the country.

Makeba married SNCC leader Stokely Carmichael in 1968. As Carmichael moved to the left politically, he became a target of right-wing forces. Promoters cancelled Makeba's American concert and recording contracts, and in late 1968 the couple moved to Conakry in West Africa at the invitation of Guinean president Sekou Toure. In Conakry, Carmichael worked closely with exiled Ghanaian leader Kwame Nkrumah and took the name Kwame Ture in a tribute to the leaders of both Ghana and Guinea. Makeba focused her career on European and African venues.

Their distance from the United States mirrored the general eclipse of Africa among U.S. activists, in comparison with the focus on Vietnam and on domestic issues. Nkrumah's name had faded from prominence. Sekou Toure, from French-speaking Africa, had never been widely known in the United States. Even Nelson Mandela had not yet been featured in the media and was as yet known to only a few.

Despite appearances, however, the small network of African connections of the late 1960s was on the verge of expansion. Still below the radar screen of public attention that would only light up in the mid-

1980s, activists inspired by African liberation and outraged by oppression in Africa and at home were growing in numbers across the United States.

## The 1970s

Returning to the United States from Tanzania in early 1969, I found a very different climate than the one I had left several years before. The antiwar movement, the civil rights movement, and the U.S. Left were fracturing along multiple ideological and strategic lines. The debates pitted violent against nonviolent tactics, black nationalist against multiracial strategies, and various Marxist ideologies against each other. There was also conflict among many forceful, competitive personalities, often exacerbated by government provocation—a mix that was often bewildering and sometimes deadly.

### Solidarity against Portuguese Colonialism

But underneath this turmoil a broad consensus on key African issues continued to grow among activists. Support for the liberation movements that had taken up arms against Portuguese colonialism and the white settler regimes was the first common denominator. The second was support for campaigns to challenge corporate complicity with Portugal, Rhodesia, and South Africa. It was possible to target these companies and banks directly at a time when official sanctions against South Africa were still a distant goal.

In the 1970s, Tanzania, with its leader Julius Nyerere, profoundly influenced activists and others who were beginning to take an interest in the continent. Among the general American public, however, not even Tanzania and Nyerere could command the level of attention that Ghana and Kwame Nkrumah had received in the 1950s and early 1960s. The novelty of African independence had passed, while the ongoing wars in Southern Africa received little attention and no regular coverage in the establishment media. Even the names of the countries engaged in liberation struggles—Guinea-Bissau, Cape Verde, Angola, Mozambique, Namibia, Zimbabwe—remained exotic or obscure. When the Committee for a Free Mozambique distributed a button with the slogan "Free Mozambique" in 1971, people asked, "Who's Mozambique?"

Amilcar Cabral, leader of the African Party for the Independence of Guinea-Bissau and Cape Verde (PAIGC), first came to the United States in February 1970, just a year after Mondlane's assassination. Cabral made only brief visits to the United States before he himself was assassinated by Portuguese agents in January 1973. But he provided Africa activists with guidance and inspiration disproportionate to the time he spent, strengthening their commitment to solidarity with the liberation movements.

Eduardo Mondlane had taught at Syracuse University in the early 1960s and a memorial lecture had been established in his honor. Cabral was the invited lecturer in 1970 and spoke on "national liberation and culture." Because the PAIGC had established liberated territories in the small Portuguese-occupied colony of Guinea-Bissau, it had credibility as a movement actively fighting for a country's independence. Cabral stressed the importance not of military action as such, but of the cultural and political renewal of African people. Like his contemporary Frantz Fanon, Cabral stressed the physical and psychological violence perpetrated by the colonialists and internalized by the colonized. His impressive personal presence added weight to his message. Publication of his speeches and accounts of the liberated areas by distinguished Africanist scholars such as Basil Davidson made Cabral one of the most influential thinkers for both American and African activists seeking perspective.

One of the keynotes of Cabral's message, paralleling Robeson's in an earlier generation, was that Africa was part of a worldwide struggle for justice. The enemy, the PAIGC stressed, was not the Portuguese people or whites as such, but the structures of oppression embodied in Portuguese colonialism. Cabral consistently reached out to potential allies across racial as well as ideological lines without ever downplaying his confident pride in African identity or his own movement's distinctive views.

After his lecture at Syracuse, Cabral visited New York, where he met informally with a group hosted by ACOA. Gail Hovey's notes of the gathering record that he spoke very specifically about the impact of colonialism on his country and then talked about life in the liberated zones, how the local villages were organized for education, medical care, and so on. He said that although they hadn't

Amilcar Cabral speaks on receiving an honorary degree from Lincoln University in Pennsylvania, 1972. Distinguished alumni of the university include Ghana's first president, Kwame Nkrumah, and Nigeria's first president, Nnamdi Azikiwe.
*Photo by Ray Lewis for Africa Information Service.*

Madison was already an activist campus and town. In May 1968, some 300 students had sat in at the administration building to demand withdrawal of university investments in Chase Manhattan Bank. And it was not alone in early actions against investment in South Africa. In 1968–69 there were demonstrations at Princeton University, Cornell University, Spelman College, and the University of California at Santa Barbara. Nor were radicalized students and faculty the only sectors responding to African liberation. Within U.S. churches, as well, the campaign to divest funds from South Africa was growing, while support for liberation movements became an issue for churches worldwide.

Endorsements by the Organization of African Unity and the United Nations strengthened the legitimacy of the liberation movements. So too did actions by global religious institutions. In July 1970 Pope Paul VI met with Amilcar Cabral and liberation movement leaders from Angola and Mozambique. In September 1970 the World Council of Churches, whose membership comprised 253 Protestant and Orthodox churches including almost all the major U.S. denominations, announced $200,000 in grants to groups fighting racism. The recipients included liberation movements in Guinea-Bissau, Angola, Mozambique, South Africa, Namibia, and Zimbabwe. Despite a storm of conservative protest, including a 1971 *Reader's Digest* article attacking the World Council, the grants continued. In October 1970 the United Nations General Assembly overwhelmingly affirmed the "inherent right of colonial people to struggle by all necessary means" for their freedom. The roster of negative votes—South Africa, Australia, New Zealand, Great Britain, and the United States—graphically illustrated the rift between a handful of powerful Western governments and broad world opinion.

planned it that way, men and women were equal partners. The women had insisted on their role in the movement and were now a fundamental part of it. From New York, Cabral traveled to Washington, where he testified before the House Subcommittee on Africa chaired by Representative Diggs. In 1972 Cabral visited again, receiving an honorary doctorate at Lincoln University and meeting with supporters in New York.

I was not on the East Coast for either of Cabral's visits. But I was part of a local Madison Area Committee on Southern Africa in Wisconsin that was campaigning actively in favor of his movement. The same week that Cabral spoke in Syracuse, the University of Wisconsin's Luso-Brazilian center hosted a Portuguese government film on Portugal's "overseas provinces." The 200 protesters we organized with the African Students Union and the Black Council outnumbered the original audience and turned the event into a teach-in on Portuguese colonialism. An exiled Portuguese poet joined us in denouncing the Portuguese fascist regime and affirming common ground with African liberation.

## The Movement Grows

During the 1970s, new immigrants from sub-Saharan Africa to the United States more than tripled, from less than 3,000 a year to more than 10,000 a year. Still a small fraction of immigrants in comparison to those from other continents, this group nonetheless included many politically conscious and well-educated activists whose influence on American activists was disproportionate to their small numbers. The Cape Verdean community was a special case. Numbering more than 300,000 and centered in New England, it included families who had immigrated centuries before as well as recent arrivals from the islands. Despite differences between these two groups, Amilcar Cabral's stature contributed to a new sense of pride arising from their country's drive for independence.

Not only were Africans coming to the United States; Americans were going to Africa. They included thousands of Peace Corps volunteers and smaller numbers from other programs who returned and spread out around the country. Their experiences and views were diverse, but almost invariably they testified that the impact of Africa on their lives outweighed any contribution they might have been able to make to African development. Despite the Peace Corps' official independence from political direction, some U.S. officials as well as critics saw the volunteers as tools of U.S. foreign policy. But in the political climate of the 1960s and early 1970s, these work and study-abroad programs and the experiences they provided became fertile ground for movement recruiting.

These years also saw the development of the women's liberation movement and the rise of feminism in the United States and around the globe. The civil rights movement, by its example, and the 1964 Civil Rights Act, which outlawed discrimination on the basis of gender as well as race, contributed directly to the parallel movement for women's rights. The women's movement often meant different things for black women than for white; there were fierce debates in both communities about ideology, strategies, and tactics. For women involved in Africa solidarity work, the two movements intersected closely. The engagement with Africa sometimes provided a meeting place where black and white women could find common ground.

Women of different generations often had different priorities. Older women on both sides of the Atlantic tended to argue that the nationalist struggle or the civil rights struggle had to take precedence. Younger women often felt that including equal rights for women could not be postponed and was in fact central to both the goals and the strategies of the movement. Wrestling with such issues as they worked for civil rights and national liberation, women helped to shape the debate about what a transformed society might look like.

Johnny Makatini, African National Congress representative in the United States, speaks at a United Nations press conference, August 25, 1981. *UN Photo.*

How people were drawn into solidarity work with Africa varied for each African country, as the liberation movements drew on specific networks to make connections in the United States. Namibia was a case in point. Illegally occupied by South Africa, Namibia was the most blatant example of South African defiance of United Nations rulings. With fewer than a million people in 1970, Namibia was little known in the United States; few Americans had ever been there. Nevertheless, the South West Africa People's Organisation, known as SWAPO, drew hundreds if not thousands of Americans into active support of its cause. From 1964 to 1975, Hage Geingob, who two decades later became prime minister, actively represented SWAPO from his base in New York while studying at Fordham University and then serving in an official post at the United Nations.

South Africa helped indirectly to mobilize additional support for Namibia by expelling successive Anglican clergy who opposed the apartheid regime there, beginning with Bishop Robert Mize from Kansas in 1968. Throughout the 1970s and 1980s, Bill Johnston of Episcopal Churchmen for South Africa (later Episcopal Churchpeople for a Free Southern

Africa) was an indefatigable campaigner for Namibia. After the African Lutheran Bishops of Namibia issued an open letter in 1971 calling for South African withdrawal from their country, many Lutherans in the United States also became involved in active support for Namibian independence. In 1978 Namibian students at Wartburg Theological Seminary in Dubuque, Iowa, were among the founders of National Namibia Concerns, which reached out to congregations across the Midwest and nationally.

It was during the 1970s that the challenge to U.S. investments in South Africa, which began in the 1960s and reached its peak in the 1980s, first

Paul Irish of the American Committee on Africa, Chris Root of the Washington Office on Africa, and Roberta Washington of the Southern Africa Committee at the Conference to Support the Peoples of Zimbabwe and Namibia held in Maputo, Mozambique in May 1977. *Photo courtesy of Richard Knight.*

spread across the country. Banks and corporations responded initially with indifference, then defended their involvement as contributing to the reform of apartheid. Church financial officers and top officials, and later university administrators, followed a similar path, moving from disregard to study commissions to reform proposals. Activists who identified with African liberation, in contrast, argued that U.S. corporate involvement prolonged the apartheid regime's viability, and they demanded that companies withdraw until apartheid was ended.

The focus on corporate withdrawal rather than government sanctions came in part because activists had concluded that there was little or no hope of gaining U.S. government support for sanctions against apartheid. The Nixon administration was even more unequivocal in its tilt toward the white regimes of Southern Africa than its Democratic predecessors had been. There were also strategic advantages in focusing on particular companies. It was possible to make an impact. Although denying that they had been influenced by pressure, Chase Manhattan and nine other banks canceled a $40 million revolving loan to the South African government in 1969 after four national church agencies threatened to remove funds from the banks. Moreover, corporate-focused campaigns like this gave the opportunity for decentralized actions.

The number of actions in the early 1970s was small in comparison to the wave of campus protests that would erupt after the Soweto student rebellion in June 1976. But the information base and the repertoire of strategies and tactics were already well developed. In 1970 the ACOA published "Apartheid and Imperialism: A Study of U.S. Corporate Involvement in South Africa." Over the first half of the 1970s there was a proliferation of reports from the U.N., church agencies, activist groups, congressional committees, and others, detailing the involvement of dozens of companies not only with South Africa but also with Portuguese colonialism in Africa.

Most church agencies hesitated to demand withdrawal or to withdraw their own investments in companies. Many turned to shareholder resolutions to raise the issues. This strategy was institutionalized when the National Council of Churches founded a Corporate Information Center in 1971 to coordinate information and action on such issues; it became the Interfaith Center on Corporate Responsibility in 1972. Another group, the Investor Responsibility Research Center, was founded in 1972 by universities and other institutional investors with the mandate to provide them with "impartial" research to use in responding to protests and shareholder resolutions.

Identification with Africa took many forms among African American activists on campuses and in cities during the early 1970s. Some focused primarily on culture or history, with emphasis on Africa's past, including the symbolically important civilization of ancient Egypt. Others looked mainly for connections to current African issues. Some were already on the way to academic careers and fighting the battles that would lead to new programs of black studies, Afro-American studies, or Africana studies. Others were turning to local politics, both militant protest and participation in the electoral arena. Despite the differences, however, there was common ground in support for those fighting apartheid and colonialism.

This movement, with a presence in almost every city and on almost every university campus, would provide one of the natural constituencies for anti-apartheid action when apartheid gained national attention in the 1980s. In the nexus of connections that gave political content to the African liberation message in the 1970s, Tanzania was the foremost crossroads where U.S. activists met Africans, including those involved in the liberation movements across Southern Africa. It was in President Nyerere's Tanzania that the Organization of African Unity had established its Liberation Committee, and all the liberation movements from white-ruled Southern Africa had offices there.

## A Pan-African Vision

Bob Moses of SNCC arrived in Tanzania in 1969. He was joined by three other SNCC veterans the next year: Charlie Cobb, Courtland Cox, and Judy Richardson. The three of them had founded the Drum and Spear Bookstore and the related Center for Black Education in Washington, DC, with the support of veteran Pan-African intellectual C. L. R. James and Tanzanian ambassador Paul Bomani. Drum and Spear was a space where community activists and local schoolteachers could mingle with diplomats, writers, and artists; it was also a base for regular interchange between Washington and Dar es Salaam over the decade. It had ties to parallel institutions in other cities around the United States. Drum and Spear established a close relationship with the newly formed Tanzania Publishing House, and Drum and Spear staffer Geri Marsh (later Geri

Augusto) served as Washington correspondent for Tanzanian newspapers.

In May 1972, the African Liberation Day coalition mobilized as many as 30,000 demonstrators in Washington, 10,000 in San Francisco, and 20,000 elsewhere, as Joseph Jordan recounts in chapter 4. The origins of the coalition also go back to the Dar es Salaam crossroads, and in particular to the Mozambique Liberation Front, Frelimo, which relied on Tanzanian support for its liberation war to the south. In August and September 1971, Robert Van Lierop, an African American lawyer in New York and an activist on the board of the ACOA, traveled with Frelimo guerillas into liberated territory in Mozambique, accompanied by cameraman Robert Fletcher. Owusu Sadaukai (Howard Fuller), of Malcolm X Liberation University in Greensboro, North Carolina, accompanied them part way. When Sadaukai raised the prospect of black Americans coming to help fight in Mozambique, Frelimo president Samora Machel reportedly told him that what was needed was work back in the United States. "If you could play a role in that," Machel reportedly said, "it would help us much more than sending folks over here" (Waller 2002, 54–55).

Van Lierop's film *A Luta Continua* was shown hundreds of times to community groups, black studies classes, and church groups. Frelimo representative Sharfudine Khan, based in New York from 1968 to 1975, reached out effectively to both black and white constituencies. Many new groups became involved in this period, from the Committee for a Free Mozambique in New York to the Committee for the Liberation of Angola, Mozambique, and Guinea-Bissau in Chicago and the Southern Africa News Collective in Washington. Even so, solidarity with the movements fighting Portuguese colonialism never gained mainstream media attention. Most of the local black nationalist or Marxist groups that received the message enthusiastically had little opportunity to follow up with ongoing ties to Mozambique or other African countries. Nor were there any ideological or rhetorical formulas for transplanting a revolutionary united front from an African to an American environment.

## Complex Networks

African liberation movement leaders visiting the United States were more accustomed to meeting representatives of Western European support networks that had clearly defined political alliances. They found the United States a bewildering contrast, despite the common ground they had with their African American supporters in experiences of racism and repression and despite a shared view of the war in Vietnam as a manifestation of American imperialism. U.S. radicals, black or white, were unable to build political forces capable of quickly changing their own communities or speedily stopping the Vietnam War. Much less were they able to have a material impact on the balance of power in Africa. Geographic dispersion and racial and ideological fragmentation made it difficult to see much potential in these scattered groups for countering Washington's alliance with the white minority regimes.

Nonetheless, by the 1970s the liberation movements and their supporters did have some allies within the halls of power in Washington. Representative Diggs became the chair of the House Africa Subcommittee in 1969. By 1971 the number of African American representatives in Congress had more than doubled, to 13, and Diggs and his colleagues created the Congressional Black Caucus. With veterans such as fellow Detroiter John Conyers and newcomers such as Ron Dellums from Berkeley, California, this small band took on the responsibility of bringing to national attention not only the interests of their urban constituencies but also the concerns of the black world at large.

Diggs also co-chaired the 1972 National Black Political Convention in Gary, Indiana with Richard Hatcher, mayor of Gary, and black nationalist Amiri Baraka of Newark, New Jersey. Diggs unambiguously endorsed the movement consensus in favor of isolating South Africa and supporting the African liberation movements. His trips to Africa and the extraordinary investigative work of his staff attorney Goler Teal Butcher ensured that the critique of U.S. policy was based on reality rather than rhetoric.

At that time, neither the Black Caucus nor the Africa Subcommittee had enough weight in Congress to prevail over entrenched interests. They were unsuccessful, for example, in their attempt to deny South Africa a sugar quota giving it special access to the U.S. market, even though their efforts won the backing of Senator Edward Kennedy. And the public paid little attention. But the caucus and subcommittee provided an essential point of reference and a communication channel for both old and new activists identifying with African liberation.

This was true despite the turmoil of the decade, which saw increasing divisions between black community activists and black elected officials on domestic issues and electoral politics. Black militant organizations succumbed to government repression and internal disputes. The antiwar movement splintered even while helping hasten the end of the war. The Republican Party moved even further to the right, while much of the Democratic Party fled from a liberal label. The "Black Power" label was as likely to serve as justification for black business promotion as for community activism.

Nevertheless, the networks linking Africa activists in churches, communities, congressional offices, and universities continued to grow. This growth was nurtured, and the pace determined, by African as well as American realities.

One example, which Joseph Jordan discusses in his chapter on the 1970s, is the discovery by a small group of workers at the Polaroid Corporation in Cambridge, Massachusetts, that the company's South African subsidiary was providing equipment and film used in the apartheid pass law system. The campaign against Polaroid gained national prominence, but it was just one example of a pattern repeated many times during the decade in which local activists took their own initiatives. They sought out information and identified local targets embodying the U.S. connection to the white minority regimes in Africa. They built local ad hoc groups or coalitions, invited speakers, showed films, sold literature, and raised money or goods to be sent to support the liberation movements. Although most groups lasted only a few years as formal organizations, they had lasting impact through the minds they changed and the informal networks they created.

At the 1972 Azalea Festival in Norfolk, Virginia, over 500 people protested when the military port city honored Portugal as a member of the North Atlantic Treaty Organization (NATO). They distributed 50,000 leaflets calling for "Portugal out of NATO, NATO out of Norfolk" and denouncing U.S.

# the southern PATRIOT

VOL. 32, NO. 5     MAY, 1974     PUBLISHED BY SOUTHERN CONFERENCE EDUCATIONAL FUND (SCEF), LOUISVILLE, KY.

# Coal From South Africa

## Apartheid in The Mines

*The following article is taken from a memorandum written by Tom Bethell of the United Mine Workers of America. It describes the new development of coal imports from South Africa, the threat this is to the job security of U.S. miners, and the added strength it will give to the repressive apartheid policies of the South African government.*

Arrangements are currently being made to bring substantial quantities of low-sulfur steam coal into the United States from the Republic of South Africa. This move on the part of the coal and utilities industries requires a strong response on the part of the UMWA, because it takes jobs away from American miners and because coal is produced in South Africa under conditions very close to slave labor. (Continued on page 7)

## Alabama Miners Say "No"

BIRMINGHAM, Ala.—Almost 1,000 people took part in a rally and picket line here on May 22. They were letting the stockholders of the Southern Company know that they were opposed to coal being imported from South Africa.

The occasion was the annual stockholders' meeting of the Southern Company, a holding company which owns Georgia Power Company, Alabama Power Company, Mississippi Power Company, and Gulf Power Company.

At issue was a contract signed by the Southern Company to import 2 million tons ($50 million worth) of coal from South African coal producers over the next 3 years. The first shipment will be brought into the Port of Mobile in mid-July and burned at generating stations in Florida.

Rank and file members, particularly from District 20 of the UMWA and other unions, as well as people from various community organizations made the rally the largest and most militant gathering in Alabama in over a decade.

The coal companies employing District 20 members reported absenteeism at around 90%. The miners said they were not on strike but that they were "taking time' off to take care of business."

Approximately 100 miners went to the state capitol in Montgomery to see elected government officials. Governor Wallace was out of town and the politicians told the miners that they couldn't do anything to prevent American corporations from importing coal.

At the Birmingham picket line the men were angry, and they manifested their attitude both in their conversation and in the slogans on their signs: "Pull the switch on Southern Co.", "Stop Southern Company Imperialism" and "No Slave Coal".

After two hours of picketing, the miners held a rally on a corner of the hotel lot. Acting as coordinator was Andy Himes of the Selma Project, an Alabama political action group which worked in the last United Mine Workers election to help throw out the corrupt Tony Boyle machine.

Among the speakers was Mrs. John Marchant, the wife of a retired miner from Brookwood, a coal town

outside Birmingham. Mrs. Marchant talked about the lynchings, lockouts, and "yellow dog" (anti-union) contracts the companies had used against the miners in the twenties and about how her own brother had been killed in a roof fall in the thirties. She said it was profit that they had to fight then and it was profit they had to fight now.

Don Stone of the Black Workers Congress spoke about the conditions in the South African coal fields and stressed the importance of fighting in both places against the same enemy, the monopoly capitalist corporations.

Andy Himes wound things up with a statement about how the Company was not only chiseling the miners of Alabama out of jobs but that the electric ratepayers of the Southeast were being expected to pick up the tab. "They say that they're concerned about Alabama because they live here too. Well, that's a damn lie. Look at the top ten stockholders of the Southern Company. They're all New York City banks and all they care about is more profit."

*(Information from Andy Himes and the Georgia Power Project).*

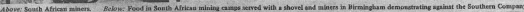

*Above:* South African miners.    *Below:* Food in South African mining camps served with a shovel and miners in Birmingham demonstrating against the Southern Company.

# Plans For North Carolina Demonstration

RALEIGH, N.C.—The National Alliance Against Racist and Political Repression (NAARPR) has declared the state of North Carolina a "national disaster area" and announced a massive demonstration to be held July 4th in Raleigh.

The demonstration's theme is "To End Capital Punishment and Free Political Prisoners". Over 10,000 people are expected to come from all parts of the country.

North Carolina, it has been said, best exemplifies the reformist spirit of the New South. This is the misconception based on the liberal traditions of three

STOP Racism and Repression

July 4th 1974
National Demonstration
State Capitol
Raleigh, North Carolina

famous academic communities — Duke, Chapel Hill, and Raleigh — and the gains once made by trade unions in the textile and tobacco industries — gains since wiped out.

The truth about North Carolina is that it is the state most vigorously renewing its efforts to use the death sentence for crimes such as first degree burglary and rape. Its thirty-one persons on death row are almost half of the nation's condemned prisoners.

Butner, N.C., is the site for the development of the Federal Center for Correctional Research (formerly called the U.S. Behavioral Research Center). The United Church of Christ's Commission

for Racial Justice has warned that, "prisoners will be chosen and shipped from around the country to Butner, to be experimented on. Drugs, brain-washing and hypnosis will be used on 'uncontrollable' prisoners to develop methods to control other uncontrollables — inmates and non-inmates."

Charlotte, Wilson, and Ayden, N.C. have been the scenes of mass jailings and beatings of black high school students protesting school conditions and racism. In 1971, black students demonstrating for a black studies program had to defend themselves in a Wilmington church for four days from the attacks of white (Continued on page 5)

The *Southern Patriot*, a radical newspaper in Louisville, Kentucky, headlined a demonstration against the importation of South African coal by the Southern Company, May 1974. The protest in Birmingham, Alabama, was organized by District 20 of the United Mine Workers, other unions, and their supporters. *Photo courtesy of Ken Lawrence.*

collaboration with the Portuguese wars in Africa. After the U.S. Congress passed the Byrd amendment in 1971 allowing the importation of chrome from white-ruled Rhodesia in violation of U.N. sanctions, longshoremen's unions and local activists repeatedly blocked chrome imports. In 1974 the United Mine Workers launched a protest against imports of South African coal to Alabama. Annual meetings of corporations were beset not only by church-sponsored shareholder resolutions but also by local demonstrators. Gulf Oil was boycotted because of its investments in Portuguese-ruled Angola, General Motors and scores of others because of their strategic involvement in the South Africa economy.

Even before student actions spread around the country in the late 1970s, the number, diversity, and shifting patterns of local groups and coalitions were beyond anyone's capacity to track. As in the 1960s, the New York–based ACOA was still the most prominent national point of contact and source of activist-oriented research. But neither the ACOA nor any other group could realistically aspire to create a coherent national organization or even a stable national coalition. Even in the 1980s, despite vastly greater national attention and eventual impact, this fundamental reality apparent in the early 1970s did not change.

By the mid-1970s, after the African Liberation Support Committee that had organized the African Liberation Day marches fractured over ideological disputes, the prospects for centralization were so remote that few even considered trying. Activists were aware that the de facto model of decentralized networks had many weaknesses. And yet, as recent studies of dispersed networks are showing in many fields, such networks can have hidden strengths. Functioning in a society that was profoundly divided, the networks supporting African liberation sometimes showed unexpected capacities for growth, rapid communication, and consensus building.

The networks included not only local groups and activists around the country but also new national groups that collaborated with the ACOA and the House Africa Subcommittee as resources and reference points. In 1972 the ACOA worked with churches and labor unions to form the Washington Office on Africa. The following year Tami Hultman and Reed Kramer, based in Durham, North Carolina, founded Africa News Service, which joined the monthly *Southern Africa* magazine out of New York as essential communication tools for Africa activists. The American Friends Service Committee, based in Philadelphia, set up a Southern Africa program in 1975 that regularly brought veteran activist Bill Sutherland from Dar es Salaam for speaking tours around the United States, benefiting from his long activist experience and contacts on both sides of the Atlantic. And in 1977, discussions within the Congressional Black Caucus culminated in the formation of TransAfrica, an African American lobby on Africa and the Caribbean headed by Randall Robinson.

The mix of strengths and weaknesses displayed in U.S. Africa solidarity networks depended above all on the African country involved. It was easier to find consensus on Guinea-Bissau, Mozambique, and Namibia, where there was one dominant lib-

Ruth Brandon interviews President Samora Machel of Mozambique for *Africa News*, New York, October 1977.
*Photo courtesy of AllAfrica Global Media.*

William Minter

eration movement. But none of the three had even a faint chance of gaining prominence in U.S. media or policy arenas. In the case of South Africa, pervasive divisions in the liberation forces were outweighed by the visibility of South African repression, the moral clarity of the anti-apartheid message, and the large number of people speaking out for freedom.

But in both Angola and Zimbabwe, divisions in the national independence movements were projected into the U.S. arena, leading to disunity among activists. In Angola in particular, the internal divisions paralleled with uncanny precision the fractures among potential liberation supporters in the United States. Jonas Savimbi of the National Union for Total Independence of Angola (Unita) touted his black nationalist credentials, decrying the prominence of white and mixed-race Angolans in the Popular Movement for the Liberation of Angola (MPLA). Savimbi's ties with China enhanced his appeal to the rising Maoist strand among U.S. radicals. And Unita could also rely on personal ties with missionaries of the United Church of Christ and the United Church of Canada, both long active in Angola.

Unita's alliance with South Africa and the CIA in the 1975 conflict in Angola that followed the withdrawal of the Portuguese thus came as a shock to its supporters. Almost all U.S. activists most deeply engaged in African issues took a clear stand against the U.S. intervention in the oil-rich African nation. We applauded when liberal academics and members of Congress also mobilized and added sufficient political weight to bar the United States from continuing its covert military involvement. And we celebrated when the MPLA, with Cuban assistance, fought off South African troops, mercenaries, and its Angolan rivals. Only a few activists stuck by Unita, some later following it into the far-right circles of the Reagan revolution.

The absence of significant movement ties with newly independent Angola, however, left the door wide open for Reagan's alliance with South Africa in attacking that country. The Angolan government never established a working relationship with its potential supporters in the United States. And even at the height of the anti-apartheid movement a decade later, South Africa's deadly wars on its neighbors were barely known to most activists, much less to the wider public.

U.S. activists were more engaged in supporting liberation movements in Zimbabwe, where the white Rhodesian regime continued in power until the end of the decade. But the U.S. right wing also mobilized to support the white regime. The ACOA and the Washington Office on Africa worked with both congressional allies and longshoremen to try to block imports of Rhodesian chrome. Journalists with *Southern Africa* magazine and Africa News Service exposed the involvement of U.S. companies in providing Rhodesia with oil and helicopters. Both the Zimbabwe African National Union (ZANU) and the Zimbabwe African People's Union (ZAPU) fostered support groups in cities around the United States. In 1979 Congress came close to lifting sanctions, after Ian Smith successfully persuaded Methodist bishop Abel Muzorewa and Congregational pastor Ndabaningi Sithole to break with other nationalists and serve in token roles in his white minority regime. Nevertheless, most U.S. church people involved with Southern Africa, with multiple ties to the liberation movements and their own sources of information, stood firm for keeping sanctions.

This history has been little researched. But it is clear that the scattered efforts of activists still added up to only marginal impact on national public debate or policy regarding Zimbabwe. As many as 1,000 American mercenaries fought for the white regime in Rhodesia, openly applauded and aided by magazines such as *Soldier of Fortune*. Along with Rhodesian troops, they were involved in massacres of hundreds of Africans, both inside Rhodesia and at refugee and guerrilla camps in neighboring countries. For the U.S. media and the Jimmy Carter administration, nevertheless, these were non-issues. Nor were activists able to mobilize many outside their ranks to pay attention.

If it was difficult to gain a large audience and support for Southern Africa, the obstacles were even more daunting in relation to independence movements elsewhere on the continent. In the case of Western Sahara, a former Spanish colony illegally occupied by Morocco, Morocco continued to block a referendum that would lead to independence. In the case of Eritrea, a former Italian colony, it was again a neighboring African state, Ethiopia, that stood in the way of independence, annexing the territory as a province in 1962 and setting off a 30-year

Demonstrators at Harvard Medical School call on the university to divest its holdings in companies involved in South Africa, March 1985. *Photo © Ellen Shub.*

war. While individual Americans visited both territories and provided some coverage in the press, U.S. activists concerned with the two countries lacked vehicles for organizing and were never numerous enough to have much impact in either case.

## The Impact of Soweto

Thus, while those activists most deeply involved saw an interconnected and Africa-wide array of issues, that perspective rarely reached the wider public. Only for South Africa did the movement succeed in influencing a critical mass of Americans. The first decisive stage of that expansion began with students, who responded to the Soweto student uprisings in South Africa in 1976. For many Americans, television coverage of police shooting down students evoked the classic images of violence against civil rights marchers from the 1960s. Sam Nzima's photograph of 12-year-old Hector Pieterson, dying in the arms of Mbuyisa Makhuba while his sister Antoinette runs along beside them, became an icon of the movement, appearing in newspapers around the world and on countless posters. Over the

next three years thousands of student demonstrators confronted university administrators at more than 100 campuses around the United States, demanding divestment of funds invested in companies involved in South Africa.

Just as televised police violence in Birmingham and Selma had dramatized the Southern civil rights movement for potential activists and politicians, so the apartheid state's violence served over the next decade as a powerful recruiting tool for anti-apartheid activism. Spring 1977 saw almost 300 arrested at Stanford University, and an early victory was won at Hampshire College in Massachusetts when trustees sold $215,000 in stock in response to student protests. The murder of Black Consciousness leader Steve Biko, at the beginning of the 1977–78 school year, gave further momentum to the student movement. Total divestments by universities jumped to more than $25 million a year in 1978 and 1979.

No one has yet told the full story of these student protests, in large part because it has as many chapters as there were campuses involved. Each local

William Minter

protest was driven by events in South Africa and fed by multiple connections to the ACOA and other central network nodes. Each involved some mix of predominantly black and predominantly white groups of student activists, often bolstered by faculty members and veteran community activists. The student protests were indeed tied to each other and to parallel divestment campaigns in churches and communities. But that linkage came from common themes and interlocking communication networks as much as from efforts at national coordination.

By the end of 1978, the Committee to Oppose Bank Loans to South Africa, a national network spearheaded by the ACOA and the Vietnam-era antiwar group Clergy and Laity Concerned, included local groups in at least 11 cities. The South Africa Catalyst Project at Stanford had published its own guide to divestment actions. Regional conferences of anti-apartheid activists had been held in the Northeast, Midwest, and Southeast, and on the West Coast, and plans were laid for nationwide protests in April 1979.

In this period there still seemed little chance that U.S. companies or their shareholders would actually respond to the demand to withdraw from South Africa. Shareholder resolutions from churches were increasing, and they often included calls for withdrawal as well as more moderate demands. But civil rights veteran Andrew Young, who served as the Carter administration's ambassador to the United Nations from 1977 to 1979, was a passionate advocate of business reform rather than sanctions to abolish apartheid. The Reverend Leon Sullivan, who had urged withdrawal from South Africa as a General Motors board member in 1971, opted instead in 1977 to ask companies to endorse a set of principles committing them to improve conditions for their workers in South Africa.

On this front, however, activist networks successfully maintained and expanded a strong consensus in favor of full sanctions against apartheid. Slogans such as "Break All Ties with Apartheid," "US $ Out of South Africa Now," and "Stop Banking on Apartheid" had appeal and credibility. A response required neither ideological agreement nor detailed knowledge of African geography. At a summit conference of Black Religious Leaders on Apartheid in April 1979, for example, delegates rejected Rev.

Sullivan's plea to endorse his principles. Instead they supported the Reverend William Howard, president of the National Council of Churches and the ACOA's board chair, who urged that U.S. investors withdraw from South Africa until the white supremacist government abandoned apartheid. The conference, chaired by the Reverend Wyatt Tee Walker, former top aide to Martin Luther King Jr., also adopted a resolution supporting the use of "any means necessary" to overthrow the apartheid state.

By the end of the 1970s, the Lancaster House agreement had paved the way for the transformation of white-ruled Rhodesia into independent Zimbabwe in 1980. Over the next decade, as action against apartheid intensified inside South Africa, South Africa also waged an immensely destructive series of wars against neighboring African countries. The Reagan administration in Washington tilted toward South Africa in these wars and actively joined Pretoria in intensifying the war on Angola. The anti-apartheid movement reached new heights, culminating in the congressional vote to override President Reagan's veto of sanctions in 1986. Despite this achievement, however, the means to turn anti-apartheid sentiment into sustainable solidarity with Africa continued to elude activists.

## The 1980s

Ronald Reagan was sworn in as 40th president of the United States on January 20, 1981. Ten days later, South African army commandoes raided the Mozambican capital of Maputo, killing 13 members of the ANC and a Portuguese bystander. Yet when Reagan's new secretary of state, Alexander Haig, spoke of the need to retaliate against "rampant international terrorism," he was not speaking about the South African cross-border attack. Nor was he referring to the apartheid regime's sponsorship of the Mozambican National Resistance (Renamo), which was then escalating its terror campaign targeting civilians, schools, and clinics as well as economic targets inside Mozambique. Rather, he was alluding to the presumed threat from the Soviet Union. In May of that year Chester Crocker, the architect of President Reagan's policy toward South Africa, wrote in an internal briefing paper, "The chief threat [to cooperation, stability, and security] is the presence and influence in the region of the Soviet Union and its allies" (cited in TransAfrica 1981). South Africa, Crocker argued, had a shared interest with the United States in thwarting Soviet goals.

Over the two Reagan terms, Crocker's approach to South Africa would be called "constructive engagement." It became, in effect, the more moderate of two emphases in play. Proponents of constructive engagement held out the hope that negotiated reforms in apartheid and the independence of Namibia could contribute to the administration's primary goals of rolling back Soviet influence and ousting Cuban troops from Angola. No one in the Reagan administration gave much heed to the view, prevalent in Africa and among activists, that the Cuban troop presence was a legitimate response to the South African threat to Angola. But Crocker at least hesitated to give Pretoria a "blank check" and sometimes counseled restraint, particularly toward Mozambique.

The other approach was advocated by those farther to the right, such as William Casey at the CIA, officials at the Defense Department, and a network

of right-wing political activists. It was based on the unwavering belief that all opponents of the Pretoria regime were terrorists. This faction embraced South Africa's allied insurgents including Unita in Angola and Renamo in Mozambique as "freedom fighters" deserving unconditional support, along with the contras in Nicaragua and the mujahadeen in Afghanistan. President Reagan himself joked that "sometimes my right hand doesn't know what my far-right hand is doing" (Barrett 1984, 61). The limited political spectrum of Reagan's Washington left little space for the view that the apartheid regime itself was the real threat to stability and security in the region.

Although the turn to the right in Washington put progressive movements on the defensive, it also clarified what was at stake and energized both long-term activists and new movement recruits. The nuclear freeze campaign against the nuclear arms race drew over a million demonstrators to New York in June 1982 and was endorsed by 275 city governments and 12 state legislatures. Central America

The corner outside the South African Mission to the United Nations was officially renamed Nelson & Winnie Mandela Corner in 1984. From left: unidentified woman; New York City council members Robert Dryfoos and Wendell Foster, who sponsored the name change; J. M. Makatini, the ANC representative to the United Nations; SWAPO deputy representative H. P. Asheeke; ANC deputy representative David Ndaba; and ACOA executive director Jennifer Davis. *Photo by Joshua Nessen.*

William Minter

solidarity groups around the country mobilized in opposition to U.S. support for the contras in Nicaragua and for military regimes in Guatemala and El Salvador. On the domestic front, Jesse Jackson's 1984 and 1988 presidential campaigns built grassroots support and alliances, as did the election of Chicago mayor Harold Washington in 1983. Both were signs of the potential for broad progressive alliances prominently featuring African American initiatives.

It was in this context that the anti-apartheid movement gained momentum during the 1980s. On Africa, as on domestic and other international issues, activists not only faced the opposition of the dominant Republican administration. They also had to contend with opposition or indifference from the congressional leadership of the Democratic Party, which was the majority party in the House of Representatives for both Reagan terms and gained majority control of the Senate in Reagan's last two years.

The success story of the 1980s, as recounted by David Goodman in chapter 5, was the buildup of political pressure that led to legislated sanctions against South Africa by the U.S. Congress. The story also includes scores of private economic actions signaling a loss of confidence in the apartheid regime. These were successful because of the extensive connections that had been forged between the United States and South Africa over many decades. It was not just that many South Africans had come to the United States and that South Africa's acts of repression against its own people kept hitting the headlines. The economic connections between the two countries meant that in virtually every community in the United States, local activists could do something on their own to help end apartheid. They could take money out of a bank that loaned to South Africa. They could make sure their pension fund was not invested in companies that operated there. For the rest of Africa, with very few exceptions, there were no equivalent organizing handles.

This was a painful reality for those of us who had worked in or visited Mozambique. We were conscious of the destructive furor of apartheid's regional wars. We saw the promise and hopes of the early independence years battered by the relentless assault of South African–backed insurgents on villages, clinics, schools, and railways. The number of civilians killed during this period in Mozambique,

Angola, and other countries in the region, and the additional deaths due to famine and disease, are impossible to estimate with any precision. But it is undeniable that the death toll numbered in the hundreds of thousands or even in the millions, and that these deaths went virtually unnoticed by the American public and policy makers.

Independent African states, meanwhile, made decisive contributions to the liberation of South Africa from apartheid. Tanzania and Zambia played early roles, followed by Botswana, Angola, Mozambique, and Zimbabwe, joining in a group that became known as the Frontline States. They provided inspiration and indispensable rear bases for the movement inside Namibia and South Africa, although their support for armed guerrilla action varied according to their circumstances. But although these regional dynamics were known to longtime activists, communicating them to the broader public proved almost impossible.

On South Africa, nevertheless, the anti-apartheid movement became a force to be reckoned with during the 1980s. The movement involved multiple networks, not centralized in any one organization but linked well enough so that the various strategies and tactics adopted reinforced each other. The movement built on background knowledge and personal ties to South Africa, dating back several decades, and continuously expanded. The visibility of resistance to the minority regime inside South Africa reinforced the message; so too did the brutality and intransigence of the regime's response.

## The Anti-Apartheid Convergence: Core Organizations

In the 1980s, four organizations were the cornerstones for national anti-apartheid action. In Washington, TransAfrica, the most recently founded, continued under the leadership of its first director, Randall Robinson, throughout the decade. The Washington Office on Africa (WOA) chose Jean Sindab to succeed Ted Lockwood as director in 1980. After Sindab left in 1986 to direct the World Council of Churches Programme to Combat Racism, Damu Smith and then Aubrey McCutcheon directed WOA. In 1980 civil rights activist Jerry Herman became coordinator of the Southern Africa program of the American Friends Service Committee (AFSC) in

Delegation from Actors/Artists Against Apartheid following 1988 Senate hearings. From left: actor Danny Glover, Washington Office on Africa director Damu Smith, Senator Carl Levin of Michigan, actress Alfre Woodard, actress Mary Steenburgen, legislative aide Jackie Parker. *Photo courtesy of Jackie Parker.*

Nobel Laureate Bishop Desmond Tutu, right, with Randall Robinson of TransAfrica at demonstration at the South African embassy in 1984. *Photo © Rick Reinhard.*

William Minter

Philadelphia. And in New York, with the retirement of George Houser in 1981 after more than 25 years of leadership, the work of the American Committee on Africa and its tax-exempt educational affiliate, The Africa Fund, was directed by two South African exiles. Jennifer Davis became the executive director after many years as research director, and Dumisani Kumalo, who first joined the organization for a 10-week national speaking tour in 1979, continued as projects director throughout the decade.

These organizations played complementary and overlapping roles as they interacted with wider networks of activists, specialized groups, and what would now be called "civil society." All four shared basic ideological and policy positions on Africa. They supported comprehensive sanctions against apartheid and the legitimacy of the liberation struggles in Namibia and South Africa, the remaining outposts of white supremacy. They opposed U.S. intervention in independent Angola and Mozambique and lobbied against the Reagan administration's backing of Pretoria's regional wars. As the decade progressed, the general tendency was to give increasing support to the ANC and the United Democratic Front in South Africa, without excluding ties to other liberation tendencies such as the Black Consciousness Movement or the Pan Africanist Congress (PAC). The four organizations sought to build support for the anti-apartheid cause from as wide a range of Americans as possible.

Race was one differential between the groups, but in a more complex way than a simple distinction between black and white. TransAfrica's mandate was to represent the African American community and to lobby on issues related to Africa and the African diaspora in the Caribbean and Latin America. Thus it was understood to be an African American organization. In principle and in fact, the other three groups were multiracial in the composition of their leadership, staffs, boards, and constituencies. Yet in the convoluted context of racial perceptions in U.S. society, they were often seen both by the media and within the movement as historically "white" organizations. This image persisted even when black staff or board members played the most important leadership roles.

What counted most in practice was not such general perceptions but the specific organizational histories, locations, and personal ties of people in each

organization's circles, including both black and white Americans as well as exiles from Southern Africa. The relationships featured both cooperation and rivalry; indeed, the movement working on African issues was hardly a harmonious family. Cherri Waters, who worked in the early 1980s at TransAfrica Forum, the educational affiliate of TransAfrica, was a close friend and adviser of Jean Sindab at the Washington Office on Africa. She said it this way: "If you think that the anti-apartheid movement was full of people who worked and played well together and who liked each other—no way. Get over it. . . . There were just lots of individual and institutional issues. But when push came to shove, their collective efforts had an impact" (Waters 2003). Still, the fact that the four organizations brought assets that were largely complementary, and that all generally acknowledged this good fit, made it possible to curtail turf battles despite the inescapable competition for constituencies and donors.

ACOA/Africa Fund's assets included well-established links to diverse networks across the country and in New York and a long history of leadership on the demand to cut economic ties with South Africa. New York City housed the United Nations, the National Council of Churches, and, at that time, the headquarters of most of the major Protestant denominations. Representatives of SWAPO and the ANC were easily accessible, as were sympathetic African ambassadors and the staff of the U.N. Centre against Apartheid and Council for Namibia. ACOA's Religious Action Network, headed by Rev. Wyatt Tee Walker of Canaan Baptist Church in Harlem, gave the organization access to leading black clergy in the city. Walker also provided a connection to the nationwide network of Progressive National Baptist congregations and others he knew from his earlier role as director of the Southern Christian Leadership Conference for Martin Luther King Jr. As interest rose in the anti-apartheid cause, the ACOA/Africa Fund also became the principal contact point for progressive trade unionists and politicians dealing with the issue.

On the campaign for divestment and economic sanctions, it was the ACOA/Africa Fund that provided information exchange and strategic consistency for the wider circles that became involved. The Africa Fund published a regularly updated list of U.S. companies involved in South Africa, providing in effect a shopping list of targets for local activ-

AFRICA

Annie King, ACOA's longtime office manager, provided organizational memory and stability. She is shown here in January 1989 with South African United Democratic Front leaders Murphy Morobe, left, and Mohammed Valli Moosa. *Photo courtesy of Jennifer Davis.*

ists. And the ACOA hosted events such as the June 1981 two-day conference of 42 legislators from 22 states, who met with U.N. officials, activists, organizers, and trade unionists to discuss strategies for attacking investments in apartheid. Georgia state senator Julian Bond, veteran SNCC activist and future executive chairman of the NAACP, keynoted the event with a call to "end American complicity with this international crime" (1981).

The AFSC, with a long history of engagement in both overseas relief and peace activism, was also by the 1980s an essential link in anti-apartheid networks. Given the Quaker insistence on consensus and reconciliation, there were many in the organization who had doubts not only about support for African liberation movements but also about the confrontation involved in demands for divestment. But the group also had the unique advantage of having offices around the country, almost all of which served as gathering points for progressive activists involved in many different issues in their communities and regions. The AFSC's work on

Africa also built on the energy of the group's Third World Coalition that had been founded in 1971.

Visits by Bill Sutherland from Tanzania continued from the 1970s into the 1980s, and the AFSC was also one of the first groups to host Bishop Desmond Tutu on a U.S. tour. Sutherland recalls that the AFSC, itself a winner of the Nobel Peace Prize, regularly nominated Tutu for the award, years before he received it. Based in Atlanta, Thandi Luthuli-Gcabashe, daughter of the 1960 Nobel laureate Chief Albert Luthuli, ran the AFSC's peace education program for the U.S. South from 1981 to 1996. AFSC offices in Seattle, Portland, Baltimore, Ohio, western Massachusetts, and North Carolina, to name only a few, were centers of local anti-apartheid activism.

Despite their location in Washington, DC, neither WOA nor TransAfrica was close to the centers of power in the nation's capital. They had good access to allies in Congress, such as the members of the Congressional Black Caucus and the handful of other representatives and senators—mainly Democrats but also a few Republicans—who showed consistent interest in Africa. But their influence even with these individuals depended in large part on their relationships to constituencies both inside and outside Washington. Both worked with other groups in the wider anti-apartheid movement, cosponsoring events such as the June 1981 conference on state and local divestment. From 1979, the two co-hosted the monthly strategy session of the Southern Africa Working Group, which at the height of the movement brought more than 40 groups together to coordinate pressures on Congress. Each also had its own networks of contacts in the local Washington community and around the country.

In addition to its ties to the national church denominations and a few trade unions that were its principal financial sponsors, WOA distinguished itself by its emphasis on coalition building combined with grassroots mobilization as the prerequisites for influence on Congress. Its leaders were a regular presence not only in the halls of Congress but also in rallies at churches and community centers. WOA repeatedly stressed the connection of apartheid with other issues, from Namibia and the regional wars in Southern Africa to domestic racism. Working with close allies such as Willis Logan, who directed the Africa office at the National Council of Churches in New York, WOA spoke out against complacency and urged stronger action from the churches.

For its part, TransAfrica became best known for the national media presence of its director Randall Robinson, an eloquent voice not only against apartheid but later also on Haiti and other foreign policy issues. Like the other groups, however, TransAfrica depended on networks not readily visible to television audiences. TransAfrica was consistently the central contact and rallying point on African issues for national African American leaders. It retained particularly close ties to the Congressional Black Caucus and built links to politically conscious celebrities in film, music, and sport. And when Robinson sought local support for the demonstrations that launched the Free South Africa Movement in November 1984, he could turn to the experienced local organizers of the Southern Africa Support Project.

Beginning in 1984, the high level of national and world media focus on South Africa, particularly on television, motivated movement activists and was a decisive factor in the buildup of political pressure. The daily demonstrations in Washington, Ted Koppel's week-long series of *Nightline* programs broadcast from South Africa in March 1985, and the apartheid regime's open intransigence all helped keep the story alive. The debate on sanctions became in effect a referendum on racism.

## The Anti-Apartheid Convergence: Wider Networks

What made this period different from previous decades was that South Africa became not only an international and national news story but a local story. And the involvement of musicians, film stars, and sports figures caught the attention even of those unlikely to follow political news.

Local activists turned to the national anti-apartheid organizations for information and occasional visiting speakers. But even when there was direct affiliation with a national body, as in the case of AFSC offices and TransAfrica chapters, the dynamic behind the activism was locally rooted. Ad hoc coalitions depended on local relationships and on local activists with a history of involvement in Africa solidarity as well as other progressive causes. It was the capacity of the movement to engage these far-flung local forces, not the existence of a single anti-

apartheid organization, that drove the movement's powerful impact on the U.S. Congress and on the business community.

In the United Kingdom and some other countries, the "Anti-Apartheid Movement" was a single, national organization. But in the United States there was no such organization, and the use of capital letters indicating an organizational name would be a misleading guide to historical reality. The diverse and hard-to-track currents involved—students, politicians, trade union groups, church groups, celebrities, and many others—were part of no unified organizational structure. Yet all are central to the movement's history.

By the early 1980s, several generations of students had come and gone since the anti-apartheid demonstrations of the mid-1960s. The post-Soweto wave of student actions was beginning to win results. By the end of 1979, universities on both coasts and in the Midwest states had divested over $50 million in stocks of companies involved in South Africa. Over the next five years universities divested over $130 million more, and in 1985 alone more than 60 universities divested some $350 million. The Africa Fund counted more than 150 universities involved in divestment campaigns during the 1980s. Protest tactics such as the building of "shanties" spread from campus to campus (Soule 1995).

Student organizations were often short-lived, and they were often divided along racial lines even when the demands for divestment were identical. Only a few of the students involved went on to pursue sustained activism in solidarity with Africa. But large numbers carried the basic message with them after they graduated, whether their career tracks took them to politics, the academic world, or some other business or profession. As the issue gained even more prominence in the 1980s, veterans of student activism were to be found in local and state governments, on congressional staffs, and even among new members of Congress.

States leading the way, through both student action and the divestment of public funds, included Massachusetts, Connecticut, New York, Michigan, Wisconsin, and California. And they were just the beginning. In 1991 The Africa Fund compiled a list of 28 states, 24 counties, and 92 cities that had enacted legislation for divestment from South Africa. In each

Artists and Athletes Against Apartheid at a press conference arranged by the Organization of African Unity, September 14, 1983. From left: Gregory Hines, Tony Randall, Arthur Ashe, Rose Elder, Randall Robinson, Franklin Williams, Harry Belafonte, Joel Grey. *UN Photo.*

of these cases, and an unknown number more where the legislation failed, local coalitions placed the debate on South Africa onto the local political agenda.

Specialized groups and national networks in many different sectors of society also took up the issue. National groups that played important roles included the Interfaith Center on Corporate Responsibility, which coordinated church action on stockholders' resolutions and divestment, and the Southern Africa Project of the Lawyers' Committee for Civil Rights Under Law, which supported political prisoners and documented South African abuses. Church groups and celebrities were particularly important because of their wide impact on the public. Church groups tended to have closest ties with ACOA and WOA, while celebrities both white and black were likely to be more closely linked to TransAfrica. And people in each of these sectors also had their own political commitments and their own links with counterparts in South Africa and elsewhere on the continent that shaped their involvement.

Three South African church leaders, Anglican archbishop Desmond Tutu and Reformed Church leaders Beyers Naudé and Allan Boesak, were so omnipresent at church gatherings in the United States that some insiders jokingly referred to them as the "holy trinity" of anti-apartheid action. While particularly persuasive within their own denominational bodies, each was able to reach wider audiences. "Black theology" and the Kairos document released by South African religious leaders in September 1985 were studied in U.S. seminaries, college religion classes, and church study groups. They provided theological reflection on and religious grounds for opposition to apartheid, just as liberation theology provided a similar resource for progressive organizing in Latin America.

Each denomination with historical connections to Southern Africa worked within its own particular structures and relationships. Within the Lutheran Church, for example, Namibians studying at Lutheran schools in the Midwest sparked a national network supporting Namibia's indepen-

William Minter

dence from South Africa. Network members raised the issue of Namibia at the Democratic presidential primaries in Iowa in 1984 and 1988 and consistently pushed the divestment issue at national meetings, despite opposition from denominational leadership. Eventually, recounts Dumisani Kumalo (2005a), even many Reagan Republicans were persuaded to support SWAPO, telling their representatives that the SWAPO guerrillas, far from being "communist terrorists," were "good Lutherans."

Celebrities who joined the anti-apartheid drive did so most often in the context of the movement's call to boycott South Africa. Like the divestment movement, the cultural and sports boycott was important both for its direct effects on South Africa and because it repeatedly raised the issue of apartheid in the United States, forcing debate. Although it reached its height in the 1980s, it built on currents from previous decades. In New York, for example, the Patrice Lumumba Coalition joined with the National Black United Front to protest artists who violated the boycott to perform in South Africa. Actor Danny Glover, who played Nelson Mandela in a 1987 television film on Mandela's life, had been a leader in the Black Students Union at San Fran-

Dennis Brutus testifies at the United Nations in 1967 on behalf of the International Defense and Aid Fund World Campaign for the Release of South African Political Prisoners and as president of the South African Nonracial Olympic Committee. *UN Photo.*

cisco State in the late 1960s. Consciously placing himself in the politically progressive tradition of figures such as Paul Robeson and Harry Belafonte, Glover has been a consistent supporter of African liberation, maintaining close ties to TransAfrica in particular over the years.

Danny Schechter, a former activist with the Africa Research Group in Boston who became a media commentator and news producer, coordinated the *Sun City* record and video produced by Artists United Against Apartheid in 1985. Named for the luxury casino in Bophuthatswana that featured in the South African regime's public relations drive, *Sun City* was explicitly political, calling on artists to boycott the casino ("Ain't gonna play Sun City!"). The Africa Fund distributed proceeds from the *Sun City* sales to the liberation movements and to anti-apartheid work in the United States. Schechter, who had taken on the video project without telling his employer while a producer at ABC's *20/20* news program, went on to produce the weekly television show *South Africa Now* from 1988 to 1991.

The sports boycott also gained impetus, although it remained less central to the movement in the United States than in Britain, Australia, and New Zealand, where rugby and cricket tours of South African teams ignited nationwide protests. In the 1970s South African exile Dennis Brutus and U.S. sports activist Richard Lapchick took the anti-apartheid message around the country. Tennis star Arthur Ashe had hoped to influence South African sport by visiting the country, only to discover that such visits were ineffectual. He joined the more than 6,000 protesters at the Davis Cup match in Nashville, Tennessee in March 1978. In 1983 Ashe agreed to join Harry Belafonte to chair Artists and Athletes Against Apartheid, a coalition of groups coordinated by TransAfrica to support the cultural boycott.

Dennis Brutus himself well illustrates how the South African cause reached Americans through the intersection of activist and other networks. A central figure in the global campaign to boycott South African sport after he went into exile in 1966, Brutus based himself in the United States, first at Northwestern University near Chicago and then at the University of Pittsburgh. One of Africa's leading poets, he won world renown for his prison and exile poetry, and he was one of the founders of the African

Proceeds of Sun City album and video sales benefit the ANC, January 1987. Tilden LeMelle, president of The Africa Fund, presents ANC president Oliver Tambo with a check for over $100,000 to be used for educational and cultural projects benefiting South African refugees. Singers Harry Belafonte, right, and Little Steven look on.
*Photo by David Vita.*

Literature Association in the United States. A tireless campaigner speaking to audiences around the country, Brutus won political asylum in 1983 despite a two-year effort by the U.S. immigration authorities to expel him.

After 1985, the South African government increased restrictions on news coverage, barring television camera crews, but to no avail. Anti-apartheid pressures in the United States and worldwide built steadily as the struggle inside South Africa escalated. Events there continued to have an impact on the U.S. movement through multiple channels: the core national organizations, the mass media, and the scores of other personal and organizational networks that by mid-decade linked Americans with South Africa.

**Invisible Wars, Invisible Continent**

The same convergence did not materialize, however, for the countries targeted by South Africa's regional wars or for other crises confronting the continent.

For the core organizations and for Africa activists whose involvement preceded the victories over Portuguese colonialism in 1975, the regional dimension was fundamental. They were aware that freeing South Africa was the culmination of the decades-long continental and global drive for freedom from colonial-

ism and white minority rule. After the burst of independence in the 1960s, the focus of action on Africa had narrowed to the southern region. And as first the Portuguese colonies and then Zimbabwe gained independence, South Africa and its occupation of Namibia became the center of political action.

For most of the U.S. public, however, the relevant fact was that South Africa had repeatedly gained world attention, more than any other nation on the continent. Although the attention was intermittent, it began with the Sharpeville massacre in 1960 and continued through the Soweto uprising in 1976–77 and the resurgence of resistance in the 1980s. Both the message and the images of black resistance and white oppression resonated with the history of the civil rights movement in the U.S. South.

While opposing South Africa's attacks on Angola and Mozambique was always part of the activist message, this was not easy to communicate to wider constituencies, whose awareness of South Africa was shaped largely by television coverage. With very limited resources, all the groups found themselves, like it or not, concentrating on the simpler anti-apartheid message. Unlike in the case of South Africa, movement actions on other African issues never passed the threshold needed to have a decisive impact on the Washington policy scene.

In the case of Mozambique, for example, small networks of activists included *cooperantes* who had worked with Frelimo in exile in Tanzania or after independence in Mozambique. They raised funds to assist the country, supporting medical clinics, sending doctors, and providing other small-scale support for development projects. Just as important, U.S. activists mobilized public pressure to keep Mozambique off the target list for U.S. covert intervention, and they exposed South Africa's backing for the Renamo guerrillas opposing the Mozambican government. In 1987, when Mark van Koevering, an American Mennonite aid worker, reported the massacre of 424 villagers at Homoíne, which he had managed to escape, U.S. activists successfully publicized the Renamo atrocity.

More significant, however, were the efforts of the Mozambican government itself. Veteran Mozambican diplomat Valeriano Ferrão, who had been my colleague as a teacher in the Frelimo school in Tanzania before independence, arrived in Washington as ambassador in 1983 and quickly reinforced contacts with U.S. supporters. The Mozambican government also hired Prexy Nesbitt, who had earlier been program director of the World Council of Churches Programme to Combat Racism and special assistant to Chicago mayor Harold Washington, as a consultant in 1987. Through these contacts and others, the Mozambican leadership made a concerted and successful effort in the 1980s to maintain its ties with the core networks of Africa activists.

This was only part of a multifaceted Mozambican government drive to win friends and neutralize enemies in the United States. Maputo also reached out to the administration and to Congress, including right-wing lawmakers, and to business interests and humanitarian agencies. The strategy was defensive and admittedly fell short of decisively engaging the United States to stop South Africa's military support for Renamo. Nevertheless, Frelimo succeeded in building strong sympathy far beyond the ranks of its initial support from activists. The far-right supporters of Renamo failed to gain credibility and were frustrated in their attempts to win U.S. endorsement and support.

In contrast, the Angola government, with few personal networks and little knowledge of the U.S. context, had no equivalent involvement from U.S. activists, and approached the United States in a quite different manner. This was so despite the fact that in the mid-1970s progressive forces in the United States had succeeded in achieving a congressional ban on U.S. covert intervention in Angola. This ban was enacted in 1975–76 after it became publicly known that South African troops had also joined the war for power in Angola as Portugal withdrew, backing the same Angolan groups as the CIA.

In the 1980s, Jonas Savimbi continued to lead Unita in its war on the MPLA and the government in Luanda. Because the MPLA was aligned with the Soviet Union, Savimbi became the darling of the Reagan administration and far-right networks. The core U.S. activist groups opposed U.S. intervention and support for Unita, but they could muster almost no constituency on this issue. Without broader public awareness of the Southern African political context, the conflict in Angola was delinked from that in South Africa, even for most anti-apartheid activists. If Angola appeared on the average American's mental map at all, it was probably closer to Cuba or to Afghanistan than to South Africa.

Strikingly, the Angolan government made little or no effort to reach out to U.S. civil society or even to Africa activists. When Luanda did try to influence the U.S. political scene, it worked almost exclusively through expensive public relations firms or through its good contacts with U.S. oil firms. The array of right-wing forces lobbying for continued U.S. intervention was probably so powerful that they would have prevailed in any case. But there was practically no visible countervailing public pressure.

If it proved difficult to transfer anti-apartheid energy to solidarity with Mozambique and Angola, building a movement for solidarity with other African countries was an even more daunting prospect. For the most part, the public remained ignorant of or indifferent to intense U.S. involvement in countries as diverse as Liberia, Zaire, and Ethiopia.

The Cold War was still decisive in shaping American involvement on the continent, along with economic interests in oil and other mineral resources. In the 1980s the U.S. government was heavily involved in support for dictator Samuel Doe in Liberia, a country intimately tied to the United States since the nineteenth century. Mobutu Sese Seko in Zaire (now Congo) not only provided a corridor for U.S. intervention in Angola but had long been notorious for his plutocratic and dictatorial exploitation of his own people. Cold War competition was even more intense in the Horn of Africa than in Southern Africa. Yet in none of these cases was there a significant public movement to demand that U.S. policy contribute to human rights and social justice.

In general, the core Africa activist organizations in the United States, stretched for resources even to keep pace with the growing anti-apartheid movement, regretfully accepted their lack of capacity to act on other issues. The ACOA took on a limited involvement in supporting the independence of Moroccan-occupied Western Sahara. And Randall Robinson of TransAfrica was arrested in a lonely protest against the Ethiopian dictatorship in 1989, an action that was totally overshadowed by the police attack on students in China's Tiananmen Square (R. Robinson 1999, 157). But none of the organizations mounted sustained campaigns or educational programs on other African crises during these years.

Individual exiles and small exile groups from some African countries did organize among themselves. But few reached out beyond their own ranks to try to mobilize American supporters. By far the most effective were Eritrean exiles supporting their country's independence from Ethiopia. But their primary focus was on directing resources back to their own movements. American journalist Dan Connell first traveled to Eritrea in 1976 and went on to found Grassroots International in 1983 specifically to provide material aid and other forms of solidarity to the Eritrean people. Few other American supporters became engaged, as most activists shied away from the complexities and divisions of the conflicts in that region.

When famine in the Horn of Africa did gain attention in the mid-1980s, televised coverage made little or no connection to the political issues in the region. *We Are the World*, featuring an impressive array of 45 music stars, in 1985 became the fastest-selling album in music history. It eventually raised over $60 million for famine relief and related causes. Yet, like the parallel Live Aid concert the same year, the message reinforced the stereotypical image of dependent Africans receiving charity. Miriam Makeba, then living in West Africa, com-

mented, "Everyone in Africa is thankful for this aid. But we listen to the lyrics, and we wonder: What is this? 'We are the world,' the stars from America sing. But who is the world? Where are the singers from Africa, Europe, the East, the Third World? They are all Americans singing 'We are the world'" (Makeba and Hall 1987, 233).

The anti-apartheid movement was successful in the 1980s largely because it had such an obvious enemy in the apartheid state and such readily available action targets in the United States. Many activists had a critical mass of knowledge and ties to South Africa, and there was a roadmap of how Americans could contribute to a struggle led by Africans. In the next decade, as victory over the apartheid regime was finally achieved, activists would face the challenge of finding new forms of solidarity that went beyond South Africa and were based on new African realities.

## The 1990s

"Free Mandela! Free Nelson Mandela!" For decades these words in chant and song were a rallying cry for activists around the world. On February 11, 1990, after 27 years, it finally happened: Nelson Mandela walked out of Victor Verster Prison in Paarl and a new chapter in South Africa's history began. The drama of Mandela's release attracted unprecedented worldwide attention. Just weeks later, on March 21, the 30th anniversary of the Sharpeville massacre, South Africa officially relinquished authority over Namibia, which gained independence under an elected government led by the liberation movement SWAPO. Four years later, Mandela took office as the elected president of South Africa.

These victories were generations in the making, and the extent to which they were long overdue simply increased the intensity of celebrations. Activists outside of Southern Africa recognized that those who had resisted tyranny inside South Africa

Board members and supporters of the American Committee on Africa/The Africa Fund in New York in 2000. From left: Robert Boehm, Robert Browne, Carl Hooper, Peter Weiss, and Huoi Nguyen, Browne's wife. The occasion was a reception hosted by U.N. ambassador Dumisani Kumalo in honor of Jennifer Davis. *Photo by Suzette Abbott.*

William Minter

and Namibia were responsible for this moment but that anti-apartheid forces around the world had also played a part. Nelson Mandela traveled to greet his supporters on repeated overseas visits, where he was welcomed as a conquering hero. Yet amid the jubilation it was understood that this was a rare moment to be savored, and that the struggle was by no means over. Both Namibia and South Africa faced monumental challenges to overcome the legacies and distortions of occupation and apartheid.

In the United States, these victories closed one period of solidarity and opened a new period, one marked by the absence of any unifying framework. Indeed, during the 1990s questions multiplied for American activists focusing on Africa. Answers were tentative and fragmentary, and the movement's capacity to mobilize public pressure was much reduced from the high of the 1980s. Yet the need for action was as great as ever. This was exemplified most horrifically by the genocide in Rwanda in 1994, with as many as 800,000 people killed in a few months. And Rwanda was only one of several crises afflicting the continent. There was also continued war in Angola, new wars in West Africa, and—little noticed in the 1990s but already taking an enormous toll—the spread of HIV/AIDS.

Ironically, factors leading to the success of the "anti-apartheid" convergence also contained the seeds of future weaknesses. Core Africa activists around the country, despite their diversity, most often saw the anti-apartheid cause within the context of wider advocacy for human rights and social justice in Africa and at home. But it was the narrow, and negative, anti-apartheid message that enabled activists to build organizational coherence and public awareness. Both the simplicity of that message and its reinforcement by the intransigence of the apartheid regime suited it

for media amplification and policy impact. And the dual strategy of national sanctions and local divestment allowed for creative pressures to be developed at all levels of the movement.

During the complex transition period from Mandela's release in 1990 until the April 1994 democratic elections that brought him into office, both the anti-apartheid message and the sanctions/divestment strategy had some continued relevance for South Africa. But that relevance rapidly waned, and was gone by 1994. The new problems to be confronted would require rethinking, both about continued inequality in South Africa and about the many issues facing the rest of the continent.

## South Africa: Transition and Beyond

The four years following Mandela's release were both perilous and confusing. The dominant forces in the South African regime and among South Africa's business community did, at last, opt to abandon the apartheid framework for a new order with equal political rights for all. But there were significant currents within the regime determined to sabotage such a transition, or at least maximize their influence in it, through covert violence.

Gathering in support of South African political prisoners, Israel Baptist Church, Washington, DC, 1991. Aleah Bacquie, left, coordinator of the ACOA's Religious Action Network, confers with Rev. Morris Shearin, center, and a church deacon.
*Photo © Rick Reinhard.*

issues were tangled and often technical: how to shape the new constitution, how to shape thinking about future economic policy, how to control political violence and establish a new security order merging the personnel of the former regime and its opponents. With regard to international relations, there was both the immediate question of when to shift from calling for sanctions and divestment to attracting new investment and aid, and the long-term issue of how far to go to win the confidence of Western investors and the global financial establishment.

Among American anti-apartheid activists, Gay McDougall of the Lawyers' Committee for Civil Rights Under Law was one of the few who was on the inside of the process in South Africa. She first came to know South African and Namibian exile leaders while studying international human rights law in London in the late 1970s. Later, at the Lawyers' Committee, she evaded South African restrictions and indirectly funneled as much as $2 million a year into South Africa and Namibia to support political prisoners. For the constitutional negotiations she provided international research resources for the ANC team, and she was chosen as one of five international members of the 16-person commission that managed the 1994 election.

"Unlock Apartheid's Jails." Activists demanding freedom for political prisoners deliver keys to the South African embassy in 1987. Gay McDougall of the Lawyers' Committee for Civil Rights Under Law, left, stands with Jennifer Davis of the American Committee on Africa. Behind McDougall are Damu Smith of the Washington Office on Africa (in tie) and Rob Jones of ACOA (in hat). *Photo © Rick Reinhard..*

Even more important, it was a time of intense jockeying for both political and economic advantage in the post-apartheid era. The most important arenas of competition were the negotiating table and the formal and informal debates over policy within the leadership of those forces contending for power. The

Such high-profile involvement by an American activist was the exception, however. Under presidents George H. W. Bush and Bill Clinton, the U.S. government dramatically stepped up its involvement, seeing a peaceful transition in South Africa as a high priority for both strategic and political reasons. U.S. foundations and others with resources saw new opportunities in South Africa; they ranged from small and large businesses to individual philanthropists to professionals, educational institutions, and church agencies. But most grassroots activists had few resources to offer apart from their time and political commitment. And the core groups that had previously helped provide information and direction faced rapidly declining financial support, as donors seemed to conclude that the need for such work had already ended.

The first President Bush lifted official U.S. sanctions in mid-1991. However, the movement was largely able to maintain a consensus in favor of local divestment actions to serve as continued pressure until Nelson Mandela formally called for the lifting of sanctions in September 1993. As violence escalated during the transition period, U.S. anti-apartheid groups publicized charges by the ANC and human rights groups inside South Africa that the killing was covertly orchestrated by the regime. This, they noted, demonstrated that the South African government was not acting in good faith to end apartheid and negotiate with the African liberation movements. Sanctions therefore needed to be maintained. But the debate over lifting sanctions was complicated, as the media celebrated President F. W. de Klerk's willingness to change and the ANC itself sent mixed signals to its supporters abroad. Official Washington and the U.S. media also gave little credence to evidence of a covert "third force" behind the disorder, preferring to accept the simplistic label of "black-on-black violence."

The decline in the movement's capacity for mobilization was in a sense inevitable as victory approached. In South Africa itself, negotiation and compromise were on the agenda. But for some activists, working behind the scenes during Mandela's initial U.S. tour in 1990, there were also early indications that it might be time to disengage. Competition to be on Mandela's schedule was intense in every single city visited. At times the political significance of the trip seemed overshadowed by the jockeying for a position close to the South African leader. To make it more complicated, the ANC

ACOA board president Wyatt Tee Walker with actress Alfre Woodard, left, ANC representative Lindiwe Mabuza, and filmmaker Spike Lee at a luncheon with the Congressional Black Caucus, March 1991. As pressure to lift sanctions against South Africa intensified, The Africa Fund organized a delegation to tell Congress to keep the sanctions in place. *Photo © Rick Reinhard.*

ACOA director Jennifer Davis and ANC president Oliver Tambo at a reception organized by ACOA/Africa Fund, January 1987. *Photo by David Vita.*

delegation itself included not only the commanding figures of Nelson and Winnie Mandela but also organizational bureaucrats. Some of these officials made it very clear that their future agenda for the United States would focus on business and government ties and include little or no role for solidarity activists.

Activists had been accustomed to dealing with South African exiles within the context of mutually understood political solidarity. As movement leadership in South Africa transitioned into a new period, preparing to assume power, new imperatives necessitated new ways of working. It was a time of often confusing signals and misunderstandings. Lines of communication became increasingly frayed without the steady hand of Oliver Tambo, who had presided over the ANC's international relations from 1960 until he was disabled by a stroke in 1989, followed by his death in 1993.

Still, American activists and the broader public that had rallied to the anti-apartheid cause continued to follow developments in South Africa. Hundreds of Americans, most with a history of involvement

in activist networks, participated as nongovernmental observers in the 1994 election. Thousands more traveled to South Africa over the decade, simply to breathe in the atmosphere of a free South Africa or to seek jobs, business ties, or other opportunities to contribute to building a new society. The activist Fund for a Free South Africa, originally established by South African exiles, spun off Shared Interest, an organization focused on providing credit guarantees for jobs and housing. For some years the ACOA was able to use its ties with state and city legislators to help foster relationships with elected officials in provisional and municipal governments in South Africa and the region. The Bay Area contacts noted by Walter Turner in chapter 6 had their counterparts in universities, communities, and professional associations around the country.

Yet such efforts were no longer situated within the context of a movement that could craft a coherent message or even sustain regular communication, much less coordination or complementary strategies, among individual activists and activist groups. By the time of the 1994 South African elections, TransAfrica had transferred its primary energies to the crisis in Haiti; its director Randall Robinson was engaged in a hunger strike to protest the U.S. policy of expelling Haitian refugees. WOA was trying to focus public attention on the continuing crises in Angola and Zaire. There was also the problem of resources. In some European countries, movement organizations related to Africa could count on government subsidies to finance their continued engagement with post-apartheid South Africa. But American movement groups had no funding flow to support such a shift.

At a deeper level, the developing impasse went beyond limitations in organizational resources. It brought to mind the dilemma of the civil rights movement following the political civil rights victories of the 1960s. With no common vision or strategy for winning social and economic rights that could lead to broader transformations in American society, that movement had fragmented. The anti-apartheid movement of the 1980s, with its commitment to fundamental political rights, had provided an opportunity to revisit the unifying spirit of the 1960s. But it had not tackled the fundamental issues of building a more just society.

Part of the problem was the fact that the movement had focused so intensely on race, commented Gay McDougall. But it was also, she said, that Americans in general believe in civil and political rights but not in economic and social rights: "We don't believe that people should have a right to livelihood, to health, shelter, homes." The anti-apartheid movement had not dealt with the tough questions about the future, she reflected. "I don't want to be too harsh here because I think that we did real good with what we saw out there to do. But it was, in many ways, a shallow movement politically" (McDougall 2005).

The Africa Fund sponsored a national consultation on U.S. policy toward Africa in Washington, DC, in April 1997. From left: Karen Boykins-Towns of the NAACP, Richard Knight of The Africa Fund, and Gugile Nkwinti, speaker of the legislature of South Africa's Eastern Cape Province. *Photo courtesy of Richard Knight.*

In the late 1960s and early 1970s, many African American and other activists had looked to Africa for inspiration, especially to Tanzania or to the liberation movements in Guinea-Bissau or Mozambique. By the 1980s the hopes that these countries might provide a new model for just societies had been shattered, if not by war then by the stubborn persistence of poverty. Despite the celebration of Mandela and the new South Africa, it was clear by the mid-1990s that South Africa too faced intractable dilemmas and internal debates about how to deal with the apartheid legacy of social and economic inequality.

Few American activists followed the South African debates about post-apartheid economic policy in detail. Fewer still had a firm opinion on whether the conservative economic policies adopted by the new South African government were necessary compromises or a betrayal of revolutionary hopes. Almost all were well aware that the media celebration of the South African miracle concealed stubborn realities of institutional racism and economic inequality still to be addressed. But neither in South Africa nor in the United States were there clear strategies for dealing with these issues, much

less a vision for how grassroots activists on both sides of the Atlantic might be involved.

## African Crises in a Decade of Indifference

What then of the rest of Africa? Both the major anti-apartheid groups and the overwhelming majority of dedicated activists saw their involvement as part of a broader vision of freedom and justice, whether this was defined primarily in terms of Pan-African unity, global justice, or a U.S. foreign policy based on human rights rather than global dominance. On this wider front, the need for continued action was undeniable. But the Africa solidarity movement in the public eye had been narrowed to the anti-apartheid message focused on South Africa. In the 1990s it became clear that a movement with identified constituencies and viable strategies to take on the new Africa-wide challenges had yet to be built.

The most dramatic indication that this was a new time—and that there was no U.S. movement ready to engage it—came in April 1994, the same month as South Africa's election. Gay McDougall remembers how, in the midst of managing the election in the conflict-ridden province of KwaZulu-Natal, she saw television images of bodies floating down a river

Memorial site in Rwanda at Ntarama Church, where approximately 5,000 people were killed in April 1994. "For the policy makers in Washington," reflected Rwanda specialist Alison des Forges, "Rwanda was simply not an issue that created enough noise for them to pay attention." *Photo by Samuel Totten.*

> We at Human Rights Watch had been involved since 1991 in trying to influence policy. We had seen small-scale massacres. We had documented the involvement of people in the government and in the military, and we had documented the growth of the militia. So we had been attempting already, for many months, to persuade governments and international agencies to be concerned and to take a stand on this issue.

When they finally reached top officials at the National Security Council (NSC) in the weeks after the killing began, they found officials trying "to find reasons not to do anything":

> We did have one discussion with another staffer at the NSC, a military officer seconded to the NSC. We talked to him about this issue. He, to my great shock, talked about this genocide as age-old tribal hatred, as something that was perhaps almost inevitable, the kind of thing that happens in Africa and it's regrettable, but after all, we can't really do anything about it. . . .

> It upset me, because here at the highest policy-making levels in the U.S. government was a military officer, who was presumably giving his advice to policy makers, who had so little conception of what was happening in Rwanda that he could mistake a modern-day genocide, designed and carried through by a group of political actors for their own benefit—that he could mistake that for so-called ancient tribal hatreds, which, in fact, were neither ancient nor tribal in the case of Rwanda. . . .

With Monique Mujawamariyaw, who had escaped from Rwanda in the days after the killings began, des Forges spoke with Anthony Lake, President Clinton's national security adviser:

> He listened very carefully for perhaps half an hour, very intently. But at the end of the half-hour, I had the impression that he was not moved to change his ideas all that much. So I said to him, "Look, I have the feeling that we are not getting very far in trying to get some change in U.S. policy. What do we need to do to be more

in Rwanda. "What in God's name is going on?" she wondered (McDougall 2005). By the end of the year, she was working with the International Human Rights Law Group (now Global Rights) on programs that included supporting human rights advocates in the Great Lakes region of Africa.

The failure of governments to respond to the genocide in Rwanda has been amply documented. African governments, the United Nations, and major powers including the United States either took too little action too late, or, even worse, blocked proposals for action that could have saved hundreds of thousands of lives. The general public indifference certainly made this inaction possible. But there has been little analysis of reasons for the failure to generate public pressure that would have required governments to respond. Human rights groups such as Amnesty International and Human Rights Watch provided information about what was happening, and a small number of activist academics familiar with the region spoke out. But the groups that had been part of the anti-apartheid movement were almost totally unprepared to act. "We, along with the whole world, allowed that situation to happen," Bay Area anti-apartheid and AIDS activist Gerald Lenoir reflected (2005).

Alison des Forges, an academic specialist on the Great Lakes and an adviser to Human Rights Watch, had been in close touch with Rwandan human rights activists. With her colleagues she had briefed U.S. officials on the threat of genocide. She recalled effective?" He said, "Make more noise," and I think that was the essential message throughout here—that for the policy makers in Washington, Rwanda was simply not an issue that created enough noise for them to pay attention. (des Forges 2003)

The U.S. movement had worked for decades to make enough "noise" to get the U.S. government to take action against apartheid South Africa. In 1994 the cry for Rwanda was only a whisper, emanating from a handful of individuals and groups. The movement lacked the infrastructure of information, networks, and committed and informed local activists able to respond to action alerts or press releases. Only a handful of Americans or African exiles—and almost no organized local groups—were even minimally informed about the complexities of Rwanda and its neighbors. In this context, there were no strong voices to challenge the wide indifference to African deaths or the stereotypical portrayal of the genocidal political project of Rwanda's leaders as the product of "ancient tribal hatreds."

Rwanda, one might argue, was particularly remote for Americans. French-speaking, it was of little economic or strategic significance to the United States and even lacked a history of U.S. Cold War intervention. But the entrenched indifference to Africa and the lack of a movement capable of breaking through to capture public attention applied virtually across the board. Liberia, Somalia, and Zaire, which had been favored U.S. Cold War clients, slid further into crisis in the 1990s. In each case small groups of activists and exiles with personal ties mobilized, aided in the case of Zaire by the notoriety of longtime dictator Mobutu Sese Seko. Human rights groups and humanitarian organizations put out reports and calls to action, as did the Washington-based progressive Africa organizations.

But these crises did not evoke the engagement of more than a fraction of those who had come out against apartheid. Nor did the parallel resurgence of pro-democracy activism across the continent, from Benin to Kenya, attract much interest. When media attention did come—as in the case of the attacks on U.S. troops in Somalia in 1993 and, eventually, the crisis in the Great Lakes in 1994—the images tended to reinforce stereotypes of African irrationality and chaos. This was of little help in building a framework with which to mobilize activists for new Africa policies.

Even for those who were interested in Africa, it became more difficult to obtain nuanced coverage of the continent through traditional channels. Africa News Service, founded in 1973 as an outgrowth of the activist Southern Africa Committee, was forced to end print publication in 1993 for lack of financial support. The publication would find a new home on the Internet, eventually transforming itself into allAfrica.com. But in 1995 the government- and business-funded African American Institute shut down *Africa Report*, the only remaining regular national magazine on Africa—yet another indication of the marginalization of African concerns during the decade.

## A Changing Africa and Globalization

Although little visible to most Americans, including anti-apartheid activists, new currents were stirring in Africa in the 1990s as civil society organizations and pro-democracy movements gained momentum. The loss of Cold War support for dictatorial regimes created the potential not only for new conflicts, but also for new thinking. Freed of the constraints of Cold War dichotomies, more and more Africans demanded that universal human rights apply to them, regardless of the exemptions claimed by many of their rulers.

On issues relating to conflict, human rights, and democracy, an increasing convergence of views across the political spectrum was developing on both sides of the Atlantic. In February 1990, the same week Nelson Mandela left prison, delegates from a wide range of organizations across the continent gathered in Arusha, Tanzania, for a session supported by the United Nations. They adopted the African Charter for Popular Participation in Development and Transformation, which demanded an opening up of the political process and the political accountability of the state. The winding down of the Cold War made it more apparent that ideological rhetoric and external backing, whether from the left or right, had often served as a cover for the self-interest of elites.

New coalitions brought together nongovernmental activists with innovative officials in international agencies and governments to push forward global issues that were of particular interest to Africa. New Internet-based communication tools facilitated outreach and coordination across geographic and institutional boundaries to maximize the impact. In the campaign for an international landmines treaty, for example, governments such as Canada and Mozambique worked with international activist networks to mobilize support. By 1997, 121 countries had signed the treaty, although the United States remained a holdout.

The growing agreement on issues related to conflict, human rights, and democracy was not matched by parallel concurrence on economic and social rights for Africa. African scholars and civil society groups, including the churches, denounced the failure of the cutbacks and privatization schemes being imposed on Africa by the World Bank and rich-country creditors. The Arusha conference directed its call for democratization not only to African governments but also to international agencies imposing outside economic agendas, notably the economic orthodoxy of the "Washington consensus." But in Washington such critical views found little favor. Instead, the principal policy alternative to a business-as-usual development agenda emerged from the right under the slogan "trade, not aid." Many of those organizing to pressure officials for more attention to the continent regarded radical critiques of U.S. economic policies as inappropriate and inconvenient. They hoped instead for a larger share for Africa in the established economic order.

Neither Africa nor developing countries more generally were anything but marginal to the debate as the General Agreement on Tariffs and Trade was transformed into a new, more powerful World Trade Organization (WTO) in 1995. There was little room for dissent from economic orthodoxy in the Clinton administration, which also pushed through the North American Free Trade Agreement in 1994.

The African Growth and Opportunity Act, which eventually passed in 2000, provided some limited additional access to U.S. markets for selected African countries, stressing the potential benefits of trade. More significantly, it dominated and narrowed public debate on Africa in the second half of the 1990s. Progressive nongovernmental organizations either opposed the bill or called for amending

it to exclude the conservative economic policies it imposed. Some in the Congressional Black Caucus also took this position, but many within this group were moving toward greater emphasis on working within the conservative economic policy assumptions of the era. The debate provided little opportunity for discussing structural changes needed both in Africa and in the world economic order.

One of the groups that tried to bring other perspectives into the debate was the Africa Policy Information Center, the educational affiliate of the Washington Office on Africa. In early 1997, Imani Countess, who directed the two organizations from 1991 to 1997, took the initiative to bring together a group of activists from a variety of backgrounds to debate the way ahead in building "constituencies for Africa" that could counter the marginalization of the continent in policy debates (Countess et al. 1997). Participants identified a division among those working to counter the marginalization of Africa, comparable to trends that had developed in the civil rights movement at the end of the 1960s. On the one hand, many groups in Washington argued that what was essential was to get "more for Africa," to move Africa into the "mainstream" of global development. The majority of the activists at the gathering, however, argued that "more" attention for Africa was not necessarily "better." The crucial question was on what terms Africa would be involved. Working for Africa, the participants agreed, required actions to oppose the status quo of global economic inequality.

Opposition to the inequalities of globalization sparked well-publicized protests at the Seattle WTO summit in 1999. Among the WTO protesters, Africa gained relatively little attention. Yet Africa is the continent predicted to be most disadvantaged by increased trade liberalization. Without accumulated investment in infrastructure, human capital, and industrialization, African countries exporting primary commodities stand little chance of competing with the richer nations of the West or with the rising Asian powers.

In the 1990s AIDS in Africa was only beginning to become visible to activists in the United States and other rich countries. Thus Africa activists applauded as the veteran AIDS activist group ACT-UP targeted the Clinton administration in 1999 and 2000 for its hostility to the use of generic drugs. At the end of the decade, however, wider consciousness about AIDS in Africa was just beginning to emerge.

## New Directions in Solidarity

Through the end of the 1990s, then, no single issue provided a focus as clear as the earlier anti-apartheid push. Nor did the networks linking potential activists for Africa match the reach or complexity of the anti-apartheid convergence of the 1980s. But there were some encouraging efforts, notably the Nigeria pro-democracy movement and the largely church-based Jubilee movement for debt cancellation. These gave some indication that it was still possible to mobilize Americans in significant numbers for solidarity with Africa. And increasingly, Africa was part of the agenda for American activists and organizations focusing on global issues, from trade to genocide to AIDS.

One campaign that did develop during the decade, described in more detail in Walter Turner's chapter on the 1990s, was solidarity with the movement for democracy in Nigeria. It replicated, on a smaller scale and for a shorter period, many of the characteristics of the anti-apartheid movement, although racial division between oppressors and oppressed was not a factor in Nigeria. From the installation of the dictatorship of General Sani Abacha in 1993 until the return to civilian rule in 1999, pro-democracy campaigners inside Nigeria and the charismatic figure of Ken Saro-Wiwa in the Niger Delta attracted a mounting wave of support in the United States and worldwide. In the U.S. context, the diverse forces involved did not come together in one centralized group. But lines of communication were strong, fostered by groups such as The Africa Fund in New York and by regular meetings of the International Round-table on Nigeria in Washington. The large community of Nigerian immigrants in the

United States produced many activists. Many of the organizations and networks that had made up the anti-apartheid movement were drawn to the Nigeria issue, while environmental activists and trade unionists were drawn in by the role of U.S. oil companies.

But few other countries in Africa—whatever the scale of their crisis or legacy of U.S. involvement—could match the convergence of factors promoting action around Nigeria. Among the many issues that needed attention, probably the most successful in gaining grassroots support were the campaign for an international landmine treaty and the campaign to cancel Africa's debt. The debt cancellation issue, which continued into the next decade, was closely linked with other issues of global economics and carried the potential to raise fundamental questions of inequality. But it was not easy to explain in simple terms, and activists were hard-pressed to find ways to build a wider movement.

The debt campaign was initiated by the worldwide Jubilee 2000 movement, named for the biblical concept of a jubilee year in which property is returned to its rightful owner. The All Africa Conference of Churches called the debt burden "a new form of slavery as vicious as the slave trade." But in the

Nigerian activist Dr. Owens Wiwa of the Movement for the Survival of the Ogoni People and Stephen Mills of the Sierra Club speak at the University of Alabama, September 24, 1996. *Photo by John Earl.*

United States, despite the engagement of significant numbers of church activists and of many others who had been involved in anti-apartheid networks, the hope of having a major impact by the millennium year 2000 met with disappointment. Creditor countries and the World Bank proved obscure as targets, making it difficult to attract much media attention or mobilize large numbers of activists. And the largely white church networks involved were too limited a vehicle, as they were unable to tap into either black activist networks or the new and diverse set of African immigrant organizations.

Africa did not figure prominently in the debates about globalization that were gaining momentum at the end of the decade, highlighted by the Seattle protests in 1999. Nevertheless, by the end of the decade there was a rising consciousness about issues of both domestic and international equality. The 1990s also saw new developments that would change the context for U.S.-African relations and could possibly provide the basis for new movement in subsequent decades. Just as new personal and organizational ties in the 1950s and 1960s intensified U.S. contact with Africa, in the 1990s the expansion of the Internet and the wave of new African immigration presented new opportunities for communication.

It took decades before the seeds planted in the 1950s and 1960s could bear fruit in a movement large enough to have an impact on U.S. policy. At the end of the 1990s, the challenge of forcing fundamental changes in U.S.-African relations and in global patterns of inequality was as great as the challenge of opposing colonialism and apartheid had been—possibly greater. No one had found a way to craft the messages or build the networks that could foster a powerful movement for justice and full human rights for both Africans and Americans. Yet the signs during the decade were in some ways encouraging. The number of people in the United States who were involved in small-scale actions of solidarity already exceeded that of previous decades. Many were new immigrants who were sending support to families or communities at home in Africa and closely following developments there. This provided links that potentially could converge again to form a movement capable of making larger changes. It was clear that the battles against injustice inside the United States and inside African countries were not isolated

and disconnected, but were linked to the need to change an international order that some of us were beginning to describe as "global apartheid" (Booker and Minter 2001).

This chapter and this book stop with the turn of the millennium. Our brief reflections on the subsequent period and the potential for the future are presented in an afterword. The new century has already brought events and developments that stand to profoundly affect both Africa and the broader global context: 9/11, the worldwide spread of HIV/AIDS, the war in Iraq, a new level of U.S. strategic interest in African oil, the emergence of the African Union, the crisis in Darfur, and more. In the years following the 1990s, the organizational configuration also changed. Africa Action emerged from the merger of ACOA, The Africa Fund, and the Africa Policy Information Center. Other groups changed leaders, and new issue coalitions developed. The catastrophe in New Orleans in 2005 provided a vivid reminder that the inequality of global apartheid has its counterpart at home. How to build an effective challenge on either front is an unresolved question.

From our review of the previous five decades, it is abundantly clear that those committed to Africa must take a long-term perspective. The connections emerging now, we are convinced, are important not just for what can be accomplished in this year and this decade. Just as connections made in the 1950s, 1960s, and 1970s contributed years later to the end of the apartheid regime, the ties now being forged can, if nourished, help make possible a world in which everyone can enjoy the same fundamental rights to freedom and justice.

*Oral sources for chapter 1 include interviews with Robert S. Browne (2003), Jennifer Davis (2004, 2005), Sylvia Hill (2003, 2004), Reed Kramer (2005), Ben Magubane (2004), Gay McDougall (2005), Prexy Nesbitt (1998), Robert Van Lierop (2004), Cherri Waters (2003), Cora Weiss (2003), and Peter Weiss (2003).*

William Minter

Chapter 2

# The 1950s:
# Africa Solidarity Rising
*Lisa Brock*

In the summer of 1979, I attended my first demonstration in solidarity with the people of Africa. Little did I know that this would be the first of many such actions, or that out of it would grow my intellectual and political work for the next 20 years. The Southern Africa Support Project in Washington, DC called the demonstration to protest the presence in Washington of Bishop Abel Muzorewa. Recently installed as leader of what was briefly called Zimbabwe-Rhodesia, Muzorewa was in town to gain support for his government, which had been established to forestall genuine majority rule in Zimbabwe.

Even before, I had been involved in domestic anti-racist issues, as a student at Howard University and as a member of the National Alliance Against Racist and Political Repression. I had begun to see the connections between the local and the global, especially in terms of racism, sexism, power, and imperialism. Meeting Dennis Brutus, while I was a graduate student at Northwestern University, solidified my growing sense of internationalism with concrete action. It was at Dennis's urging that I became a co-chair in Chicago of the Stop the Apartheid Rugby Tour in 1981, and I never looked back. I came to understand that I was part of a tradition of activists and intellectuals who had made that same political and personal journey.

In this chapter about the 1950s, I will present three "lions," activists who preceded me on this

journey and emerged as leaders: George Houser, Bill Sutherland, and Charlene Mitchell. For each of them, but in very different ways, the 1950s was a determining decade that shaped the work they would engage in for the next half century.

From the vantage point of the twenty-first century, it is important to grasp that the 1950s was a messy dance of a decade. The Cold War was omnipresent, both shaping and being shaped by rising demands for freedom and civil rights on the African continent and in the United States. The struggles against racism, colonialism, and nuclear proliferation were intertwined. Enormous, almost impossible, hopes and dreams were placed on Africa and African leaders by Americans, especially African Americans, who wanted to believe that colonialism and racial oppression were finite and vulnerable.

As I began to explore the 1950s, probably most revelatory for me was the discovery that virtually all U.S.-centered activists and scholars whom we identify with the civil and human rights movements consciously saw themselves as working in solidarity with the peoples of Africa. The list is far too long to name in full but includes Paul and Essie Robeson, St. Clair Drake, Thurgood Marshall, Sidney Poitier, Ella Baker, Billie

Lisa Brock
*Photo courtesy of Lisa Brock.*

Holiday, and Harry Belafonte. This discovery reinforced the need for the sort of history we present here, and it raised important questions. Why are the histories, documentaries, and biographies of these people and this era problematically constructed to emphasize the national and not the international? How does the desire for a "national narrative" obscure the evolution of an international one? Could this be one postmodern undertaking of scholar activists, to deconstruct the "imagined past" toward a reimagined future? This small essay dreams so.

## Race, Ideology, and the Fall of the Council on African Affairs

Before I present the lives and work of George Houser, Bill Sutherland, and Charlene Mitchell, a few words should be said about the Council on African Affairs. The council closed its doors in the mid-1950s, just as Houser's American Committee on Africa was opening up for business.

Formed in 1937, the Council on African Affairs was by the 1950s the largest Africa solidarity organization in the United States up to that time. Its history illustrates the power of African American solidarity with the peoples of Africa as well as the threat this solidarity posed to the American establishment. At the beginning of World War II the organization was "crafted by the left" but embraced by "the full range of black American liberals, church leaders, [and the] professional and middle class" (Von Eschen 1997, 19), as well as by black nationalist organizations. At its height, under the leadership of giants like Paul Robeson, W. E. B. Du Bois, and Alphaeus Hunton, the council had the ear of the U.S. president and drew tens of thousands to mass rallies at Madison Square Garden and Harlem's Abyssinian Baptist Church.

From its office on 26th Street in New York City, the council linked the struggle against racism in the United States with the colonization of "colored peoples" the world over. Guests from South Africa and India were honored at its events. CAA campaigns—opposing Mussolini's invasion of Ethiopia; advocating for a strong United Nations; championing workers' causes in South Africa, Nigeria, and Ghana; demanding the end of the South African mandate over South West Africa—were widely applauded in U.S., European, and African newspapers. The council in the late 1940s had varied and deep personal, political, and journalistic ties in Africa, India, the Caribbean, and Europe.

By 1952, however, the liberal-left coalition was imploding under the weight of a totalizing Cold War. Robeson and Du Bois were hounded by U.S. authorities and Hunton served nine months in jail in 1951 for his political and ideological beliefs. Labeling them as subversive and soft on communism was both accurate and effective, and it cost the council considerable support. While none professed

As the Cold War intensified, the Council on African Affairs was attacked as subversive and its leader, Alphaeus Hunton, was jailed for nine months in 1951. On his release, Hunton, left, was welcomed by his wife Dorothy, Paul Robeson, and W. E. B. Du Bois. *Photo reproduced from Hunton 1986.*

Lisa Brock

membership in the Communist Party at the time, all three men were clearly Marxist or left-leaning. And all three refused to distance themselves from friends and comrades in the U.S. Communist Party or from their belief in a détente between the Soviet Union and the United States.

Choices had to be made. At the end of the war, President Truman had indicated that he was ready to concede certain civil rights demands. But these concessions were predicated on black leadership support for, or at least acquiescence to, U.S. domestic and foreign policy. While this kind of "contradictory politics of inclusion" was not new for African Americans, the stakes were higher in postwar America (Brock 1998). This was so, ironically, because organizations like the CAA and a radicalized NAACP as well as the black media had brought international attention to the horrors of Jim Crow.

Engaged in a deepening ideological struggle with the Left, the United States was touting itself as moral leader of the free world. Yet the United States had an image problem, and this problem became especially acute as old colonial relations in Africa began to fall away and countries moved toward independence. Taking the offensive, the Truman administration set out to craft an Africa policy for the United States and to recruit American blacks to play a role in these new initiatives.

This was a game two could play. Leading black liberal groups—the NAACP, the Urban League, the National Council of Negro Women—employed a carrot and stick of their own. If the government desegregated the armed forces, for instance, they would not demonstrate in Washington; if the government appointed blacks to key government, judicial, labor, and military positions, the black press would applaud U.S. programs such as the Marshall Plan in Europe. More African Americans than ever before (although still only a handful) emerged to play roles on the national and international stage. Ralph Bunche, an early supporter of the CAA, became the U.S. representative at the United Nations and won a Nobel Peace Prize. Max Yergan, one of the original founders of the CAA, turned to the far right and even collaborated with the FBI against the CAA. Edith Sampson, a prominent attorney from Chicago, became the first African American federal judge, while Maida

Springer, a union organizer, served as the AFL-CIO's African representative for many years.

All of these African Americans became at one time or another part of U.S. State Department tours that traveled abroad to "reassure Africans and Asians that the U.S. government treated [black Americans] fairly" (Lutz 2001, 328). This was one aspect of the messy dance mentioned above. African Americans hoped their involvement in these international jaunts would lead to increased justice at home, while the U.S. government encouraged and promoted a black presence on such tours in hopes of pushing its own corporate, political, and economic goals in Africa.

Although the Council on African Affairs was harassed and charged with sedition, it refused to back off of its critique of race relations in the United States, where segregation and white-on-black violence continued. Nor would it uncritically support an emerging U.S. policy in Africa. The CAA moved its office to the more friendly environs of 125th Street in Harlem. It was the only U.S. organization in the early 1950s to offer an incisive analysis of the two major trends in Africa at that time: first, the deepening African anticolonial/antiracist struggles, and second, the desperate attempts by colonial powers to retain control.

The council paid a price for its clear questions and straightforward analysis. In October 1954, Alphaeus Hunton was subpoenaed to appear before a federal grand jury and was forced to surrender all records detailing the CAA's relationship with the African National Congress and the South African Indian Congress. The CAA's newsletter, *Spotlight on Africa*, reported that the grand jury sought to determine "whether these activities represented a violation of the Foreign Agents Registration Act" (October 28, 1954).

One of Hunton's last involvements before closing the Council on African Affairs was to attend the Asian African Conference in Bandung, Indonesia. Although he criticized the conference for not having enough African participation, he clearly identified with the Cold War weariness in the "colored" world that motivated them to find their own nonaligned path. "It is possible and practicable," he said, "for Communist, non-Communist and anti-communist to live together, meet together, speak together, and contribute toward the common good of all mankind" (Von Eschen 1997, 172).

America in the 1950s had no room for Hunton's kind of inclusiveness. For more than 15 years the Council on African Affairs had packed the churches and streets of Harlem, building support for the end of colonialism and African liberation. The American Committee on Africa began its work just as the CAA closed its doors. Although the two organizations understood the Harlem community to be a key constituency and shared a focus on Africa, ACOA did not give credit to or claim any continuity with the CAA. Silences in history speak as eloquently as words, and this omission, given the times, may suggest if not outright anticommunism on the part of ACOA, then at least a fear of being associated with communists.

## George Houser and the American Committee on Africa

Africa was rising and its people welcomed support from a broad spectrum of sources in their struggles for independence and majority rule. These included the American Committee on Africa as well as the Council on African Affairs. ACOA began as Americans for South African Resistance, which was formed in 1952 to support the South African Defiance Campaign Against Unjust Laws. In 1953 AFSAR broadened its mission and changed its name. George Houser, one of the founders, served as executive director from 1955 until his retirement in 1981, creating, with his staff and board of directors, what was to become the most successful U.S. Africa solidarity organization of the next 50 years.

George Mills Houser was born in 1916 in Cleveland, Ohio, the son of Methodist missionaries. By the time he finished college, he had lived in the Philippines, New York, California, Colorado, and China. Influenced by the social gospel his father preached, Houser entered the world of activism through his faith. He followed in his father's footsteps, entering New York's Union Theological Seminary to become a minister himself.

The outbreak of World War II opened a new chapter in Houser's life. Called to register for the draft before the United States was formally at war, he was one of eight seminary students who refused

to register. They were arrested and sentenced to a year and a day in federal prison. Upon their release from prison, the seminary asked them not to take any other action that would bring adverse publicity to the seminary, or at least to seek permission before acting. Houser and four others moved to Chicago instead and entered Chicago Theological Seminary.

While Houser was in prison, A. J. Muste, a leading pacifist, visited him and offered him a job with the Fellowship of Reconciliation (FOR) in Chicago. FOR was an international pacifist organization that had been established in 1914, and Houser took up the position when he arrived in Chicago. In 1943, through his involvement with FOR, he helped found CORE, the Congress of Racial Equality. With offices on Chicago's South Side, CORE would become a key organization in the fight for desegregation and civil rights in the 1960s. Foreshadowing what was to come, FOR and CORE conducted the first Freedom Ride in the U.S. South in 1947 and launched campaigns to desegregate restaurants, pools, and beaches, beginning in Chicago.

In this way Houser discovered his life's path. "I realized, well, I am not just looking around for a church. I've got a vocation going here." Houser became a national FOR/CORE organizer and returned to New York in 1946. It was a natural step for him to move from this work to work on South Africa.

> I was on the national staff of the FOR working with Bayard Rustin and others. Bill Sutherland was a good friend of ours. . . . We had been on many projects together—antiwar, antirace, what have you—in the New York area. Bill came back from London saying that he had met a representative of a South African publication who was connected with the African National Congress of South Africa and there was a big campaign coming up. I said to myself . . . defiance against unjust laws was very much like some of the CORE activities, civil disobedience against Jim Crow laws here, against apartheid laws there.

I interviewed George Houser at his modest home in Pomona, New York in 2004. Gray-haired, with sparkling eyes, he talked about the 1950s. For him, just as for members in the CAA, the connection between fighting racism in the United States and in South Africa was too obvious to ignore.

Americans for South African Resistance was formed with Don Harrington of the Community Church and the Reverend Charles Y. Trigg of the Salem Methodist Church in Harlem, along with Norman Thomas of the Socialist Party and Roger Baldwin of the American Civil Liberties Union. Houser, although still working for FOR and CORE, began a rich correspondence in February 1952 with Walter Sisulu and Yusuf A. Cachalia, leaders of the African National Congress and South African Indian Congress respectively, the two organizations leading the Joint Planning Council for the Defiance Campaign. He also wrote to many others, including people in the ANC, the Unity Movement, and the South African Institute of Race Relations. All wrote back, welcoming AFSAR'S support for their work in South Africa. During this flurry of letters, Z. K. Matthews, a Fort Hare professor and ANC leader, came to spend a year at Union Theological Seminary. He passed on to AFSAR the letters he received from his son Joe, leader of the Defiance Campaign in the Cape Province. Matthews and Houser become friends, and on his return to South Africa Matthews remained an invaluable contact.

This correspondence was to set the agenda for AFSAR: information dissemination and raising funds. The ongoing vehicle for both was a small newsletter called *AFSAR Bulletin*. It kept its readers informed of the stages of the Defiance Campaign and solicited donations for those who were putting their lives on the line in South Africa. During its brief and somewhat irregular run, it managed to reach some 2,000 to 3,000 people scattered around the country. With the *Bulletin*, AFSAR was able to raise around $2,000, which it sent to the campaign. One woman from Arizona sent her diamond ring with a note saying, "use this to raise funds for the cause." The immediate cause was legal defense and support for families whose breadwinners were imprisoned for defying unjust laws.

In spring 1952, AFSAR held its first big event in support of the Defiance Campaign. Hosted by Adam Clayton Powell Jr. at his Abyssinian Baptist Church in Harlem, the event drew more than 800 people, black and white. A featured speaker was actor Canada Lee, who was starring in a Broadway production based on the South African novel *Cry the Beloved Country* (Paton 1948). He had just returned from South Africa and spoke passionately of what he had experienced. After the program, Houser recalls, a motorcade of nearly 50 cars drove from Harlem all the way down to the South African consulate at 58th Street to hold a lively demonstration.

As the Defiance Campaign was winding down in spring 1953, a group came together to decide what to do next. Houser, Harrington, Thomas, Baldwin, and Muste were joined by George Carpenter, Africa secretary of the National Council of Churches; Professor Rayford Logan of Howard University; Peter Weiss, a lawyer and director of the International Development Placement Association; James Farmer, a

George Houser, left, and Bill Sutherland greet each other at Houser's 90th birthday party in Nyack, NY in 2006. Over more than 60 years, the two met time and again on the road they each traveled for African liberation.
*Photo courtesy of George Houser.*

founder and later director of CORE; and Walter Offutt of the NAACP.

This mix of religious, civil rights, socialist, and pacifist leaders was Houser's natural community, and it would continue to be the core constituency of the organization they were about to create. Calling itself the American Committee on Africa, the infant organization proclaimed that "one of the world's continents is missing from America's consciousness . . . The ACOA is being organized to help bridge this gap between Africans and Americans" (Houser 1989, 63).

The Community Church of New York on 35th Street and Park Avenue gave ACOA office space. George Shepherd, who had been traveling in Uganda and was well known to the founding committee, agreed to be temporary volunteer executive. They decided that Houser should travel to Africa to become more familiar with conditions on the ground. From May to October 1954, he traveled to London and from there to West and Southern Africa, establishing contact with leaders and movements and conducting hundreds of hours of interviews. Upon his return, he became the executive director. Lydia Zemba joined him as a second staff member, leaving a job at Doubleday to work for an organization with a nonexistent budget.

Supported by small contributions, ACOA spent the first year finding its feet and defining its work. In a document dated April 21, 1955, it announced a three-point program comprising education, action, and projects. The vehicles for education would be its journal *Africa Today*, as well as a speaker's bureau, special literature on topics of importance, and public conferences. Action would focus on influencing the course of American foreign policy. This would involve a considerable amount of time spent at the United Nations working with African petitioners. ACOA's projects included an African Leadership Lecture Program, which began organizing speaking tours for emerging African leaders (Shepherd 1956).

For projects, a fund was established and began by supporting two African education initiatives. In South Africa, the imposition of "Bantu education" nationwide forced most mission schools, which provided education for Africans, to turn over their operations to the government. ACOA provided support to Father Trevor Huddleston, who was fighting to keep his integrated St. Peters school independent. In

the Gold Coast, soon to become Ghana, Bill Sutherland called for support for village education. An old friend of FOR, CORE, and now the ACOA, he had moved to the Gold Coast in 1953.

Both fundraising campaigns achieved some success. By mid-1956, $10,000 had been sent to Huddleston (Houser 1989, 65). In September 1958, just a year after Ghanaian independence, 515 books and several records were shipped to Accra by the New American Library. Cora Weiss, married to board member Peter Weiss, was volunteering for ACOA. She cultivated contacts with publishers, national library associations, and record companies, asking them to defray the cost of shipping material aid to Ghana (C. Weiss 1958).

The third major initiative was the South African Defense Fund, established in response to the infamous Treason Trials. Among the 156 people put on trial were a number of ACOA contacts including Z. K. Matthews, Walter Sisulu, Yusuf A. Cachalia, and Albert Luthuli. ACOA drew on the prestige of its national committee, which included emerging civil rights leader Martin Luther King Jr., Congressman Adam Clayton Powell Jr., actor Sidney Poitier, Senator Hubert Humphrey, and African American baseball pioneer Jackie Robinson. The fund continued after the trial, and ACOA contributed about $75,000 to legal defense over the years (Houser 1989, 120–21).

In another highly successful initiative in the 1950s, ACOA sponsored a tour by the Kenyan labor leader Tom Mboya. Only 26 at the time, Mboya was a rising star in a dazzling constellation of brilliant young African leaders engaged in the anticolonial nation-building endeavor. First belonging to Jomo Kenyatta's Kenya Africa Union, by his 1956 tour he was the elected general secretary of the newly formed Kenyan Federation of Labor. Kenya had been front-page news since 1952, when the Mau Mau rebellion erupted on the scene. Chapter 1 describes this armed insurgency that shook British control and seeped into the consciousness of 1950s America. Tom Mboya, a leader who appeared willing to pursue a moderate, nonviolent path of action, seemed to many Americans to offer a welcome alternative.

The ACOA sponsored two tours with Mboya. The first, in August–September 1956, was heavily geared toward trade unions. Mboya spent time with many regular workers and trade union leaders and

Meeting Kwame Nkrumah. At the first All-African People's Conference in Accra in 1958, the ACOA delegation was photographed with the Ghanaian president. From left: John Marcum, Homer Jack, George Houser, Nkrumah, Frank Montero, Bill Scheinman. *Photo courtesy of George Houser.*

also met Walter Reuther of the United Auto Workers and George Meany, the highly influential national president of the AFL-CIO. Back in Kenya in December, Mboya wrote Houser that the Kenyan Federation of Labor had received a $35,000 grant from the AFL-CIO to build a trade union center. "At least one important aspect of my trip has been fulfilled," he wrote. "For this the ACOA must take some credit" (Houser 1989, 83).

During the second trip begun on April 8, 1959 and ending "thirty-five days and about 100 speeches later" (Houser 1989, 88), Mboya became one of the most well-known African leaders in the United States. He established contacts in the highest echelons of the U.S. government and the civil rights community. Because of this trip, Mboya saw the achievement of a second goal: the ACOA was able to facilitate, through the formation of the African-American Students Foundation, an airlift of Kenyan

and other East African students to U.S. colleges and universities. The fundraising appeal to charter a flight to bring the 81 students to the United States was led by Jackie Robinson, Harry Belafonte, and Sidney Poitier (Okoth 1987, 88).

On September 6, 1959, 61 men and 20 women arrived in New York and were met by a contingent led by Robinson, who himself gave $4,000. "I have had few more rewarding experiences in my entire life," Robinson said. "As they talked in the same quiet calm, self-assured way with which Tom Mboya made such a hit on his recent tour here, I couldn't help but feel that here undoubtedly was a whole group of potential Tom Mboyas, Kwame Nkrumahs and Nnamdi Azikiwes" (Okoth 1987, 88). Returning to their home countries, many of the students went on to become part of the first generation of civil servants who would help run their countries after independence. It was one of the few women, Wangari Maathai, who would become the most outstanding leader, winning the 2004 Nobel Peace Prize for her groundbreaking environmental work in a far different period of Kenya's history.

Tom Mboya, his tours, and the student airlift program, while hugely successful for the ACOA, became controversial soon after, a reflection of the strange political space that Mboya and the ACOA found themselves in during the Cold War. In an effort to influence an emerging U.S. policy, the ACOA had taken Mboya to Washington to meet Vice President Richard Nixon, Senator John F. Kennedy, and State Department officials, among others. Over the next few years Mboya would move closer and closer to the United States government, establishing a relationship with the CIA. He eventually affiliated his Kenyan Federation of Labor with the U.S.-backed International Confederation of Free Trade Unions, which guaranteed some funds, rather than with the Eastern European–backed World Federation of Trade Unions (Richards 2000, 8). He was touted in establishment circles as the anticommunist spokesman for Africa (Wechsler 1959).

Cora Weiss, who directed the African-American Students Foundation and its airlift, came to know Mboya well. Reminiscing in 2003, she described herself as "Miss Innocent" in the 1950s. ACOA did not know of Mboya's connection to the CIA, she said, though she remembers driving him to what she suspects now was an appointment to pick up a check: "If we had known, we probably wouldn't have had anything to do with him" (C. Weiss 2003). For reasons that remain unclear, Tom Mboya was killed by a fellow Kenyan in 1969.

ACOA during its first few years emerged as the premier U.S. Africa solidarity organization. It did so through sophisticated coalition building, through work with the young United Nations, and by cultivating good relationships with emerging African leaders. ACOA held public events and sponsored speaking tours for these leaders. Houser's continued travel to Africa, where he developed an expertise on regional conflicts, was critical to the organization's development. Its regular publication of *Africa Today* and *Africa-UN Bulletin* as well as numerous analytical pamphlets began to build an educated constituency on Africa in the United States.

The ACOA also continued to review and evaluate its projects, work, and internal structures. The only

significant power struggle came in the 1950s. Would ACOA give priority to support for the African liberation movements and include on its board men like A. J. Muste, who were pacifists and socialists? Or would it focus on a more mainstream constituency, with public relations and lobbying of Congress and the State Department as its main priorities? The issue came to a head at a March 1959 meeting of the board of directors at which Eliot Newcomb, arguing for the more conservative strategy, ran for chair against the incumbent Don Harrington. Newcomb, associated with the fundraiser Harold Oram, was narrowly defeated on a vote of 14 to 15, opposition to him having been organized by Peter Weiss. Houser believes that if the vote had gone the other way, ACOA would have distanced itself from the liberation movements and he would have been out of a job (Houser 1988).

The 1950s was a strange time. Not only was ideological conformity demanded, but false accusations could destroy individuals and organizations. ACOA's success stemmed in large part from its careful navigation of these charged waters. Under Houser's leadership, the organization, while unalterably opposed to McCarthyism, declined to work in collaboration with communists or communist organizations. Houser was very focused on getting noncommunist liberals involved in the cause of African freedom (Houser 1989, 13). When I asked him why there had been no contact with the Council on African Affairs, he said it was because of their connection to the communist Party. He told me that he saw those in communist parties in both the United States and South Africa as defenders of Soviet policy, which he did not support. But Houser also said that the driving motivation for his involvements were his religious orientation and his belief in nonviolence, not anticommunism.

When he visited South Africa in 1954, Houser saw that white communists were playing an important role, keeping the national struggle from being simply antiwhite. He called it a "real tragedy" that there were practically no militant noncommunist South African whites involved. This discovery increased his determination to recruit white liberals to the anti-apartheid struggle (Houser 1954).

He was able to achieve this goal. The ACOA and the U.S. civil rights movement succeeded in getting a wide range of white Americans interested and engaged in the nonviolent struggle for racial justice, both in the United States and on behalf of Africa. And while Houser sought to get more whites involved, he clearly had no intention of building a white organization. Although he came out of a nonracial movement, Houser understood that historically Africa had been an issue of concern mainly to Pan-Africanists and African Americans. But the United States was a majority white country, and if U.S. policy was to be affected, Houser believed, members of the majority group had to be engaged. The fact that he managed to accomplish this *and* gained the respect of black politicians, entertainers, and athletes was clearly significant for this time in African and U.S. history.

Over the next decades, the space for ideological debate increased in the United States. At the same time, the number of African liberation movements asking for support proliferated. ACOA took the position that it was not the prerogative of an American organization to judge the legitimacy of these movements. Instead, it took its direction from the Organization of African Unity (OAU), working with any movement that the OAU recognized. A number of these movements had strong ties to the Soviet Union and were heavily influenced by communist ideology. In 1969, in an exception to its policy of following the OAU lead, ACOA endorsed the primacy of the MPLA and directed its support for Angolan liberation to this movement. Houser himself became friends with many South African communists. How could he not? If the ACOA was going to do its work, it had to engage with Africans on their own terms.

## Two Voices: Charlene Mitchell and Bill Sutherland

*It was a glorious time, it was.*

—Charlene Mitchell, speaking of the seating of independent Ghana at the United Nations in 1957

*My life, living it, has helped some people. You know, by actually going and living in Africa, I have very often been a bridge between the African American movements and the African movements.*

—Bill Sutherland

Charlene Mitchell and Bill Sutherland had connections with the Council on African Affairs and the American Committee on Africa respectively. The lives of these two African Americans represent examples of committed journeys shaped by political beliefs and engaged activism. Charlene Mitchell was born in Ohio in 1930. She joined the Communist Party at age 16 and ran for president on that ticket in 1968. Bill Sutherland was born in New Jersey in 1918 and became a believer in nonviolence. He grew up knowing, from family stories passed down through the generations, that his ancestors came from Nigeria, and he had even met distant cousins from that country at family reunions. As a young man he decided to move to Africa, and he lived there for much of his life. Of the 1930s and 1940s, both Mitchell and Sutherland remember racial experiences in the United States. Of the 1950s, they both remember Africa.

At an early age, Sutherland moved into the all-white community of Glen Ridge, New Jersey, where he says he experienced "a great deal of ostracism and discrimination" because of his race (Sutherland and Meyer 2000, 3). Searching for a place to fit in and trying to find his own way, Sutherland was drawn to the local Congregational Church, whose young white Southern minister was a pacifist and a socialist. The minister and his congregation invited Sutherland to become a member of the Young People's Society. He also recalls attending an African American church with his father and hearing a fiery speaker from India who spoke of Gandhi's civil disobedience campaigns. He was so excited by this that he reported on it in his social studies class, much to the dismay of his white teacher who, he remembers, seemed intent on defending British colonialism. Another teacher gave him the seminal work by W. E. B. Du Bois, *Black Reconstruction in America* (1935), and Sutherland remembers it having a tremendous impact on his young mind (Sutherland and Meyer 2000, 8).

While in high school Sutherland became involved in the junior NAACP and in youth groups that focused on international relations and socialism. In college he joined the Student Christian Movement and met David Dellinger, who would become a major figure of the anti–Vietnam War era. Dellinger was also the principal founder of the Newark Ashram, a Gandhian-based community center, which Sutherland joined. When the United States initiated the military draft in 1940, Sutherland, Dellinger, and other members of this community decided to resist. All of them, like George Houser, were sentenced to jail. But Sutherland and Dellinger spent almost four years in prison, while the others served only a year. Upon his release in 1945, Sutherland helped found the New York office of CORE at the same time that Houser was working with CORE's national office in Chicago.

Charlene Mitchell spent most of her youth in Chicago. Her father was active in the local NAACP, in Chicago machine politics, and in the Communist Party. Charlene belonged to a cluster of integrated, mostly communist, youth in Cabrini. Cabrini, she remembers, "was a big integrated [working-class] community and it was wonderful." At age 13 she joined an organization called American Youth for Democracy, and she took her first political action with this group. It was 1943 and the neighborhood theater, the Windsor, was a segregated facility. She and her friends were frustrated and insulted that as a mixed group they could not sit together. So they integrated the theater using, as it turned out, the same tactics being used at a similar time and in the same city by the older CORE activists, including Houser.

The theater's seating pattern required the African American patrons to sit in the balcony while the white patrons sat downstairs. One day Charlene and her friends simply exchanged places. The management could not tell the white kids they couldn't sit in the balcony. Even if management required the African Americans to return to the balcony, that section would still be integrated by the presence of whites. Others joined the effort and before long the management gave in and ended segregated seating.

This kind of activity was part of the broader Double V campaign initiated by African Americans during World War II, in which they sought to use the war effort strategically in the struggle against racism and segregation at home. With African Americans fighting in Europe just as white Americans were, African American activists called for a victory against Hitler in Europe and a simultaneous victory against lynching and second-class citizenship in the United States.

In the interviews conducted for this chapter, Sutherland and Mitchell recalled the 1950s as a decade of great hope and great sadness—hope for African freedom on the one hand, and sadness and disillusionment at the rise of Cold War hostility on the other. In 1950 Sutherland joined the Peacemakers, a group of radical war resisters opposed to the Korean War. Their members organized on street corners in Boston and New York. As is often the case during war, antiwar efforts were not well received, and the resisters heard taunts of "Tell it to the Russians." So Sutherland and the others decided to do just that. They organized a bicycle trip from Paris to Moscow on which Sutherland was joined by Dave Dellinger, Ralph DiGia, and Art Emory, all of whom he had known from the Ashram in Newark. Their goal was to "call upon the young men on both sides to lay down their arms and refuse to fight" (Sutherland and Meyer 2000, 5).

While Sutherland may not have persuaded many to resist war, the contacts he made on this trip would have far-reaching consequences. He met a number of Africans, students and others, who explained colonialism to him and talked about their struggle against it. Their enthusiasm for African liberation was infectious.

Sutherland describes one such encounter:

> I met this man who was the editor of the *Bantu World*. And he was the one who told me that there was going to be the Defiance Campaign Against the Unjust Laws. And then I came back and told George [Houser] and Bayard Rustin about it, and they were CORE executives . . . and that was the beginning of Americans for South African Resistance. (Sutherland and Meyer 2000, 4)

Returning from his travels, Sutherland was disillusioned by what he found at home. "The possibilities of progressive social change looked rarer and more remote. . . . Everyone was knuckling under to [Senator Joseph] McCarthy." In Africa, by contrast, it seemed that there was "a real possibility to put the values we were talking about into practice . . . and I had a vision of Africa so idealistic" (Sutherland and Meyer 2000, 7).

Sutherland decided to move to Africa. He traveled first to London to get his visas and papers. There he met George Padmore, the well-known Pan-Africanist and writer for the *West African Pilot*, one of the most important African newspapers. Its founder,

Nnamdi Azikiwe, like many other Africans, had traveled to the United States, where he had attended the historically black Lincoln University. He had gone home to found the newspaper and take part in the struggle for independence. In 1953 Sutherland took up residence in the Gold Coast, which was moving toward independence under the leadership of Kwame Nkrumah and the Convention People's Party.

Sutherland found in Nkrumah's pamphlet, *What I Mean by Positive Action* (1949), many of the same "intensified nonviolent methods of struggle" that he had come to embrace (Sutherland and Meyer 2000, 30). Sutherland became friends with Komla Agbeli Gbedemah, one of Nkrumah's trusted comrades, and he married Efua Theodora, a Ghanaian poet and teacher. When Ghana became independent in 1957 with Nkrumah as its first president, Sutherland became progressive America's unofficial ambassador to the new nation.

Sutherland could not have played this role at a more significant time. Because Ghana was the first sub-Saharan African colony to gain independence, thousands of people attended the inaugural celebration. Sutherland suggested that an invitation be extended to the young civil rights minister Martin Luther King Jr., and King and his wife Coretta accepted. They were afforded a deference and attention on this trip that they had not experienced at home. Even Vice President Richard Nixon, the head of the U.S. delegation, who had ignored King's efforts to communicate at home, treated King like an ambassador in Ghana and invited him to Washington for private talks.

Sutherland recalls that the changing of the guard in Ghana made a deep impression on King, so much so that Nkrumah's powerful words would later come to be identified with King himself:

> On that fateful night in 1957, [when] the British flag was lowered, and the flag of Ghana was raised, Nkrumah, dressed in traditional kente cloth, his fist waving in the air, tears streaming down his face, shouted over and over again: "Free at Last, Free at Last, Free at Last." (Sutherland and Meyer 2000, 35)

Martin Luther King chose these same words to close his historic "I Have a Dream" speech at the March on Washington in 1963.

Bill Sutherland (holding photo of Kwame Nkrumah) with his wife and three children in Accra in 1957. From left: Efua Theodora, his wife, with Esi and Ralph, and family friend Margaret Cartwright holding Amowi. *Photo by Willis E. Bell. Courtesy of Bill Sutherland.*

Those who attended Ghana's independence celebration were a veritable who's who of African American leaders, including A. Philip Randolph, Adam Clayton Powell Jr., Ralph Bunche, and Mordecai Johnson. Shirley Graham Du Bois, Dorothy Hunton, and Essie Robeson attended on behalf of their husbands, whose passports had been confiscated by the U.S. government.

Sutherland would continue to be progressive America's unofficial ambassador in Ghana for the next few years, especially during the pivotal All-African People's Conference held in 1958, at which almost every African country and liberation movement was represented. At this conference huge debates unfolded about the future direction of Africa, with Nkrumah emerging as a leading Pan-Africanist voice.

But the climate in Ghana was changing, with intrigue and splits in the Convention People's Party leadership and among the Ghanaian people. By the time of the CIA-inspired murder of Patrice Lumumba in the Belgian Congo in 1961, Sutherland had begun to sense that it was time to move on. After a year or two in Israel he moved to Tanzania, where he would live for the next 30 years.

Charlene Mitchell, somewhat younger than Sutherland, initially came to understand the African liberation struggle not by traveling or living in Africa but through the teachings of the Communist Party. "I was taught that the struggle in Africa was part of the struggle for socialism all over the world. And that it would never be complete unless the colonialists were forced out of Africa."

However, not everyone on the left agreed with Mitchell on the importance of Africa. She read as much as she could get her hands on. She read *Freedom Magazine*, and later the journal *Freedomways*. She read Alan Paton's *Cry the Beloved Country*, anti-imperialist literature on the Belgian Congo, and the writings of Robeson and Du Bois. Alphaeus Hunton made a particular impression on Mitchell, she recalls. It was not only about Africa, it was about the world economy: cocoa and coffee, for example, and how the West was paying so little for what they got.

It was a dangerous time to be a member of the Communist Party, especially for black communists. African American party members went to jail, among them Ben Davis, who had been a city councilman in Harlem, and Henry Winston; both had been very active in the anti-apartheid movement. It was clear that the intent was to jail anybody who was openly a communist.

Seeing what was happening, people became frightened, and many members of the party went underground. Mitchell was one of them. She moved from Chicago to St. Louis in 1952 and lived there under an assumed identity for nearly two years. She particularly remembers the execution of Ethel and Julius Rosenberg, who were tried, convicted, and sentenced to death on charges of spying for the Soviet Union.

> I was in St. Louis. Nobody knew I was a communist. When I heard the news that the Rosenbergs had been executed, I cried. I was completely alone, just completely alone. The people from whom we had rented an apartment were African Americans, they were Catholic, very conservative. So I couldn't tell them I was crying because of the Rosenbergs. And it was one of my most difficult times.

Mitchell emerged to live first in Los Angeles and then in Harlem. When asked what she remembers of the African liberation struggle after her time underground, she beams and says "Nkrumah!" She took great pride in the seating of Ghana at the U.N. "It was a glorious time," she says, with people wanting to be around him, to help build his nation.

I asked Mitchell about the impact of the Cold War on her African solidarity work in the 1950s. Of course it was impossible then to be open about membership in the Communist Party and remain involved in a mass movement; as an admitted communist you'd be kicked out of the movement and probably arrested. Her experience with ACOA was that it did not welcome members of the party. From Mitchell's point of view it was an illogical position: "What is it that communists ever did to the anti-apartheid movement," she asked, that would mean party members could not be involved?

Houser based his anticommunism on opposition to the Soviet Union. Mitchell argued that most people, especially people of color, joined communist parties not out of love for the Soviet Union but because they believed socialism to be the necessary response to capitalism and oppression. Mitchell also said that over the years the ACOA became more inclusive, especially under the leadership of Jennifer Davis.

In 1960 Mitchell was able to travel. And like Sutherland and Houser, her life was expanded by what she learned. In London she went to see Claudia Jones, a member of the Leading Committees of the Communist Party who had been deported from the United States. Through Jones she met Yusuf Dadoo, who had been a member of the South African

With President Kwame Nkrumah at Government House in Ghana, 1958. From left: Alphaeus Hunton, Shirley Du Bois, Nkrumah, and Eslanda Robeson.
*Photo reproduced from Hunton 1986.*

Lisa Brock

Indian National Congress and was now a member of the ANC and a leader of the South African Communist Party. These meetings and exchanges in London helped her see the connections between imperialism, Africa, and the world, and appreciate that solidarity between the United States and Africa is always a two-way street.

> Africans did not all come from either princesses or princes or from slaves. They were workers, they were farmers, they were people. And they fought for freedom from day one. But we [in the West] seem to see [Africans] only as a bunch of people who need help; [we don't see] that they have been of assistance to the whole world's development and that a lot of the wealth in the world has come from those workers. Africa opened its doors to me, more as part of the movement and solidarity with us as we were with them. And I always saw that as an equal thing, because I would learn so much from it.

Mitchell would continue on that two-way street for decades. In the United States, she continued as a leader in the Communist Party from the late 1950s until she left the party in the late 1980s when she too began to question many of its domestic and international policy positions. In Africa, her closest link was with the ANC and the South African Communist Party. Because of the international connections between communist parties and her personal relations with ANC exiles and activists in the United States, Mitchell was among those invited to international conferences and asked to help host delegations visiting the United States.

Assessing the contribution of Mitchell and others in the Communist Party remains difficult, because throughout the entire Cold War period membership in the party could have unwelcome consequences. It is not known how many Communist Party members were involved in African solidarity work in the United States because many, fearful of repression, were not open about their membership. Nevertheless, veteran activists with links to Communist Party networks in the labor movement and other local struggles were almost always valued participants if not leaders of local anti-apartheid coalitions. Their ideological grounding in class analysis, their mass organizing skills, and their strong links within the black community were a significant part of ongoing African solidarity activity.

Sutherland stayed in contact with a wide range of people and political movements reflecting various ideologies. While he played an important role in the founding of Americans for South African Resistance, which became the ACOA, his most consistent organizational link in the United States was with the American Friends Service Committee. Based in Dar es Salaam, he served formally as Southern Africa representative for the organization between 1975 and 1982 and traveled each year to the United States for extended speaking tours. In this period and later in the 1980s, when he occasionally returned for speaking engagements, the AFSC was one of a handful of organizations that served as national contact points for anti-apartheid activists. Although not specifically focused on Africa, it had the unique advantage of having offices around the country. Sutherland's speaking tours helped to link diverse sectors of activists across racial and ideological lines

Angela Davis, left, and Charlene Mitchell visit Soweto during their trip to South Africa as guests of the African National Congress and others in 1991. *Photo courtesy of Charlene Mitchell.*

and increased participation by minority activists within the AFSC itself.

Sutherland also put the AFSC in touch with Desmond Tutu. The organization used its position as 1947 recipient of the Nobel Peace Prize to repeatedly nominate Tutu for the prize, which he eventually received in 1984.

On his return from South Africa in October 1954, George Houser articulated an understanding that would remain important for the American Committee on Africa over the years. Putting aside the question of communism, Houser said that the struggle against colonialism "cannot be understood unless one recognizes it as revolutionary in nature" (1954). This fundamental conviction was common ground for Houser, Mitchell, Sutherland, and others of their generation who supported African liberation.

Zambian president Kenneth Kaunda serves tea to Bill Sutherland, right, in Lusaka in 1977. *Photo by Harry Amana. Courtesy of the American Friends Service Committee.*

*Oral sources for chapter 2 include interviews with George Houser (2004), Charlene Mitchell (2004), Bill Sutherland (2003, 2004), and Cora Weiss (2003, 2005).*

Lisa Brock

# Alphaeus Hunton ✎
# *Why Worry about Africa?*

## Alphaeus Hunton

"Dear Sir, I have come upon a copy of your paper *New Africa*. I have read and re-read with fervent interest the articles contained therein. First, allow me to ask a question. Why in the world would one worry about the racial conditions in Africa when we as a minority group catch hell in this country? Chances are that I'll never make it to Africa, therefore, I'm not the least bit interested in what goes on over there, but very concerned about conditions here at home.

I would appreciate an answer to this question and also any literature you have concerning the problems of our illustrious race, and additional information from your organization."

Alphaeus replied:

You ask why one should worry about racial conditions in Africa, when as a minority group we catch hell in the U.S.A.? It is a question that arises frequently, although usually asked by liberal minded white people instead of Negroes.

The answer is two-fold. First, we have to be concerned with the oppression of our Negro brothers in Africa for the very same reason that we here in New York or in any other state in the Union have to be concerned with the plight of our brothers in Tennessee, Mississippi or Alabama. If you say that what goes on in the United States is one thing, quite different from what goes on in the West Indies, Africa or anywhere else affecting black people, the answer is, then you are wrong. Racial oppression and exploitation have a universal pattern, and whether they occur in South Africa, Mississippi or New Jersey, they must be exposed and fought as part of a worldwide system of oppression, the fountain-head of which is today among the reactionary and fascist-minded ruling circles of white America. Jim-Crowism, colonialism and imperialism are not separate enemies, but a single enemy with different faces and different forms. If you are genuinely opposed to Jim-Crowism in America, you must be genuinely opposed to the colonial, imperialist enslavement of our brothers in other lands.

Our great leaders from Frederick Douglass to Paul Robeson have emphasized and re-emphasized this lesson in both word and deed. It was Douglass' support of the Irish people's freedom struggle in his day that made it possible for Britain to rally the British workers to fight [with] the North in the Civil War. The workers of England took their stand on the side of Lincoln and emancipation. This leads to the second important part of the answer.

It is not a matter of helping the African people achieve freedom simply out of a spirit of humanitarian concern for their welfare. It is a matter of helping the African people, because in doing so we further the possibility of their being able to help us in our struggles in the U.S. Can you not envision what a powerful influence a free West Indies or a free west Africa would be upon American Democracy? . . .

William Alphaeus Hunton Jr., who led the Council on African Affairs and edited its publications from 1943 to 1955, was born in 1903 in Atlanta, Georgia. His parents, William Alphaeus Hunton Sr. and Addie Hunton, were national and international leaders of the YMCA and YWCA respectively. The younger Alphaeus Hunton graduated from Howard University, received a master's degree from Harvard University, and taught English at Howard from 1926 to 1943. He was active in the National Negro Congress and moved to New York in 1943 to work for the Council on African Affairs.

As editor of the council's magazine *New Africa*, Hunton received a letter from a reader questioning the group's emphasis on Africa. According to James H. Meriwether (2002, 271), the letter was written in July 1950. The letter and Hunton's reply are included in a book by Hunton's widow.

Reprinted from Dorothy Hunton, *Alphaeus Hunton: The Unsung Valiant* (Richmond Hill, NY: D. K. Hunton, 1986), 60–62.

Dorothy and Alphaeus Hunton in Conakry, Guinea, in 1962.
*Photo reproduced from Hunton 1986.*

# E. S. Reddy ∾
# *Behind the Scenes at the United Nations*

## E. S. Reddy

I was already interested in the anti-apartheid movement in the 1940s, when the struggle in South Africa took on new forms and Indians and Africans were cooperating in the struggle. During the Second World War, the United States and Britain talked about four freedoms in the Atlantic Charter, but those freedoms didn't apply to India or South Africa. As Indians we were very much interested in South Africa, because a lot of Indians were there and they were treated as second-class citizens or worse. And of course Nehru was talking about South Africa, Gandhi was talking about South Africa and so on.

I arrived in New York in 1946, shortly before the Indian passive resistance and the African mine labor strike in South Africa. I learned from a friend that there was a Council on African Affairs in New York with a library that got newspapers from South Africa. So I began to go to the council almost every week and look at the newspapers. That is how I met Dr. Alphaeus Hunton, a very fine man. He was head of research at the council at that time, later executive director. We became good friends.

In June 1946, India complained to the United Nations about racial discrimination against Indians in South Africa and the matter was discussed in November and December of that year. A delegation led by Dr. A. B. Xuma, president-general of the African National Congress, came from South Africa to advise the Indian delegation and lobby the United Nations. Paul Robeson, who was chairman of the Council on African Affairs, hosted a reception for them and I met the delegation. The council organized a demonstration in front of the South African consulate in New York. I was in contact with the council, and took a group of Indian students to join the demonstration.

When the Indian delegation came to the United Nations in '46 for the first time—the free Indian delegation—they said the main issues in the world for us are colonialism and racism. They were not interested in the Cold War. India felt very strongly about discrimination in South Africa, and also took up the question of South West Africa [Namibia]. It not only tried to get support from other countries, but tried to build up support from the public, especially in Britain and the United States.

All those who supported India's freedom now began to support African freedom, because solidarity can easily be transferred when the basic issue is freedom. The people who were in the solidarity movement for South Africa in those early days were mostly the people who were in the solidarity movement with India.

In 1952, after the African National Congress decided on the Defiance Campaign, India and some Asian and African countries got together and asked the United Nations to discuss the whole question of apartheid. By

Coming to the United States from India in 1946, E. S. Reddy was both a witness to and an important participant in the international struggle to end apartheid in South Africa. He went to work for the United Nations Secretariat in 1949 and served there for 35 years. From 1963 to 1984 he was the U.N. official in charge of action against apartheid, first as principal secretary of the Special Committee Against Apartheid and then as director of the Centre against Apartheid.

United Nations action both legitimated and was influenced by the momentum of popular mobilization against apartheid. Reddy was probably the most consistent and influential of the U.N. officials working behind the scenes, ensuring that the United Nations not only represented governments but also helped build bridges between liberation movements and their supporters in the United States and other countries.

Inspired by his own country's struggle for independence, he first connected to Africa through the Council on African Affairs in New York. Later, when African countries gained influence at the United Nations, he was able to use his position in the Secretariat to work closely with the American Committee on Africa and Episcopal Churchmen for South Africa in New York, and with other groups around the United States and around the world.

E. S. Reddy spoke with Lisa Brock in New York City on July 20, 2004.

that time I was working in the U.N. Secretariat, and my boss called me in for a chat. He said, "Don't you think it's illegal to bring that up? It's an internal problem." So I said, "No, I don't think so. I think it's a matter of how you interpret the charter." Because you know when the U.N. charter was signed, the real India was not there. And we had a different attitude towards the charter than some of the Western countries; it's a psychological thing. He didn't like that at all. He said I was prejudiced, not objective. Supposedly U.N. staff should be objective, neutral and all that sort of thing. So he moved me from research on South Africa to the Middle East.

The atmosphere in the U.N. was terrible for many years, until the sixties. It changed after many African countries became independent and joined the United Nations. Third World countries became a majority. So the situation was much better when the Special Committee Against Apartheid was established and I was appointed secretary.

The Western countries refused to join the Special Committee. As a result, all the members and I thought alike. Not only were we against apartheid, but we supported the liberation struggle and opposed Western collaboration with South Africa. The members of the committee, who were delegates of governments, and I could work together as one team. That could not happen in other committees where the members were divided and the Secretariat was supposed to be neutral.

Coming from India, with the influence of Gandhi and Nehru, I felt that we had a duty not only to get India's freedom, but to make sure that India's freedom would be the beginning of the end of colonialism. Rightly or wrongly, I had a feeling that I had not made enough sacrifice for India's freedom, so I should compensate by doing what I could for the rest of the colonies. That feeling was in the back of my mind.

The real opportunity came when I was appointed secretary of the Committee against Apartheid in 1963. Other officials were not interested, as they felt the committee was worthless. I wanted to give the best I could and I did for more than 20 years.

Soon after the committee was formed, we had a private meeting of the officers. I explained to them what I knew of the situation in South Africa and what I thought the committee and the United Nations could do. The chairman was Diallo Telli from Guinea, who later became secretary general of the Organization of African Unity. He liked my presentation, and said, "Look, Mr. Reddy, we are small delegations, we are terribly busy with so many things, so many issues, documents and meetings and so on. We don't have the time or the staff to do research. So you study the situation, you propose to us what we should do, and we'll say yes or no."

So our relationship developed into tremendous confidence. Most of the resolutions were written by me. Reports were written by me. Even speeches were written by me for many years. But I can't claim too much credit because nothing would have happened unless the chairman and other members took the responsibility and made the necessary decisions.

And I told them, "Look, I'm a very junior official in the U.N., so there is a limit to what I can do. I will get into trouble if it gets known that I did this or that. You have to take the responsibility for everything." That they very loyally did. And of course they obtained credit for all that I quietly and often secretly helped them in doing. So with their protection I was able, for instance, to discuss with the liberation movements about their needs and the possibilities in the United Nations, contact anti-apartheid groups and seek their advice and help, and propose initiatives for the Special Committee.

I was very lucky that I had a job doing something I believed in; it has given me a lot of satisfaction. In the course of my work, I was able not only to help the liberation movements, but to develop closest cooperation with anti-apartheid groups because their activities in promoting public opinion and public action against apartheid were crucial for the effectiveness of the United Nations.

It could have been an extremely frustrating job because whatever we did, repression was getting worse in South Africa year after year and people were suffering. But I was not frustrated.

Once a proposal I suggested did not get enough support and I was depressed. Robert Resha, a leader of the African National Congress, was with me. He said, "E. S., why are you frustrated? We are not frustrated. It's none of your business to be frustrated. We are going to win." So I kept that in mind.

We were able to win small victories and help people. For instance, we set up a fund for scholarships, we set up a fund to help the political prisoners and their families. And they developed into big things. Thousands of South Africans got scholarships. The fund for the prisoners was my idea. And millions of dollars started coming in after a while. Every day we could see that this fund was helping a prisoner or his family, financing defense in a trial and so on. We could derive some satisfaction from what we could do. So we had faith that we were going to win, and that faith never left me.

E. S. Reddy made the U.N. Centre Against Apartheid an indispensable resource for the anti-apartheid movement.
*Photo by Nils Amar Tegmo.*

# Robert S. Browne ~
# A Voice of Integrity

## Charles Cobb Jr.

With training in economics from the University of Chicago and the London School of Economics, Bob Browne founded three organizations that served as critical, radical voices around economic issues. The Black Economic Research Center founded in 1969 sought to pull in other black economists for black economic development projects, and it published the *Review of Black Political Economy*. The Emergency Land Fund founded in 1971 fought to protect black land ownership and reverse its decline, especially in the rural South. Also in 1971 he founded the Twenty-First Century Foundation to "promote strategic black philanthropy." He helped organize the 1967 National Conference on Black Power and presented proposals at the 1972 National Black Political Convention for black economic empowerment. Respected by both radicals and moderates, Browne explored the issue of how demands for reparations to African Americans could be channeled into workable programs for economic development.

Browne worked for the U.S. aid agency in Cambodia from 1955 to 1958, and in Vietnam from 1958 to 1961. On his return to the United States, he was one of the earliest active opponents of the war in Vietnam. As he explained in an article in *Freedomways* in 1965, his marriage to his Vietnamese wife, whom he met in Cambodia, gave him an insight shared by few other Americans at the time. "The fact that I was a non-white, Vietnamese-speaking member of a Vietnamese family frequently made me privy to conversations intended only for Vietnamese ears, and provided me an unusual measure of insights . . . which led me to become a constant and vigorous critic of the United States policy" (Browne 1965, 152–53).

His introduction to Africa, interrupted by the time in Southeast Asia, came first in Chicago and then in New York. In a tribute to Paul Robeson published by *Freedomways* in 1978, Browne wrote:

> My earliest recollection of Paul Robeson is from news stories about him in the Chicago Defender, which I read avidly as a child growing up on Chicago's South Side in the late thirties and the forties. The stories were full of Robeson's views on Africa—views which described a different Africa from the one the movies and the white press described.
>
> I sent for literature from his organization, the Council on African Affairs, and I devoured it avidly, for Robeson wrote and talked about the Africa which I wanted to believe [in]. Thanks to him, I discovered Africa a full two decades ahead of most of my contemporaries.
>
> In 1942, I was privileged to meet Robeson when he came to Champaign-Urbana to sing at the University of Illinois. Few of the black students could afford to buy tickets to the university's cultural events. However, after his performance Robeson met with a number

Robert S. Browne, who died in 2004 at the age of 79, was a leading thinker and activist best known for his work on black economic development in the United States and for his early leadership in opposing the Vietnam War. He also had a lifelong commitment to Africa and was one of the original founders of the American Committee on Africa. To the end of his life he served as a mentor to other activists. People of many political persuasions trusted him for his personal and intellectual integrity and his respect for all those with whom he worked.

Charlie Cobb recalls Bob Browne's remarkable life, drawing on Browne's writings and on a 2003 interview by William Minter.

of us at the Alpha house and I recall how his presence electrified us as had no one else's. . . .

I was to meet him on a couple of later occasions when he visited Chicago, for he usually stopped with the Hansberrys and Lorraine [author of *A Raisin in the Sun*] would invite a group of us over to see him. By this time he was being overtly persecuted by the federal government and his stirring bass voice had been banished from America's major concert halls.

His admiration for the Soviet Union, which had been acceptable (grudgingly) to Washington during the brief wartime interlude, was clearly unacceptable in the cold-war climate of the fifties, but for us the validity of his anti-imperialist message was merely enhanced by the consternation he caused in Washington. . . .

Browne spent the year 1952 traveling in Europe, North Africa, and the Middle East, after a short course at the London School of Economics. The trip "internationalized" him, he said in a 2003 interview, and he returned not to Chicago but to New York. He became one of the founders of the American Committee on Africa and a regular participant in the group of volunteers helping out with mailings and other work in the years before he moved to Cambodia. On his return, he joined the board of directors of the organization and continued to be a part of its activities even when his own work took him away from African issues or away from the New York area.

Browne worked both inside and outside of the political and economic establishment. In 1980 the U.S. Treasury Department appointed him as the first U.S. executive director of the African Development Bank in Côte d'Ivoire. Debt and the economic conditions in developing nations, especially African nations, figured prominently among his concerns. With Robert Cummings of Howard University, he wrote an early critique of World Bank policies in Africa (Browne and Cummings 1984). He was Jesse Jackson's adviser on economic policy during his 1984 presidential campaign and from 1986 to 1991 he was staff director of the Subcommittee on International Development, Finance, Trade and Monetary Policy of the House Banking Committee.

"The global trading system handicaps Africa," wrote Browne in a 1995 paper criticizing export restrictions, import duties, and agricultural subsidies to U.S. and European farmers. "While African countries may open their economies more widely to imports and investments from other countries, they may not have the capacity to take advantage of new opportunities for exports in sectors other than primary commodities.

"Unfortunately, the architects of the global trading system, including the United States, display very little sensitivity to these issues," he continued. Nevertheless, "it is in the long-run interest of all peoples [to close] the yawning gap between economic conditions in Africa and in the United States."

**Robert Browne.** *Photo courtesy of the 21st Century Foundation.*

# Peter and Cora Weiss ✍
# *"The Atmosphere of African Liberation"*

## Gail Hovey

This profile highlights two activists who have played significant roles in the Africa solidarity movement and other progressive causes for over 50 years. Emphasizing their involvement in Africa issues, particularly in the 1950s and 1960s, it draws in part on interviews with Cora Weiss by William Minter in 2003 and by Gail Hovey in 2005, and on an interview with Peter Weiss by William Minter in 2003.

For most of those who know Peter and Cora Weiss, personally or by reputation, Africa is not the first connection that comes to mind. Since the 1960s, Cora Weiss has been prominent in the peace movement. She was an early member and one of the national leaders of Women Strike for Peace, which played an important role in bringing an end to nuclear testing in the atmosphere. Cora also served as co-chair of the massive November 15, 1969 mobilization in Washington, DC to end the war in Vietnam, and she was one of the leaders of the June 12, 1982 antinuclear demonstration that drew an estimated 1 million people to New York City. She has been president of the international Hague Appeal for Peace since its founding in 1996. Lawyer Peter Weiss has taken the lead in national and international groups of lawyers opposing nuclear weapons and in the Center for Constitutional Rights, which has pioneered human rights law on both domestic and international fronts since its founding in 1966.

In the 1950s, however, it was Africa and the excitement of the independence struggles that inspired their engagement in international issues. The "atmosphere of African liberation" and the personal contacts they made during the decade, recalled Cora Weiss, set the trajectory for their lifelong involvement with global issues.

Peter Weiss was 13 when his family, fleeing the Nazi onslaught, left Vienna for France in 1938. They reached New York in 1941, where he attended high school before being drafted into the army and later working with the U.S. military government in occupied Germany. After graduating from Yale Law School, he directed the International Development Placement Association, a predecessor of the Peace Corps. That job took him to West Africa, where he established close contacts with nationalist leaders such as Nnamdi Azikiwe of Nigeria. This experience consolidated the progressive internationalist views that he had absorbed at the Foundation for World Government started in 1948 by Stringfellow Barr, former president of St. John's College, Peter's alma mater.

Cora Weiss first came into contact with Africa as an undergraduate at the University of Wisconsin in Madison in the early 1950s. She met law student Angie Brooks from Liberia, who later became the first woman to head the U.N. General Assembly. Cora worked with African and Indian foreign students to organize a speakers' bureau that sent students around the state to talk about their countries. The speakers earned $10 per speech, which helped with their school expenses.

In 1957, the newly married couple spent months traveling through West Africa. It was Peter's second trip and Cora's first. In the 1950s, they also became actively involved with the work of the American Committee on Africa in New York. Peter later came to serve as president of the organization, while Cora took on ambitious projects as a volunteer. She organized a 1,000-person dinner for President Kwame Nkrumah at the Waldorf-Astoria in 1958, an event co-sponsored by ACOA with the NAACP and the Urban League. She also coordinated the Africa Freedom Day rally at Carnegie Hall in 1959, featuring Tom Mboya of Kenya. From 1959 to 1963 Cora directed the African-American Students Foundation, which brought almost 800 East African students to study at U.S. colleges and universities.

Over the next decades, Peter and Cora Weiss continued their involvement with Africa even as their primary attention turned to other issues. They had been close friends with Eduardo and Janet Mondlane when the Frelimo leader worked at the United Nations from 1957 to 1961, and they maintained close ties with the family after Eduardo was assassinated in 1969. They met Oliver Tambo on his first visit to the United States in 1962 and became friends with him and his family. The Samuel Rubin Foundation, which Cora Weiss directed, was part of a small cluster of progressive funding organizations and individuals that paid attention to Africa even when African issues were not in the news. Typical of its progressive vision was its support for Robert Van Lierop's film *A Luta Continua*, a documentary on Frelimo filmed in liberated Mozambique that became an exceptional educational and organizing resource. The foundation was also consistently an important source of support for The Africa Fund.

Cora was associated with Hampshire College in Amherst, Massachusetts, the first U.S. college to begin divesting its holdings in companies operating in South Africa. In 1977 Adele Simmons, the new president of the college, asked Cora to become a member of the board of trustees. Simmons's predecessor, Charles Longsworth, had failed to win student trust, and the Committee for the Liberation of Southern Africa had occupied the college administrative offices in May of that year. During the occupation, Longsworth had finally acted, reluctantly announcing that Hampshire would sell stocks in the offending corporations. Following her appointment to the board, Cora became a member of the Committee of Hampshire on Investment Responsibility, which set guidelines firmly establishing the ban on South African investment (Dayall 2004; Shary 2004).

Present at the founding of ACOA, Peter Weiss encouraged George Houser to take the position of executive director in 1955. An active board member and longtime president of the board, Peter provided important leadership, fully supporting the need for close working relationships with the liberation movements. Peter also provided legal expertise on a number of occasions. In 1967 he assisted two South Africans, attorney Joel Carlson and recently arrived exile Jennifer Davis, who were working frantically—and as it turned out, successfully—to save the lives of 37 Namibians who had been charged under South Africa's Terrorism Act. In 1972 Peter was succeeded as ACOA president by black community leader Judge William Booth, a former New York City commissioner for human rights. Peter remained active on the board into the 1990s (Houser 1989). He also served on the board of The Africa Fund until it merged into Africa Action in 2001.

In a 2003 interview, Peter recalled that his early interest in Africa came from his involvement with the Foundation for World Government, where he quickly concluded that a world so divided economically could never function under a world government. His focus had turned to economic disparities and the attempt of the new African countries to climb out of the condition that had been imposed on them by the colonial powers. The world today, he insisted, confronts the same issue: to address "the gulf between the rich and the poor, both internally and globally."

Cora Weiss in Dar es Salaam, probably in 1965. Back row, from left: Pascoal Mocumbi, Eduardo Mondlane, Weiss, Amilcar Cabral. Others in the photo are not identified. *Photo courtesy of Cora Weiss.*

# Chapter 3

# The 1960s: Making Connections

## *Mimi Edmunds*

I had to go to Africa to understand America.

Sitting in Sproul Hall Plaza on the University of California's Berkeley campus, arm in arm with someone I don't know, I'm just a little nervous. It's October 1, 1964, and I'm in my first year at Berkeley, having just transferred from a small women's college on the East Coast. Suddenly we hear a hundred or so motorcycles roaring down Bancroft Avenue.

I had never been in a demonstration. I hadn't gone on the Freedom Rides in the South, and in fact I hadn't yet voted. I didn't really understand why the United States was in Vietnam. But I had learned something about segregation and discrimination growing up in rural Maryland.

Other Berkeley students had just returned from working with SNCC and CORE during the Freedom Summer of 1964. They included Jack Weinberg and Mario Savio, graduate students who had been registering black voters in Mississippi. They were fired up to right the injustices they had seen, and they began recruiting students for a variety of causes on and off campus. Their activities included picketing the *Oakland Tribune* for discrimination. University president Clark Kerr and the University of California Board of Regents capitulated to pressure from

the newspaper's owner and publisher, William Knowland, and outlawed all political activity on campus. Savio and Weinberg wasted no time in challenging the new prohibition.

Jack Weinberg sat down at his now-unauthorized recruitment table. He was arrested and put in a police car. Mario Savio climbed up on top of the police car and called for us all to sit down in the name of the right to practice free speech. As we blocked the police car from moving, we could see the phalanx of shiny police motorcycles at the university gates, waiting and watching. We continued to sit as night came on.

We didn't know it then, but we were participants in the birth of the free speech movement, one of the many expressions of *the movement* that would define a decade and, to an extent, a generation. The movement of the 1960s embraced not only civil

Mimi Edmunds with Kenyan members of parliament Charles Murgor and Joseph Chemjor, about 1967. The MPs were among the elders who termed Mimi and her sister Dorsett "daughters of the Rift." *Photo by Dorsett Edmunds.*

rights activism but also anti–Vietnam War protest, along with efforts to counter cultural complacency with "free love, drugs, and rock 'n' roll." Some of us were radically secular; others had strong religious connections.

The sit-ins that began in the South in 1960 helped make the civil rights movement a moral center of political action in the United States for much of the decade. In the South, in particular, the term "movement" had a spiritual dimension. The church was a meeting place and a safe haven; prayer, preaching, and song lent courage and inspiration. "Movement" also meant moving ahead and together, the opposite of retreat, fragmentation, and passive acceptance of the status quo. "One isolated battle had given way to many scattered ones," writes the historian Taylor Branch. "Now in the Mississippi jails [the Freedom Riders] were moving from similar experiences to a common experience. Students began to think of the movement as a vocation in itself" (1988, 485).

I am going to explore the significance of the 1960s by telling the stories of four people—Mary Jane Patterson, Bernard (Ben) Makhosezwe Magubane, Prexy Nesbitt, Mia Adjali—and a bit of my own story. As a group we are black and white, women and men, born in the United States and in Africa. We represent more than one generation of activists, both through our own experience and through the work and influence of our families. We are not so much typical as illustrative of the wide diversity of people who were fortunate enough to be engaged during this tumultuous decade. What we have in common, and what sets us apart from most activists involved in the movement, is our connection to the new Africa that was emerging in the 1960s. The bond that was created then continues today.

We also shared, by the end of the decade, understandings about the world we lived in: that the United States was an imperialist power, and that, for U.S. policy makers, Cold War imperatives trumped verbal commitments to freedom in Africa.

Africa was a beacon of hope in the decade: 28 countries gained political independence, 17 in 1960 alone. In the United States, historic civil rights legislation was passed, and entrenched systems of racial discrimination were actively challenged as never before. There was a sense of freedom rising. At the same time, Washington's preoccupation with the Cold War led to policies that contributed to conflict and instability in Africa—in the Congo, in the Portuguese colonies, and in the white settler states of Rhodesia, South Africa, and South West Africa. By decade's end it was clear that the U.S. government was trying to limit the scope of independence in Africa as well as the pace and extent of change in the United States itself. Those of us active in the decade wrestled with these realities. We made decisions to be engaged in struggles for justice, many of us leaving home to do so.

## From California to Kenya

A year after the demonstration in Sproul Hall Plaza, the alienation I felt about the war in Vietnam and the injustices in my society made

Mimi and Dorsett Edmunds served as Peace Corps volunteers in Kenya's Great Rift Valley in the mid-1960s. Here Dorsett reads to children. *Photo courtesy of Mimi Edmunds.*

me want to live and work in a non-Western culture. I was one of many young idealists who went away to better understand my home country and to do something that I thought might contribute to a better world.

I received an invitation from the Peace Corps to teach secondary school in Kenya. What I didn't know was that my twin sister Dorsett had applied the very same day, and the Peace Corps, thinking we were the same person, sent her an invitation to Kenya as well. In the end, we both went. I was posted to a young secondary school, Chepterit, on the western slope of the Great Rift Valley near the Ugandan border, 200 miles from Nairobi. Dorsett went to a Harambee school 60 miles north, also high up on the western escarpment of the Rift.

For two years I taught high school girls at Chepterit and boys in the neighboring boys' school six miles south on a dirt road, preparing them for higher studies or the workforce. None of them wanted to go back to the farm. It was a poor province, but the students were driven to get an education, and while many of them may have lacked a pair of shoes, their writing and reading skills were better than my kid brother's back in the States. It was difficult to keep books in our small library. *The Autobiography of Malcolm X* regularly went missing.

I was struck by how little of their own country's history these students knew, and by how well they could recite British monarchical and constitutional history. Even three or four years after independence, the students were not learning Kenyan history. I decided to create a branch of the East African History Society in my local district.

During school breaks I worked in health programs, inoculating hundreds of people against infectious diseases, especially in the Maasai Mara region. Because Dorsett and I were posted to neighboring districts, we probably got to know twice as many people in the province as we might have otherwise. Many of my students were cousins of her students. The local elders decided that since our parents had allowed their twin daughters both to come, they needed to adopt us as "daughters of the Rift," and so they did. And so we were, and are.

## Mary Jane Patterson: Missionary on Two Continents

*Our involvement in the civil rights movement is what sent us into our involvement about apartheid. I am convinced of that.*

—Mary Jane Patterson

Not everyone active in the 1960s was new to these issues. Mary Jane Patterson was in Kenya at the same time as I was, but she came with decades of experience as a leader in her church and in the civil rights movement. "What sent me to Africa," she says, "was the Presbyterian Church. . . . The church in Kenya wanted a missionary who had worked in the American civil rights struggle. They did not care what the race of the missionary was, whether white or black."

Mary Jane Patterson was born in Marietta, Ohio in 1924. Her mother was a librarian and her father worked in the post office. From her parents, she recalls, she received a sense of history and a "can do" attitude. Ohio lacked the patterns of segregation that existed in the Deep South, but Patterson does remember the Ku Klux Klan coming to town in 1936 or 1937, when she was 12 or 13. Only a few blacks lived in Marietta, but they all went downtown, including Mary Jane and her father, and successfully broke up the Klan gathering.

Patterson entered college in 1940, but once the war began she left her studies to take up work in the Curtis Wright airplane factory in Columbus. "I was Rosie the Riveter until the end of the war," she says. Only in 1954, 14 years after she started, did she complete a BA in philosophy and a BS in accounting at Ohio State University. She returned to school later to earn a degree in social work, having discovered that this field, not accounting, was her real interest.

Patterson became an activist in the Presbyterian Church and took a leading role in the church's growing involvement in the civil rights movement. Through the NAACP she learned about apartheid. But Patterson's first priority was not Africa; it was her church and civil rights. The Bethany Presbyterian Church in Columbus was fighting discrimination in housing. "One suburb would not sell houses to Negroes or Jews, and our church along with Christian, Methodist, and Unitarian churches got involved in desegregation in housing—that was around 1948. The civil rights movement really began in the church in the late forties."

In 1960, at just 36, Mary Jane Patterson became an elder in Bethany Presbyterian Church. "They asked me to be an elder, because they wanted me to say the same thing on the floor of the presbytery that I'd say in the street about civil rights." It didn't take long for Patterson to earn a reputation at the national level. In 1963, Margaret Shannon of the church's Commission on Ecumenical Mission and Relations contacted her because they needed a social worker for Nairobi. But Mary Jane Patterson had another priority.

> I said no, even though I was interested in Africa. I cannot, I am going to help organize the March on Washington in Ohio. What we did was interfaith—Protestant, Catholic, Jewish. . . . I can't tell you how many busloads of people we got to go to Washington from Ohio, and when we came back, we were heroes!

The church asked her to go to Kenya again in 1964. Again she turned down the request because of her commitment to the civil rights struggle at home. Patterson spent six weeks in Hattiesburg, Mississippi, registering voters. "Ohio is a state where African Americans, or Negroes, or colored, whichever they were, had been voting since the 1850s, since before the Civil War. My grandmother and my great-grandmother voted. That was normal for Ohio." So there was no hesitation in her mind; she had to go to Mississippi in the summer of 1964.

Finally, in 1965, Margaret Shannon pressed her one more time to accept the invitation to work in Kenya. And she did, she says with a laugh, "after a two-martini lunch." Patterson arrived in Nairobi in September 1966.

Patterson served as a social worker with the Presbyterian Church of East Africa, doing work similar to her earlier YWCA activities in Columbus. With her Kenyan co-worker Mary Kirobi, she set up a hostel where girls could begin their education, and then helped them go on to high school or vocational school or find a job. The pair worked at the Eastleigh Community Center in Nairobi and Patterson lived in the city's Delamere flats.

Mary Jane Patterson
*Photo by Mimi Edmunds.*

Living and working in Africa had special meaning for Patterson and laid the foundation for her future work lobbying for a better U.S. foreign policy toward Africa. Still, she always knew she would be an outsider.

> I wasn't one of those crazy African Americans who went over and kissed the soil and said, "God, I'm home." You can't be home if you've been in the diaspora for 14 generations! You're not home. Home is where you are for 14 generations!

Even so, there was a deep connection. Patterson could relate to the idea of African roots. Slaves came from East Africa as well as West Africa. A museum in the Tanzanian port of Bagamoyo (often translated as "lay down your heart") highlights the town's role in the slave trade. Patterson remembers the Swahili phrase "moyo ya Afrika"—heart of Africa.

> Kenyans would say, "You look like us," and I did, I do. Well, I was young and pretty. [*Laughs.*] When you go out to an African village, they have you sit—all guests—with the elders, but the women would always say "You're our daughter!"

Reflecting on those years, 1966–68, she says, "I loved it. They only had had their independence for three years. And oh, the hope. *Harambee!* Swahili for 'let's all pull together.' The joy of it all. . . . It was such a great time."

In 1968, Patterson's sojourn in East Africa was interrupted by the crisis in the United States that followed the assassinations of Martin Luther King Jr. and Robert Kennedy. When Rev. King was killed, President Jomo Kenyatta held a memorial ceremony at St. Andrews Presbyterian Church in Nairobi in which Patterson participated. "You couldn't get in the church, it was so crowded," she recalls. Awareness of Martin Luther King reached deep into the Kenyan countryside. On a trip upcountry Patterson was stopped by villagers who told her of the violence in Chicago following King's assassination. They said to her, "We heard on the radio. The mayor of Chicago said 'shoot to kill.'"

Patterson was called home, along with 100 other Presbyterian missionaries. She arrived to find the country "going crazy" in the summer of 1968. She put her things in storage, certain she would be returning to Africa in six months. The church sent her first to Chicago and then to California. Ronald Reagan had been governor since 1966, and according to Patterson, he had "wrecked education, wrecked mental health, and was on the way to wrecking the environment." She came to understand that she would not be returning to Kenya, at least not right away. She resigned from her mission board assignment, saying, "California needs missionaries worse than Kenya does."

One of the challenges for Patterson in the late 1960s was the rise of the black nationalist movement, the Black Panthers, with their ideology of violent struggle.

> It made sense in terms of an old Frederick Douglass saying that nothing happens without struggle. It can be peaceful; it can be violent. Power conceded nothing . . . I had known that saying since I was a child. My Dad used to say it. Although I couldn't go along with [the stress on violence], because it had not been a part of my background, it did make sense.

In 1971 Mary Jane Patterson became associate director of the Washington Office of the United Presbyterian Church in the USA. She quickly assumed principal responsibility for international issues, including Africa, and continued to place Africa high on the agenda when she became director of the office in 1975, a post she held until her retirement in 1989.

Working with contacts in the church, in Congress, and in progressive political circles, Patterson was a stalwart supporter of the campaigns to cut off U.S. support for apartheid and minority rule in Southern Africa. She represented the United Presbyterians on the board of the Washington Office on Africa, which had been founded in 1972 by the American Committee on Africa with church and trade union involvement. WOA's mission was to support African liberation by lobbying in Washington, and Patterson chaired its board of directors during the critical years of 1978–84. Patterson was a consistent counselor and mentor for three of WOA's directors: Ted Lockwood, Jean Sindab, and Damu Smith.

To this day, Mary Jane Patterson, now in her eighties and living in a retirement community, takes every invitation to speak on Africa and civil rights. She never fails to make the connection between the struggle for basic human rights in the United States and in Africa. Today, she says, the most devastating threat the continent faces is HIV/AIDS.

## From Kenya to New York

Returning to New York after the Peace Corps, I found my way to the basement of Washington Square Church, where the Committee of Returned Volunteers had formed as an anti-imperialist branch of the antiwar movement. It was 1969. We broke into geographic regions and in time formed the Committee for a Free Mozambique. Sharfudine Khan, representative at the United Nations for the Mozambique Liberation Front, met with us regularly as we organized to build support for Frelimo. With the Southern Africa Committee, we met representatives from the Southern African liberation movements—MPLA from Angola, PAIGC from Guinea-Bissau, SWAPO from Namibia, and the ANC from South Africa. Our goals were to build solidarity and support for the liberation movements and raise consciousness about colonialism and apartheid and about U.S. political and economic support for both.

For the next 10 years I continued my involvement with Africa in a number of ways. I returned to

Sharfudine Khan, Frelimo's representative at the United Nations, built support for the struggle against Portuguese colonialism. *UN Photo.*

the continent twice, meeting with leaders and other members of Frelimo. In the United States I worked on *Southern Africa* magazine and *Africa Report*. But I wanted to know more, to understand more, to do more. I decided to return to graduate school in anthropology at the University of Connecticut. Bernard (Ben) Magubane became my professor and my political mentor. I was one of innumerable students who benefited from the fact that contacts with Africa in the 1960s were not one-way: Americans were going to Africa, but Africans were also coming to the United States.

## Bernard Makhosezwe Magubane: Educator in Exile

*History has a way of throwing long shadows. The experiences of Afro-Americans and of the black people of South Africa share a great deal in common.*

—Ben Magubane, *The Ties that Bind*

Ben Magubane barely made it out of South Africa in December 1961. The year before, South African police had fired on a group of peaceful protesters, killing 69 and wounding hundreds in what came to be known as the Sharpeville massacre. The March 21 police attack and the government crackdown that followed changed the struggle for freedom and majority rule in South Africa, making clear that non-violent protest alone would be futile. Both the ANC and the Pan Africanist Congress (PAC) were banned, their leadership forced underground or into exile. The preparation for armed struggle accelerated.

A secondary school teacher in Durban since 1951, Magubane had also been an ANC activist and had attended Defiance Campaign rallies. When the government introduced Bantu education in 1953, enforcing full racial segregation in schools, he joined with ANC members Johnny Makatini, Fred Dube, and Mazizi Kunene to discuss what to do. He had to decide if he would work for this new system. Concluding that he could not, he went to night school, taking all his subjects at once to speed up the process while still teaching a full load during the day. Because of this effort he was able to enroll in the non-European section of the University of Natal, and he completed a master's degree in sociology in the late 1950s.

Married with three children, Magubane felt it was too dangerous for him to stay in South Africa in the repressive climate after Sharpeville. He had received a scholarship from the Institute of International Education in the United States. Magubane was able to secure the necessary papers and passport with the help of two leaders of South Africa's Liberal Party: anthropologist Leo Kuper, for whom he had worked as a research assistant before Kuper moved from Durban to Los Angeles, and the writer Alan Paton.

In December he told his mother his plans and left for Johannesburg. The next day the Special Branch of the South African police came looking for his house. Warned by children in the neighborhood, his mother got there first; she gathered all his political pamphlets and literature and made a huge bonfire.

When Magubane arrived at the Johannesburg airport on December 21, 1961, the Special Branch was waiting for him. They delayed the plane for three hours, trying to decide whether he should be detained. Finally they allowed him to leave, but his passport, good for only a year, was never renewed. He was exiled from his country and was not able to return until the end of the apartheid regime, 30 years later.

Emotionally, it was extremely hard for Magubane to leave South Africa. It was, he recalls, "one of the most exciting periods in South Africa's history as the bomb [of resistance] had exploded." Just before leaving, he had heard Mandela speak from the underground. Still, because of his family, he felt he had no choice. After he arrived in the United States, a visit to Harlem reminded him of home. "I saw how black folks lived, and the housing was just as bad" as in South Africa.

Magubane headed to the University of California at Los Angeles (UCLA), where he earned a second master's in sociology and advanced to candidacy for the PhD within three years. At about the same time, Martin Legassick, a white South African associated with the ANC who had studied history at Oxford, also arrived at UCLA.

In 1964, Legassick and Magubane had similar reactions to the news that ANC leaders Nelson Mandela and Walter Sisulu had been sentenced to life in prison. "It was a terrible moment, especially for those South Africans so far away and overseas," says Magubane. The devastating event solidified their friendship, and they organized a demonstration at an office of the South African tourist bureau that was located on an affluent stretch of Beverly Drive. The demonstration made the Los Angeles papers the next day, including a photograph of Magubane carrying a placard denouncing South Africa.

It was the beginning of his political activism in the United States. With Legassick, Magubane founded a grassroots anti-apartheid group in Los Angeles, perhaps the first such local group in the United States. Among their activities was the collection of clothing for the ANC in Tanzania, which they shipped through ACOA.

Long before coming to the United States, Magubane had been interested in African Americans. During World War II he had seen black and white American sailors walking around Durban, a regular port of call. Through his reading—*Ebony* magazine was readily available in South Africa—he became aware of racism, segregation, and the murder of Emmett Till. Young Ben and his friends would go to

see American movies, especially if there were black actors in them, even if blacks played the "buffoon" as they usually did, he says. Magubane also became familiar with American culture through his fondness for American jazz. He claims to have one of the best collections of records, including Duke Ellington, Louis Armstrong, Nat King Cole, and many others.

Once in the United States, Magubane took advantage of opportunities to deepen his understanding. He met Ethel Nance, W. E. B. Du Bois's West Coast secretary, who gave him an autographed copy of the writer's thesis on the Atlantic slave trade, which he cherishes. At the time, he was not familiar with Du Bois's work, but once introduced to it he

PROTEST — While Beverly Hills went about Christmas shopping, pickets appeared yesterday at Wilshire and Beverly Drive to object to conditions in South Africa. Tourist office was confronted with offenses, tourists were urged to go elsewhere and abstain from buying South Africa goods.

Ben Magubane, then a student at UCLA, leads a protest march in Los Angeles after Nelson Mandela and Walter Sisulu were sentenced to life in prison in 1964.
*Photo courtesy of Ben Magubane.*

read Du Bois "ferociously" and still does to this day. He met Bill Sutherland and drove to the Bay Area to hear the speeches of Mario Savio. He followed developments in the civil rights movement and went to speeches by Martin Luther King Jr. In 1963 he was introduced to Malcolm X after hearing him speak in a mosque in Watts. The experience had a powerful impact on him, Magubane says.

In 1966 Magubane completed the doctoral thesis that would later become a book, *The Ties That Bind* (1987), an exploration of the connections between African Americans and Africans. With PhD in hand, Magubane was ready to leave Los Angeles. He had kept in touch with fellow students Siteke Mwale and Arthur Wina, who had returned to Zambia after that country's independence in 1964, Mwale to become foreign minister and Wina minister of finance. At their suggestion, Magubane accepted a position in the sociology department at the new University of Zambia, beginning in March 1967.

Magubane says he needed to return to the African continent. He missed home and wanted to be closer to South Africa, even if he could not go there. His family had joined him in Los Angeles in 1965. But now his four daughters were growing up, and he wanted them to be closer to South Africa as well.

It was a dynamic time in Southern Africa, the best of times, says Magubane. A large community of South Africans lived in Lusaka. Jack Simons, author of *Class and Colour in South Africa* (1969), was teaching sociology at the university. Every Sunday Magubane and Simons would meet at Simons's house to discuss Southern Africa and other issues. These conversations had a great influence on his thinking. He says he "unlearned" much of what he had been taught in political science and sociology at UCLA and reconsidered what he understood about the political economy of race.

These new ideas would become the basis for *The Political Economy of Race and Class in South Africa* (1979). Magubane dedicated the book to his parents, who "sacrificed every penny to put me through school," and to his grandparents, "whose fireside stories about the Zulu War of 1879 and the Bambatha Rebellion of 1906 made an indelible mark on my mind." With this scholarly work he broke with authorities in his field in South Africa, taking up a Marxist perspective that would alienate a number of liberal scholars, including some of his early mentors. In the 1960s and 1970s, Magubane recalled, many liberal scholars bashed the liberation movements, criticizing them as ineffective. He charged them with ignoring the complex, historically determined realities that the movements confronted and underestimating their long-term potential.

He also published papers, including "The Crisis in African Sociology" in *East African Journal* and a criticism of the theory of social pluralism in *African Review*. Out of this work came an invitation from James Farris to apply for a position at the University of Connecticut at Storrs. He joined the Department of Anthropology at the end of the decade and was finally granted a green card, allowing permanent residency in the United States. For the first time he could travel easily, speaking about apartheid and South Africa all over the country.

Magubane was one of many political exiles whose presence in the United States in this era helped educate Americans about the liberation struggles in Southern Africa. In January 1969 many of those exiles gathered in Raleigh, North Carolina for the newly established Kennedy-King Memorial Forum of the Chief Albert Luthuli Memorial Fund. The week-long conference was held at Shaw University, where the Student Nonviolent Coordinating Committee had started in 1960. It was organized by ANC supporter Rev. Gladstone Ntlabati and gave a forum to exiles supporting both the ANC and the PAC. Speakers included James Forman of SNCC, who later that year would issue the Black Manifesto, demanding reparations from churches to address the economic injustice still facing the black community. Magubane was invited to the conference but was unable to attend because he was then in Zambia.

Today Magubane is one of the distinguished elders among South African social scientists. He directs the South Africa Democracy Education Trust, an ambitious research project documenting the history of South African liberation from 1960 to 1994. By 2007, the project had published two volumes on the 1960s and the 1970s, based on extensive new primary research, and was completing a third volume on international solidarity with South Africa.

In the fall of 1971, before I studied with Magubane at the University of Connecticut, I had enrolled in a graduate program in anthropology at Northwestern University. While in Chicago, I worked with activists and returned volunteers to found the Chicago Committee for the Liberation of Angola, Mozambique, and Guinea-Bissau. This committee held demonstrations, carried out grassroots education, and produced posters and other materials to support this work. A leading member of the group was Prexy Nesbitt, who brought to our committee a personal knowledge not only of the city of Chicago but of the movements in Africa we were organizing to support.

## Prexy Nesbitt: Activist Networker Extraordinaire

*I was not only studying history; I felt like I was living it. . . .*

—Prexy Nesbitt, reflecting on the first International Conference on African History in Dar es Salaam, 1965

In 1965, Chicago-born Prexy Nesbitt, a junior at Antioch College in Yellow Springs, Ohio, was enrolled at the University of Dar es Salaam in Tanzania for a year abroad. Nesbitt's arrival in East Africa continued his extended family's long history of activism and interest in international affairs, especially in Africa.

Nesbitt's parents, Rozell William Nesbitt and Sadie Alberta Crain, had met at the University of Illinois in the late 1930s. His father, the third of five brothers, was finishing a BS in engineering, and his mother was getting a degree in education. Both parents became teachers. Before Prexy was four years old, the five Nesbitt brothers bought a large house on Chicago's west side, on Albany Street in the North Lawndale neighborhood, for all the Nesbitt brothers and their families.

Today Lawndale is almost entirely black, but back then its residents were mainly working-class and lower-middle-class Jewish families. The Nesbitts broke the color bar in the neighborhood elementary school. After Prexy completed the fifth grade, his parents transferred him to the private Francis Parker school after his father discovered that the teacher in the neighborhood school was absent from the classroom and Prexy was—as he remembers it—doing the teaching.

Sadie Nesbitt, his mother, worked for years as a counselor and social worker at the YWCA and Hull House, as well as in the public school system; she later served on the board of directors at Francis Parker. She helped start the Urban Gateways program to bring artists and writers into the public schools for lectures and performances. An educator with broad multicultural and international sensibility, she was a role model and inspiration for her son.

Nesbitt's extended family provided additional models of engagement with African and civil rights issues. His father's uncle, Rufus Barker, was a follower of the Jamaican-born Pan-Africanist leader Marcus Garvey. Prexy's uncle, George, was an attorney in Champaign County and either a member of or very close to the Communist Party. George Nesbitt was one of the African American soldiers who attempted to integrate the U.S. army at the officer level during World War II. For his efforts he was sent to an isolated post in Australia. When he returned from the war, he helped draft the legal case for the integration of public housing in Chicago. Another uncle, Lendor, was a physician who later cared for patients in the Black Panthers' free medical clinic on Chicago's West Side.

As a young boy in the 1940s and 1950s, Nesbitt was taken to meetings to hear W. E. B. Du Bois, Alphaeus Hunton, Paul Robeson, Cisco Houston, the Weavers, and Pete Seeger. In 1958 Rozell Nesbitt took his son to hear Kwame Nkrumah speak. But Prexy Nesbitt's first personal encounter with Africa actually came earlier, in the mid-1950s, when Eduardo Mondlane, who would later become the leader of Frelimo, visited the Nesbitt home on Albany Street. The Nesbitts belonged to the Warren Avenue Congregational Church, where the pastor was Edward A. Hawley, a good friend of the Nesbitt family. Hawley had been a pastor in Oberlin, Ohio, when Eduardo Mondlane was a student there, and they were close friends.

Mondlane began graduate work in anthropology at Northwestern University in 1953. He and Janet Rae Johnson were already engaged. Not only was she white, she was considerably younger than he was, and her parents did not approve of the match. Nevertheless, the couple was married by Ed Hawley in 1956. With few places to socialize, they enjoyed the interracial community of the Warren Avenue church, and they came to the Nesbitt building. "Eduardo and Janet were very accepted in the living room of Aunt Peggy and Uncle Lendor," says Nesbitt. While he only vaguely remembers meeting them, he certainly remembers the lively discussions.

In high school, Nesbitt was active in the baggage porters' union through his father and his uncle George, who had helped form a black redcaps' union. In his first year at Antioch College, he was arrested for sitting in the barber chair of a segregated barbershop. In 1964 he was set to go to Mississippi for Freedom Summer, but his mother stopped him. Prexy was a large man, six foot one, with a commanding presence, and his mother had a real fear that he would be killed. The murder of Emmett Till was still fresh in her mind; moreover, a young black man recently had been sledge-hammered to death by a gang of whites on the corner of 55th Street and Kedzie right there in Chicago. She told her son he would have to find another family to send him through college if he went south that summer.

Nesbitt could go to Africa with her blessing but not to Mississippi. He had chosen Antioch because of the opportunity it offered to take the junior year overseas. Tanganyika had achieved independence in 1961 under the leadership of Julius Nyerere, known as Mwalimu, or Teacher. In the 1960s the country seemed to offer a model for postcolonial Africa, with its philosophy of African socialism and self-reliance and its support for the liberation struggles to the south. It became a mecca for young Americans, especially African Americans. Even so, few foreign students were enrolled at the University of Dar es Salaam in 1965, and Prexy Nesbitt was the first African American to study there.

Nesbitt's family connections preceded him to Tanzania. Ed Hawley had left Chicago and become pastor to Southern African refugees in Dar es Salaam. Nesbitt's instructors in African history at the university, Terence Ranger and Irene Brown, were also involved in support work with the liberation movements. Through them and through Ed Hawley and Bill Sutherland, Nesbitt quickly became engaged. He spoke at a school in Dar es Salaam for refugees from Southern Africa, choosing as his topic Malcolm X, who had been assassinated earlier that year.

When the white minority government in Salisbury, Rhodesia, made its Unilateral Declaration of Independence from Britain in November 1965, Nesbitt joined a student protest made up largely of Tanzanians, with a sprinkling of Kenyans and Ugandans. The students mounted a symbolic attack on the British embassy, burning a Rolls Royce and the British flag. They were hauled off to jail, then released. When they returned to the university, President Nyerere came to formally reprimand them for their actions and call for an apology. But as he was leaving the room, the president turned around and winked at the student protesters.

That same year, Nesbitt was asked to be the sole student representative at the first International Conference on African History, organized by Terence

Prexy Nesbitt in Geneva in 1981 or 1982, while on the staff of the World Council of Churches Programme to Combat Racism. *Photo courtesy of Prexy Nesbitt.*

Ranger at the University of Dar es Salaam. "It was an emerging field at that very time, and I felt like I was living history," Nesbitt recalls.

Returning to the United States at the end of the academic year, Nesbitt led the Antioch Committee on Southern Africa along with Martie Houser,

George Houser's daughter. The committee raised the issue of Antioch's connections to companies involved with South Africa. It would take a decade, but Antioch College became one of the earliest colleges to divest.

That fall, pursuing a doctoral degree on a fellowship at Columbia University, Nesbitt studied with Marcia Wright and Thomas Karis. He co-edited a citywide black student newspaper, and during the demonstrations of 1968, he urged black students to link up with white students as they took over buildings. Locally, they were protesting the expansion of Columbia into the Harlem neighborhood; some also wanted to expose the war-related research the university was engaged in. Nesbitt was arrested and lost his fellowship. Throughout his political activism, Nesbitt says, he was buoyed by his family's support. When he was sitting in protest in Hamilton Hall, his father, Rozell Nesbitt, came to visit. A bystander remarked, "They should throw them all in jail." Rozell Nesbitt turned to the man and said, "Well, they better start with me, because that's my son up there!"

The lawyer for the arrested students was Robert Van Lierop, an African American attorney who was also becoming interested in Africa's liberation movements. Two years later Van Lierop would travel to Mozambique to make the film *A Luta Continua*, which became an organizing tool for Southern Africa support groups.

With Sharfudine Khan, Frelimo's representative at the United Nations, Nesbitt had been exploring the possibility of returning to Tanzania to work for Frelimo at its secondary school in Dar es Salaam. Eduardo Mondlane, the Frelimo leader, was instrumental in making this happen. It wasn't until they sat down for a meal together that Nesbitt realized he had met Mondlane years before, as a youngster back in Chicago.

Due to internal struggles within Frelimo, Nesbitt was not able to teach as expected at the school. Instead, he worked with Southern African refugees through Ed Hawley at the Tanzanian Christian Council. He also worked with Jorge Rebelo, Frelimo's information secretary, helping edit *Mozambique Revolution*. But in 1969 Prexy's mother, Sadie Nesbitt, died suddenly, and he returned to Chicago.

Prexy Nesbitt's personal and political lives would be linked twice by tragedy. In 1969, the year his mother died, Eduardo Mondlane was assassinated. In 1973, his sister Roanne called to tell him that Amilcar Cabral had been killed. Four months later, Roanne was killed. For Nesbitt, these deaths are forever linked.

Back in Chicago in 1970, Nesbitt became the first field staff for ACOA, organizing anti-apartheid groups in the Midwest. In 1972 Robert Van Lierop and Nesbitt founded the Africa Information Service in New York and published a book of Amilcar Cabral's writings and speeches, *Return to the Source* (1973b). Nesbitt worked for ACOA a second time in 1977–79, coordinating the national Committee to Oppose Bank Loans to South Africa.

When he joined the staff of the World Council of Churches in Geneva in 1979, Nesbitt became part of its highly controversial Programme to Combat Racism. Among other things, the program provided humanitarian aid to liberation movements fighting racial oppression. He brought to the position a network of contacts with the Southern African movements, and he had credibility within many member churches of the World Council because of the numerous church audiences he had addressed over the years.

Some years later, in 1986–87, Nesbitt made similar linkages at the local level when he worked as a special aide to Harold Washington, the first African American mayor of Chicago. Above all, Nesbitt was skilled at bringing people together. He maintained a vast network of organizations and individuals around the United States and in Africa and Europe. He was a bridge builder, able to work with blacks and whites alike and with a wide array of sectors ranging from church people and trade unionists to elected officials and members of liberation movements. Reflecting in 2003, he said:

> I'm very interested in trying to pass on to this next generation how you cannot let these kinds of tensions—racial, ethnic, religious—divide people from fundamental goals that can only be reached by people banding together and overcoming the social barriers and the polarization. That's the only possible future that we have, to bring in real change in the United States.

## Mia Adjali: United Methodist Women and African Liberation

*To go from Algeria to Connecticut to Mississippi in the fifties was the most extraordinary experience.*

—Mia Adjali

Like Mary Jane Patterson's work with the United Presbyterians, Mia Adjali's life work with the United Methodist Church illustrates the contributions made to African liberation by people of faith and the institutional church. The daughter of Norwegian missionaries, Mia Aurbakken spent her childhood in Algeria, where her parents worked for the Methodist Church. She attended college in the United States and in 1960 began working with the Methodists at the United Nations in New York. In 1967 she married Boubaker Adjali, an Algerian journalist and filmmaker who had participated in his country's war of independence from French colonialism. Each of them has been involved in African issues for over half a century.

Mia Adjali grew up on three continents. The family spent the turbulent years of World War II in Algeria. "There was no way we could return to Norway, as the North Sea was mined," she recalls. When the war ended her family was able to travel to Norway and on to the United States, where her parents studied at the Kennedy School of Missions in Hartford. Her mother died in 1947 and the family returned to Norway, but by 1948 they were back in Algeria, where Adjali's father remarried and she finished elementary school. She continued her studies in France and then entered Millsaps College, a Methodist school in Jackson, Mississippi.

"To go from Algeria to Connecticut to Mississippi in the fifties was the most extraordinary experience," she says. "I had the chance to be living in societies that were going through severe changes and confrontations." When Algeria became independent in 1962, Adjali recalls, her father commented that "in the United States only people living in Mississippi in the fifties could really understand what was happening in Algeria."

Millsaps was a progressive, albeit all-white college where professors raised the consciousness of the students and the community around the issues of racism, civil rights, and integration. In 1959, her senior year, Adjali chaired a committee that organized a series of lectures on integration. The first guest was Dr. Ernst Borinski, a professor of sociology at Tougaloo College, a black college near Jackson. The audience that night was small, just a few students and a reporter from the new daily newspaper in Jackson. The reporter turned out to be the son of the president of the White Citizens Council, and the next day Borinski's talk hit the headlines. The newspaper blasted the lecture series for giving him a platform, noting angrily that Dr. Borinski had said that segregation was "unchristian."

The repercussions were statewide and jeopardized the college. Millsaps officials reluctantly gave in and cancelled the following speakers in the series, replacing them with a person who championed segregation. Adjali had to introduce the well-known Mississippi lawyer John Satterfield, who later would oppose the admission of James Meredith to the University of Mississippi. This time the classroom was packed, mostly with people from Jackson. Satterfield began by saying, "All that will be said tonight will be in the name of Jesus Christ." He went on to justify segregation, citing the Bible as his authority.

With her experience in Algeria and Mississippi, Adjali compares the relationship of the colonialist and the colonized to that of plantation owner and slave. "It is a strange relationship," she says, best described by Lorraine Hansberry in *The Drinking Gourd* (1960) and by Martinique-born psychiatrist Frantz Fanon. Fanon worked in an Algerian hospital and joined the National Liberation Front (FLN) after the 1954 outbreak of the French-Algerian war, serving as ambassador to Ghana for the provisional Algerian government. The experience led him to write his best-known book, *The Wretched of the Earth* (1961), which became a primer for those trying to understand the quest for liberation. The book was at the heart of the argument in the 1960s over the movement from nonviolence to armed struggle as the only means to end intransigent colonial oppression.

In 1960 the Methodist Church established the Methodist Office for the United Nations, three rooms and a walk-in closet on East 46th Street and First Avenue in Manhattan. A college graduate that year, Adjali was invited to New York to work

Mimi Edmunds

at the new office as a staff member of the Women's Division of the Board of Missions of the Methodist Church, arguably the most progressive force within the denomination.

It was an exciting period for Africa. Of the nations that became new members of the U.N. in 1960 and 1961, 19 were African states. Adjali began meeting African delegates to the U.N., developing close relations that continued in the following decades. She also met with representatives of the movements still struggling for liberation. One of her first contacts was with the Algerian FLN, whose office was located down the street from her own office.

In December 1960, tension and excitement filled the air as Resolution 1514 (XV), "Declaration on the Granting of Independence to Colonial Countries and Peoples," was introduced in the U.N. General Assembly. The most critical—and controversial—elements were the concept of the right to self-determination and the call for "a speedy and unconditional end [to] colonialism in all its forms."

The night before the vote on the resolution, Prime Minister Harold Macmillan of Britain called President Dwight Eisenhower. Concerned about Southern Rhodesia and the consequences of independence for its minority white population, Macmillan urged Eisenhower to abstain on the vote. The U.S. abstention came as a surprise, as the entire U.S. delegation had favored the resolution. Dr. Zelma Watson George, a social worker from Chicago and a member of the U.S. delegation to the U.N. General Assembly that year, had been authorized to assure African delegates of United States support for the decolonization resolution. When the resolution passed with a few abstentions, mostly countries that still had colonies, delegates stood to applaud. Dr. George joined them, standing up in the middle of the seated U.S. delegation.

It wasn't long before the American vote was neutralized. The new president, John F. Kennedy, agreed to have the United States participate on the Committee of 24 for Decolonization, a body set up to carry out the resolution. Adjali says that while many people remember 1960 as the year Khrushchev took off his shoe in the U.N. General Assembly and banged it on his desk, she remembers it as the year of the decolonization resolution—and Zelma Watson George standing to applaud.

By 1963, Adjali and the Women's Division had moved into the Church Center for the United Nations on First Avenue, directly across from the United Nations. For the rest of the decade and into the 1970s and 1980s, the new Methodist Office for the U.N. served as a hospitality center for the liberation movements. They had desks available with phones, typewriters, and access to duplicating equipment. One person had special privileges: Dr. Eduardo Mondlane, a Crusade Scholar of the Board of Missions of the Methodist Church and the first president of Frelimo. During his trips to New York and the United Nations Mondlane would "nationalize" Adjali's office, and she became his temporary secretary. While Oliver Tambo, president of the ANC, never used a desk, he sometimes needed other

Dr. Zelma Watson George, center, was a member of the U.S. delegation to the United Nations when the decolonization resolution was introduced in the General Assembly in December 1960. *UN Photo.*

services. One evening he had a number of telegrams to send, and Adjali's office was ready to help.

Representatives of the liberation movements also came to the Methodist Office for the United Nations when the Methodist U.N. Seminar Program invited them to address youth or adult seminars. They would describe colonialism or apartheid in their countries and the process for freeing their people. The Methodists (and later the United Methodists, after the 1968 merger of the Methodist and Evangelical United Brethren Churches) involved the liberation movement figures in consultations about decolonization and apartheid in the United States and in countries with United Methodist Churches, many of them under colonialism. Missionaries who spoke out in those countries and had been expelled by the colonial powers also shared important information about the situations they had witnessed.

Mia Adjali in her office at the Church Center for the United Nations. *Photo courtesy of Mia Adjali.*

Adjali's office helped the liberation movement representatives prepare their speeches for presentation to the United Nations' various committees dealing with decolonization or ending apartheid. "We often ended up typing their U.N. speeches and duplicating them," Adjali recalls. "It was in my office that the ZAPU and ZANU representatives wrote their first joint speech, shortly before independence in Zimbabwe. Paragraph by paragraph, the speech was negotiated, and page by page it was typed by Jennifer Dougan, my assistant, to be ready for the 3:00 p.m. session of the Security Council."

Adjali and the Women's Division worked with the ACOA, led by George Houser, a United Methodist pastor, to bring pressure for a change in U.S. policy. The churches realized they had a critical role to play in influencing Washington, and Adjali believes they provided important support for the liberation struggles during these years. Of central importance to this work was the church presence at the United Nations.

United Methodists from all over the country came to New York to attend seminars on decolonization and many other issues related to racism and social justice. A good number of them took back to their communities and churches a deeper understanding of world issues and a renewed commitment to engage locally in liberation support and anti-apartheid campaigns. Adjali came to direct this work, becoming the executive secretary for global concerns of the Women's Division of the General Board of Global Ministries of the United Methodist Church and the main representative for the board at the U.N. She held these positions until her retirement in 2006.

For many Protestant and Catholic churches with a missionary presence in Africa, the anticolonial period required a rethinking of roles, a redistribution of resources, and a shifting of control to African leadership. In relation to Southern Africa, where the struggle for majority rule was protracted and difficult, church denominations had to decide whether or not to be in solidarity with the struggle for freedom and whether or not to support armed struggle. Mia Adjali spoke with unflinching clarity on these matters, her personal experience providing her with understanding that came only later to many others in the United States.

By the end of the 1960s, the emergence of independent African nations gave all of us a sense of achievement and of hope. At the same time, the continuing struggle in Southern Africa deepened our understanding of what remained to be accomplished on the continent and of the role U.S. political and economic interests would play in the process. Whether we entered the 1960s as newcomers or as experienced activists, we ended the decade knowing that the work in which we had been engaged was unfinished. Eduardo Mondlane signed his letters *A luta continua*, the struggle continues. It became our byword and our challenge.

---

*Oral sources for chapter 3 include interviews with Mia Adjali (2004), Ben Magubane (2004), Prexy Nesbitt (1998, 2003), and Mary Jane Patterson (2004).*

Janet and Eduardo Mondlane with two of their children in Mozambique in 1961.
*Photo courtesy of Oberlin College Archives.*

# Harry Belafonte ∾ A Committed Life

## Charles Cobb Jr.

For Harry Belafonte, artistic achievement does not and should not mean political disengagement. "My social and cultural interests are part of my career. I can't separate them," says Belafonte. Paul Robeson was a major influence on Belafonte and other African American artists in the late 1940s and 1950s. Many of these artists, like Ossie Davis, Ruby Dee, and Sidney Poitier, were involved with the American Negro Theater in New York. So was Belafonte. "When I first met [Robeson], I was quite young. And he embraced those of us in our little group of cultural activists in New York. And he came to see a play that we were in, and at the end of the play, he stayed behind to talk to these young people, of which I was one. And he said to us, 'You know, the purpose of art is not just to show life as it is, but to show life as it should be'" (2004a).

Belafonte's political commitment started even earlier, during his years growing up in Harlem and Jamaica. His Jamaican-born mother, says Belafonte, "embraced Marcus Garvey and the struggles against oppression of Africans" (2002). Belafonte was also a veteran of World War II, a war that shaped many young African Americans who would emerge as civil rights leaders in the 1940s and 1950s. "In the victories that came out of that war, those of us who participated came back to our homes with the expectation that there would be generosity, that we would be rewarded for our commitment not only to our nation, but to its principles of democracy. However, we found that such generosity was not available" (2000).

Belafonte's first record album, *Calypso*, sold more than a million copies in 1956, the first album ever to do so. It stayed at the top of the charts for an unprecedented 31 weeks. That was the year of the Montgomery, Alabama bus boycott against racial segregation. Belafonte quickly lent his growing prestige to the boycott and to the young leader it had thrust forward—Martin Luther King Jr.

His interest in Africa, meanwhile, was growing, inspired partly by culture and partly by the emergence of the newly independent African nations. When the Peace Corps was founded in 1961, the Kennedy administration sought credibility for the fledgling organization. Belafonte became one of its advisers, but with a clear-eyed view of the corps' real value. "Most people thought the Peace Corps was a chance for America to show how beautiful we were as a people, our great generosity. I viewed the Peace Corps another way: Get enough Americans to go to these countries and live for two years with indigenous peoples in environments where [these volunteers] learned something else altogether and bring them back to America to educate their own communities. To point out that their own humanity was inextricably bound to the humanity of the peoples of the developing world" (2004b).

For many in the African American community, support for African liberation has been closely linked to the civil rights struggle in the United States. One of the clearest examples of this connection is the life of singer-activist Harry Belafonte, whose advocacy for Africa spans decades. This profile draws on published and broadcast interviews with Belafonte in 2002 and 2004 and on speeches he delivered in 2000 and 2004.

Involvement with the Peace Corps helped deepen his Africa experience. "And then I began to go to Kenya. [I learned] what Jomo Kenyatta went through in the Mau Mau uprising and I became very friendly with Tom Mboya." Throughout his career, Belafonte maintained contacts with African leaders, intellectuals, and artists, both those in independent Africa and those from countries still under white minority rule.

During the intense years of civil rights struggle in the South, Belafonte not only lent time and resources to the movement but encouraged movement interest in Africa. In 1964, Belafonte sponsored a visit to West Africa by SNCC leaders Fannie Lou Hamer, John Lewis, Julian Bond and others.

Belafonte became increasingly visible as an opponent of apartheid. He introduced South African musicians Miriam Makeba and Hugh Masekela to U.S. audiences and supported their on-stage denunciations of the racist regime. In 1983 he was co-chair with tennis great Arthur Ashe of Artists and Athletes Against Apartheid. His 1988 film and record album, *Paradise in Gazankulu*, focused on children victimized by apartheid and had a significant impact. After Nelson Mandela was released from prison, Belafonte played a key role in organizing his visit to the United States and was his official host.

At age 78, he continues to speak out. "Whether it is Kosovo, whether it is Somalia, whether it is Rwanda, whether it is Kampuchea, wherever we have been in the world, we still see man's inhumanity and our work is far from over" (2000).

Harry Belafonte.

# Charles Cobb Jr. ✍
# *From Atlanta to East Africa*

## Charles Cobb Jr.

As I came of age, the things that are dramatic in my memory are the 1954 Supreme Court decision, the events in Little Rock, and the events in Montgomery, Alabama, and tangled in there are the independence of Ghana and the Mau Mau struggle in Kenya. I remember the *Pittsburgh Courier* used to run a little box on the front page that talked about the conflict in Kenya, the conflict in Congo, the Sharpeville demonstrations, Lumumba, Tshombe, Kasavubu, all of which were happening when I was in high school. These things were part of my consciousness, growing up.

A lot of us in 1960 and '61 who were in college were caught up in the student sit-in movement, which was more or less a spontaneous movement, though not quite as spontaneous as some historians would suggest. I was living in Massachusetts and had been picketing the Woolworth's in support of Southern students in 1960. The students who were protesting in Greensboro and Nashville had the greatest dramatic impact; they were shown on television and so forth. People my age were strongly affected by that because it was, for our generation anyway, the first time in the South that we saw blacks taking the initiative.

By the time the Freedom Rides happened, I was at Howard University, literally sitting on the grass on campus and reading in the student newspaper about the Howard students who had been involved in the Freedom Rides. Somebody gave me a leaflet about a sit-in demonstration in Maryland, which I went to, and I became involved in that way.

The name that kept coming up was SNCC, simply because that was an organization that the students had formed. There was a discussion going on among a lot of students about whether sit-ins would really change anything, whether you should commit a real chunk of time to working in the South. What made up my mind was a very small blurb in the *New York Times* which talked about a voter registration project in Mississippi, run by Bob Moses in fact. The story was about the fact that Moses had brought some people down to register to vote and had gotten beaten up. And it struck me that more than sitting at lunch counters, this was probably something important, and I began to cast about for a way to get into that. . . .

What we were organizing people to do was to register to vote, mainly because that was the most legitimate thing. The law was pretty clear, at least the federal law: all people have the right to vote . . . But we were also organizing in a deeper sense. Mississippi at that time, Alabama, the Arkansas Delta, the north of Louisiana, the northern Florida panhandle, the whole Black Belt South, southwest Georgia: If you were black and living in those areas, you were really living almost in a state of paralysis. . . . As an orga-

Charles Cobb Jr., one of the editors of this book, was a field secretary for the Student Nonviolent Coordinating Committee in Mississippi from 1962 to 1967. He moved to Tanzania in 1970. This excerpt from an interview with Cobb traces the beginnings of his involvement in the civil rights movement and his introduction to Africa.

Excerpted from an interview with Charlie Cobb by Julius Scott, a graduate student at Duke University, in the spring 1981 issue of *Southern Exposure* (Institute for Southern Studies, Durham, NC).

nizer the idea, the *real* idea behind organizing, was to begin to get people in motion around something, just to break that paralysis.

It was in '63 that we really started to become aware of Africa, as I remember. Oginga Odinga, who was at that time the vice president of Kenya, was touring the United States, and one of the places he visited was Atlanta, Georgia. A whole bunch of us went to see him, just because he was an African leader. There was no political assessment of Kenya, or any of that. He was a black guy who was a vice president of a country, and we had just never seen that. He was staying at some posh hotel in downtown Atlanta, and he saw us. We had this talk, and shook his hand; it was a big thing. Afterwards we decided to go have coffee at a restaurant next door to the hotel, and we were all refused service. We were kind of high on meeting this black leader, and so naturally we refused to leave the restaurant, and we all got arrested. Oginga Odinga became a known name in the organization. There were songs written about him. Because of this incident, discussion started.

Then in '64 Harry Belafonte, who was a supporter of SNCC and other organizations, arranged a trip to Africa for some SNCC people. It was a big thing, and built the discussion more and more in the organization. In the media by this time you're starting to get the whole business with Rhodesia and the Unilateral Declaration of Independence, and all this was filtering into the organization.

> ## Oginga Odinga
>
> I went down to the Peach Tree Manor
> To see Oginga Odinga
> The police said "Well, what's the matter?"
> To see Oginga Odinga.
> Oginga Odinga, Oginga Odinga
> Oginga Odinga of Kenya
> Oginga Odinga, Oginga Odinga
> Oginga Odinga of Kenya.
> Uhuru, uhuru
> Freedom now, freedom now
> The folks in Mississippi
> Will knock you on your rump
> And if you holler FREEDOM
> They'll throw you in the swamp.

Our expanding consciousness of Africa and the discussions within the organization revolved around two key words: power and alternatives. All along we were asking ourselves whether what we were doing was really going to provide the answers for blacks. You work in a county, or you work in some rural town, and because you're working some blacks get killed or shot, something like that. And you inevitably ask yourself, "Is it really worth it? If they actually get this vote, what will it really mean for them? Is what we are about, making blacks Democrats or Republicans, is that really freedom, is that liberation?" And that question really became very intense in 1964, in the aftermath of the Democratic Party convention in Atlantic City, where clearly, legally and morally, the black delegation that we had organized as the Mississippi Freedom Democratic Party should have been seated. By any standard, it should have been seated and wasn't. It didn't have anything to do with the merits of our case; it had to do with politics that were at play at that particular convention. As a consequence, coming out of that convention a few people were looking around for alternatives.

What we had learned essentially was that the things that affected blacks in Ruleville, Greenwood, or Sharkey County, Mississippi, didn't just stop at the county line or the state line. What we really had was a national structure. The sheriff and the Ku Klux Klan and White Citizens Council were all tied into the Congress and the president, and even if we got everybody registered to vote in Sunflower County it wasn't going to provide the complete answer for black people. We were beginning to see the relationship between economics and politics.

Then the question became—and this began to lead us into Africa and more broadly into the Third World—where do we find alternative designs for organizing ourselves as a people? So Africa then begins to loom very large, partly because we were meeting poor people from ZANU and ZAPU and ANC, and African students. They would talk to us about their situation, and they knew what we were talking about and we knew what they were talking about, and there was something to share there. We began to talk to people more and more about independent institutions. The question of power—Black Power—became a discussion. The question of race intensified.

The work in the counties went on pretty much the same way it always had, but in addition our own broadening consciousness entered into those discussions. For Fannie Lou Hamer to go to Guinea the way she did didn't lead to some African institution developing in Ruleville, Mississippi, but perhaps it made Africa a little less alien to our friends and neighbors. Julius Lester and I went to Vietnam, people went to different parts of Africa, people went to Cuba, to Puerto Rico. We had taken a position on the Vietnam War, and we were becoming interested in the African liberation movement.

As a field secretary for SNCC, I came into contact with journalists and saw what they wrote. Inevitably one says, "I can do a hell of a lot better than that." I traveled widely; I was in south Asia and Africa. It seemed to be important to begin to figure out ways to communicate what I'd seen.

In 1969 I was teaching school in the United States and decided to go to an African country long enough to really learn something about it. I chose Tanzania simply because it seemed to be the place where the liberation movements were concentrated and because I just happened to know more Tanzanians than anybody else. And one of the things I started to do was write.

The thing that I learned in the South, which I didn't know before going into it, was that what looks simple turns out to be complex. The same thing is true about rural Africa. And if you want to write about it, as I did when I got to Africa, or if you want to organize it, which is what I did in Mississippi, then you have to learn to deal with these complexities.

From left: SNCC workers Stokely Carmichael, Charlie Cobb, and George Greene at a demonstration in Atlanta, Georgia, December 1963. *Photo by Danny Lyon/Magnum.*

Charles Cobb Jr.

# Walter Bgoya ✑
# From Tanzania to Kansas and Back Again

## Walter Bgoya

At the end of July 1961, I and several hundred other African students left our different countries on scholarships offered by the African American Institute. I was placed at the University of Kansas. Before going to the university I stayed for a month with a generous and deeply religious white family in a little town called El Dorado. The stay with this family offered me the first experience of living in the United States.

I was taken to church every Sunday and stood in line with the priest after service to shake hands with the whole congregation, as the African student who was staying with the Cloyes. Not having seen any black person in the church, I was intrigued and asked my hosts if there were any black people in the town. Yes, I was told, there were Negroes (the term in use then), but they had their own churches. I thought it strange that there were separate churches for black and white people, but I did not want to embarrass my family any further so I did not pursue it. I did, however, ask if I could meet a family of black people and arrangements were made.

The visit did not go well, unfortunately, perhaps because neither they nor I were prepared for it. Only one member of the family greeted and sat with me—quite uncomfortably, it was obvious. The others went on with their business, oblivious to my presence, not even greeting me, which as an African I found insulting. Perhaps the fact that I had been brought there by a white family made me part of the white world with which they had problems. I was deeply disappointed. I learned later that relations between Africans and African Americans were complicated and that it would take special efforts to make friends with people of my own race.

Going to the university in September was the beginning of four years of intense involvement in the struggle against different forms of racial discrimination at the university and in the town surrounding it, leading to the 1964 takeover of the administration building. Protesters were arrested, tried, and acquitted. The story has been told in *This Is America? The Sixties in Lawrence, Kansas*, by Rusty Monhollon (2002). The struggle at the university exposed me to unpleasant experiences with rightist groups, including the John Birch Society and the Ku Klux Klan, who burned a cross outside my apartment. I was called all sorts of names in threatening letters and phone calls—I was a "communist" and a "foreign agitator"—and I was advised to take these threats seriously. But while my involvement in a leadership position in the campus civil rights movement was deeply resented by right-wing white people, we had great support from liberal and progressive white students and faculty members.

Walter Bgoya is the managing director of Mkuki na Nyota, an independent scholarly publishing company in Dar es Salaam, and chairman of the international African Books Collective. From 1972 to 1990 he directed the Tanzania Publishing House, which played a major role in making Dar es Salaam a center for progressive intellectuals from around the world. Its publications included Walter Rodney's *How Europe Underdeveloped Africa*, Agostinho Neto's *Sacred Hope*, Samora Machel's *Establishing People's Power to Serve the Masses*, and Issa Shivji's *Class Struggle in Tanzania*. In this essay, written for *No Easy Victories*, Bgoya reflects on his experiences and work in the 1960s.

I returned to Tanzania in 1965, having learned many lessons from my years in the United States. I had immersed myself in the struggle for rights and human dignity regardless of my status as a foreign student. I rejected the notion that as a foreigner I had no business getting involved in black people's struggles; after all, I was not spared the indignities of racial discrimination in housing or refusal of service in restaurants and other places. I learned to speak up and to challenge authority when I believed it was wrong. Back home, my outspokenness did not endear me to my superiors at the Ministry of Foreign Affairs, where I was assigned to work, or to politicians who did not accept that their ideas could be challenged. A one-party state under the Tanganyika African National Union (TANU), Tanzania was hierarchical and authoritarian, and one was expected to conform and to do as one was told.

It was clear after a short time in the foreign ministry that I needed to make some alliances at the workplace and outside if I was to survive. A group of youth leaders had been invited by Mwalimu Nyerere soon after the 1967 Arusha Declaration (TANU's policy on socialism and self-reliance) to form the TANU Study Group, a kind of think tank for the ruling party. I was asked to join and we met once a week on Sundays to discuss current political and economic issues, both national and international, and to forward recommendations to the party leadership.

Major issues during that period were the struggles for liberation from Portuguese colonialism in Angola, Mozambique, and Guinea-Bissau; settler colonialism in Rhodesia (Zimbabwe) and South West Africa (Namibia); apartheid in South Africa; and issues in other places such as French Somaliland (Djibouti), Comoros, Sahara, and, outside Africa, East Timor. The Vietnam War, the struggle for admission of the People's Republic of China to the United Nations, the Soviet Union's invasion of Czechoslovakia in 1968, and support for Cuba were among the other issues that exercised us. In the Ministry of Foreign Affairs I was assigned to the Africa desk and it was there that I had the opportunity to meet and work with liberation movements and their leaders. I also worked with the OAU's Liberation Committee, which had its headquarters in Dar es Salaam.

Not all Tanzanians supported the government's policy of supporting the liberation movements. There were some high officials and politicians who thought Tanzania was unduly exposing itself to dangers and was expending financial and other resources it could ill afford in support of the wars of national liberation in Africa. They did not say this openly—who would dare question Mwalimu Nyerere? Nevertheless they slowed things down, frustrated the more radical supporters of the liberation movements, and even occasionally resorted to calling them CIA agents as a way to discredit them.

Relations between the Tanzanian government and the liberation movements were generally good but difficult situations did sometimes arise, especially where there were two or more liberation organizations from the same country. Cold War politics influenced debates and decisions in international forums inside and outside Africa. There were also contradictions. On one hand, the liberation movements were grateful for the support they enjoyed from Tanzania and from Mwalimu Nyerere; on the other hand, they feared that Tanzania might exert undue influence on their "internal affairs." A good example of this was the response of the liberation movements to the 1969 Lusaka Manifesto.

The document, which had been written by Nyerere and adopted by the leaders of the Frontline States, put forward the position that the heads of state would dissuade the liberation movements from continuing the armed struggle if the Portuguese and South African regimes accepted the principles of independence and majority rule and agreed to start the process of negotiations to that end. The liberation movements were incensed by this position. In the first place, they argued, it had been taken without consulting them. Second, the decision on the means by which to pursue the struggle was a sovereign decision that only they and no one else could take. Third, each struggle had its own character and there could not be one position that would fit all.

The Lusaka Manifesto was adopted by the OAU. We argued with the liberation movements that armed struggle was not an end but a means toward an end, and if that end could be secured peacefully, there would be no reason for war. But the liberation movements never quite accepted the position. In 1971 I had the honor to be assigned to draft the Mogadishu Declaration, which nullified the Lusaka Manifesto. The declaration argued that since the Portuguese colonialists and the apartheid regime had not responded positively, frustrating the hopes of the OAU, there was no alternative but to continue to support the armed struggle.

The 1960s and 1970s were exciting times in Tanzania's history. Because of Mwalimu Nyerere's leadership and his desire to build an African socialist society based on the African concept of *ujamaa*, he attracted many Western intellectuals. For African Americans, Tanzania came to embody many of their historical aspirations, including the possibility of returning to Africa to stay, which a few of them did.

African Americans coming to Tanzania often arrived with names of individuals and institutions to contact, including in some cases the foreign ministry, and I was privileged to be one of the individuals who was contacted. It was a period of mutual discovery between those African Americans and Tanzanians, with unresolved questions and frustrations but also fulfillment, especially in 1974 around the time of the Sixth Pan-African Congress. Some members of the Drum and Spear group—Charlie Cobb, Anne Forrester, Courtland Cox, Geri Stark (Augusto), Jennifer Lawson, Kathy Flewellen, and Sandra Hill—stayed for short periods of time. Others, such as Bob Moses and Professor Neville Parker, stayed longer and made invaluable contributions to Tanzania in the field of education. Bill Sutherland stayed the longest, followed by others such as Monroe Sharp and Edie Wilson. Walter Rodney, who was at the University of Dar es Salaam, had great influence on discussion and debates around the period of the Pan-African Congress.

I left the foreign ministry in 1972 to join and manage the Tanzania Publishing House. There, my involvement in liberation support activities actually increased, as I was now less constrained by diplomatic and civil service orders. Publishing became another front in the struggle. Looking back after the end of apartheid and the liberation of the continent, we salute those who bore the brunt of the enemies' blows, and we remember with respect and pride those who paid the supreme price. Among those who worked together, friendships and comradeship endure, along with a feeling of connection to a larger network. On all continents there are still many who remain committed to freedom and to inevitable victory of the next stage of the African revolution. As before, victory will not be not easy, but it is essential.

From left: Kathy Flewellen, Geri Augusto, and Walter Bgoya, in Dar es Salaam, 1974. Flewellen and Augusto were among the organizers of the Sixth Pan-African Congress. Bgoya was then director of the Tanzania Publishing House. *Photo courtesy of Loretta Hobbs.*

Walter Bgoya

# Miriam Makeba ✑ "Mama Africa"

## Gail Hovey

*My life, my career, every song I sing and every appearance I make, are bound up with the plight of my people.*

—Miriam Makeba, *Makeba: My Story*

As a teenager in South Africa, Makeba listened to Ella Fitzgerald and Billie Holiday on a wind-up record player. Her older brother Joseph, a saxophone and piano player himself, introduced her to the American jazz greats and taught her American songs. When she would sing with Joseph, she recalls, "sometimes I don't even know what I'm saying, but I put my all into it" (Makeba and Hall 1987, 21).

Makeba learned how to sing from the musicians she performed with, having had no formal musical training. Among the first were her nephew Zweli's band, the Cuban Brothers. They were not from Cuba, had never been there, had never met a Cuban, and none of them were brothers; the name was a fantasy from the movies.

Her first paying job was with the Manhattan Brothers, a popular group in South Africa in the 1940s and 1950s. The contacts she made landed her a small role in Lionel Rogosin's film *Come Back, Africa* (1959). Rogosin, an American filmmaker, took Makeba and the film to Europe. While in London she met Harry Belafonte, who came to a screening of *Come Back, Africa*. Makeba told him that all his songs had been translated into South Africa's African languages. He told her to get in touch with him if she came to the United States. Rogosin wanted Makeba to do just that, but her visa only allowed her to travel in Europe. In no time, Belafonte arranged for her visa and she entered the United States in November 1959, at the age of 27.

It was overwhelming. Within a week she appeared on the *Steve Allen Show* in Los Angeles and opened a four-week run at the Village Vanguard in New York's Greenwich Village. Belafonte became her guardian; she called him Big Brother. He brought guests to hear her sing—Sidney Poitier, Duke Ellington, Diahann Carroll, Nina Simone, and Miles Davis. After she sang, Makeba says, their applause was like thunder, and it electrified her.

Press reviews compared her to Ella Fitzgerald, Ethel Merman, and Frank Sinatra. Belafonte praised her as "easily the most revolutionary new talent to appear in any medium in the last decade." *Time* magazine wrote, "She is probably too shy to realize it, but her return to Africa would leave a noticeable gap in the U.S. entertainment world, which she entered a mere six weeks ago" (Makeba and Hall 1987, 89).

Catapulted to international fame, Makeba remained first of all a South African. She was in New York when she heard about the Sharpeville massacre. Two of her uncles were among the 69 dead. In the same year Makeba's

Perhaps more than any other public figure, Miriam Makeba embodies the connections between the African and North American continents and the gifts each has to give the other. Her life also illustrates the harassment and alienation suffered by many of those who spoke out publicly against apartheid. This profile of Makeba draws on her autobiography and on published memoirs by her two husbands, Hugh Masekela and Stokely Carmichael.

mother, who was ill, phoned that it was time for Makeba's nine-year-old daughter Bongi, who lived in South Africa with her grandmother, to join her mother in the United States; she did soon after. Not long after that Makeba's mother died.

Makeba applied to the South African consulate for permission to return for the funeral. She watched as an official stamped her passport "Invalid," placing her permanently in exile.

> For an instant my breath catches in my throat as I realize what has happened . . . I am not permitted to go home, not now, and maybe not ever. . . . Everything that has gone into the making of myself, gone. . . . I have gone too far. I have become too big. . . . I have not said a word about politics in all the newspaper stories about me. But I am still dangerous. . . . I am in exile. I and my daughter alone in a West that is bright and rich but is foreign to us. I hold Bongi tight and try to protect her from the terrible things I feel. (Makeba and Hall 1987, 98)

Makeba's troubles with the authorities, South African and American, were just beginning. She accepted an invitation to address the United Nations Special Committee Against Apartheid on July 16, 1963. "My country has been turned by the Verwoerd Government into a huge prison," she told the committee. "Therefore, I must urge the United Nations to impose a complete boycott of South Africa. The first priority must be to stop the shipment of arms. I have not the slightest doubt that these arms will be used against African women and children" (Makeba and Hall 1987, 112).

With this speech, Makeba was no longer just a brilliant entertainer. She became the voice of Africa's oppressed people. Immediately the apartheid government banned the sale of her records in South Africa. But African leaders reached out to her and she became friends with the heads of newly independent states like Kwame Nkrumah, Sekou Toure, and Julius Nyerere, as well as leaders of liberation movements like Eduardo Mondlane and Amilcar Cabral. It was an exciting time, as one after another African nation became independent. "There is so much hope and promise," she rejoiced. "It is the dawn of a new age" (Makeba and Hall 1987, 92).

In May 1964 Makeba married South African musician Hugh Masekela, and they welcomed many into their home in New York. Masekela recalls:

> The African community, especially the diplomatic and exile population, was growing in leaps and bounds, and our place had become a home away from home for many people from these groups. Students, ambassadors, musicians, actors, writers, dancers, and activists. . . . The civil rights and African-American communities held a special place in their hearts for her. More than that, people of all nationalities . . . recognized and loved her with a sincerity I have seen reserved only for a few very special people in the world. Miriam was extraordinarily special then, and always will be. (Masekela and Cheers 2004, 169–70)

But life with Makeba was not easy, Masekela says, and the couple divorced. Although her increased outspokenness did not go unnoticed by the U.S. and other Western governments, it was not until 1968, when she married the radical SNCC leader Stokely Carmichael, that Makeba's career was seriously threatened. The bad news came in a phone call from her manager Bob Schwaid. Her bookings were being canceled right and left (Makeba and Hall 1987, 159).

Carmichael was surprised. "I hadn't expected this. I'd figured, at most, some people would criticize her. Racists might boycott her shows, maybe stop buying her records. But this? All at once? It had to be an organized campaign. . . . It had to be organized across the industry" (Carmichael and Thelwell 2003, 653–54). Indeed, according to Ekwueme Thelwell, who completed Carmichael's autobiography after the SNCC leader's death, actions of the Internal Revenue Service later made clear that the federal government played a role in the continuing harassment of Makeba (654).

At almost the same time, Martin Luther King Jr. was assassinated in Memphis. Makeba had been performing in Los Angeles, but she immediately got on a plane to return home to Washington, DC, where she and Carmichael lived. Washington was in flames, black neighborhoods under military curfew. With the sirens and occasional gunfire, it "seemed to her like South Africa all over again" (Carmichael and Thelwell 2003, 656).

Makeba and Carmichael decided to act on a long-held dream and move to Africa. They had begun their relationship in Guinea, and President Toure had long encouraged them to live in his country. Makeba lived the next two decades in Africa, performing there and in Europe. She served as a member of the Guinean delegation to the U.N. General Assembly, an opportunity that again allowed her to speak out about South Africa.

By the time Miriam Makeba returned to South Africa in 1990, after 30 years of exile, she was known as the Empress of African Song and, more simply, as Mama Africa. She was welcomed home personally by Nelson Mandela. Her first concert in South Africa was held in 1991 and was a huge success. It was followed by a world tour that included the United States and Europe.

It was her friend Philemon Hou, a fellow South African musician, who taught Makeba a poem she repeated with her grandchildren while still in exile (Makeba and Hall 1987, 198):

Miriam Makeba addresses the United Nations Special Committee on the Policies of Apartheid, March 9, 1964. *UN Photo.*

> We are an African People
> An African People!
> An African People!
> We are an African People
> And don't you forget it!

# Media for the Movement ∾ Southern Africa Magazine

## Gail Hovey

*If you care about civil rights in the United States, you need to care about the freedom struggles in Southern Africa.*

—Hank Crane, Africa Secretary, World Student Christian Federation

When the National Student Christian Federation, the student movement of the mainline Protestant churches, met for its annual summer meeting in Chicago in 1964, the students in attendance were well aware that this was Freedom Summer. Many of us had already been involved in one aspect or another of the civil rights movement. At that meeting we heard a new challenge from Hank Crane, who had grown up in Congo, the son of Presbyterian missionaries who had arrived there in 1912. Crane's father-in-law and mother-in-law, Roy and LeNoir Cleveland, were also missionaries; although they were white Southerners, they had been recruited to go to the Congo by African American missionary William Sheppard. Sheppard and others in the Presbyterian mission in Congo's Kasai area had been active in exposing the grisly horrors of King Leopold's rubber trade in the Congo at the beginning of the twentieth century (Hochschild 1998, 164–65; Kennedy 2002; Phipps 2002). Before Crane spoke to us in 1964, he had spent several years traveling around Africa for the World Student Christian Federation, based in Northern Rhodesia, which would become independent Zambia that October.

Crane found a receptive audience in the students that day. In the fall we took up his challenge to focus on liberation in Southern Africa. David Wiley, then a graduate student at Princeton University and Seminary, who had worked with the Student Christian Movement in white-ruled Southern Rhodesia in the early 1960s, and Ken Carstens, a white South African Methodist minister in exile since 1961, began the process of educating us, explaining the workings of the apartheid state and setting the larger Southern African context. We continued to meet on a weekly basis, first to educate ourselves and then to determine what action to take. Although this new Southern Africa Committee (SAC) was initially intended to be national, limitations of time and money quickly narrowed our membership to students at East Coast schools, especially Union Theological Seminary and Columbia University in New York City.

When Students for a Democratic Society called for a demonstration at Chase Manhattan Bank in the spring of 1965 to protest Chase loans to South Africa, we were ready to participate, as were SNCC and CORE. Chase was chosen as a target not only because it was a leading member of a consortium of banks that provided a revolving loan fund to the South African government, but because it had been instrumental in resolving the crisis in the South African economy after the Sharpeville killings in 1960.

Gail Hovey, one of the editors of this book, was a founder of *Southern Africa* magazine and an original member of the Southern Africa Committee. She remained involved with the magazine from 1964 to 1975. During the two years she spent in Africa, living in the Northern Transvaal from 1966 to 1967, she regularly sent information to the magazine in New York without the knowledge of the South African authorities.

Revealing our preference for reconciliation, and also our naiveté, Southern Africa Committee members insisted that an effort be made to negotiate with the bank before taking action against it. At a lunch appointment in Chase's swanky dining room, we were hosted by a vice president for public relations. I was amazed to discover that we knew more about Chase's involvement in South Africa than he did. Instead of addressing the support provided by the bank to the apartheid regime, he wanted to talk about the possibility of scholarships for South African students.

For some of us it was a revelatory moment, the beginning of an education in the nature and power of international capital. Our argument that supporting a more just society in South Africa would be in Chase's long-term interest cut no ice. What mattered was profit in the short term and co-opting Africans through scholarships and capitalist economic development. SAC joined the demonstration in front of the bank and some of our members were among the 49 arrested.

Our next target was First National City Bank, now Citibank, which was a part of the same revolving loan fund. SAC members talked with bank officials, seminary and university administrators, faculty, and students. We asked people to withdraw their accounts if the bank had not met our demands by a specified date. We also approached the denominations and church agencies that had their offices at the Interchurch Center in New York, asking them to withdraw accounts. This campaign continued in collaboration with the American Committee on Africa, the initial public withdrawal involving some 70 accounts by individuals and a $20,000 withdrawal of Barnard College's student council fund. We saw this strategy as an effective way to confront the public with the issue of American involvement with apartheid. We gave up our illusions about convincing the banks to change their ways of doing business. It would take more years and radically increased pressure that ultimately affected their bottom line before the banks would finally end their loans to South Africa.

In 1965, most Americans knew very little about apartheid or about the countries of Southern Africa. As a new convert to concern about the region, I found it instructive that the November 11, 1965 Unilateral Declaration of Independence in Rhodesia received such minimal coverage in the U.S. press. SAC understood that the declaration was a daring and desperate effort on the part of whites, under the leadership of Ian Smith, to perpetuate minority rule in the British colony.

Convinced of the seriousness of the crisis in Rhodesia and of the need for information, we started what quickly became a biweekly news summary on Southern Africa. At first our sources were mostly British. Before long we established contact with the Zimbabwean nationalist movements and in time subscribed to publications printed in Southern Africa by the liberation movements and by the regular press. What began as the "Rhodesian News Summary" evolved over the next three years into *Southern Africa* magazine.

When the NSCF became the University Christian Movement and then went out of existence as a national movement in 1969, SAC became independent and continued as a cooperative. The quality of *Southern Africa* magazine improved significantly over time with the involvement of ACOA staff member Janet Hooper and graduate student Susan Geiger, both of whom had spent time in Africa, and South Africans Stephanie Urdang and Jennifer Davis, among others. The committee operated on a shoestring and was subject to FBI infiltration and IRS investigation, and it finally ceased publication in 1983. But for 15 years the magazine provided its readership, some 4,000 subscribers, with information on the progress of the liberation struggles and analysis of U.S. governmental and economic involvement with the region.

Unlike *Africa News*, which emerged from a North Carolina branch of the Southern Africa Committee, *Southern Africa* magazine was primarily a vehicle for communication within the movement rather than something intended for a broad public audience. In the period before Africa rated even minimal media attention, it was a vital resource, joining Liberation News Service and the *Guardian*, both also based in New York, in keeping African freedom on the movement agenda.

The women in the *Southern Africa* magazine collective were also involved in the emerging women's movement in New York and made connections between that movement and the anticolonial and anti-apartheid movements in Africa. We learned from and reported on the roles African women were playing in national liberation struggles. The connections we established resulted in, among other things, Stephanie Urdang's *Fighting Two Colonialisms: Women in Guinea-Bissau* (1979) and her later book on women in Mozambique, *And Still They Dance* (1989). Another committee member, Susan Geiger, went on to teach women's studies at the University of Minnesota and wrote *TANU Women: Gender and Culture in the Making of Tanganyikan Nationalism, 1955–1965* (1997). These books, among others, preserved and made available to future generations the essential contribution of women in the history of African resistance, knowledge of which was in danger of being lost.

Stephanie Urdang of the Southern Africa Committee was invited to travel to liberated areas of Guinea-Bissau with PAIGC in 1974. Here she speaks with her translator, Mario Ribeira. *Photo courtesy of Stephanie Urdang.*

# Chapter 4

# The 1970s:
# Expanding Networks

*Joseph F. Jordan*

In 1972 I was a 20-year-old psychology major at Norfolk State University, a historically black institution in Virginia. One day a visiting white South African lecturer came to campus. In his speech, he referred to the lesser capabilities of "our blacks"—meaning black South Africans—compared to U.S. blacks. I still remember the students' anger. One of us challenged the visitor by asking him what he meant by "our blacks." Was he suggesting some kind of ownership? The lecturer, visibly perturbed by our contempt, tried to forge ahead. But it got worse.

He launched into an explanation of the physical characteristics of some black South African women, the so-called Hottentots (the term is a derogatory reference to the Khoikhoi people driven into the Kalahari Desert by the first wave of white settlers). According to the lecturer, these women were able to weather periods of privation and scarcity by storing fat in their buttocks! We didn't riot; we simply tuned him out. As far as we were concerned, he had nothing to say that we needed to hear. While few of us could have spoken in depth about South Africa and the situation there, we were familiar enough with racism to know a racist when we heard one.

The South African's disturbing visit was an important moment for me because it demonstrated both my ignorance about Africa and my lack of political sophistication. The Vietnam War and the draft of young men like me was another indicator

that I needed to become more politically engaged. Some of my high school classmates, who had either been drafted or had volunteered for military service, had returned home in body bags, forcing me to think about their senseless deaths. I vowed never to participate in a war unless I was fighting for something I believed in, something for which I was willing to die.

I still hadn't connected Vietnam to South Africa, though, or the situation in either of those places to the one at home. At Norfolk State we were more concerned with the racism we encountered each day than with racism 4,000 or 5,000 miles away. It wasn't until I began graduate study at the much larger Ohio State University in 1973 that the relationship between Southern Africa and the United States became clear to me. That was partly because there were many foreign students on campus, and a substantial number of them were from nations in Southern Africa.

At Ohio State, where I was a member of the All-African Student and Faculty Union (AASFU) and co-editor of its monthly newspaper, *Our Choking Times*, my consciousness and activism increased. In AASFU I participated in heated political debates about competing liberation groups in South Africa, Angola, and Zimbabwe.

Joseph Jordan
*Photo courtesy of Joseph Jordan.*

And since this was the era of Black Power, black students like me also debated what allying with the white Left in the United States might mean.

As our sense of the world we lived in developed, we began to see that local cops or sheriff's departments weren't all we had to confront. Challenging the U.S. government seemed an increasingly important task that those of us trying to support Southern African liberation movements would have to shoulder. The giant multinational corporations we were being educated to serve seemed a dominant force in Southern Africa, maintaining the status quo. Support for Southern African liberation meant we would have to challenge them. South Africa, where many U.S. corporations were concentrated, took on special importance. Given South Africa's powerful political and economic role in the region, we knew that if African revolutionary movements were successful and the apartheid nation fell, black majority rule would become a reality throughout Southern Africa. We also recognized South Africa's role as a regional terrorist that attacked and destabilized independent African nations in an attempt to guarantee its own security.

It was a great learning period for me and for others like me. We had first been influenced by black radical organizations, notably the Black Panthers and the All-African People's Revolutionary Party. These had succeeded groups like the NAACP, CORE, SNCC, and the Southern Christian Leadership Conference (SCLC), which had largely focused on civil rights in the U.S. South. Although we didn't make the connection until later, during the 1960s civil rights activists like SNCC's James Forman had already recognized a relationship between the oppression of blacks in the United States and in Southern Africa. Indeed, the "one man one vote" slogan SNCC had used for its Southern voter registration campaign was borrowed from Zambia's independence struggle. By the 1970s SNCC no longer existed, and CORE changed for the worse under new leadership. The NAACP was still focused on its decades-old approach to civil rights, and the SCLC had declined after the assassination of King. But militant and thoughtful activists who had been shaped by these organizations remained active, forming a kind of loose political network or set of interconnecting networks.

Activist and scholar Geri Augusto, who took part in protests on the Howard University campus in the late 1960s, recalls these networks as complex and multigenerational. Her mother and father had been active with CORE and SNCC in Dayton, Ohio. Augusto herself became involved with the DC-based Center for Black Education, an independent school and community education center. Later, while living in Angola, she was one of the key contacts in Africa for the Southern Africa Support Project (SASP) of Washington, DC.

Augusto emphasizes the myriad interconnections between activists, individuals as well as groups. At the Center for Black Education, she recalls, there were old SNCC people, a few people who had been involved in the student strike at San Francisco State, and others with links to the Black Panthers or to black nationalist Maulana Ron Karenga's U.S. organization.

> This whole thing is a story of networks and nodes and density and connections. I think complexity theory is probably a good frame for looking at how black activists got created and how they got hooked into other nodes and sets of institutions and activities across the country.
>
> A quick summary of complexity theory is many agents interacting in a field or a system or a space. Each one has its own logic, its own culture, its own interests, but for whatever reason, it has, from time to time, to interact with any number of others. And then they come to share certain kinds of things, like you might share a set of ideas or beliefs. Or you might come together from time to time to work on a purpose, like all of us came together for that first African Liberation Day. We [all] came together where there was mutual interest.

If the roots of the anti-apartheid movement were planted in earlier decades, the 1970s was the decade in which those roots began to grow, shaping the course of the movement in the 1980s and into the 1990s. In my own case, involvement with African liberation pushed me away from my own uncritical politics into a more disciplined analysis and approach to struggle. By the end of the 1970s I had left Ohio State for Howard University in Washington, DC. There I joined SASP, a stalwart in DC's black community, serving as its co-chair for several years.

Many people representing a range of political positions were part of the 1970s anti-apartheid movement in the United States. But the movement was primarily shaped by activists who recognized the importance of local organizing and local strategies. In many cases these were designed to coincide with the national focus of organizations like the African Liberation Support Committee, AFSC, ACOA, the Washington Office on Africa, and, beginning in 1978, TransAfrica. Close attention was paid to the use of local, national, and international media.

Veterans of the civil rights movement, in particular, brought useful skills and experiences to this phase of the movement. Frank Beeman was a key figure in the Southern Africa Liberation Committee, a small group founded in East Lansing, Michigan in 1972. He recalls that, for him, anti-apartheid work "just seemed to be a natural shift from the civil rights movement."

> Older organizations and their members, who had been involved with Africa far longer than our student generation had, helped connect us to groups in various communities around the country. The ACOA, in addition to Washington lobbying, also funded field programs, working in Chicago with Prexy Nesbitt and in New York, building bridges to the black activist communities in those cities.

ACOA and other experienced activist groups brought sophisticated strategies and tactics to our attention. As early as 1966, for example, the National Council of Churches and its member churches began using their institutional power to challenge investment in South Africa. Although this was only a beginning, it pioneered the strategy of targeting individual corporations involved in South Africa.

Another member of SASP, Mark Harrison, served as program director for the United Methodist Board of Church and Society and as human rights coordinator for Clergy and Laity Concerned. He remembers that in the religious community, "the growth of activity was uneven, and mostly unstructured except for the work of some key groups at the national level." Even so, he notes that the religious community led the way. "As early as 1976, before the divestment issue became nationally prominent, the Christian Church (Disciples of Christ) had adopted a strong resolution on divestment and on bank deposits by member congregations and agencies" (Harrison 1995). Church activism encouraged our own, and we in turn pressed church groups to become more active, despite the conservatism of some denominations.

At the national level, labor unions were reluctant to join our effort because they maintained a strong anticommunist stance inherited from the Cold War. Yet the rank and file members in local branches often adopted a more militant anti-apartheid attitude than the leadership. At the local level, direct action was carried out by groups like the Dodge Revolutionary Union Movement and the League of Revolutionary Black Workers, both operating in the auto industry in Detroit.

In Cambridge, Massachusetts, the Polaroid Revolutionary Workers Movement was formed for the express purpose of taking action on South Africa. In 1970, two black employees at the Polaroid Corporation in Cambridge, Ken Williams and Caroline Hunter, had discovered that Polaroid was selling its instant photo technology for use by the South African military and police. They organized the workers' movement, which demanded that Polaroid stop doing business in South Africa and turn over its South African profits to African liberation groups. Working with South African exile Chris Nteta, who was based in Boston, they gained not only local but international attention. They testified before the United Nations and at the House Africa Subcommittee in Washington. Polaroid responded with an "experiment," improving conditions for its black workers in South Africa. The experiment ended five years later when it was revealed that Polaroid's distributor was violating Polaroid's commitment not to sell directly to the South African government.

In 1972 black longshoremen, in an alliance with black students, held demonstrations at ports in Burnside, Louisiana, aimed at preventing ships from unloading Rhodesian chrome. Similar actions were held at ports in Baltimore, Boston, and Philadelphia.

An emerging figure in the early part of the decade was Randall Robinson, a brilliant young student at Harvard Law School. In 1971 he teamed up with Chris Nteta, then a student at Harvard

**the southern PATRIOT**

VOL. 30, NO. 4   APRIL, 1972   PUBLISHED BY THE SOUTHERN CONFERENCE EDUCATIONAL FUND (SCEF), LOUISVILLE, KY.

## Historic Protest in the Deep South
# Dockworkers Slow Ore Ship

By KEN LAWRENCE
(Staff Correspondent)

BURNSIDE, La.—One of the most significant events of this period in the South occurred here this spring when black dock workers refused to unload a ship full of chrome ore from Rhodesia.

The ship was finally unloaded by other workers but only after a historic protest by black workers and students.

It appeared to be the first time that black Americans had refused to unload a ship bringing imports from a country run by racists and imperialists.

The protesters said the ore is the product of the oppression of the people of Rhodesia. They called on all citizens to join them in opposing the exploiting of Africans by U.S. corporations and the U.S. government policy which encourages this exploitation.

"Racism abroad, like racism at home, must be resisted with all the power and strength that we have," one of the black organizers of the protest declared. "Black Americans will not tolerate a Vietnam in Africa!"

Chrome ore is among 12 items specifi-

—Photo by James W. Terry, III

cally barred from trade with Rhodesia under a resolution passed by the United Nations Security Council in 1966.

The resolution was aimed at the white rulers of Rhodesia, known to Africans as Zimbabwe. The Rhodesian government has been harsh in its repression of black people, who make up 95 per cent of the population.

The United States had voted for the boycott resolution, but the U.S. Congress and President Nixon got around it with the Military Procurement Act of 1971.

In early March, Africans notified friends in New York that an Argentine vessel, the *Santos Vega*, was on the way to Burnside terminal with 25,000 tons of the ore. The New Yorkers notified movement people in Louisiana, who went into action.

An alliance was formed between the predominantly black locals 1830 and 1833 of the International Longshoremen's Association (ILA) and an organization of faculty members and students at Southern University in Baton Rouge called the Committee of Blacks Against Oppression.

The ILA, an AFL-CIO affiliate, refused to unload the "hot cargo" and the Committee organized a mass demonstration at the Burnside terminal. More than 300 Southern University students joined the demonstration.

In the face of this massive protest, the *Santos Vega* didn't dock on March 15, as

(Continued on page 2)

Front page of the *Southern Patriot* shows black dock workers in Louisiana who refused to unload a ship carrying chrome ore from Rhodesia, April 1972. *Photo courtesy of Ken Lawrence.*

Divinity School, to form the Pan-African Liberation Committee. The group called for Harvard to divest from Gulf Oil, which was providing the colonial Portuguese government with funds to wage wars in Angola, Mozambique, and Guinea-Bissau. In April 1972 Robinson, Nteta, and 36 black Harvard undergraduates took over the building that housed the office of the newly appointed president, Derek Bok. The takeover lasted six days, ending when Harvard agreed to send what would prove to be a fruitless fact-finding mission to Angola.

By the mid-1970s new voices, including those of students, were making themselves heard. Grassroots groups in the United States were forging close working relationships with the liberation organizations in Southern Africa, including South Africa's ANC and PAC, Angola's MPLA, Mozambique's Frelimo, and Namibia's SWAPO, among others. These ties influenced our political thinking, guiding

us to a more radical stance on an array of Southern African issues.

An anti-apartheid and Southern Africa support community was growing internationally, and this also had an impact on the growth of the movement in the United States. Contacts with counterparts in Canada, Great Britain, and other parts of Europe, as well as in Africa itself, influenced the strategies and tactics of U.S. activists. Cultural and economic boycotts as well as the campaign for sanctions gained momentum from the continuous interaction between groups on both sides of the Atlantic.

Broadly speaking, this phase of the anti-apartheid and Southern Africa liberation movement was probably the most radical, mirroring the political sensibilities of the era. As the U.S. governing establishment moved away from the liberal domestic policies of the Kennedy-Johnson administrations, the crackdown on domestic dissent and the escala-

Joseph F. Jordan

tion of the war in Vietnam had a radicalizing effect. Equally important were developments in Africa. The Cold War conflict between the United States and the Soviet Union, having festered throughout the 1960s, raged across the continent in the 1970s. The settler colonies of Southern Africa were allied with the United States and apartheid South Africa, ostensibly in the name of fighting communism. All continued to turn a deaf ear to the growing chorus of voices demanding African majority rule.

## The Influence of the Liberation Movements

At various times in the mid-1970s, liberation movement leaders visited Ohio State University and many other U.S. colleges and universities to talk about the struggle in Southern Africa. They included, among others, ANC stalwarts like Johnny Makatini and Thabo Mbeki and SWAPO leaders Sam Nujoma and Theo-Ben Gurirab. These voices from the front added a measure of validity and contributed mightily to campus organizing and public information work.

As the Southern Africa liberation movements grew in sophistication, they also challenged U.S. support groups to move beyond an idealized and simplistic image of the struggle. They encouraged us to develop a political analysis capable of critiquing the various forms of colonialism, neocolonialism, and imperialism supported by the U.S. government. This challenge opened up the intellectual space for us in the support movement to debate the concept of "solidarity" and how best to organize ourselves to be most effective.

What emerged as a crucial domestic task, as we in SASP often said, was to make the struggle in Southern Africa real and not something that was remote and unrelated to our daily lives. Frank Beeman says his organization knew that "people would do what was right if they knew the truth, if they knew what was actually happening." Bringing the Southern African struggle home depended on maintaining close ties with the people involved in and leading those struggles in Africa. Those ties in turn depended on face-to-face contact, often in the course of U.S. visits by the liberation leaders. George Houser, a founder and former director of the ACOA, recalls:

We made contacts with liberation movements our primary focus. This began with the ANC and Indian Congress leadership in South Africa—Sisulu, Cachalia, Luthuli, Tambo, Z. K. Matthews, Manilal Gandhi and later Mandela, and so many others. We can still recite the initials and acronyms by which the movements were commonly known [but] it's easier to use names of leaders—Nkrumah, Azikiwe, Mondlane, Cabral, Nyerere, Kaunda, Kenyatta, Mboya, Nkomo, Mugabe, Kozonguizi, Nujoma, Neto, Lumumba. Each name conjures up memories. I recall when Sam Nujoma, [who was to become the first president of Namibia], came to New York after escaping from the then South West Africa after the Katatura uprising of 1959. One of the first places he came was to our office.

If the task was to make the struggle in Southern Africa real, Robert Van Lierop's documentary film *A Luta Continua* (The Struggle Continues) accomplished it brilliantly. Based on his travels inside Mozambique with Frelimo in 1971 and released the following year, the film was a spare cinema verité record of Frelimo's struggle. Its impact was far-reaching, as it brought the battlefield of Mozambique and the struggle against Portuguese colonialism to the U.S. public as well as to viewers in other countries. Van Lierop recalls:

It was smuggled into Portugal by Frelimo. They used it there. It was also smuggled into South Africa. And prior to the Soweto uprising it was shown by the Black Consciousness Movement and others in South Africa. And they began to use some of the slogans—*a luta continua*, which was, as you know, the way Eduardo [Mondlane] always signed his letters. That was why we chose that title.

Van Lierop recalls showing the film in venues throughout the United States, including in prisons and on a Navajo Indian reservation.

I can remember an outdoor screening in Harlem. We put some sheets as a screen, and screened it—I can't remember the exact street, but I think it was around 132nd Street. And Guebuza was there, and Guebuza stood on top of a car to address the crowd [Armando Guebuza, a top Frelimo leader in the 1970s, would be elected president of Mozambique in 2004].

Dr. Sylvia Hill, an educator and one of the original organizers of the Southern Africa Support Project, also recalls that *A Luta Continua* had a transformative effect on her when she first saw the unfinished version of the film in 1971.

> I remember distinctly looking at that film and envisioning social change based on a science, much like when I first saw the *Battle of Algiers* in San Francisco with Jimmie Garrett, [and] a whole bunch of Black Student Union folks. I remember for the first time having this sense that you can have a science of change because you have to think methodologically about what you're doing. It's not just haphazard and just occurring willy-nilly.

Van Lierop had already been involved in anti-apartheid and Southern Africa work before the 1970s and had served on the board of the ACOA in the late 1960s. With Prexy Nesbitt, he founded the Africa Information Service (AIS), which provided valuable research material for organizations interested in Africa work. In October 1972 Van Lierop used AIS to bring together PAIGC leader Amilcar Cabral with about 120 African Americans to discuss the liberation struggle in Africa (Cabral 1973a). AIS was never able to realize its full potential, but it produced a number of important documents including a collection of speeches by Amilcar Cabral, *Return to the Source* (1973b), republished in 1974 by Monthly Review Press.

## A Watershed Moment: The Defeat of Portuguese Colonial Rule

Cabral had returned to Guinea-Bissau from exile in Angola in 1956 to found the African Party for the Independence of Guinea-Bissau and Cape Verde. During 1970 he traveled to the United States for a series of public and private engagements (see chapter 1). In a 1965 published interview, Cabral had already articulated PAIGC's understanding of the role of solidarity with progressive forces in support of revolutionary struggle.

> Our solidarity goes to every just cause in the world, but we also derive strength from the solidarity of others. . . . [We] have a fundamental principle that consists in counting above all on our own efforts, our own sacrifices. But, in the objective framework of Portuguese colonization, dear friends, we are also aware that our struggle is not solely ours in the present stage of man's history. It is one that comprises all of Africa, all of progressive humanity. This is why we, . . . confronting the peculiar difficulties of our struggle, and in the context of current history, have realized the need for concrete help from every progressive force in the world. . . . We expect only that aid which each is able to offer to our struggle. This is our ethic of help.

Cabral returned to the United States in 1972 for a historic appearance at the United Nations, where he was welcomed as the de facto leader of Guinea-Bissau and Cape Verde. On both trips he met informally with supporters in the activist community. Because of these contacts, he had a large influence on the thinking of many in the anti-apartheid and Southern Africa support movement. Cabral used his keen theoretical insights into the process of liberation to build a movement based on the realities of the people of Guinea-Bissau and Cape Verde and the concerns of their daily lives under colonialism. As one writer noted: "Cabral's revolutionary strategy emphasized the political mobilization of the masses around practical material issues rather than grand theoretical ideals" (Meisenhelder 1993, 40).

Cabral's conversations also ushered in a renewed and often heated debate in movement circles about the process and practice of solidarity and, in particular, about the role of race. There was tension over the various forms of radicalism that were shaping black struggle in the United States, and over some of the forms of black nationalism that some activists embraced. Much of this came to a head in the split over Angola, between those in the United States who supported the MPLA and those who supported Jonas Savimbi's Unita. The debates revealed an overall lack of coherence and the absence of a coordinating structure for the U.S. movement. These weaknesses would continue to plague the movement even though it was able, ultimately, to play a vital role in the eventual fall of apartheid as well as in the liberation of other Southern African states.

Amilcar Cabral's assassination by agents of the Portuguese secret police in 1973 was a tragedy for the entire Southern Africa liberation support movement. His brilliance as a revolutionary theorist and his legacy of principled leadership helped change the way the movement defined its role in liberation struggles in Africa and elsewhere. The assassination also meant the loss of an important political voice that advocated for Africa's liberation movements here in the United States. Nevertheless, while he didn't live to witness it, I like to think that Cabral knew that the Portuguese fascist state was about to fall. And so it did, on April 25, 1974, just over a year after his death. Portugal's new rulers moved quickly to recognize the independence of Guinea-Bissau and to begin the transition to independence in Cape Verde, Angola, São Tomé, and Mozambique.

We in AASFU were buoyed by the dictatorship's demise and the birth of the new nations. The independence of the Portuguese colonies allowed us, for the first time, to celebrate national liberation to which our support work in the United States had contributed. The Portuguese defeat also vindicated our choice to support the MPLA, Frelimo, and the PAIGC over other groups that had vied for our backing. Against the backdrop of the Cold War, questions had been raised, both inside and outside of government, about our support for movements on the political left, seen by the U.S. government and some civil rights organizations as "communist." Equally controversial, especially to many in the non-violent civil rights movement, was the decision to support groups that had taken up arms. The victories in Mozambique, Angola, and Guinea-Bissau helped justify our support for armed struggle against colonial rule. It was clear that victory did not mean a bloodbath of retribution.

But the Cold War context remained, so that even in this moment of accomplishment and celebration the liberation process faced a new danger. The Cold War would play out in decidedly hot and vicious wars aimed at destabilizing Angola and Mozambique. These two countries were targets because they were providing bases and support for the continuing liberation struggles in Namibia and South Africa. As early as August 1974, the CIA had begun funneling aid to the National

The All-African Student and Faculty Union organized in solidarity with African liberation at Ohio State University in Columbus during the 1970s. At this fundraising event Joseph Jordan is at the center playing the cabaça. *Photo courtesy of Joseph Jordan.*

Front for the Liberation of Angola (FNLA), led by Holden Roberto. South Africa, aided by the United States, was assisting Unita in the south of Angola, as well as backing insurgents in Mozambique.

Meanwhile, Roy Innis, who had replaced Floyd McKissick as chair of CORE, forced many Southern civil rights movement veterans out of the organization. He announced that CORE was now recruiting black Americans to fight in Angola against the MPLA—effectively inviting African Americans to fight on the side of the apartheid state. We thought, what foolishness! Doesn't he know what a mercenary is? Doesn't he know what mercenaries have done in Africa?

The AASFU meetings in the fall of 1976 were the scene of heated debate. Savimbi's appeal to the most narrow aspects of black nationalist sentiment was attractive to some in the African American activist community. At the same time, liberation movements with Soviet backing were looked on with suspicion by some, not only because the Soviet Union was communist, but also because it represented an alien presence in Africa and ran counter to the Pan-African politics that were popular at that moment.

Looking back some years later, I recall the temporary confusion in our ranks. A member of the All-African People's Revolutionary Party who visited one of our gatherings looked me straight in the eye and asked who were the "correct" forces to support in Angola. I think we spent several hours denouncing Jonas Savimbi, leader of Unita, and talking about his ties to the CIA and to South Africa.

The warfare in Angola would go on for almost a quarter century. The battles to control this resource-rich nation would eventually involve five U.S. presidents, numerous other leaders from around the world, and tens of thousands of innocent, noncombatant Angolans. The counterrevolutionary war was even more devastating than the revolutionary war for independence in terms of the damage it inflicted on the country. Those of us in the U.S. movement struggled with thorny questions: What could we be *for*, now that national liberation had been achieved? We watched in dismay as the superpowers fanned the flames of civil conflicts designed to tie up resources, split once unified movements, and neutralize solidarity forces in the United States and elsewhere.

## Strategy and Tactics

In practice, one of the most important answers came from South Africa. On June 16, 1976, students in the South African township of Soweto took to the streets in opposition to the apartheid regime, sparking a wave of protests around the country. The response from the regime's security forces was brutal. Over the following eight months, according to low-end estimates by the government-appointed Cillie Commission of Enquiry, 575 people died, 451 of them as a result of police action. Within four months people in over 160 African communities around the country became involved in resistance, at least 250,000 people in Soweto alone. Despite the banning of organizations, arrests, and torture, by 1977 the regime had only succeeded in imposing a temporary calm. The continuing resistance inside South Africa evoked a worldwide response and the solidarity movement entered a new phase, gaining mass support and high visibility.

There were political divisions among opponents of the South African regime, of course. Some U.S. activists were strongly allied with the ANC, others with the PAC, the Black Consciousness Movement, or the Unity Movement. But these differences were almost always eclipsed—at least in public—by the common ground found in opposing U.S. collaboration with apartheid. The drama of resistance in South Africa and the brutality of regime actions such as the killing of Steve Biko in prison in 1977 were powerful incentives to unity.

The latter half of the 1970s saw the beginnings of high-profile campaigns targeting state and local governments, churches, universities, and other institutions. The goal was divestment, the withdrawal of funds or selling of stock in banks and corporations operating in South Africa. *Divestment*, it was hoped, would lead to *disinvestment*, the actual exit of a bank or corporation from South Africa. Along with divestment campaigns, sports and cultural boycotts proliferated, aimed at isolating South Africa on the international scene. Such campaigns and boycotts were important actions for many groups, both national and local. But most never saw themselves as working only or primarily toward those objectives. While some groups were founded specifically to work for divestment, disinvestment, and sanctions, with only occasional involvement in the broader

Joseph F. Jordan

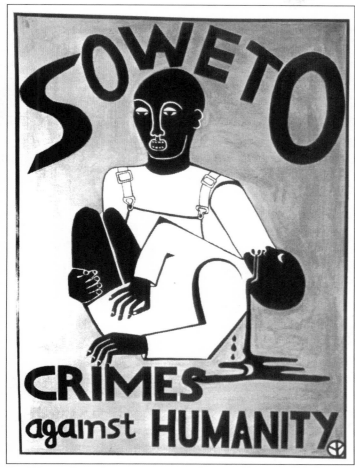

Sam Nzima's photo of 12-year-old Hector Pieterson, the first person killed by police in the student uprising of 1976, was shown around the globe. Artist Birgit Walker created this graphic based on the photo, and ACOA used it for an anti-apartheid calendar in 1978. *Photo courtesy of Richard Knight.*

other people had landed on one of the uninhabited beaches of Great Britain, could it have been claimed by the explorers? He replied that using our logic the United States would belong to the Indians. Without hesitation we responded, you're damn right!

We also worked hard to support the sports and cultural boycotts on campus and picketed any event featuring South African performers or performers who had played in South Africa. In the winter of 1976, Arthur Ashe sponsored white South African tennis players in an exhibition at French Field House on the university campus. That winter like all Ohio winters was frigid, yet we bundled up with our leaflets and staked out the facility. We were even able to recruit non-AASFU members to help distribute the flyers to white and black attendees. To our amazement, some of the black attendees, as well as most of the white attendees, balled up the flyers and threw them back at us. Although disappointed, we pressed on. It is a moment that remains in my consciousness, 30 years later. Ashe subsequently changed his position on South Africa and supported the sports boycott.

Many U.S. companies stayed in South Africa, leading some analysts to say that the divestment, disinvestment, and boycott campaigns failed to achieve their goals. But even a casual look at these efforts refutes such argument. These campaigns had several objectives. The first was to make participation in the movement accessible and easy for individuals and organizations that might be reluctant to fully commit to the entire range of activities that were part of movement work. Support for disinvestment and divestment campaigns could be as simple as casting a shareholder vote or signing a petition.

A second objective was to expose U.S. state and corporate complicity with apartheid, which was hard to defend under any circumstances. Denying South Africa and the other outlaw regimes in the region safe corporate cover helped raise the consciousness of many beyond the activist community. This "public" strategy not only embarrassed corporations, it also helped garner additional exposure for the work of the movement.

Finally, these campaigns did eventually have economic repercussions, both directly on U.S. corporations and by building support for the demand that the U.S. Congress pass economic sanctions against South Africa. The movement has never claimed that

movement, most of the groups saw these strategies as means to more radical transformation.

The growth of divestment campaigns provided new opportunities for organizations and individuals to become involved in the anti-apartheid fight. At Ohio State University, from 1975 until I left in 1979, AASFU and *Our Choking Times* continually pressed the university administration to divest the institution's holdings in companies and funds that did business in South Africa. We encountered resistance that was as much cultural as political. In one confrontation with the administration over these and other issues, we were met by an assistant to the president of the university. As we explained to him our position on South Africa, he said that he had heard that no blacks inhabited the Cape of Good Hope when the Dutch arrived, therefore it had been open territory. We then asked him, if Africans or any

Tim Smith, right, testifies at the United Nations, November 4, 1976. From 1976 to 2000 Smith led the Interfaith Center on Corporate Responsibility, a faith-based coalition of institutional investors who were key players in the divestment movement. *UN Photo.*

Shareholder resolutions were widely used in the 1970s. For example, on January 27, 1973 the Church Project on U.S. Investments in Southern Africa filed resolutions with 11 companies. Groups involved in supporting this initiative included the American Baptist Churches, the National Council of Churches, the United Presbyterian Church in the USA, the United Methodist Church, the Episcopal Church, and the Unitarian Universalist Association.

As the push for divestment and disinvestment continued to grow, many activists were surprised to see the introduction of the Sullivan Principles in 1977. The brainchild of Rev. Leon Sullivan, a Baptist minister, the Sullivan Principles presented a dilemma for the anti-apartheid movement in the 1970s and early 1980s. Sullivan pitched the principles as an alternative to divestment and disinvestment that would offer corporate interests an opportunity to reject the mandates of apartheid in the operation of their business interests in South Africa.

In Sullivan's view, disinvestment and divestment would harm blacks in South Africa. A better strategy, he believed, would be to work through corporations that could, by their presence and size, bring about crucial societal changes. Numerous corporations rushed to sign the principles and then argued that because they were signatories they had rejected apartheid, so divestment and disinvestment campaigns were no longer relevant.

Many of us disagreed with Sullivan's reasoning, even though the principles garnered wide support in some liberal corners. We felt that the issue was not simply workplace conditions but the question of majority rule; once that was achieved, the nation could then select the policies that investing companies should follow. Sullivan himself later renounced the principles and declared that sanctions against

divestment or disinvestment strategies alone were effective, but it is clear that these actions functioned as part of a comprehensive strategy that hastened the end of colonialism and settler rule.

A 1970 ruling by the Securities and Exchange Commission that allowed shareholders to submit resolutions on specific social responsibility concerns opened the door to anti-apartheid activists, including elements within the National Council of Churches. The church council established the Corporate Information Center in 1971, which became the Interfaith Center on Corporate Responsibility (ICCR) in 1972. ICCR played a pivotal role, encouraging Protestant and Catholic churches and religious orders to challenge support for apartheid.

Investors introduced these concerns at shareholders' meetings through two main types of resolutions: fact-finding resolutions, which requested that the corporation disclose its operations in South Africa or create an investigative committee to examine the impact of its corporate activities on black South Africans, and calls for unconditional termination of all activities in South Africa (Culverson 1999, 87).

Joseph F. Jordan

South Africa would be the only way to force that nation to change its ways. Nevertheless, Sullivan's supporters still claim that the principles played a key role in the dismantling of apartheid.

## The Link between Organizing and Community Consciousness

Organizations like the Southern Africa Support Project in Washington, DC understood that popular education was important. Divestment campaigns and boycotts, as well as opportunities for direct-action protest, helped raise awareness of the connections between the U.S. economy and the colonial and apartheid machinery. This knowl-

Divestment demonstration, New York, 1977. The Committee to Oppose Bank Loans to South Africa was established by ACOA, AFSC, and Clergy and Laity Concerned. At this June 24 demonstration, a member of the Furriers Joint Council joined the march. His union would withdraw more than $11 million of pension and welfare funds from a bank making loans to South Africa. *Photo by David Vita.*

edge would become important in the 1980s when SASP and others coordinated the demonstrations at the South African embassy. They found a receptive audience among people whose consciousness had been raised during the campaigns of the 1970s. It was clear that education, especially at the local level, was a crucial part of organizing that could pay off, sometimes in unanticipated ways.

Cherri Waters, a former staffer at TransAfrica, emphasized the important role that local organizing groups played in building the movement:

> There were these little Africa focus groups all over the United States that nobody outside that city and that group knew anything about. Certainly, that was true in DC with SASP . . . And the divestment campaign also pulled together and recreated that. The other source of continuous interest would have come out of the churches. And it was the action at the level of the people in the pews that ultimately got the people in the hierarchies to pay

attention to these issues—not the other way around.

These were new voices, and while many of these individuals may have been somewhat unfamiliar with the political details of Southern Africa, a good number were already skilled in organizing work. Many of the black leaders of the movement were former members of SNCC or other civil rights organizations that had been active in the 1950s and 1960s. Still others had participated in revolutionary black nationalist, cultural nationalist, or other radical organizations that emerged with the call for Black Power in 1966. Their approach to the struggles in Southern Africa was greatly influenced by their experience with struggles in their own communities against racist oppression and segregation. The fit wasn't always perfect. The liberal push for reform in U.S. communities was not at all the same as the revolutionary struggle to overthrow governments in Africa. African liberation movements and their supporters often found Marxist analyses the best guide to understanding their realities. But for white and

More than 1,000 people participated in a May Day march in Boston, Massachusetts, to protest apartheid and U.S. involvement in South Africa on April 30, 1977. Organizers included Youth Against War and Fascism and the African National Congress. Sponsors included several state representatives and labor officials.
*Photo by Dick Wheaton.*

black liberals, Marxism was anathema. And many black radicals saw it as an alien philosophy that had little relevance to African realities or struggles. Still, a good number of organizations embraced the vision of a free, egalitarian, and socialist Africa that Marxism seemed to promise.

Despite the difference in context and in understandings, the role of the U.S. government in opposing liberation in Southern Africa made for common ground between the liberation movements and Americans questioning their own country's direction. This required building alliances that cut across divisions in the United States and reaching out to distinct sectors of U.S. society, including public office holders, church groups, advocacy organizations, and community-based groups. Special efforts were made to encourage solidarity with the black community as well. This close engagement encouraged the development of many activists who eventually became dedicated and effective workers for Southern African liberation.

## Emerging Activism in the Black Community

The decade of the 1970s saw the creation of an unprecedented number of new organizations in black communities that focused specifically on South Africa and Southern Africa. In addition, many black organizations that had never expressed a specific interest in Southern Africa work began to turn their attention to the crisis that was growing in the region.

Older, conservative, middle-class black organizations like the NAACP, the Urban League, and a number of national religious organizations also expressed support for liberation struggles in Africa. One of the vehicles for this expression was the American Negro Leadership Conference on Africa (ANLCA), which had been founded a decade earlier in 1962. Believing that pressure from the black community was needed to change U.S. policy toward Africa, the American Committee on Africa proposed creation of the organization to civil rights leaders, including Roy Wilkins of the NAACP, Whitney

Joseph F. Jordan

Young of the National Urban League, Martin Luther King Jr., labor and civil rights pioneer A. Philip Randolph, James Farmer of CORE, and Dorothy Height of the National Council of Negro Women. Ted Brown from the Brotherhood of Sleeping Car Porters became executive director. Under his leadership the ANLCA worked to establish an Africa program for each civil rights organization and to make an impact on U.S. policy toward Africa. The organization was active in the 1960s and early 1970s, laying a foundation for subsequent work.

During the first half of the 1970s, determination grew stronger within the black community to support South Africa's anti-apartheid struggle as well as the liberation struggle intensifying across Southern Africa. Groups such as the African American Solidarity Committee of Chicago, the African Liberation Support Committee, and the Harlem-based Blacks in Solidarity with South African Liberation were formed. Their radical agendas aimed not only at supporting Southern African movements but also at challenging U.S. foreign policy at many different levels.

The rhetoric and objectives of the liberation movements tended to push black organizations toward more radical analysis and actions than domestic struggle did. In order to be effective advocates, black Americans were obliged to commit to constant study that both informed and critiqued the practice they had followed in previous movement work. Even many of the most conservative black organizations came to understand that the movements in Namibia, Mozambique, Angola, Zimbabwe, South Africa, and Guinea-Bissau/Cape Verde were not struggling merely to achieve civil rights in their countries but were engaged in a fight for a nation.

With the rise of a new black consciousness in the United States, the traditional civil rights organizations faced a demand for a more pronounced commitment to the South African and Southern African support movements. They had seen their influence weakened by the radicalization of the black community, particularly among young people. Regaining their place as recognized opinion leaders was directly related to their ability to stake out a more progressive position on issues that were important to blacks. Because of this, support for African struggles became as much a strategic move for these organizations as it was an expression of their strongly felt convictions.

The Third World Women's Alliance rallied at the Federal Building in San Francisco in 1979 to protest U.S. complicity with the apartheid regime. Leading the chant, from left, are Michele Mouton, Letisha Wadsworth, and Attieno Davis.
*Photo courtesy of Nunu Kidane and Women of Color Resource Center.*

Activists focused on Southern Africa began to increase their work with the social justice groups that had emerged with the rise of black consciousness that followed Stokely Carmichael's call for Black Power in 1966. Much of the work of these groups was concerned neither with Southern civil rights nor with South Africa. Increasingly, though, they included support for Southern African liberation movements as part of their overall activism. Their important support is almost always overlooked when scholars assess the work of the black community in the period 1970–79. These organizations included the well-known Black Panther Party for Self-Defense; the African Heritage Studies Association, a group formed by dissident black members of the African Studies Association; the African American Scholars Council; the Coalition of Black Trade Unionists; *Black Scholar* magazine; and the Black World Foundation. Other organizations that became prominent during the decade were the Congress of Afrikan People, whose founding convention in Atlanta on September 6–9, 1970, drew 3,500 people, and the National Black Political Assembly, established in October 1972 after 10,000 delegates had attended the National Black Political Convention on March 10–12, 1972, in Gary, Indiana.

The launching of the Congressional Black Caucus (CBC) meanwhile heralded the rise of black legislative power. Formed in 1969, the CBC was made up of black congressional representatives who immediately began to take an active interest in Southern African issues. The caucus came to prominence in 1971 when it presented a list of 60 recommendations on various domestic and foreign policy issues to President Nixon. Detroit congressman Charles Diggs, one of the founders of the CBC and its first chairperson, also chaired the House Subcommittee on Africa from 1973 to 1978. From that position he consistently advocated independence for the former Portuguese colonies and for majority rule in the other Southern African states controlled by white minorities. He and his staff became key allies of anti-apartheid groups, as well as those concerned with Southern Africa in general. In 1976 Diggs and others pushed for the creation of a black American lobby for Africa and the Caribbean, leading to the birth of TransAfrica.

## African Liberation Day and the ALSC

Perhaps the most dramatic example of black U.S. activism on Africa during this period was the campaign for and organization of African Liberation Day (ALD). This was one of the few instances in which a black campaign for African independence garnered mass support nationally.

In the summer of 1971, a group of black activists, influenced by a strong Pan-Africanist consciousness, traveled to Mozambique's liberated areas to spend time with Frelimo, the leading revolutionary force in that liberation struggle. They included Owusu Sadaukai, one of those who had founded Malcolm X Liberation University/African People's Liberation and Technical Institute in October 1969, originally in Durham, North Carolina. After returning home from Mozambique, Sadaukai convened a gathering in Greensboro that then launched African Liberation Day the following spring. Marches on May 27, 1972 under the ALD banner drew 60,000 demonstrators in cities across the

United States and in Canada and the Caribbean, with over 30,000 taking part in Washington, DC alone. The day is still vivid in the memory of Geri Augusto:

> That march went from what was Meridian Hill Park, next to a Howard University dormitory—and from thenceforth it became Malcolm X Park—on down to the Washington Monument. . . . It was a glorious and large occasion and for many radical black groups across the country, it put the whole question of African liberation square in the middle. At that time it wasn't just about anti-apartheid at all, it was about all of [the Southern African countries].

African Liberation Day rally in Washington, DC, 1972. *Photo © Jim Alexander.*

Energized by the success of the first ALD, the organizers launched the African Liberation Support Committee (ALSC) at a conference in Detroit in Sep-

Joseph F. Jordan

tember 1972. The organization held its first international steering committee meeting in South Carolina in June 1973. The following year, a second conference in Greensboro, North Carolina, was attended by 51 local committees from 27 states and six countries.

In those heady early days, ALD and the ALSC seemed to represent the greatest possibilities yet for a mass movement in the black community geared toward the liberation of South and Southern Africa. The May observances of ALD continued to grow: 1973 saw demonstrations in over 30 cities, drawing an estimated 100,000 participants. In New York, Manhattan borough president Percy Sutton proclaimed May as African Liberation Month. He named the intersection of 7th Avenue and 125th Street in Harlem "African Liberation Square." Also in 1973, ALD expanded to include the launch of the United African Appeal and a stronger call to boycott Portuguese products and Gulf Oil, whose operation in Angola was fueling the Portuguese military (*New York Times*, May 20, 1973, GN54).

May 1974 saw another pivotal event in the struggle to build a mass constituency for the liberation movements in the black community. The ALSC sponsored a conference at Howard University, "Which Way Forward in Building the Pan African United Front?" The event attracted over 700 attendees and was followed the next day by an ALD march with over 10,000 participants.

The conference was significant not only for the sizable attendance but also because of the intense debate among the participants. These discussions reflected disagreements within the movement as a whole that would lead to the splintering of the ALSC and the ALD movement several years later. They focused in part on the struggle between the various ideologies and political tendencies that had emerged in the ranks of black activists, related especially to the struggle underway in Angola but also to Africa advocacy work more broadly. Some of the debate was constructive, helping to challenge ahistorical views of Africa and movement support for authoritarian regimes such as Uganda's Idi Amin. But the

African Liberation Day rally in Washington, DC, 1977. *Photo by Stan Sierakowski.*

arguments often became violently divisive. One consequence was that by the mid-1970s various political and ideological conflicts disrupted meetings of erstwhile allies and found their way into the pages of publications like *Black Scholar* and *Black World*.

In the summer of 1974, soon after the Howard University conference, the Sixth Pan-African Congress—"Six PAC"—was held in Tanzania. It was the largest of the Pan-African congresses ever held, and the first since 1945. Yet the unresolved rifts within the ALSC that had erupted at the Howard conference carried over to Six PAC. There were other differences too, such as whether movements opposed to existing governments in the Caribbean and Africa would be officially welcomed at the event. This created political tension with the host country, Tanzania, and with other participating African governments, limiting the effectiveness of the gathering. Despite these disappointments, the experience was invaluable for the U.S. participants as an introduction to the real world of Africa's struggles, and many black activists mark their participation in Six PAC as the turning point for their activism on South and Southern Africa. Many returned to the United States and took leading roles in the growing anti-apartheid and broader solidarity movement.

Despite a strong and experienced organizational and leadership structure, the ALSC saw its national influence waning by 1975. By 1977 ALD too had become a victim of factionalism, with ALD marches being held under the auspices of two separate groups who vied for the support of the black community. *Washington Post* staff writers Cynthia Gorney and Juan Williams openly derided the ALD march and its participants in the newspaper. Although the story was riddled with inaccuracies, its publication signaled that the influence of the ALSC had diminished considerably (*Washington Post*, May 29, 1977, D1).

Beyond fundamental ideological conflicts, an array of other factors, including class and regional differences, affected the ALSC and the black activist movement as a whole. These disagreements were not limited to the black community, however. Similar debates raged within many groups in the wider movement throughout the 1980s and into the 1990s.

While the ALSC's influence was declining, that of TransAfrica was on the rise. Launched on May 20, 1978, TransAfrica was officially a product of a 1976 Congressional Black Caucus Conference, but it really existed because of the efforts of Congressman Diggs and his House Africa Subcommittee. It was intended to be an effective domestic lobby on Africa issues for the black community. Upon its launch it released a position paper that, among other demands, called on the United States to cease treating African nations as "pawns in a game of geopolitical roulette between the major powers." The paper also addressed Southern Africa economic cooperation, the Horn of Africa, and U.S. relations with the Caribbean. TransAfrica soon became the preeminent organization that was articulating a common position for black Americans on U.S. foreign policy toward Africa and the African diaspora. TransAfrica also became a prominent voice outside the black community as it entered into strategic partnerships and coalitions with other groups and forged strong relationships with the most progressive of the Southern African liberation organizations.

TransAfrica's first director, Randall Robinson, who had first gained prominence in the early 1970s, would also become a central figure in the anti-apartheid and Southern Africa support movements in the 1980s. The birth of TransAfrica along with the demise of the ALSC ushered in a new phase of the movement in the black community.

Many activists formerly associated with the ALSC and the Six PAC movement went on to found or join other organizations. Their previous work served as important preparation for the challenges of the next two decades. SASP found that the study/work collective model of organization was a successful way to build a strong local movement with national and international connections. This model allowed groups to build on their strengths and minimize some of the weaknesses of the movement in the 1970s, including its inability to resolve some of the deep ideological and philosophical differences within its ranks. These realizations proved to be of great importance to the development of the more broadly based anti-apartheid and Southern Africa advocacy movement that emerged in the next decade.

*Oral sources for chapter 4 include interviews with Geri Augusto (2005), Frank Beeman (2003), Sylvia Hill (2003, 2004), George Houser (2004), Robert Van Lierop (2004), and Cherri Waters (2003).*

Joseph F. Jordan

# Remembering Nyerere ✑

## Charles Cobb Jr.

Toward the end of the 1960s, many of us who had been involved in the Southern civil rights movement were looking for ideas. New ideas seemed scarce in America just at the moment we needed them most. The political establishment here—integrating rapidly—was saying, enough of this talk of poor people taking control of their own destiny, making decisions about their lives. Instead, they said, "learn to think like us and act right and we'll make a place for you."

I wish I had time to talk about the rejection of the Mississippi Freedom Democratic Party in 1964, or the way the federal government injected itself into Mississippi in the late 1960s.

We were thinking "black," I say unapologetically and without elaboration, and Africa seemed to be the direction to point ourselves toward to find the ideas we needed—just Africa. Down there, struggling on Mississippi back roads and plantations, we knew very little about the continent. For some of us, Kwame Nkrumah was the president of all of Africa. There were words that meant Africa to us: Lumumba. Mau Mau. Sharpeville. Freedom fighters. Liberation struggle. Fanon. We didn't know very much, in truth.

*Ujamaa* and *uhuru*—those two words meant Africa to us also. It was Julius Nyerere's Tanzania that reached out to my generation, demanding that we think about this Africa that Africans were trying to fashion. Although necessarily there were ideas and processes specific to Tanzania underway in that then-new East African nation, the Africanness reached through to us. Something larger seemed to surround local Tanzanian efforts. *Kujitegemea*, or self-reliance, was a term that reached many of us via President Nyerere's important writings on education for self-reliance. The concept seemed bigger than Tanzania, and relevant to my neighborhood too. Ujamaa seemed to be more than a Swahili phrase defining rural cooperative efforts in Tanzania.

And think about it. These two terms, ujamaa and self-reliance, are now part of our political lexicon. They are still ideas we can work with—Tanzania's contribution to our idea of struggle.

And no, I am not going to get into the question of who "our" refers to. Or who "we" are. I do not know that President Nyerere thought of himself as a Pan-Africanist. But he certainly saw himself as an African contributing to, if I may use an old phrase that I still like, "the redemption and vindication of the race."

Tanzania's streets and roads housed much political opinion: Southern African liberation movements, opponents of neocolonial African regimes, and, yes, political refugees from Afro-America. And there certainly is a

Julius Nyerere, often called Mwalimu or Teacher, led Tanganyika to independence. He retired as president of the Republic of Tanzania in 1985 and died on October 14, 1999. Charles Cobb Jr., one of the editors of this book, spoke at a memorial gathering for Nyerere in Boston, Massachusetts, on November 21, 1999.

straight line connecting today's liberated nations of Southern Africa and President Nyerere's commitment to their liberation. And, if I may speak personally, there are few conversations in Africa I consider more important than those that many of us held with Tanzanians. They were patient with what surely must have seemed a strange and confused lot of distant cousins from America who washed up on their shores. Benjamin Mkapa, the current president of Tanzania, then a newspaper editor, was one of those Tanzanians. We owe Mwalimu Nyerere some thanks for opening instead of locking the doors to his house, and I am here to publicly acknowledge the debt.

It was in Tanzania, a crossroads of Africa and Africans, that a lot of us learned that political struggle was necessarily about more than color. And that political struggle was about more than being against something. The essential discussion in Tanzania centered on how human resources could be mobilized and organized. For me, anyway, it was the first time seeing what it meant for a state, a government, and a nation to commit to all of its people.

And let me say quickly that judging Tanzania now in terms of its successes and failures in this regard is less important than applauding Tanzania, the Tanzania of Nyerere's vision, for its commitment. For Africans in America like myself, the value of seeing an African effort like this was sustaining. And the final chapter on the effort has not yet been written.

Bill Sutherland, right, meets with President Julius Nyerere, left, and the deputy foreign minister of Tanzania, Dar es Salaam, 1977. *Photo by Harry Amana. Courtesy of American Friends Service Committee.*

Remembering Nyerere

# Charles Diggs and Goler Butcher ⁊
# *Taking the Lead on Africa in the U.S. Congress*

**William Minter**

embers of Congress are under constant pressure to pay attention to issues close to home. This is particularly true of those in the House of Representatives, who are elected by specific districts within their states. Focusing on foreign policy rarely brings political rewards or campaign contributions. But Africa became a central focus for the Congressional Black Caucus, which grew from five House members and a lone Senator in 1968 to 23 House members and no Senator two decades later. This happened largely because of the direction set by the CBC's founder, Charles Diggs Jr., with strong reinforcement from his younger colleague from California, Ronald Dellums. The tradition of strong, competent staff for the House Africa Subcommittee, which continued through the 1980s under Diggs's Michigan colleague Howard Wolpe, was launched with the early leadership of Goler Butcher.

Elected to Congress for a first term beginning in 1955, Diggs came from a prominent Detroit African American family. His father had established a leading mortuary business and had been one of the black pioneers in state Democratic Party politics. When the younger Diggs came to Congress, he was one of only three African American members, and he was conscious of the obligation to stand up for black people everywhere, not just in Detroit. His grandfather, a Baptist pastor in Mississippi in a county next to the one where Emmett Till was killed, had been a missionary in Liberia for a year in the early 1880s.

Diggs gained national attention from his presence at the Till trial in 1955, and he continued to take a leading role on national civil rights issues as he gained seniority. In 1969 he took the initiative to create the Congressional Black Caucus. He took on the chairmanship of the congressional subcommittee that oversees the District of Columbia in 1972, and he played a key role in bringing local elected government to that black-majority city that still lacks its own voting representation in Congress. Diggs also became the first black congressman to visit Africa when he was chosen to join the U.S. official delegation to Ghana's independence in 1957. He returned to Africa on his own to attend the All-African People's Conference in Accra in 1958. In 1959 he became the first black to serve on the House Foreign Affairs Committee. He joined the Subcommittee on Africa immediately and became its chair 12 years later, in 1971.

At just this time, the incoming Nixon administration was replacing official indifference toward white minority rule in Southern Africa with a more decisive tilt in favor of the white regimes. In 1971, as a member of the U.S. delegation to the U.N. General Assembly—part of a tradition of bipartisan representation—Diggs decided it was time to make a decisive stand against U.S. policy. On December 17 he held a press conference at the

In the 1970s and 1980s, the Congressional Black Caucus and the Subcommittee on Africa of the House Foreign Affairs Committee were the two key government institutions in Washington keeping a consistent focus on African liberation. Without the efforts of a handful of individuals, however, this probably would not have happened. Talk to anyone familiar with the congressional scene on Africa during these years, and you will hear two names again and again: Representative Charles Diggs Jr. of Detroit and his first staff counsel for Africa, Goler Teal Butcher.

Sources for this profile include a biography of Diggs by Carolyn DuBose (1998) and an article about Butcher by J. Clay Smith Jr. (2000).

United Nations. He denounced the recently signed Azores agreement with Portugal as "a partnership in the subjugation of the African people" and announced his resignation. Administration officials, including then U.N. ambassador George H. W. Bush, were outraged.

In the 1970s Diggs traveled repeatedly to the continent. He organized committee hearings on a wide range of African issues, forcing administration officials to present their views and providing a forum for critics. The foundation for this work was laid between 1971 and 1974 by Goler Butcher, who had already won a reputation as a leader in international legal issues. Graduating from the Howard University School of Law in 1957—the sole female graduate—she joined the legal staff of the Department of State in 1963, the first black person to serve in that unit. At the Africa Subcommittee, she was key to ensuring that questions addressed to administration witnesses and criticisms of administration policy were solidly based on detailed data.

Butcher left the subcommittee staff in 1974, but she continued her involvement with African issues and her ties with congressional allies. In 1975 she was one of the lawyers challenging a Civil Aeronautics Board ruling that allowed a South African Airlines flight to New York. During the Carter administration she served as assistant administrator for Africa in the U.S. Agency for International Development, and she then became professor at the Howard Law School, where she stayed until her death in 1993. She continued to provide advice on Africa to members of Congress and to groups such as the Lawyers' Committee for Civil Rights Under Law. In 1989 she served as an election monitor in Namibia.

Diggs was forced to resign from Congress in 1980 after being convicted of fraudulent financial mismanagement of his office budget. Many were convinced that the conviction was unjust and that white colleagues guilty of similar

Congressman Charles Diggs of Detroit and his associate, Goler Butcher, as he resigns from the U.S. delegation to the United Nations in 1971 to protest Nixon administration support for South Africa and Portuguese colonialism. *Photo courtesy of South African Research and Archival Project, Howard University.*

Charles Diggs and Goler Butcher

abuses would not have suffered a similar penalty. In the 1980s he withdrew from political involvement. But he never lost the respect of his colleagues or of Africa activists, who paid tribute to his work at his death in 1998.

Diggs and Butcher are significant not just for their individual commitment and contributions, but for illustrating the complex ways in which Africa solidarity moved into the mainstream as the anti-apartheid movement grew. They were among a much larger cohort of African American politicians and professionals who gained entry, if only marginal, into the corridors of Washington power in the wake of the 1960s civil rights movement. Diggs and Butcher paved the way, in the words of Sylvia Hill (2004), for "young black activist types, . . . internationalists in some sense, whether they defined it as Pan Africanist or anti-imperialist, . . . [people who were not] careerist in the traditional sense of the word." This group may have been a minority, even among their African American peers in Washington. But they retained bonds of mutual trust with the activist groups. The continuous interchange between activists and Congress over two decades was one of the keys to the capacity of the anti-apartheid cause to make an impact.

# Durham, Durban, and AllAfrica ✍ Reed Kramer and Tami Hultman

## Reed Kramer

Tami and I had gone to Africa in late 1969 on the Frontier Internship program sponsored by the United Church of Christ (UCC), United Methodist, and Presbyterian churches. We were assigned to assist the Methodist Church of South Africa in launching a racially integrated youth leadership training program. Called "Give a Year of Your Life," it brought two dozen young people together in Durban for three months of intensive training, followed by nine months as youth leaders in their congregations. We weren't trained for the challenge of helping young South Africans—some older than we were—negotiate their first relationships across racial lines as equal partners. But there was lots of good will, as well as tears and agony. So the courses became a learning laboratory that prefigured the post-apartheid era in many ways.

Steve Biko, then a medical student, was one of the first people we met in Durban. He was kind enough to speak at the leadership course, where his charisma made an enormous impression. He and other founding activists of SASO, the South African Students Organization, drew us into their circle and gave us extraordinary insights into the emerging political culture of black consciousness. Most of them went on to become deeply engaged in their communities. For example, a woman student, Vuye Mashalaba, who was on the initial SASO executive committee, became a beloved doctor in one of the roughest townships outside Durban.

Tami and I had access to a minivan provided by the churches, and we would often load up a group of students and drive up the coast, north of Durban, where you could get beyond the apartheid signs and go to the beach. We were also privileged to be there at the time of an explosion of black cultural projects. The Theatre Council of Natal, founded in 1969, united African, Indian, and Coloured students across ethnic lines to produce workshops and drama and poetry events. We saw the first performance of Welcome Msomi's stirring play *Umabatha* in an outdoor amphitheater under a full moon. It's now a South African classic that has been performed all over the world.

Our other assignment, which was not public, was to document the role of U.S. companies in South Africa's economy, research we undertook on behalf of the Southern Africa Committee and the Interfaith Center on Corporate Responsibility. While in South Africa we spent three months at a time in Durban and then three months on the road, gathering data on dozens of the largest U.S. companies. In Port Elizabeth, for example, we visited all the auto assembly plants, interviewing everybody from managing directors to shop floor workers.

The data and photographs we collected were used by organizers of the first shareholder resolution against General Motors in 1971. After our

AllAfrica.com is the largest free-access source of African news on the World Wide Web. By 2007 it was posting some 1,000 stories daily from African newspapers and other sources. The predecessor to allAfrica.com, AfricaNewsOnline, was one of the first public Web sites. But few allAfrica.com readers are likely to know that its origins can be traced back to the 1970s, to Durban, South Africa and Durham, North Carolina.

Reed Kramer, the CEO of AllAfrica Global Media, and Dr. Tamela (Tami) Hultman have guided these news services through more than 30 years. Kramer reflected on these experiences in a 2005 interview with William Minter. This brief recollection is adapted from the interview and also draws on a 2003 article by Hultman.

return, the research formed the basis for a book, *Church Investments, Corporations and Southern Africa* (Corporate Information Center 1972). Our photos were used and reused in the divestment movement. I remember one ubiquitous photo of a General Motors police van carrying black prisoners. We were chased a few times while taking pictures of police or military facilities, but we always managed to get away.

It was an irony that when we were expelled from South Africa, in March 1971, it had nothing to do with our research. The government at that point hadn't realized the sensitivity of economic information. Our visas were revoked, along with those of other foreigners working with denominations belonging to the World Council of Churches, after the council gave humanitarian grants to Southern African liberation movements such as Mandela's ANC.

For six months after being expelled we visited groups working on Southern African issues in several African countries, discovering how little information was available and how hungry people were for it. In Nairobi we worked with the Africa region of the World Student Christian Federation. From José Chipenda, one of its regional secretaries, we got our first real training in photography, a skill we've made the most of ever since. In Lusaka we worked with a Zambian organization and discussed with the top leadership of the ANC what we had learned in South Africa, particularly about American companies, but also about the rise of the Black Consciousness Movement. In Dar es Salaam we began our journalism career, writing for the Tanzanian daily paper edited by Frene Ginwala, an exile who became speaker of the South African parliament after apartheid. We were in the fortunate position of knowing both the activists arising inside South Africa and a network of outside contacts who wanted to support them.

After two years investigating the role of U.S. companies in South Africa and a year in New York writing up our research, we returned to Durham, North Carolina, in 1972, initially working as a local branch of the New York–based Southern Africa Committee. The concept of a news agency focusing on Africa stemmed from frustration with the lack of news and information. Africa News Service was born through a small grant from the UCC Commission for Racial Justice, directed by the Reverend Charles Cobb Sr. and sustained by his colleague, UCC Africa secretary Larry Henderson. It subsequently received other church and individual contributions, as well as foundation grants.

The initial target audience for Africa News Service was the American public. Tami had visited 13 African countries on a Presbyterian student seminar in 1966, before I met her, and remembers meeting a small boy, about 10, in a village on the lower slopes of Mount Kilimanjaro. He queried her group incessantly about civilian casualties in the war in Vietnam, U.S. support for apartheid, and whether the CIA had been involved in the assassination of Kennedy and the overthrow of Nkrumah in Ghana. The contrast between his knowledge of the outside world and most Americans' lack of familiarity with Africa made an indelible impression. But in 1973 we could see that many people in the United States were eager to know more about Africa, if given a chance.

We based ourselves in Durham because that's where we had gone to university and first became involved with community issues. In 1968, after the assassination of Martin Luther King, I had helped organize a demonstration that began with a march to the Duke University president's house. All 300 of us were invited in and we spent two nights. The protest ended with 1,500 people—a significant percentage of the student body—staging a four-day silent vigil on the Duke quadrangle. Supported by many of the faculty, we stayed until the trustees agreed both to raise wages for nonacademic employees and to negotiate with the mostly black employees union. There were also continuing black student movement protests, and Tami and I had been lucky enough to have roommates who were leaders of that group. So when we went to South Africa, we'd had a bit more exposure to the racial issues in our own society than was the case for many white Americans our age.

We began Africa News Service by mailing out news scripts for radio stations to read on the air. In those days, news from Africa could be several days old and still seem fresh! Black radio networks, a commercial all-news network, and college stations were among the subscribers, along with public stations. We also began reporting for National Public Radio in its early years. As interest in Africa grew, stations wanted the news faster. In response, we converted a closet in the old house we were renting—it had large walk-in closets—into a recording studio. Somewhere we got a castoff reel-to-reel recorder and began taping our own reports, which we fed to stations over a telephone line.

We gathered news by phone, often getting a more accurate story than reporters on the scene. One dramatic example was the 1976 Soweto uprising, when journalists were barred from the township. We called friends and contacts and recorded eyewitness accounts. In one call I particularly remember, a woman explained that the news stories about random destruction were wrong. "I can see the smoke from the pass office," she said. "It's where they keep the records that control our lives, and that's why it was torched." Protestors knowingly targeted places they regarded as instruments of oppression, but most coverage portrayed them as marauding mobs.

We also monitored shortwave radio broadcasts. With an array of antennas in the backyard and on the roof, we could pull in stations from Africa and Europe, along with the Africa services of the BBC and the Voice of America. The bloodless Portuguese revolution of April 25, 1974, which ended the dictatorship, was played out on Radio Portugal. We recorded the music and the announcements and used them in a radio show. We could listen to Radio South Africa and many other broadcasts in French and English. In addition, we inherited a bank of teletype machines that could decode radio signal transmissions and spit them out as wire copy. That was another cost-efficient way of getting news out of Africa.

At the time, major media basically worked one way. If you had a correspondent somewhere, you got a story. If you didn't, and you wanted a story, you'd pick up a wire story, if there was one; if there wasn't, the story probably wasn't newsworthy anyway. That was the thinking.

Over the years, the constituency for Africa grew incrementally, but significantly and visibly. Most dramatic was the growth of the anti-apartheid movement. When we started *Africa News* there was an active anti-apartheid movement, and we were very much aware of it and knew many of the people. All over the country, there was hard work going on, but it was completely below the radar of media coverage and invisible to most Americans. It managed to have episodic impact when it organized actions such as sit-ins at the South African embassy in Washington. But slowly the movement grew on campuses. It grew in the black community. It grew among churches and synagogues. It grew with involvement of the Congressional Black Caucus. And eventually the media responded.

Our use of technologies to gather news grew out of necessity. We wanted the news, and a growing number of people across the country wanted the news. We didn't have the budgets to fly in and out of places or to hire lots of correspondents, so we figured out a way. The telephone was a good, affordable, low-tech tool, though there were times the line got cut because we couldn't pay the bill. We were also early adopters of fax machines, which had the advantage of allowing us to avoid South African censors, who routinely intercepted our telephone conversations.

The Africa News Service staff in Durham in 1985. Back row, from left: Jim Lee, Katherine Somerville, Debbie Jackson-Rickettes, Lise Uyanik, Pat Ford, Barbara Neely, Reed Kramer. Front row, from left: Mills Crossland, Charles Cobb Jr., Tami Hultman, Susan Anderson, William Minter, Charlie Ebel, Seth Kitange. *Photo courtesy of AllAfrica Global Media.*

Around 1976, we started producing for broadcast through direct telephone feeds rather than printed news scripts. We immediately heard from our nonmedia subscribers—church agencies, libraries, government offices, anti-apartheid groups—who said, "Wait, we still want this news." That's when we started a print publication, which became a biweekly newspaper. We continued to produce, edit, and consult for radio and television. We still report occasionally for public radio or appear on CNN and other networks.

The newspaper continued until 1993, when issues of sustainability forced us to move more aggressively to become an online service. We had begun electronic publishing in late 1983 on the NewsNet bulletin board, almost a decade before the emergence of the World Wide Web, and in 1991 on LexisNexis. Around 1993 we were approached by the newly formed America Online (AOL) and had extensive discussions. They wanted us to create a closed channel for them, but in the end we thought it better to be on the open Internet. So we launched a Web site instead.

We began early on and continue to this day to work with African journalists, some very brave and dedicated people among them. They were always ready to work with us. These days it's common to hear reporters interviewing other reporters who are in some place of breaking news, but it wasn't a widely used technique at the time. The relationships we developed with African media professionals were an early form of what we do now in a more formal way, by working with 125 African news organizations at allAfrica.com. Through those ties, users of our Web site have easy access to news gathered by African journalists across the continent. Large information wholesalers also distribute the daily news feeds we provide, reaching an even larger global audience. The resulting revenues from advertising and from royalties are split between AllAfrica and the participating publishers. We hope it will continue to grow and become sustainable.

Throughout these years we have drawn on our early African experiences and on the skills we learned from and with our African colleagues. AllAfrica, which has pioneered several aspects of information technologies and won international prizes, was founded with mostly African funding and with prominent African media professionals as executives. It is built on the legacy of people from the United States traveling to Africa and learning from the people they came to know in the cauldron that was the struggle against apartheid.

# "The Angolan Question" ✍ Walter Rodney Speaks at Howard University, 1976

## Walter Rodney

I would like to come to the situation in the U.S. and to look at the types of responses, and to look at what I consider to be some fairly horrendous mistakes which were made by certain forces in this country in their approach to the Angolan question.

Again I will dismiss at least one element. We can dismiss those who are attempting to hire black mercenaries for the FNLA and Unita. When this individual [Roy Innis, who took over the Congress of Racial Equality in 1968] purports to be organizing black mercenaries to go and fight in Africa, and then we know that mercenaries cost, whether they are black or white—and we know that this particular black functionary cannot afford to pay anybody—we know that these black mercenaries would have been paid by imperialism, to go and fight in Angola.

But I think we can dismiss that as an aberrant phenomenon—as the expression of a particularly reactionary and unresponsive force within the black American political environment. So we should really concentrate attention on those elements that are serious. With serious people, one engages in serious debate. And I think there were a large number of serious people throughout the Afro-American community [who supported Unita] when they should have been lending uncompromising support to the MPLA at that particular historical juncture.

It was immediately obvious that there was a startling coincidence—a startling convergence—between the positions of certain individuals who call themselves progressive, revolutionaries, and who in fact regarded themselves as the essence of revolution—yet their positions converged with that of U. S. imperialism. And this amazing historical convergence needs to be understood.

I assume that there are elements within the audience who took that position, and I'm not going to engage in any abuse of those elements. I am simply going to say I believe the position was historically completely incorrect. I will indicate how I believe that error took place

The first thing is Unita gained a certain popularity in this country in the very late sixties and the early seventies, particularly in the period of the rise of the African liberation movement, and the like. I was following the process, so I know that they were becoming more exposed and more popular in this country. And that they used certain very opportunist political tactics and techniques. They simply appealed to the growing black consciousness by saying, "Inside of Angola we stand for the elevation of the black man to a position of dignity and rule, and the MPLA stands for the elevation of whites and mulattoes over the indigenous African people." That was the standard line in the late sixties and early seventies.

Walter Rodney, best known as the author of *How Europe Underdeveloped Africa* (1972), was a highly respected revolutionary scholar and activist from Guyana who taught at the University of Dar es Salaam from 1968 to 1974. This excerpt is from "The Lessons of Angola," a speech that Rodney delivered at Howard University on April 22, 1976, just a month after South African troops had withdrawn from Angola after their first unsuccessful invasion.

In their war for independence, which began in 1961, Angolans were divided. The National Front for the Liberation of Angola (FNLA), based among Kikongo-speaking people in the north, had ties to Mobutu Sese Seko of Zaire and to the CIA. The Popular Movement for the Liberation of Angola (MPLA) had a national appeal, with its strongest base among Kimbundu-speaking people in the Luanda area. It was closely allied with Frelimo in Mozambique and the PAIGC in Guinea-Bissau, and it had support from the Soviet Union, as well as from most solidarity groups in Western countries. Jonas Savimbi's Unita claimed leadership of Umbundu-speaking Angolans but secretly collaborated with the Portuguese military during the last years before independence.

Portuguese control began to crumble in 1974, and rivalry between the three groups led to war the next year. U.S., Zairian, and South African military intervention in favor of the FNLA and Unita was countered by Cuban forces and Soviet supplies aiding the MPLA. After Angola's independence in 1975, the victorious MPLA soon gained international

*continued on next page*

recognition, except from the United States and South Africa. The U.S. Congress barred further U.S. military involvement in Angola, and the South African troops also withdrew. But the wars that followed, with a series of South African invasions as well as internal conflict, continued until 2002, with Unita being backed by the CIA and apartheid South Africa until the mid-1990s.

It was the war in 1975–76, however, that most provoked division among liberation supporters outside Angola, particularly in the United States. Rodney's commentary explains the issues.

And they would then say, "Look at the MPLA. It has so-and-so, who is in its executive, who is a white, who is a Portuguese. It has so many mulattoes who are on the Central Committee, it has so-and-so who is married to a white woman, President Neto, so on and so forth."

And in the context of the U.S., I think that those are very telling points. In the context of the black struggle in this country, when brothers and sisters were going through that terrible period of self-identification, trying to extract themselves out of the dominant white culture, I think that those points made a great deal of impact.

Particularly because the MPLA was not really seeking to influence the Afro-American population. Or much of the American population.

So that is one reason why the Unita gained in popularity. And when we examine that very carefully, we must of course admit that to declare blackness is a very easy thing to do. I mean the same character who was mobilizing black mercenaries was also in the forefront of declaring his blackness—and he would call himself Garveyite, and so on and so forth.

To declare for blackness is one of the easier things to do. Once one— uh—recognizes the opportunities inherent in that situation [*laughter*].

But surely we need to go further than that. We need to examine, firstly, whether the reality in Angola was the reality as portrayed by Unita. We need to go further and ask whether the historical experience of Angola could be so easily assimilated into the historical experience of black people in the U. S. that Afro-Americans should run to make a judgment on Angola on the basis of some knowledge they had that so-and-so was married to a white. Or that so-and-so was a mulatto.

Because the central understanding that we must reach is that any situation must be examined on its own historical merits. What is called "race" in the U. S is not the same thing as [what] might be called race in Angola. In fact, in this country, those who are all called black, or used to be called Negro—if they went to Angola, they would be distinguished, many, as mulattoes. If we want to understand Angola and the complex of the relationships between social strata and race, etc., we must then understand Angola. We cannot sit in Washington or in Detroit and imagine what we are seeing around the block is Angolan society.

And this seems to me to be one of the mistakes which the brothers made when they tried to transform a very simplistic understanding of black-white relationships in the judgment of whether they would support the MPLA or support Unita.

One is reminded here of some of the things which Fanon wrote in regard to Africa, when he was talking about the pitfalls of national consciousness. He was talking about the pitfalls of African national consciousness. Now we can apply that to the pitfalls of black national consciousness. Which is to say that national consciousness is clearly a liberating force, but at a certain point it can provide blinkers. It can turn into blinkers and constitute a barrier for further understanding of the real world.

The second and more widespread factor, and one that ultimately proved to be most decisive [for many black progressives], was the notion that Unita was a Maoist movement. And these left forces who [opposed the MPLA] were moving from the starting point of supporting Marxism-Leninism, Mao Tse-Tung thought.

In their own words, they have a vision and an analysis of contemporary society wherein they identify as the principal contradiction that between the two superpowers. They argue further that the more dangerous force is Soviet socialist imperialism, because it's more covert, it's more subtle, and because it ultimately can be more powerful, since capitalist imperialism is on the wane. And therefore, in a situation in which the Soviets are involved, one has to take a stand on the opposite side.

Now, what is my disagreement with that position? I shall not go into all my disagreements, because I do not want any sort of global confrontation. I am not in favor of trying to resolve all the problems of the world at the same time, in a single stroke. So that I'm not going to attempt to deal with that postulation about the principal contradiction and its implication.

What we are going to ask is how does that relate to Angola with its specific characteristics. If someone holds that belief as a sincere revolutionary tenet, when that person approaches Angola, how is it that such a belief ends by placing such forces on the side of those who have for 500 years oppressed the African people?

What explanation does such a person give to the Angolans who have been engaged since 1960 in armed struggle against the Portuguese, against NATO, who, at the end of that struggle found they were faced with the South Africans and with an escalation of U.S. support to the so-called liberation movement which had been harassing the genuine freedom fighters for many years?

So that from a dialectical perspective and a scientific perspective we struggle and work to discover the correct line. It is only from a theological perspective that one *knows* the correct line because of revealed truth. And it seems to me that the limitations of that position were very clearly revealed in the Angolan situation. I have not seen a single analysis from forces claiming that they had the "correct" line, which meant opposing the Soviets—not a single analysis of what was going on *inside* of Angola. It was purely external. And I do not believe we can proceed on that basis.

Walter Rodney speaks at Yale University, 1972.
*Photo © Jim Alexander.*

# Robert Van Lierop ∽
# *A Luta Continua*

## Robert Van Lierop

My father was born in Suriname, and his father was Dutch. My grandfather had actually been in South Africa and had participated in the Boer War. My father had been to South Africa, subsequently, as a merchant seaman. Didn't like it. And he told me about it, about what was wrong with South Africa. He always told me a lot about other parts of the world and always talked about colonialism. He hated colonialism, and he had a lot of firsthand experience with colonialism.

After working as a chauffeur and truck driver my father went into the dry cleaning business in Queens, and made a really successful go with that. I didn't want to take over my father's dry cleaning business when he retired, and he eventually sold it. Interestingly enough, he sold it for less money than he could have got. He had two buyers, one white and one black, and he sold it to the black person for less money because he felt that it was important to keep a business opportunity for black entrepreneurs.

I was very much influenced by Malcolm X. I didn't know Malcolm, but I was very influenced by his journeys to Africa and what he saw and wrote about and spoke about. I became determined to go to Africa after law school.

Having met Eduardo Mondlane and coming under his sway, one didn't easily walk away. He was a very captivating and larger-than-life personality. When Sharfudine Khan came to stay [to represent Frelimo at the United Nations in 1968], I was one of the people that Eduardo told him to contact. The three of us would sometimes talk about what could be done to increase people's knowledge and awareness of Frelimo. The idea of a complete media treatment came up—articles, photos, even a film documenting the struggle.

I was not a film director, and I had no previous experience or knowledge about film. My initial assignment was to find somebody to do it. I asked quite a few people I knew who were filmmakers. None of them seemed to have time to take it on.

I had been involved in the area of private offerings for theatrical ventures at the law firm where I worked, and I used that approach to raise money for the film. I actually met Carol Ferry because she was a client of the firm, and Peter Weiss did a lot of work with partners of the firm. And so Carol put money in the project, and Peter and Cora Weiss did; they were the two biggest sources of funds. The churches also put some money into the film, primarily the United Methodist Church, the Episcopal Church, and the United Presbyterian Church in the USA.

Bob Van Lierop doesn't know how many copies of his film *A Luta Continua* (The Struggle Continues) were made, or how many times it was shown. But there is no doubt that for many in North America and Europe, the short film provided the definitive visual imagery that made the African liberation struggles come alive in the 1970s.

*A Luta Continua*, portraying Mozambican guerrillas fighting against Portuguese colonialism, was filmed in 1971 in the liberated areas of Mozambique, across the border from Tanzania. A sequel, *O Povo Organizado* (The Organized People) was filmed shortly after Mozambique's independence in 1975 and released in 1976.

The two films had a profound impact on black independent cinema in the United States in this period, yet their producer, Van Lierop, was not a filmmaker by training. He was a progressive African American lawyer based in New York, who launched the project in solidarity with Frelimo, opting to make the first film himself when he was unable to find a filmmaker willing to take on the task. He recruited his friend Bob Fletcher, who had been a photographer for SNCC, and credits him with most of the technical work on the film.

In the 1960s, Van Lierop's political activities had included opposition to the Vietnam War and support work in New York for SNCC. SNCC later helped put him into contact with Eduardo Mondlane of Frelimo, who encouraged the film project and whose signature slogan, *A luta continua*, provided the title. Carol Ferry and Peter and Cora Weiss were all friends of Mondlane from the early 1960s, and they were among the key financial backers of the film.

I met Bob Fletcher, who had never made a film before either, but he had been a photographer with SNCC in the South, and he had a lot of experience doing that. And Bob agreed to go.

The film was distributed by a lot of the African support committees, and also by the Southern African Committee and former Africa Research Group people, groups in Chicago. All of those people helped get the film out, as well as colleges and universities. I knew a lot of people in Europe also, and met even more—the Angola Comité in the Netherlands and groups in London and the Scandinavian countries. They helped get the film out there. The film was smuggled into South Africa and shown in Soweto before the uprising. The title of the film, *A Luta Continua*, began to appear scrawled on Soweto walls.

Most people would have said that I was too loose with it, because I didn't keep much control over distribution. I just basically let people who were willing to go out with it, use it. And I asked that the money that was raised be sent to Frelimo.

I left law and was working as a waiter down at the Village Vanguard [a club in Greenwich Village] at night, so that I'd be free in the daytime to do this work without a salary. Everything that we brought in from the film went back to the project. I just lived on the tips that I made as a waiter. And some people who knew that I had been a lawyer already said, You did this when you were in law school! What are you doing? You're a lawyer now, why are you waiting on tables? But it just seemed like the right thing to do. I wanted to do this, and this was the only way that I could support myself without taking money from the project.

Technically, we were not able to do what we had planned on doing because some of our equipment was lost crossing the river into Mozambique. We didn't have a sync camera, so we had to use a 16-millimeter spring-wound Bolex camera. That means, number one, very short takes, and number two, the sound could not be synced to the picture. So we had to do that in the editing process. Richard Skinner was the editor of the first film, and Richard had experience making television commercials, so he was very good at editing with quick cuts.

It's very gratifying, because I think that everyone would like to feel in life that he or she has contributed to something meaningful. I never was able to keep records of how many copies were made and where it was shown and all of that. But I definitely feel good, because I think that we did contribute to something that was both good and important.

Between 1971 and 1978 Van Lierop gave up his law practice to dedicate himself entirely to the Mozambique film project and related activities of the Africa Information Service, an organization he co-founded in late 1972 with Prexy Nesbitt.

The release of *A Luta Continua* in 1972 came just as the armed liberation struggle against Portugal was reaching its height. In the first half of the 1970s, before the Soweto uprising of 1976 focused solidarity efforts on South Africa, the figure of Amilcar Cabral and that of Samora Machel of Mozambique featured prominently in the rising identification with Africa among American activists, African Americans in particular. The African Liberation Day coalition, described in Joseph Jordan's chapter on the 1970s, is in part the outgrowth of Van Lierop's visit to liberated Mozambique in 1971.

In a 2004 interview with William Minter, Van Lierop talked about his background and how he became involved in filming and distributing *A Luta Continua*.

Robert Van Lierop, right, presents a check to President Samora Machel of Mozambique at the United Nations in 1977. The funds, raised from Van Lierop's film showings across the country, went to build a health clinic in rural Niassa province. In the background, from left, are Valeriano Ferrão, James Garrett, and an unidentified man. *Photo reproduced from Van Lierop 1977.*

# From Kenya to North America &
## *One Woman's Journey*

## Njoki Kamau

It was during my early years in high school in Kenya that I was first exposed to the idea that far away in the Americas lived people who were black. I was greatly fascinated by this idea. Until then, history was just another mundane class that focused on Europeans colonizing Africa and large parts of the rest of the world. The materials covered in class included David Livingstone's three missionary journeys. No effort was made to bring to the student's awareness the fact that the caravans of the so-called "slaves" that Livingstone stumbled on in the interior of Africa were Africans like ourselves. Obviously this was part of the colonizer's overall strategy to keep us disconnected from not only other Africans in the continent, but also black people in the diaspora.

In September 1976, after finishing college, I came to the United States as a Fulbright student to pursue graduate studies in management. When I arrived at Southern Methodist University, I was excited to note that my roommate was a black woman. I felt a great sense of relief, especially because I had noticed that the campus was predominantly white. When I woke up the following day, I further noticed that everyone in the apartment and building was black. I soon learned that this was where SMU housed its few black undergraduate students. SMU was not willing to place me in its graduate housing because this was reserved for their white students only.

When I complained to the housing office and threatened to call the Kenyan embassy, I was moved to the "theology complex," where there were a few international students. After a while, I decided to move off campus, only to find that an apartment that had been promised to me was given to somebody else by the time I arrived to sign a lease. When I told an Asian graduate student from Kenya, he told me that these things happened often to people of color and were classic examples of racial discrimination in the United States.

I was too new to this society to fully understand and detect racism in all situations. I began to notice in class, however, that some professors would never call on me even when I had my hand raised. It was a rude awakening, that the color of my skin had become a most significant factor in defining who I was and, to some extent, in determining my ability to fulfill my potential as a human being. Needless to say, I felt both anger and fear simultaneously. From then on, I began to live with the unsettling feeling that I lived in a society where, because of my skin color, I would be required to prove myself at every turn—in the classroom, in the workplace, indeed everywhere.

[During the time I lived in the all-black housing], black Americans in the complex, while somewhat intrigued to have me there, were not ready to embrace me yet. In a few instances, my roommate and other students in

Njoki Kamau is originally from Kenya. A women's rights activist, she is associate director of the Women's Center at Northwestern University near Chicago and has taught courses in women's studies at the university. From 1985 to 1990 she directed the YWCA Northshore (Chicago) Shelter for Battered Women, and she has been a leader in action against domestic violence.

Excerpted from "From Kenya to North America: One Woman's Journey," in "African [Diaspora] Studies," edited by Lisa Brock, special issue, *Issue: A Journal of Opinion* 24, no. 2 (1996). Reprinted by permission of the African Studies Association.

the complex would hold parties right on the doorstep of our building, and I would not be invited. In the Kikuyu culture that I come from this would have been considered unthinkable. In fact, when I tried to make friends with some of the black students on campus, I was not very successful. It slowly began to dawn on me that even though we shared the same skin color, our cultures were vastly different, and we had little information about each other's way of life. I came to the conclusion that I was not invited to the party because I was different; I was African and not black American.

Unfortunately for myself and my two fellow African students, our feelings of rejection and exclusion left us vulnerable to an internalization of the dominant culture's stereotypes of black Americans. We began to believe some of the things that we heard from whites who did strike up friendships with us. But as I grappled with the idea of giving up any hope of ever developing a meaningful connection with black Americans, it hit me that African Americans were probably also vulnerable to stereotypes about us. They had grown up on racist tales of the dark continent, and thought themselves better than Africans or at least too different from Africans to know them. I therefore decided to keep an open mind and to embark on a long journey of educating myself about black Americans as my way to bridge the impasse. I hoped that this process could open a gateway through which one day I would build strong connections with this people, whose capacity to survive continues to fill me with awe.

As if my life as a graduate student was not already complicated enough and my needs and desires to find my feet difficult enough, I could hardly believe that I had become a victim of domestic violence while at Northwestern University [where I went for a PhD in 1978]. The perpetuator was a Kenyan man whom I viewed as my "brother," Kikuyu like myself. When the police came, time and time again, they tried to encourage me to file a complaint. I could not find it in my heart to throw not only a foreign African but now a "black" brother into the throes of a colonial-like white criminal justice system. What if I was accused by the few Africans and African Americans on campus of betraying our already oppressed race? Was I not supposed to put my being African/black (race) before my being a woman (gender)? What if both communities ostracized me?

This experience became the turning point in my life. It completely shattered my former beliefs: one, that higher education could cushion me from being victimized by racism, and two, that self-identifying as an African or black could protect me from gender-based violence. I set out on a second mission to become a women's rights advocate. The question that continues to perplex me is, "When a black woman is victimized by violence, in a racist society, where should she go for help without seeming to betray the race?"

Thus my effort to become informed about African Americans has been joined with my discovery of what it means to be a woman. By connecting with a black community I have discovered a resilience, creativity, and brilliance, and a spirit that will not give up, no matter how overwhelming the odds. This has left me with a sense of deep respect and admiration for all African Americans as a people, but especially black women.

What I have learned is that there is overwhelming evidence that if one is born nonwhite in this society, and especially if one is born black, one receives the message from birth that one is somehow inferior. The misinformation campaign by the larger society is directed at all black people who live in the United States throughout their entire lives and is part of the overall strategy to keep racism in place both in the diaspora and in Africa. It is especially disturbing to note that our direct interactions with each other occur through the prism of this erroneous information. Our deep internalization of this misinformation about ourselves renders our efforts to come together very difficult. The good news is that we have begun to understand what has happened to us, and to make concrete efforts to dismantle our internalized oppression.

I have also sought to learn from all women, rich and poor, white, black, Latino, Asian, and Native American who simply want to be treated humanely. Working with women, and on women's issues, has shown me the uneasy ways in which gender, class, and race intersect and the contradictions they produce in all communities. For instance, while most black men can deeply understand racism, only a few are able to confront their own sexism. Similarly, while most white feminists experience great outrage at sexual harassment in the workplace, few show real empathy toward victims of racism.

Over the last decade, therefore, I have devoted my time to advocating for women and blacks and learning about race, class, and gender. In fact, my journey to learn brought me into an active involvement in the community on racial, gender, and cultural issues and to teaching a course on race and gender at Northwestern University. Through this involvement, I have developed deep and meaningful relationships with black Americans, which has shown me that skin color is one thing but situating oneself within the socio-political context and culture of a people is most important. I also once served as the director of the very domestic violence center that I had called for help.

When I left my home village in Kenya 19 years ago to pursue a higher education, there was nothing in my background as a young woman that could have adequately prepared me for what awaited me on this side of the Atlantic. I am fully aware that without the support of my community of black and women friends that I would never have successfully overcome the obstacles that lay in my path. I have learned the importance of belonging to a community. For us Africans who are far from home, I cannot over-emphasize how important it is to belong to and identify with a community of your choice. The community that I have chosen is the descendants of those Africans who were brought here 400 years ago. Even with its paradoxes, it has seemed to me the most right and intelligent thing to do.

# From Campus to Statehouse ∾ *East Lansing Connections*

## William Minter

T he Southern Africa Liberation Committee (SALC) was founded by campus minister Warren (Bud) Day and political science doctoral candidate Carol Thompson in 1972. Never large, it was made up of faculty and students at MSU, with a sprinkling of others from the local community. Day and Thompson moved away from Michigan in 1976 to continue their academic and activist work on Africa over the next decades in Los Angeles, Tanzania, Zimbabwe, and Flagstaff, Arizona. But the group they had started found both continuity and a solid link to national organizations through the involvement of activists at MSU's African Studies Center.

From the start these included anthropologist Bill Derman, who had already been involved with divestment campaigns in Toronto. In 1977 he was joined by African Studies Center director David Wiley and outreach coordinator Marylee Crofts, who moved from the corresponding positions at the University of Wisconsin in Madison. In the early 1960s Wiley and Crofts had worked with the interracial Student Christian Movement in then-Rhodesia, and in covert support for the then-emerging Zimbabwean nationalist groups. They were eventually declared prohibited immigrants by the white minority regime.

Michigan had other assets for mobilization on Africa. Detroit's strong African American congressional delegation, headed by veterans Charles Diggs and John Conyers, made the state a natural base for anti-apartheid action. Former governor Mennen Williams, a liberal Democrat, had headed the Africa desk at the State Department under President Kennedy, although his policy initiatives then received little support from more conservative administration officials. Elsewhere in the state, at the University of Michigan in Ann Arbor and many smaller institutions, African students and Americans who had worked in Africa were well represented. And in 1979, Howard Wolpe, a professor in African studies at Kalamazoo College, was elected to Congress to represent the district to the west of Lansing. He would later head the House Africa Subcommittee and play a key role in the adoption of sanctions against South Africa.

Within this mix, East Lansing's SALC played a key catalytic and communications role. And critical to the success of the group, its members concur, were Frank and Patricia Beeman. The Beemans, who grew up in Michigan and worked there all their lives, never visited Africa during the years they were active with SALC, though Frank Beeman was finally able to visit South Africa in 2001. He was the tennis coach and director of intramural sports at MSU from 1947 until his retirement in 1987. As director of intramural sports, he successfully spearheaded a national effort to block South African teams from intramural sports at U.S. universities. Patricia

Michigan State University (MSU) in East Lansing housed both the largest African studies program in the country and a host of specialized study centers in agriculture and other development issues. There the anti-apartheid divestment movement found fertile ground. The university's location adjoining the state capital made it ideal for the move from campus to local to state action.

David Wiley has directed the MSU African Studies Center since 1977. William Minter spoke with him and edited this brief account of the Southern Africa Liberation Committee (SALC), which led anti-apartheid efforts at MSU.

Beeman was inducted into the Michigan Women's Hall of Fame in 1999 for her anti-apartheid work in Michigan. Their initial connection to Africa was through Patricia's brother Rick Houghton, who had been an Episcopal missionary in Namibia and was expelled by the South African authorities.

Patricia and Frank Beeman were the ones who always showed up with a literature table, posters, and films on South African apartheid and other liberation struggles in Southern Africa. Their message, repeated in dozens of demonstrations and meetings and hundreds of private conversations, was not a political or ideological argument but a moral one: apartheid was wrong, and therefore any collaboration with the apartheid regime was also wrong. Claiming no status as experts but speaking as members of the community, they had credibility that came from their persistence and their integrity.

SALC's efforts first paid off in the passage of the East Lansing Selective Purchasing Resolution in 1977, which prohibited the city of East Lansing from using suppliers that were operating in South Africa. In 1978 SALC successfully campaigned for MSU to divest its stock from companies with subsidiaries in South Africa, making it one of the earliest major universities to take such action.

That same year, SALC member David Wiley met with Representatives Lynn Jondahl of East Lansing, Virgil Smith of Detroit, and Perry Bullard of Ann Arbor and developed a decade-long plan to seek state of Michigan sanctions on South Africa. They supported a Michigan state legislature resolution calling for national sanctions against South Africa, and then a series of three sanctions bills for the state of Michigan.

These acts prohibited the state from depositing its funds in banks making loans in South Africa (1979); prohibited state university and college investments in firms operating in South Africa (1982); and divested the $4 billion state employees' pension fund of any companies operating in South Africa (1988). And at MSU in 1986, SALC won their demand that the MSU Foundation divest its holdings of stocks of companies operating in South Africa.

## Frank Beeman

I came as a freshman in 1939 and graduated from Michigan State and went in the service. I came back and started as an intramural director and tennis coach in 1947. And we got involved in civil rights. We got involved with a program called STEP, Student Teacher Education Program. A group of students, in fact from Michigan State, met and went down to Rust College in Holly Springs, Mississippi. That started because Bob Green [former dean of urban affairs at MSU, who had worked with Martin Luther King] had been down through there and had been involved in voter rights.

The James Meredith march occurred in 1966 and we joined that march at Tuskegee and marched all the way to Jackson. As we turned the corner in the neighborhood, we saw the Capitol and the Capitol was ringed by soldiers in at-ease position with their shotguns. And so we marched up to the Capitol and Bob Green and other people spoke. It was quite an adventure.

Back in East Lansing, we were involved in a number of demonstrations. At that time East Lansing had a housing covenant, and they wouldn't allow any Native American or nonwhite people to move in. So our daughter and 46 other students sat in front of the police station and blocked the traffic in East Lansing.

And it just seemed to be a natural shift from civil rights to apartheid. It came about partially because of Pat's brother, who was an Episcopal priest who went to Africa and taught in Africa. He was in South Africa and in Namibia and kept us informed on how unjust things were. He gave us the straight scoop on what was happening there. So we got involved, figured that that wasn't right, that our country shouldn't be involved that way in supporting apartheid.

SALC was always a combination of students and faculty and community people. Any event that was on, the general rule was that if three people would show up then we would stay there and leaflet and hand out information. The idea behind SALC was that people would do what was right if they knew the truth, if they knew what was actually happening. And so most of this stuff that we put out was informative and educational.

It was kind of interesting, because generally, jocks weren't so much involved in civil rights and things. So we

Frank Beeman, one of SALC's most consistent activists over the years, spoke with David Wiley and MSU Africana librarian Peter Limb in 2003.

March in East Lansing, Michigan, organized by the Southern Africa Liberation Committee based at Michigan State University. *Photo courtesy of Frank Beeman and Dave Wiley.*

kind of stood out. When I would say it as a coach, people would stop and think about it, and wonder about what was all this activity. . . . maybe there must be something to this if Beeman is saying it.

SALC generally generated, at these weekly meetings that we had, probably six to 10 people really. But it became evident that with persistence, and constantly bringing this to the fore and getting the student newspaper to cover things, that the word was going out. One of the things we had was a shanty that we built out in front of the administration building, trying to get the MSU Foundation to divest. Students would come by and we had stickers that were cut out, with "No to Apartheid" and "Support Mandela."

We would have a representative at every meeting on the campus, whether it was the trustees or the faculty group and so forth. We would have a representative there to speak on the divestment proposal, so that it was constantly kept in front of their noses, actually. I can remember, in one of the trustee meetings, one of the trustees said, well, if we use the word slavery, they'd know what we were talking about. So it was constantly in front of them.

We had prepared a green book folder with a lot of information on apartheid and divestment, it must have been 20 pages. We went in early and put one at each of their places. And so they thought that that was part of the official documents that they were supposed to talk about that day.

At our literature tables very rarely was there anybody that really argued about this is wrong or this is right. One South African from the Lansing area came by and said, well, this is propaganda that you're handing out. I said, well, it may be so but it's true whatever it is. That was what made the arguments easy—because it was true. It was so wrong to have enslaved a whole nation of people, how do you argue for it?

Chapter 5

# The 1980s:
# The Anti-Apartheid
# Convergence

## *David Goodman*

It was the fall of 1978, and South Africa was about the farthest thing from my mind. I was just entering college and knew little of this distant, tortured land. A chance encounter with an anti-apartheid activist changed all that. On a sunny September afternoon during freshman week at Harvard, I was walking up the steps of the Fogg Art Museum to participate, along with a thousand or so of my new classmates, in the quaint ritual of having tea with the college president, Derek Bok. As I approached the front door, a graduate student named Joe Schwartz pressed a leaflet into my hand.

"Why don't you ask President Bok why Harvard supports apartheid?" he challenged me. He explained that Harvard had millions of dollars invested in companies doing business in South Africa. I figured there must be some explanation for this, but I was sufficiently cheeky to venture inside and go directly over to the university president. He was cradling a teacup, surrounded by a clutch of awestruck freshman. Was it true, I asked Bok, that Harvard was profiting from apartheid? The students fell silent. Bok pursed into a tight smile. He replied coolly, speaking of the importance of remaining "engaged," maintaining "dialogue," and bringing pressure on South Africa from the inside.

I was unimpressed, and frankly disgusted by his explanation. Two years after the police attack on protesting students in Soweto, the white regime that I

read about appeared to be utterly unmoved by polite pressure and the occasional diplomatic scolding. The simple reality was that the college president could not bring himself to part with such profitable investments. My anti-apartheid activism began that day.

Although I didn't know it at the time, my chance encounter was being repeated on sidewalks, in living rooms, and in workplaces all across the United States. Schoolteachers, longshoremen, investment managers, legislators, and retirees were learning of the ways that they were unwittingly supporting a racist state on the southern tip of Africa. And they were figuring out that they had the power, right in their own communities, to make a difference.

These realizations did not come about by chance. The explosion of activism in the 1980s in support of Southern African liberation was the culmination of decades of efforts, reflecting lessons learned from countless past successes and failures. The singular achievement of U.S. activism in the 1980s was the transformation of disparate African solidarity movements into a focused, multiheaded, and surprisingly successful anti-apartheid movement.

My own engagement reflected how the movement had spun off numerous local— even neighborhood—initiatives.

**David Goodman**
*Photo courtesy of David Goodman.*

As a college activist, I joined efforts to force Harvard to divest itself of the approximately $1 billion that it held in companies doing business with South Africa. I worked with Harvard's Southern Africa Solidarity Committee, helping organize demonstrations, teach-ins, debates, and fasts, and constructing a South African–style shantytown in Harvard Yard.

In 1983 I was involved in launching the Endowment for Divestiture, an alternative donation channel for Harvard alumni who wanted to pressure the university by contributing to an escrow fund that would only be turned over to Harvard after it divested from South Africa. Following college, I was active in several Boston-based anti-apartheid groups, and I participated in demonstrations aimed at stopping the sale of Krugerrands. I was mostly just a foot soldier in these efforts, one of thousands around the country engaged in the seemingly quixotic challenge of smashing the pillars that supported apartheid.

My involvement in the divestment movement led me to want to see for myself what the apartheid of my protest chants was about. Themba Vilakazi, a friend who was a longtime member of the African National Congress, told me, "You should go to South Africa if you can get in. But," he added, "when you come back, you will have a responsibility to tell people about it." In 1984, as a budding freelance journalist, I journeyed to Zimbabwe and South Africa. I chronicled what I found there for a variety of U.S. and British publications and ultimately wrote a book about that and subsequent visits, *Fault Lines: Journeys into the New South Africa* (Goodman 2002).

In this chapter, I tell the story of U.S. activism in the 1980s by focusing on representative examples of anti-apartheid activism in three key arenas: local, national, and international. At the

Anti-apartheid demonstrators fill the streets of New York City, August 13, 1985. ACOA joined with a coalition of labor, religious, and community groups led by Cleveland Robinson, secretary-treasurer of United Auto Workers District 65, to organize the event. *Photo by David Vita.*

David Goodman

local level, I take as a case study the organizing that happened in Massachusetts, which led to passage of the nation's first statewide divestment initiative in 1983. Former Massachusetts state representative Mel King and Massachusetts Institute of Technology professor Willard Johnson were at the center of these struggles. The national picture is represented here by Jennifer Davis and Dumisani Kumalo, both of the American Committee on Africa, and by the work of the Free South Africa Movement launched in Washington, DC by Randall Robinson. Finally, Ted Lockwood, who spent the 1970s as director of the Washington Office on Africa and the early 1980s as the international affairs representative for the American Friends Service Committee, fills in the international dimension of the solidarity effort.

## Global Outrage, Local Actions

South Africa may be an ocean away, but when I arrived to start college in Cambridge in 1978 it was a hotly debated local issue. Massachusetts, I quickly learned, was a key outpost of the U.S. anti-apartheid movement. The first university divestment and the first full divestment of a state pension plan took place there in the late 1970s and 1980s. Chapter 4 on the 1970s recounts the story of the Polaroid Corporation in Cambridge and how workers there made South Africa a local issue. It also relates the early organizing done by Randall Robinson while he was a Harvard Law School student and before he became executive director of the African American lobby TransAfrica.

In the late 1970s, students in Massachusetts took up the cause of South African divestment. The first school in the country to divest was Hampshire College in western Massachusetts in 1977. The Southern Africa Solidarity Committee at Harvard, of which I was a member, formed during this period. It brought members of African liberation groups to campus, held material aid drives for Zimbabwe, and sponsored concerts by Abdullah Ibrahim (Dollar Brand) and Bob Marley. Around the city, the Boston Coalition for the Liberation of Southern Africa (BCLSA) played a key role in building a larger divestment initiative. A key member of BCLSA was Themba Vilakazi, Boston representative of the ANC. In 1985 Vilakazi formed the Fund for a Free South

Africa (FREESA), which became the de facto leader of anti-apartheid work in the Boston area.

Two African American leaders played central roles in anti-apartheid efforts in Massachusetts. Mel King is a lifelong community activist in Boston. He headed up the Boston chapter of the Urban League in the late 1960s—described by a fellow activist as "the first Black Power Urban League chapter in the country"—until his election as a Massachusetts state representative in 1972.

Willard Johnson was a professor of political science at the Massachusetts Institute of Technology for over 30 years, until his retirement in 1996. The founder and head of the Boston chapter of TransAfrica and a member of the group's national board, he was a guiding force in numerous African solidarity efforts around Boston from the late 1960s onward, and he spearheaded Boston's Free South Africa Movement in the 1980s.

Massachusetts was among the first states to put issues of African liberation before state and local political bodies. In 1973–74, for example, state representative Mel King introduced a bill in the Massachusetts legislature aimed at preventing the port of Boston from handling Rhodesian chrome. This strategy was conceived during a visit to Boston by ANC president Oliver Tambo in late 1969 or early 1970. Tambo met activists at the home of Willard Johnson in suburban Newton. Among those in attendance was Mel King. Johnson recalls, "What Tambo was essentially pointing out was that there are ways to use legislative and governmental machinery at the local level on these foreign policy issues."

Mel King's focus on South Africa was a natural outgrowth of his racial justice work in Boston. He explains, "One's involvement in [anti-apartheid work] is based on one's understanding of the racial nature of this society. And so a situation like South Africa is just an extension of here. So if you're working on it here, you see the relevance of working on it anywhere it exists."

In the aftermath of the Soweto uprising, King held hearings to expose how Massachusetts investments were supporting South Africa. After a 1979 commission study revealed that the state had more money invested in companies doing business in South Africa than in companies doing business in

Massachusetts, King and a liberal white state senator, Jack Backman, filed a divestment bill. The legislation failed to pass, but King and Backman succeeded in winning a provision that barred the state from new purchases of stock in companies doing business in South Africa (Massie 1997, 539).

In 1980, King and Backman again pushed divestment legislation. Dumisani Kumalo from ACOA testified before the Massachusetts State Legislature, and the *Boston Globe* supported the bill. It failed again.

In February 1981, King and Backman sponsored a meeting of area groups, including the Catholic Archdiocese of Boston, the Massachusetts Council of Churches, the American Federation of State, County and Municipal Employees, BCLSA, and TransAfrica. The groups formed a coalition, Mass-Divest, to support legislation seeking total divestment from every bank and company doing business in South Africa. MassDivest members traveled around the state, speaking to people about the need to invest locally, not in apartheid South Africa. They created a popular bumper sticker that said "Make it in Massachusetts, not in South Africa." In late 1981 the bill passed the State Senate, but it failed a third time in the House.

In late 1982, the Massachusetts House and Senate both passed the divestment bill. It was then vetoed by conservative Democratic governor Edward King, who had just been defeated by Michael Dukakis. Mel King and Jack Backman fought off efforts to weaken the bill, and in a last-minute move before the legislature adjourned, they pulled off a dramatic veto override in both houses. "We whipped him soundly. It was the only veto of [Gov. King's] that was overturned," recalls King proudly.

Massachusetts thus became the first state to fully divest from South Africa. Within nine months, the state sold off $68 million of investments in companies doing business in South Africa (Massie 1997, 540). The action energized the national divestment movement, and other states followed suit.

Demonstrators at Boston's City Hall Plaza demand that Massachusetts pension fund monies be divested from companies doing business in South Africa, September 16, 1981. *Photo © Ellen Shub.*

David Goodman

King reflects on the strategy that finally resulted in victory:

> There had been some good organizing. There had been the union people who could tell their legislators, "That's our money." So I think it was a great coalition of forces that came together. . . . It's one of the things that you learn as a legislator, and that is that you get a good base of people who are constituents of a couple of the legislators who can go and tell them what they want. And you get enough of them, then you can make things happen.

Jennifer Davis, ACOA's executive director, noted that the experience in Massachusetts became a model for the country. For divestment legislation to succeed, she said, it was crucial to have both a black and a white legislator pushing the bill, as was the case with King and Backman.

Mel King continued his work with a historic run to be mayor of Boston in 1983. As one of scores of volunteers in his "Rainbow Coalition"—the forerunner to Jesse Jackson's same-named political operation—I was among many who drew inspiration from King's eloquence and the power of his message, linking the fights for social and racial justice abroad and at home. Many of the progressive unions and organizations that backed divestment supported Mel King's candidacy. But Boston was not then—and is still not—ready to elect an African American mayor. King finished a distant second to Ray Flynn. In 1986 King ran for U.S. Congress, finishing third in a race won by Representative Joseph Kennedy.

One of Mel King's greatest legacies was the progressive coalitions that he helped build. King was a patient, forceful, and visionary organizer. His moral authority derived from his experience fighting racism in Boston's schools and neighborhoods. When I asked him when his awareness of social justice issues began, King replied, "When I was born as a black child." When King took on apartheid, he made it clear that he was fighting the American version as well. It was a message that resonated strongly among everyone from whites in the solidarity movement to black community activists.

But the racial tensions that divided Boston were never far below the surface of the coalitions working to fight apartheid. A citywide coordinating group

that I was a part of, the Southern Africa Support Coalition of Massachusetts, foundered over racial divisions between our own members. At one point, our work against racism in South Africa ground to a halt as we turned our energy to confronting racism in our own relationships. We sought help from Joyce King, Mel's wife, who facilitated a painful, important dialogue about racism, both personal and political. The emotional conversation between the black and white members of our group in Boston reflected strains within the South African liberation movements, where there were long-standing tensions between proponents of Africanism and those advocating a nonracial approach.

Willard Johnson was determined to keep blacks and whites talking and working together when he established the Boston chapter of the Free South Africa Movement (FSAM). The FSAM had been launched on the day before Thanksgiving 1984 when Randall Robinson was arrested at the South African embassy in Washington, DC. Johnson recounts:

> I have to admit that I personally differed with Randall with regard to how the Free South Africa Movement ought to have been structured nationally. He wanted it to be very clear that this was black leadership, and the [Congressional] Black Caucus and the black elected officials were the heart of the power base. There was a certain sense that all of these other folks had been marching around the mulberry bush for a long time with no results. We could avoid that at the local level in a way, and we didn't have the same level of challenge that you would have had nationally. But we set up our steering committee for the movement here, for Free South Africa, in Boston deliberately to incorporate a variety of other groups.
>
> Now, they were all on the left. We didn't really go back and tap into the Catholic Church leadership, but we made sure that we had a number of very credible white folks involved in our steering committee. And it was a real steering committee and it made real decisions.

To activate the FSAM in Boston, Willard Johnson, Mel King, and others used the occasion of a visit by South African Anglican bishop Desmond

After a campaign to close the South African consulate in Boston, Willard Johnson displays a signed letter of resignation from the acting consul, December 4, 1984. With Johnson are Massachusetts state representative Mel King and Boston city councilor Bruce Bolling. *Photo © Ellen Shub.*

Tutu to announce that they would hold a demonstration outside the office of South Africa's honorary consul in Boston. When King, Johnson, and other demonstrators arrived for the protest, the consul agreed to meet with them. To their surprise, he met their demands and resigned on the spot.

Buoyed by this early victory, activists identified their next target: stopping the sale of Krugerrands at Deak-Perera, a national gold coin dealership. In late 1984, a delegation of four local leaders, including Johnson, met with Deak-Perera officials in Boston and demanded that they stop selling Krugerrands until apartheid was ended. A frantic conference call with company executives ensued, during which the company declined to comply. Johnson and his colleagues then refused to leave Deak-Perera's offices and were arrested. This kicked off the Krugerrand campaign in Boston, which Johnson wrongly assumed they would win quickly. The protests outside Deak-Perera, which spread to the company's offices in cities around the country, endured through a long winter.

In August 1985, with the threat of a national ban on sales, Deak-Perera finally announced that it was suspending the sale of Krugerrands. This local campaign had a direct impact on the apartheid government. Willard Johnson (1999) estimates that the

Boston campaign resulted in cutting Deak-Perera's Krugerrand sales in half; the national campaign is estimated to have cost South Africa $400 million in sales.

The combined effects of these attacks on the economic pillars of apartheid eventually became impossible for South Africa to ignore. According to Richard Knight, ACOA's longtime keeper of the numbers, "By the end of 1987 more than 200 U.S. companies had withdrawn from South Africa. Net capital movement out of South Africa was R9.2 billion in 1985, R6.1 billion in 1986, R3.1 billion in 1987 and R5.5 billion in 1988" (Knight 2004).

The FSAM in Boston disbanded in 1986 following the formation of the Boston-based Fund for a Free South Africa the year before. Divestment efforts continued with the passage of groundbreaking selective purchase legislation in Massachusetts and Boston. These laws prevented local government officials from purchasing products from companies that did business in South Africa.

In 1985, after nearly a decade of protests, and following the election of anti-apartheid candidates to its board of overseers (including, eventually, Bishop Tutu), Harvard University began a process of selective divestment. Over the next five years, Harvard sold off hundreds of millions of dollars of investments in companies that were doing business in South Africa.

Mel King and Willard Johnson insist that the local actions to bring pressure on the apartheid regime were part of a larger struggle. Johnson reflects, "The framework for us was African liberation in all of its dimensions, even liberation theology aspects of it within that framework. This is all a part of trying to organize for a free, powerful African world that was anchored on the continent itself, able to project dignity and power, but extending to all of the places where there were substantial communities of peoples of African descent."

## The Movement at Home: U.S. Anti-Apartheid Activism

In the 1980s, activists brought the issue of apartheid to the U.S. heartland. The American Committee on Africa and its tax-exempt educational affiliate, The Africa Fund, were now headed by two South African–born activists: the analytical and intense executive director, Jennifer Davis, and the ebullient and persuasive projects director, Dumisani Kumalo. They led the charge from the East Coast power centers into the 50 states. Their efforts were bolstered by the high-profile protests and arrests and lobbying efforts being organized by Randall Robinson and the Free South Africa Movement.

While Kumalo focused his work exclusively on South Africa, Davis, as George Houser's successor, provided what Kumalo calls the "intellectual

Dumisani Kumalo
*Photo © Rick Reinhard*

glue" for the organization, locating the divestment campaign in the larger context of solidarity work in Southern Africa. Kumalo, who became South Africa's ambassador to the United Nations in 1999, recounted the origins of the divestment strategy as we sat in his office in the South African Mission to the U.N. in New York.

Kumalo's own story is a classic South African reversal of fortune. A founder of the Union of Black

Journalists in South Africa who later worked for an oil company, he arrived in this country in 1977, just as South African police were closing in on him and his colleagues. His transformation from an activist who organized protests outside South Africa's New York mission to the country's ambassador is jarring, dramatic, and even humorous, a point made often by the quick-to-laugh diplomat.

Kumalo recounts the arc of activism that began in church basements and sidewalks of middle America and was eventually felt in the power centers of Washington and Pretoria. In the 1980s, he recalls, anti-apartheid activism "went local" with the state and local divestment and selective purchase campaign.

> The other campaign that even localized it more was the Campaign to Stop Banking Loans to South Africa. And Prexy Nesbitt and Gail [Hovey] and myself were involved in that. It made people ask themselves a simple question: The money I put in this bank, does it go for loans in South Africa? And of course we had these guys who could research, people like Beate Klein, and all those people who could do research into where these loans were invested. As a result there were demonstrations in places like Wyoming.

> In Wyoming, people would go picket the local bank about South Africa. First of all, picketing in Wyoming is like, what is this? What? South Africa? Where is that? But the people who are picketing are local neighbors. So it became local, the local radio station, local people. . . . It wasn't run by South Africans in the U.S. or the people outside doing it. It became a local campaign, a homegrown campaign. And all Africa Fund did was provide information.

Kumalo's organizing strategy was inspired by organizing successes in the labor movement, especially the J. P. Stevens campaign. This was an organizing drive launched in 1976 by the Amalgamated Clothing and Textile Workers Union (ACTWU) against textile giant J. P. Stevens. ACTWU organizer Ray Rogers devised a "corporate campaign," successfully targeting high-profile J. P. Stevens board members and isolating the company from its

Children protest in New York City, June 16, 1980. Rev. Herbert Daughtry of Brooklyn organized children to march across the Brooklyn Bridge to the Wall Street financial district, where they protested corporate investment in South Africa. Some 300 people took part in the demonstration commemorating the 1976 Soweto uprising. *Photo by Stan Sierakowski.*

financial backers. In 1980, J.P. Stevens settled with ACTWU, enabling 3,000 workers in 10 plants in the South to win collective bargaining rights (Corporate Campaign 2004).

In carrying out the bank campaigns, Kumalo notes, they drew on what they had learned from Ray Rogers and the other activists in the J. P. Stevens movement. He adds that the churches, along with Tim Smith and the Interfaith Center on Corporate Responsibility, also played key roles. In the 1980s, "all these things were coming together."

Drawing on the strength of other movements was critical to the success of the anti-apartheid movement. "I was responsible for putting together coalitions around the country," observes Kumalo. "Everywhere I went, the coalitions were made up of people who either had been trade union people who had done J. P. Stevens, people who were doing antiracism work in their own neighborhood, some people who were veterans of the antiwar movement.

So we had a very fertile ground, which made it very easy for us."

While Kumalo was able to tap into existing coalitions, his work remained delicate and complicated. In his travels around the country—he visited as many as 1,000 campuses and every single state—Kumalo encountered the entrenched racism of U.S. society. Trying to build a movement that was politically and racially diverse "was very, very difficult," he recalls. Again and again, Kumalo would visit cities where progressive whites and progressive blacks lived on opposite sides of town and did not work together. "I would insist, we are going to have a joint meeting. Because the issue of apartheid was the rich issue on the table. Then they eventually began to work. We really helped them forge coalitions."

The college campuses were especially divided. Most often, the white student groups would invite Kumalo because they had the money, and the black students would not be involved in the visit.

David Goodman

So I always insisted when I got to a college, I must go talk to the black college group. "Oh, they are not interested," I was told. I said, well, fine. They have a radio station—the colleges pacify black kids by giving them their radio station. I'd go there and they'd say, "Oh no, we don't do interviews." I'd say, "No, you have to do interviews." And then suddenly these kids come out in large numbers . . . But the American campuses are very segregated.

The anti-apartheid movement's finest hour was the passage by the U.S. Congress of the Comprehensive Anti-Apartheid Act of 1986 over the veto of President Ronald Reagan. The legislation imposed limited sanctions against South Africa. Kumalo explains the groundwork that led to this event:

The reason why we have the biggest success of this movement, reversing the Reagan veto on sanctions, was precisely because we had this grassroots. The South African government focused their lobbying efforts in Washington—I'm told this by current colleagues who were working against me then. But we lobbied on the ground. These senators and these congressmen were getting 10, 12 calls at the district office.

I remember Senator [Harry] Reid, who is now leader of the Democratic Party. He owes his election to us. He was at that time, I think, in Congress [running for] Senate. I know he's from Nevada, because there was a movement there led by an African American senator called Joe Neal. Senator Joe Neal was a very, very good politician in Nevada. And these guys generated calls from these rural Nevada towns to Senator Reid. And Senator Reid became the one to join in the vote overriding President Reagan.

So we knew in The Africa Fund by lunchtime that we would reverse the veto, even though the vote was in the afternoon. We knew, because we were counting on all these people. And these people are calling us from wherever they are. State representative Joseph Mitchell up in Alabama, and we had those Alabama senators that nobody said we could get. Because they were getting calls from their local voters

"Shantytown" erected on the Michigan State University campus by the Southern Africa Liberation Committee. Similar displays were built on campuses throughout the country. *Photo courtesy of Frank Beeman and David Wiley.*

and their local people saying "sanctions matter." And those people, we cultivated them easily because our movement was seen as an integral part of these movements of the time that were about justice, anticapitalism, antiwar.

[Reagan's effort to undermine sanctions came] at the wrong time for him because by that time we had done the work. We had had five, six years of really preparing the ground. So we had people in every corner in every neighborhood who were willing to rise and say this is not the way it should be done.

As ACOA/Africa Fund pursued its organizing efforts, TransAfrica, under Randall Robinson, was also looking for ways to bring the issue of apartheid to the heartland. Cecelie Counts-Blakey, legislative liaison and an assistant to Robinson in the 1980s, was an active member of the local Southern Africa Support Project in Washington. In a retrospective published in the Oakland, California–based journal *CrossRoads* a decade later, she reflected that the anti-apartheid movement

needed to do something to take it beyond the traditional solidarity networks that were its main constituency; we had to find a way to galvanize "mainstream America" and shift the parameters of the policy debate. If this could not be accomplished, anti-apartheid activists were in danger of losing the gains we had made in the economic battle against South Africa at the

Randall Robinson
*Photo © Rick Reinhard.*

local and state levels in the early 1980s.
(Counts-Blakey 1995, 11)

The Free South Africa Movement was launched in 1984 on the day before Thanksgiving with the arrest at the South African embassy of Randall Robinson, DC Congressman Walter Fauntroy, and civil rights activist Mary Frances Berry. Within a week, protests sprang up at corporations and consulates in over 20 cities. Over the course of the following year, more than 4,500 people were arrested nationwide. Getting arrested at FSAM demonstrations became a rite of passage for public figures and celebrities who wanted street credibility with progressives; scheduling these high-profile actions became a logistical headache—albeit a welcome one—for FSAM activists.

The FSAM was spectacularly successful at launching the issue of apartheid onto the front pages and energizing a grassroots base. But the meteoric rise and headline-grabbing nature of FSAM accentuated rifts within the anti-apartheid movement. Counts-Blakey reflected on this in her *CrossRoads* article:

There were many layers of tension between TransAfrica, the Free South Africa Movement, and other members of the anti-apartheid movement. FSAM, though successful in some respects, exacerbated existing tensions between TransAfrica, a relatively new Black foreign policy lobby, and the older, hardworking, solidarity organizations (American Committee on Africa, Washington Office on Africa, American Friends Service Committee). Randall Robinson, executive director of TransAfrica, led what ostensibly was an African American foreign policy lobby. But the organization was treated by the media as an anti-apartheid organization, while Robinson was depicted as the representative of the anti-apartheid movement. TransAfrica's Board of Directors expected him to devote more time to development of the organization's overall capacity, while anti-apartheid activists felt that TransAfrica should devote more of its resources to nurturing and sustaining the Free South Africa Movement.

Some activists were upset because FSAM was led by African Americans, not a multiracial coalition of traditional anti-apartheid organizational leaders. Other activists felt dispossessed as FSAM attracted new grassroots support and celebrity involvement far beyond the traditional network of long-term activists. So, even though FSAM's policy of moderation resulted in a major movement victory, many anti-apartheid activists were ambivalent, if not hostile towards it.

It may well be that FSAM, as time passes, will become a model for mobilizing public opinion and [not for how] to build lasting coalitions. It is also quite possible that FSAM was a victim of its own success and meteoric rise. FSAM represented the greatest triumph for the U.S. anti-apartheid movement but also revealed its deepest problems. In one sense it was the realization of all of the work done in the previous 30 years and could not have been successful without that groundwork. But its promise as the vehicle for bringing disparate elements of the [anti-apartheid movement] into a more coherent and con-

David Goodman

tinuous effective force was never realized. (Counts-Blakey 1995, 14)

Jennifer Davis says that "keeping some sort of coalition together" became a challenge as the anti-apartheid movement achieved success. "It was really tough keeping TransAfrica within the organizing group so that everybody would push more or less together. [Robinson] didn't do a lot of organizing, but he was a great speaker. I do think that one of the things that ACOA did was to enable that coalition to sort of keep together."

Kumalo adds,

> The drama was the Free South Africa Movement and the people getting arrested, the big names . . . The weakness of it is that it was very celebrity-oriented. But the fact that it was celebrity-oriented, it gave even more momentum to the people at grassroots level. When TransAfrica, for instance, and Randall Robinson and these guys would do things in Washington, for some African American leaders it was very important. But don't forget people like Rev. Dr. Wyatt Tee Walker of the Canaan Baptist Church who were organizing the African American churches around the country.

As the anti-apartheid movement scored victories, the South African government parried. It cultivated several African American leaders to defend South Africa's actions within America's black communities. South Africa's supporters in Congress succeeded in repealing the Clark Amendment in 1985; the repeal allowed millions of dollars in aid to flow to Jonas Savimbi, the South African–backed rebel leader waging a bloody insurgency against the government of Angola. As a TransAfrica staff person noted, "We were negotiating down to the last semi-colon on the sanctions bill [of 1986] while the policy context had shifted to a regional strategy" (Hill 1995).

Davis reflects,

> The things that were important were the ability to connect people here to what was happening in South Africa. Something happened in South Africa and people here responded. But they could respond in a directed and effective way because patterns had been established and analysis had been

done. So if you got angry and you wanted to do something, well, go and make sure that your pension fund doesn't invest in South Africa.

Kumalo offers this advice to today's activists:

> You need an action message. You need to say to people, "If you do this, it has an impact on this."
>
> You need to pick one issue. You can't be a movement that addresses everything under the sun. And through that issue, articulate concerns that are universal. The human rights of the people who are dying of HIV/AIDS, the poor—these are all common things. But you need one issue

Rev. Larry Gilley, who worked for the United Church of Christ in South Africa and in Mozambique, joins a 1985 demonstration in Washington against South Africa's war on Angola and Mozambique. *Photo © Rick Reinhard.*

that you can zero in on and say this is one thing that we should do.

For Americans, who have a very poor attention span, you need a very simplified message. And if you have information, give it in slow doses.

## American Activist in the Frontline States

When I first began my travels to Southern Africa in 1984, I headed to recently liberated Zimbabwe. With my partner (now wife) Sue M. Minter, I arrived in the quiet high-country capital of Harare with just three contact names. These were the people to whom American activists entrusted our political education, and our safety. One of those contacts was Edgar (Ted) Lockwood, who headed the Southern Africa International Affairs office of the American Friends Service Committee.

Lockwood, then 64 years old, was a bear of a man. He had a gentle but firm manner, a mix of minister and streetwise activist. In a country and region riven by political and racial tensions, where South African spies and assassins were at work, Lockwood accomplished the considerable feat of earning the respect and trust of a diverse range of political antagonists. In this suspicion-filled environment I found him a generous guide, opening doors for us to opponents of the white regime both outside and inside South Africa's borders.

Lockwood came to Southern Africa by a circuitous route and with an impressive résumé. The offspring of a Republican family and a former lieutenant commander in the U.S. Navy, Lockwood became a lawyer in the 1950s, only to quit after making partner in a law firm. He then went to seminary to become an Episcopal minister. In 1962 he took the helm of a church in Woods Hole, Massachusetts.

Lockwood traces his real awakening to issues of racism and social justice to a trip he took to Alabama in 1965. He and 90 others were responding to a call from Martin Luther King to join civil rights activists on a march from Selma to Montgomery. During the march, he recounts, "I asked somebody on the street where could I get a drink of water, and he pointed to the sewer, and said, 'You can get it down there.' I

From left: Father Michael Schultheis, S. J., Edgar (Ted) Lockwood, and Warren (Bud) Day in Harare, Zimbabwe, 1985. Schultheis was a solidarity activist based in Tanzania. Day was Oxfam America's regional director for Southern Africa, based in Harare from 1985 to 1986. Lockwood, based in Harare as the Southern Africa international affairs representative of the AFSC, was responsible for relating to the member countries of the Southern African Development Coordination Conference (SADCC). SADCC was set up by the nine majority-ruled countries of Southern Africa (Angola, Botswana, Lesotho, Malawi, Mozambique, Swaziland, Tanzania, Zambia, Zimbabwe) with the aim of reducing economic dependence on apartheid South Africa. *Photo courtesy of Carol Thompson.*

really saw face to face the raw nature of racism, and that spurred me on."

Lockwood's involvement in fair housing issues and his interest in progressive economic change—he describes himself as a "democratic socialist"—led him to move to Washington, DC in 1967. It was there that someone at the Institute for Policy Studies, a progressive think tank, asked him how his church made decisions about its investments. Lockwood had no idea. He decided to look into the matter.

Lockwood's inquiry quickly led to action. "What we did was to challenge the Episcopal Church on the issue of lending money to South Africa through banks with which they did business." Among the banks that the church invested in were Guaranty Trust Company, Chemical Bank, Chase Manhattan Bank, and Citibank, which were all part of a consortium that was making loans to South Africa. Lockwood's research revealed that the church had unwittingly "taken part in a consortium loan to the South African government of something like $40 million."

In May 1969, Lockwood, along with Bill Johnston of Episcopal Churchmen for South Africa, helped organize a protest and teach-in about South

Africa in the lobby of the Episcopal Church Center in New York City. The following year, the church established a Committee on Social Criteria for Investment and appointed Lockwood to serve on it. In May 1971 the committee persuaded the Episcopal Church to challenge General Motors to divest from South Africa, a widely publicized move that helped catalyze a national church divestment movement.

At the urging of the ACOA, Lockwood traveled to South Africa in 1971 to attend the trial of Dean Gonville ffrench-Beytagh, the Anglican dean of Johannesburg who was charged and later jailed for funneling money from the ANC and the International Defense and Aid Fund to use for social welfare. The trip was a watershed for Lockwood. Among other things, it included his first meeting with members of the African liberation movements in Zambia. He recalls how the meeting in Lusaka unfolded and what transpired on his return to the United States:

> I got in a taxi [in Lusaka] and I said I want to go to the liberation movements. They took me down to the liberation movements' headquarters which they had in a kind of compound. . . . I went in and said hello to SWAPO and ANC and they said, "You shouldn't be here. Where are you staying? We'll come up." So the ANC people sent a delegation to meet me in my hotel room. I think there were three or four people. One of them was a very sedate and dignified older person. I don't remember what his name was. One of the people was Duma Nokwe, who was the secretary of ANC at that time.
>
> And so they pumped me for what was going on in South Africa. And I told them what I knew about the trials, and what I had done, and what I had seen. And we all had a beer in my room. And then this very dignified man said, "Comrade Lockwood, you may think that what you have said is of no importance, and that you have only told us some little bits and pieces of things. But it is like a person being in the middle of a desert, and seeing a place where there is water. And you have given us water, and we have drunk it with great pleasure."
>
> It was my first chance to hear some kind of eloquence that was also quite touching

> in a way. So I felt renewed. I really didn't know very much about the liberation movements at all, but I was favorably impressed with them. And then I came home. And in 1971, in November, Bill Johnston arranged for me to make a presentation to the [U.N.] Committee on Decolonization. I think they called it the Fourth Committee. I thought it was going to be a little something in a small room with a few people. It was not at all. It was a committee of the whole of the General Assembly. . . . So that's how I got launched on South Africa, apartheid, and all that.

In 1972 Lockwood was appointed director of the Washington Office on Africa, a post that he held until 1980. His early focus at WOA was on strengthening sanctions against Rhodesia, specifically to repeal the so-called Byrd Amendment sponsored by Senator Harry Byrd. "This Byrd Amendment, in effect, said you couldn't ban critical and strategic materials from a noncommunist country, unless it was also banned from communist countries. So that meant that the United States could import the Rhodesian chrome ore and the nickel ore," explains Lockwood. WOA lost its campaign to overturn the amendment in Congress but succeeded in persuading President Jimmy Carter, who took office in 1977, to reimpose these sanctions against Rhodesia. In the end, international pressure helped force the white Rhodesian government to accept a settlement and allow free elections for a majority-ruled Zimbabwe.

Three years after leaving the Washington Office on Africa, where he was replaced by Jean Sindab, Lockwood accepted an offer to serve as the international affairs representative for AFSC in Southern Africa. Bill Sutherland, his predecessor in that post, had been based in Dar es Salaam. But with the independence of Zimbabwe in 1980, the frontline had moved closer to South Africa, and Lockwood worked out of Harare from 1983 to 1985.

In those early years, Zimbabwe was one of the most hopeful and stable of South Africa's neighbors, and it served as a strong anchor for the regional political and economic alliances confronting South Africa. The new government was breaking down segregated education, bringing more Africans into schools than the white-minority government had in the previous 90 years. Its economy grew and the government was cited internationally as a model in expanding rural health services. Harare was the regional hub for nongovernmental assistance to the region, and food surpluses were available for famine response in neighboring countries. Zimbabwean troops were sent to Mozambique to help that country against the South African–backed insurgency and to protect the trade corridor to the sea that served not only Zimbabwe but Botswana and Zambia.

It was easy to travel in the region then, Lockwood recalls, and his mandate from AFSC was broad. One of his priorities was to support the efforts of worker-owned agricultural cooperatives in the region. He felt that it was important "to try to see what it was like for people who said they wanted to live out socialism in terms of how they organized their life."

Lockwood's planning for a conference and his effort to link up members of worker-owned co-ops in Tanzania, Mozambique, and Zimbabwe brought him into direct conflict with the new Zimbabwean government. "The Minister of Agriculture headed the co-ops, and he didn't want our society of co-ops to do this conference. He tried his best to ruin it." The conference, which Lockwood says was the first nongovernmental conference in Zimbabwe since independence in 1980, eventually happened in June 1985. But it highlighted for Lockwood some of the fundamental problems with the new Zimbabwean regime. "The idea of a nonprofit, nongovernmental civic society was something that [the Zimbabwean authorities] didn't tolerate," he says. "That's part of the Mugabe problem, I think."

Lockwood was not a pacifist, and he understood the need for Zimbabwe to defend itself against South African attacks. But he also saw the dangers in the approach taken by top leaders of the Zimbabwe African National Union, the party led by Zimbabwean president Robert Mugabe. Lockwood first met Mugabe in Maputo, Mozambique during the Rhodesian liberation war. He was introduced by Eddison Zvogbo, who later became Zimbabwe's justice minister.

> [Zvogbo] explained that I had been working to restore sanctions against Rhodesia. And Mugabe looked up and said, "Eh, sanctions. What are sanctions? It

means nothing. Nothing means anything except the gun."

> He struck me as being a very violent man, and having a preference for violence. Very bright guy. But also a streak of extreme emotional bias in favor of military action. . . . And it just got more and more so. And he was not in any way a humble man. He was always fearful of his grip on power, and the grip of ZANU on power, and he did everything possible to make it a solid one-party state. In effect, he tried to do a security situation the way the Soviet Union did under Stalin. Only it didn't appear so at the time, and we didn't see it coming at the time.

Lockwood left Zimbabwe in 1985 to return to the United States, where he worked on projects for the National Council of Churches and AFSC. His experience in Zimbabwe had given him a more nuanced appreciation for the challenge of transforming a racist, authoritarian society into a nonracial, democratic one.

> It was very easy to sort of say, well, the liberation struggle, they're the heroes. They are the good people, and I don't want to hear anything bad about them. The more I stayed with it, the more I felt sympathy for everybody. How difficult it is, really, to have a peaceful society as well as a just society come out of this. . . . ZANU's adoption of a program of holy violence is just wrong. You can't do that, and carry it all on as part of your understanding of what the state is supposed to be. What is the underlying constitutional structure? If in fact what you're going to continue to do is a civil war on your political enemies, then you can't go on like that. It's horrible.

Looking back on his involvement with the campaigns for freedom in both Zimbabwe and South Africa, however, Lockwood thinks that a key lesson for activists is that one has to focus.

> My feeling is that you have to accept that you are a small part of a big movement. Accepting that means that you don't take on all of the issues that you see as possible to deal with. Concentrate your focus on one issue or two issues, and don't spend

your small degree of capital by taking on all the issues.

It's like a laser beam. A laser beam is a collection of light that will cut something. If you dissipate the light and you don't have it concentrated, you can't cut anything.

## At Decade's End

By the end of the 1980s, South Africa's prime minister F. W. de Klerk wanted the international community to believe that his country, by then reeling from military setbacks in Angola and Namibia, the effect of international sanctions, and a domestic insurrection, was on "the threshold of a new era." In an effort to prove this, he visited European capitals and also met with the presidents of Mozambique, Zaire, and Zambia. At home, he sought to consolidate power and implement a Nationalist Party five-year plan, which he spoke of as the vehicle to end apartheid and white minority rule.

But the plan that de Klerk proposed in 1989 was not one-person, one-vote in a unitary state—the arrangement that ultimately resulted from the 1994 South African elections. Instead, de Klerk proposed replacing white minority rule with a federation of

many minorities: whites, Indians, people of mixed race, and some 10 African ethnicities. He was still dedicated to a system imposed by the white minority government that had race or ethnic division at its core. De Klerk's "new era" was really a desperate effort to convince the international community to lift sanctions to avert South Africa's financial collapse.

Gail Hovey, then managing editor of *Christianity and Crisis*, reported that "foreign investment in South Africa is at a standstill and the government can raise no substantial loans abroad. On June 30, 1990, some $11 billion in loans are scheduled to come due. . . . South Africa is under extraordinary pressure to convince the international financial community, and the new administration in Washington, that sanctions should be lifted because a new day has dawned" (Hovey 1991).

The anti-apartheid movement in the United States and around the world helped ratchet up pressure on the minority government of South Africa. From shantytowns on American college campuses to the numerous universities, cities, and states that divested, to protests against businesses that were profiting from apartheid, to vigils and sit-ins at South African embassies and consulates, to winning

SWAPO president Sam Nujoma, left, with ACOA executive director Jennifer Davis, Manhattan borough president David N. Dinkins, and ACOA executive board president M. William Howard at the Municipal Building in New York City, May 1988. ACOA organized many of the events on Nujoma's schedule in New York, including a labor rally, a press conference with Dinkins, and meetings with other political, religious, and civic leaders. *Photo courtesy of Richard Knight.*

passage of national anti-apartheid sanctions legislation, the movement was crucial in helping to amplify the chorus of South African voices who were demanding simple justice in the land of their birth.

During my travels in South Africa and Namibia during the 1980s and 1990s, ordinary citizens would often tell me how important it was to them to know that the international community was on their side. "Don't forget us here in the 'Wild South,'" implored my friend Anton Lubowksi, a Namibian attorney and the first official white member of SWAPO, in a letter to me shortly before his assassination by South African agents in 1989. Coming just a year before Namibia's hard-fought independence, it was a plea for continued solidarity, one that international activists can say proudly that they heeded.

With a little more time, South Africans would finally accomplish what they had been fighting for over many generations. In a free and fair democratic election, voters at last would choose a new government that for the first time represented all of South Africa's people.

*Oral sources for chapter 5 include interviews with Jennifer Davis (2004, 2005), Willard Johnson (2005), Mel King (2004), Dumisani Kumalo (2005a, 2005b), and Ted Lockwood (2004, 2005).*

Meeting of the Bay Area Anti-Apartheid Network in the 1980s. Similar meetings were held in living rooms, church basements, college classrooms, and union halls throughout the country to organize against South Africa.
*Photo courtesy of Vukani Mawethu.*

David Goodman

# Sylvia Hill ᴧ
# From the Sixth Pan-African Congress to the Free South Africa Movement

## William Minter

At the Sixth Pan-African Congress in Dar es Salaam in June 1974, Sylvia Hill didn't have much time to follow the speeches and debates about race and class, the African diaspora, and the current status of the liberation movements. As one of the key U.S. organizers of the event, she had to focus instead on a host of logistical questions, from finding typewriters to transcribe the sessions to negotiating with translators demanding to be paid in U.S. dollars.

"Six PAC," the sixth in the series of Pan-African congresses initiated by W. E. B. Du Bois, came more than two decades after the historic Fifth Congress in Manchester, England in 1945. It was the first to be held in Africa. Hill is aware that many observers discount the congress because of the heated disagreements that were aired, particularly among delegates from the United States and the Caribbean. But there were positive outcomes, she insists. "I've read and I've heard people say that the conference didn't produce anything, and I'm like, wait, wait, wait," she said in a 2003 interview. "It was really Six PAC that led me to return and work on Southern Africa. There were a group of us who committed ourselves that we were going to work against colonialism, and it was based on the investment in this congress and the agenda of the national liberation struggle."

Hill and many of the other organizers wanted to establish direct connections between African liberation movements and African Americans. Tanzania, which hosted the event and had fostered wide participation from the United States through its embassy in Washington, was the key venue for bringing people together.

Tanzania's President Nyerere was keenly aware of the importance of people-to-people contact and of the critical contribution made by those who work behind the scenes. When national delegations to the congress were scheduled to meet with Nyerere, the all-male group of leaders of the U.S. delegation chose themselves as the five to go, despite a suggestion from veteran activist Mary Jane Patterson that Hill should be included. That night, Hill recalls,

> Ambassador Bomani [the Tanzanian ambassador to the United States] came and said to me, "There will be a car to pick you up to take you to the president. You will meet with the president alone, and when the gentlemen get there, you will already be there." I was there half an hour before they got there. I was already on my second cup of tea when they walked in and they were so stunned to see me sitting there.

On returning to Washington, Hill and a small group of fellow activists— almost all women—founded a small group called the Southern Africa News Collective, which grew into the Southern Africa Support Project in 1978.

Sylvia Hill and her fellow local activists in the Southern Africa Support Project were at the heart of the Free South Africa Movement that brought demonstrators to be arrested at the South African embassy. Hill was also one of the key organizers for the Sixth Pan-African Congress in Dar es Salaam in 1974, and for Nelson Mandela's tour of the United States following his release from prison in 1990.

Today Hill is professor of criminal justice at the University of the District of Columbia. She serves on the board of TransAfrica Forum. This profile draws on interviews with Sylvia Hill by William Minter in 2003 and 2004.

They were clear in defining their top priority as the local community. While they recognized the complementary role of national organizations focused on Africa and developed particularly close ties with TransAfrica, they argued that developing a local base of support for African liberation was essential. They raised assistance for Zimbabwean refugees in Mozambique and for the ANC exile school in Tanzania through annual "Southern Africa" weeks with radiothons, public meetings, and speaking engagements in churches and schools. It was this systematic work, Hill says, that built "a kind of social infrastructure of ties to institutions and sectors in the city" and that would later pay off in the Free South Africa Movement demonstrations.

The relationship between local groups and other groups working on different aspects of solidarity was dialectical, Hill stresses. If it had all been one large bureaucracy, "we could have never done what was ultimately accomplished." It was local organizing in combination with national media attention to South Africa—and particularly TransAfrica's presence in the national media—that enabled the Free South Africa Movement coalition to sustain daily demonstrations at the South African embassy for a year, in 1984–85. Around the country, coalitions of local activists came together and took their own initiatives, inspired by the growing publicity and informed by resources from national groups.

"People have a range of ways they express support. It's everything from sitting in front of the TV and saying, 'right on,' to physically being there. Now if you want them there, you've got to work to get them there," Hill reflects.

> What is significant, from the organizer's point of view, is that the person expresses public opposition instead of private disdain for policies. The challenge for the organizer is to find that creative space that will permit ordinary citizens to express collective opposition. It is the task of the organizer to create venues for internal feelings to be expressed publicly. This the Free South Africa Movement accomplished. And therefore, one of our profound lessons of this movement is that one should never underestimate the power of symbolic protests to create a climate for political change.

Sylvia Hill, center, and Gay McDougall were among African American activists invited by Nelson Mandela to visit South Africa in October 1991 on what was called a "Democracy Now" tour. *Photo courtesy of Sylvia Hill.*

Sylvia Hill

# Jennifer Davis &
# *Clarity, Determination, and Coalition Building*

## Gail Hovey

Jennifer Davis never planned to go into exile from South Africa. But by 1966, organizing inside the country had become very difficult. Most major organizations were banned, and an increasing number of the individuals she worked with, at both the grassroots and leadership levels, were in detention or under house arrest. Exile was never simple, she says. Activists had to grapple both with their conscience about "leaving the struggle" and with the authorities, who used the issuing of passports as a means of control.

> Leaving South Africa happened quite suddenly, in a traumatic few weeks. It started by my husband [lawyer Mike Davis] leaving to visit my brother, traveling on a valid passport. That was followed by several calls from the police indicating that they believed he had left illegally and that I would soon be subjected to some form of house arrest order, as would he if he returned. Mike had done many political cases in South Africa, including several where he was instructed by the Tambo-Mandela law firm.

In New York, Mike Davis made contact with people connected to the American Committee on Africa, and over time they helped him reestablish his legal career. Jennifer Davis arrived with their two small children and began her adjustment to life in the United States. An early experience stands out in her mind as particularly instructive. She was invited to dinner by friends of her parents who lived on Manhattan's East Side.

> They had an absolutely beautiful house with lots of original artwork, an El Greco in their dining room. One of the guests said to me—I think we were already sitting down after dinner—you must see great differences between South Africa and here. And I said, well, there are some differences, but there's not such a lot of difference. I see a tremendous number of very poor black people, and a lot of very rich white people. And she pulled herself up to her rather portly height and said, there are no poor people in America.

Davis had been speaking her mind since high school, when she dared to argue with her Afrikaans teacher about the 1948 elections. The daughter of a South African father and a German mother who left Germany in the early 1930s, she came to understand the meaning of the Holocaust from her parents and maternal grandmother. For Davis, "never again" meant that every Jew should be an activist, resisting religious and racial oppression wherever it occurred.

A member of the Unity Movement in South Africa, Davis describes herself as a very serious young woman.

Jennifer Davis and George Houser had been colleagues for more than a decade when he retired from the American Committee on Africa in 1981 and she became the organization's second executive director. A South African exile, she knew the organization well from her years as its research director and led it through the critical decades of the 1980s and 1990s.

This profile is based in part on interviews with Davis by William Minter in 2004 and 2005. It also draws on interviews with Robert S. Browne by William Minter in 2003, and with Dumisani Kumalo by Gail Hovey in 2005.

By the time I got to the University of the Witwatersrand in the early fifties, the Communist Party had already been banned. On the Wits campus much of the left debate was carried out in the Student Liberal Association, which provided the public home for many who had formerly been open party members. Unity Movement members who were functioning in something called the Progressive Forum were in hot opposition to the Communist Party, and drew their ideological framework from the Trotskyist tradition. Thus there was a lot of debate, mainly about the nature, structure, and possible transformation of South African society, but also about international issues and about broader ideas, the role of art and science, the nature of capitalism and imperialism.

In the United States Davis found a place at ACOA, where she became the research director. She established extensive files that were a resource for activists and journalists and provided the information for ACOA's and The Africa Fund's numerous presentations before U.N. and U.S. government committees. During the burgeoning divestment campaign, items like "Fact Sheet on South Africa" and "Questions and Answers on Divestment" were used in virtually every state and local campaign.

Davis's home became a temporary landing place for countless people—Africans, Europeans, and North Americans—who had been recently expelled from their countries of origin or were in New York temporarily to carry out a U.N. assignment or use ACOA's resources. One such guest was activist poet Dennis Brutus. In 1966 Brutus had just been released from the Robben Island prison in South Africa and went on tour in the United States for ACOA. Davis remembers that he used to wander around her apartment in the middle of the night, muttering poetry; her kids were fascinated by him. He later settled in the United States and spearheaded work on the international sports boycott.

Over more than three decades, Davis continued to host delegations and individuals from liberation, protest, human rights, and trade union movements throughout Southern Africa, providing the opportunity for them to inform and update activist Americans on the progress of their work.

In 1981, on the retirement of George Houser, Jennifer Davis took over the leadership of the American Committee on Africa and The Africa Fund, a position she would hold until her retirement in 2000. At the time, ACOA's board was chaired by William Booth, a black lawyer and district court judge who was a former New York City commissioner. Announcing Davis's appointment in *ACOA Action News* (spring 1981), Booth said, "She has gained a reputation as an authority with few peers in analyzing political and economic developments in Southern Africa. . . . She brings the same commitment and integrity that are characteristic of George Houser. What was so well begun will be well continued under her leadership."

It was not quite that simple. This was, after all, the *American* Committee on Africa, and according to board member Bob Browne, some people thought it was crazy to appoint a South African to head it. And not only a South African, but a white Jew. Browne went on to say that it did not remain a problem because Davis quickly won over any skeptics. But that is also an oversimplification. While serving as director, Davis traveled around the country speaking in a wide variety of venues. She had to deal with sensitive questions regarding her credibility. Although he says they didn't talk about it at the time, Dumisani Kumalo, ACOA's project director and a fellow South African, was well aware of the challenges she faced. "We were involved in a political struggle and she was a white Jewish woman in this struggle against racism. So she was up against it in the U.S., with its racism."

Davis recalls her debates on U.S. television with South African homeland leader Gatsha Buthelezi, who worked with the South African government to lobby against sanctions.

"He attacked me as the 'white lady.' He's black; I'm white. What do I know? He was arguing that we should have more investment." Davis learned the value of speaking, whenever she could, in joint appearances with a black colleague. "I developed, I think, a fair amount of credibility, but to have David Ndaba from the ANC or Dumisani Kumalo meant that me being a 'white lady' didn't matter."

Davis remained a strong advocate for strengthening sanctions and keeping them in place until there was a genuine transfer of power in South Africa. In 1989 Assistant Secretary of State for African Affairs Herman Cohen admitted, "Sanctions have had a substantial impact on persuading white South Africans of the need for a negotiated settlement" (*Wall Street Journal*, June 30, 1989). Then he argued that now was the time to lift sanctions, to reward the changes that had been made.

Davis was quick to reply. "What has changed," she said, "is the white power structure's sense of permanence and invulnerability . . . The economy is badly shaken—no growth, unemployment for whites, inflation" (1989). She called for the imposition of comprehensive sanctions.

From the beginning of her involvement with ACOA, one of Jennifer Davis's key contributions was to insist on an anti-imperialist focus for the American anti-apartheid work and for the work in support of liberation movements in the rest of Southern Africa. While affirming the importance of human rights and political prisoner campaigns, Davis insisted that ACOA concentrate on exposing and weakening the support that American institutions were giving to the white minority regimes.

Beginning in the 1970s, Davis began making trips to Africa. In August 1974 she traveled to Tanzania to spend time with Frelimo, visiting, among other places, the Mozambican movement's hospital in Mtwara.

> We were supporting, through the Rubin Foundation, the hospital in Mtwara. It wasn't a hospital, it was a small house, and they'd bring people across the border from Cabo Delgado. The staff greeted me as I came up to the building, and then they held me in the door, and they said to the respective people in the beds, this visitor is coming from the United States and she would like to come and talk with you, and is it all right? And everybody said yes, and then I went inside. I went to a hospital in Zambia where the doctors took me around and nobody ever told the patients what was happening.

Davis was enormously impressed by Frelimo. She understood them to be seriously attempting to engage the people not as victims but as participants. When Mozambique's president Samora Machel and 33 others died in a plane crash on October 19, 1986, Davis flew to Maputo to attend the funerals. ACOA's relationships with Frelimo were too enduring not to express solidarity in person. She recalls:

> Perhaps the most memorable minutes of my stay in Mozambique were 15 minutes spent with Graça Machel an hour before leaving. She had borne herself with great dignity throughout the public ceremonies. Now, face to face, she embraced me, listened to my messages of sympathy and solidarity and said, "We have always known that we had many friends, but it is good that you are here, so we can touch." Then she went on to talk about tasks ahead. (Davis 1986)

In January 1990, just before the elections that would bring SWAPO to power in Namibia, Davis traveled to Windhoek. She wanted, she says, to reconnect with individuals and groups throughout the country, to understand what might happen in the next few weeks and the ways that solidarity could continue after the elections. She went north to Oshikati, where SWAPO had strong support. She talked to a wide range of people, from Toivo ya Toivo and other SWAPO leaders to women's groups and Lutheran church activists.

Finally, in 1994, Davis returned to South Africa to serve as an official observer for the South African election. She had traveled a long distance in the three decades she had been away. A Jewish secular intellectual, she had come to lead organizations whose constituencies were most often Christian, or black, or both. That the churches were major players in the anti-apartheid movement in the U.S. was something that she had to get used to.

She came to win the respect of those with whom she worked. At a party held in her honor in 2003, one of the speakers was Harlem minister Canon Fred Williams, a board member of ACOA and co-founder with Wyatt Tee Walker of ACOA's Religious Action Network. The network was open to all religious traditions but was made up predominantly of black churches. They had answered a call from religious leaders in South Africa to protest detentions, work for sanctions and send prayers and messages of solidarity.

"Here was this Jewish woman," Williams said, "and she is the one who made it possible for the Religious Action Network to do its work, this coalition of primarily black, male clergy and their churches. The public Jennifer, cold to some, aloof, hard to connect to, yes, but so reliable as the one to look more deeply, to insist on principle, to keep focused even in the face of terrible opposition" (2003).

Jennifer Davis, left, testifies at the United Nations on South Africa's apartheid policies, November 1980. Karen Talbot of the World Peace Council was also among the witnesses from nongovernmental organizations. *UN Photo.*

Jennifer Davis

# Jean Sindab ∾
# *Connecting People, Connecting Issues*

## Gay McDougall, *International Human Rights Law Group*

I remember being with Jean in Zimbabwe in 1988 for an international conference convened to highlight the tragedy of thousands of children that were being detained in South African jails. Many of them were tortured. It was the first major anti-apartheid conference that was attended by large numbers of South Africans, many of whom surreptitiously crossed the border to attend. There were nearly 2,000 people there. Jean was asked to speak at the closing plenary—a great honor to her and to the role of African Americans in the worldwide movement. Many of the great orators of the movement preceded her at the podium—a tough act to follow. But it was Jean that brought the house down. She spoke simply and eloquently and so passionately that every person in the audience was touched and moved to give her a standing ovation.

It is hard to imagine what the international anti-apartheid movement would have been without Jean Sindab. She was such a vital part of it, whether lobbying Congress, organizing grassroots campaigns, or strategizing with activists from other countries.

One of the things that I greatly admired about Jean was that she was an internationalist. There could be no question that she was firmly rooted in the experiences of the oppression suffered by African Americans [and especially by] African American women. But she was also someone that was able to rise above a parochial view of "our" problems and see the horizon where people of many different experiences of oppression could join forces into a majority. She was a part of the lives and struggles of many different peoples around the world.

Above all else, Jean was genuine and sincere. Jean was the type of person that gave a lot of herself to what she cared about. She was blessed to have both purpose and passion in her life.

At the goodbye party we held for Jean when she moved from Washington to Geneva, I said that when I think of Jean Sindab it calls to mind other great black women of our generation: Ms. Ella Baker, Fannie Lou Hamer, and Shirley Chisholm. Jean has earned her place among them.

## Ted Lockwood, *Washington Office on Africa*

Jean succeeded me as the director of the Washington Office on Africa in the summer of 1980. She brought strengths to the office that I did not have and never would have. The fact that she was African American and bright was just the beginning of what she brought.

Her bubbling energy and enthusiasm led her to reach out to others who had not been reached in the struggle against apartheid. Organizations which we had never been able or tried to reach were glad to share in her zeal for

Raised by her mother and grandmother in Bedford-Stuyvesant, New York City's largest black neighborhood, Jean Sindab won a scholarship to attend Hunter College in 1970, at the age of 26. She went on to earn a PhD in political science at Yale University. Beginning in 1980, she directed the Washington Office on Africa and led the organization during the critical period leading up to the adoption of congressional sanctions against South Africa. Sindab directed the Programme to Combat Racism of the World Council of Churches, based in Geneva, from 1986 to 1991. After returning to New York, she coordinated work on environmental and economic justice for the National Council of Churches until her final illness. Her death from cancer in 1996 cut short a rich career of activism.

During her time in Washington, Sindab focused her work on South Africa and Namibia. In Geneva the scope expanded to include combating racism worldwide. Later, from her post at the National Council of Churches, she was one of the pioneers in raising the issue of environmental racism around the country. Many in the movement stressed the intersection of domestic and international struggles. But few matched Sindab in her capacity to make live connections that went beyond rhetoric or theoretical analysis. She was confidently rooted in her own community and values, yet insistent and skillful in bringing people together for common goals.

A celebration of the life of Dr. Nellie Jean Pitts Sindab was held on February 24, 1996 at People's Congregational Church in Washington, DC. These testimonies, from among many read at the service, focus on the distinctive contributions she made to African justice.

African interests. Even though she was fresh from academic studies, her passion for liberation was infectious and intense. It galvanized and mobilized the anti-apartheid movement. No one was a better stump speaker.

She was generous in recognizing the contributions of those of us who had preceded her at the Washington Office on Africa. She organized a spectacular tenth anniversary party for WOA that honored those contributions. Her staff were devoted to her.

Her nationalism was not narrow or racialist or doctrinaire. It stemmed from her own heritage of Christian faith and love: a love that tries to embrace not only the victims of racism but those who are the victimizers, whether they are insensitive elitists, misguided bigots, or outright enemies. She was a disciple of Christ, a beautiful child of the black church.

At the same time, she could be confrontational with those friends and allies who she felt were undercutting the cause of freedom by lukewarm support, bureaucratic indifference, racial or sexist condescension, cynicism, or snide remarks. She was confrontational with me more than once but I think we never ceased to be friends.

She never got the support that she needed. Those of us who shared the niggardly financing that marked our times appreciated her downright rage. She would storm out of meetings in ways we never dared to.

She never forgot her roots in "Bed-Stuy." The traumas she and her family had endured there fueled her passion for justice. She never suffered fools gladly. Why should she?

As my artist friend, Freddy Reynolds, would say, she was "something else." Her death is a terrible loss, but nothing so good is ever lost forever.

May she rest in peace, and may light perpetually shine upon her.

## Past and present members of the Southern Africa Support Project

The Southern Africa Support Project mourns the loss of our sister in the struggle for human rights. Her belief in the impossible, her sense of humor, and her energetic spirit will be sorely missed as we meet the challenges of tomorrow.

Despite Jean's tremendous workload as director of the Washington Office on Africa, she was always willing to help us in organizing material aid for refugees in Southern Africa and participate in our campaigns to raise public consciousness against U.S. foreign policy. Whether we asked her to join us in a picket line, attend a gospel show, chaperone a youth dance-a-thon, or co-host a radio program, she enthusiastically joined our programs. Jean did not limit her role in the struggle to only her organization's work. She valued the work of many organizations as a collective strike against injustice!

Her ability to work in coalitions was just one of her treasured strengths. We will miss her.

Current and former directors of the Washington Office on Africa gather at the National Anti-Apartheid Conference in June 1990. From left: Damu Smith (director 1986–89), Jean Sindab (director 1980–86), and Aubrey McCutcheon (director 1989–90). Ted Lockwood (director 1972–80), not shown in this photograph, was also at the conference. *Photo by Basil Clunie.*

Jean Sindab

# Public Investment and South Africa ~

## Julian Bond

Thank you a great deal for the kind and warm welcome. I think most of us who work on African issues, who are scattered throughout the United States, begin to develop a feeling of isolation and estrangement. So it is extremely gratifying to discover that we are many and diverse, that those of us represented here in fact are representatives of a larger group of people scattered throughout the 50 states of the U.S. and that our cause is just and our success virtually assured.

Among all of us who are gathered here, there is a particular group: legislators and council members, who are here as part of the responsibility of our offices because we are all sworn to uphold the public good. There certainly could be no greater good than the cause for which we gather, the advancement of the struggle for the independence of Southern Africa.

We are here to complete the process of halting American complicity in the most hideous government on the face of the planet, the one system where racial superiority is constitutionally enshrined. We gather here at a time when even the most moderate advances away from complicity are being compromised, abandoned and withdrawn.

In less than six months, the new government of the U.S. reversed even the halting Africa policies of the Carter administration and has embarked on a course of arrogant intervention into African affairs in the most hostile way. From Cape Town to Cairo, the American eagle has begun to bare his talons. Our secretary of state is a man who pounded his palms on the table like tom-toms when African affairs were discussed in the Nixon White House. Our new ambassador to the U.N. sees callers [a high-ranking South African military intelligence team that came March 15, 1981]. [First] she says she does not know [them] and then denies seeing them at all. When her visitors are discovered to have entered the U.S. illegally and their hospitality revealed to be a violation of policy, she dismisses all complaints as if the policy had been already revised.

Unfortunately, she was right. America's policies towards Africa have changed. They have changed from benign neglect to a kind of malignant aggression. In Mozambique, starvation is added to the American arsenal. On the high seas, the American oil companies, Mobil, Exxon, and Texaco have joined European interests in breaking the OPEC embargo to South Africa. On Capitol Hill there is the intensity of Soviet competition in Africa, not humanitarian concerns, which conditions American aid to the continent. Mineral rights are exchanged for human rights.

In South Africa itself there is no mistaking the increased militancy, each group adding momentum to the irresistible motion of liberation. But our concerns are here. Our cause is to take whatever action we can

At the first national Conference on Public Investment and South Africa in 1981, some 200 state and municipal legislators from across the United States attended workshops on drafting socially responsible legislation, among other topics. Held in New York City on June 12–13, the conference also drew trade unionists, investment experts, church leaders, academics, and grassroots organizers. The conference sponsors included ACOA, AFSC, the Connecticut Anti-Apartheid Committee, Clergy and Laity Concerned, the Interfaith Center on Corporate Responsibility, TransAfrica, the United Methodist Office for the U.N., and the Washington Office on Africa.

For the opening session at the United Nations, Ambassador B. Akporode Clark of Nigeria, then chair of the U.N. Special Committee Against Apartheid, welcomed the participants. The keynote address, excerpted here, was given by SNCC veteran and Georgia state senator Julian Bond.

to end American complicity with this international problem [apartheid]. Our contribution is to pull together those forces—legislators, investment experts, trade unionists, student activists, that growing constituency for freedom in South Africa—to facilitate the expansion of public prohibitions against the expenditure of public funds for inhuman purposes. In short, we intend to end American investment in evil. The evil, of course, is the system of apartheid in which four and a half million whites absolutely dominate 20 million nonwhites, denying them every vestige of humanity. As the second-largest foreign investor, the U.S. plays a key role in keeping apartheid afloat. The net effect of American investments, according to former senator Dick Clark of Iowa, has been to strengthen the economic and military self-sufficiency of South Africa's apartheid regime.

Our cause, then, is to end American complicity with this evil. But we must know the course of the rapidly shifting climate around us. The loudest voice on the Senate Foreign Relations Committee today belongs to Senator Jesse Helms, Republican of North Carolina and apologist for South Africa's fascists. The new president of the U.S. had already announced even before his nomination and election his intentions to subsidize subversion in Angola; he has sent repeated assurances to South Africa's white population that the U.S. will tolerate their genocide. He has further delayed the liberation of Namibia, rewarding South Africa's intransigence. He has made the American colossus he professes to adore bow down before a small tribe of racist tyrants.

We are here, then, to force the disengagement of our commonly held wealth from this evil. I think we all realize that this will be a difficult and time-consuming process, for we are in effect opposing the whole of American history. The current condition of American black people, political and economic, is more than well known. We gather here to ask the U.S. to honor the principle that no person's worth is superior to another, to do in foreign affairs what is yet to be done at home.

If it is difficult, our task is not impossible. Events in South Africa daily demonstrate that we are a part of a quickening struggle whose outcome has never been in serious doubt. We can make a great contribution to that struggle if all who truly believe in freedom will join us. Ours, then, is a subtle request; to ask our neighbors, the people with whom we share the country, to refuse to finance the domination of one set of human beings by another.

Surely that is a reasonable appeal. South Africa today constitutes a direct personal threat to us all. Forty years ago, Adolf Hitler demonstrated that genocide is yet possible even in democracy, even among people who look alike. It is evil supreme and we cannot allow it to continue; to be neutral on this issue is to join the other side.

State legislator Julian Bond in 1981.
*Photo courtesy of Richard Knight.*

# "South Africa Is Next to Namibia" ∽ The Lutheran Connection

## Solveig and Peter Kjeseth

*Solveig:* In 1971, Wartburg Seminary—which is where Peter taught for 36 years—in Dubuque, Iowa began to receive Namibian pastors who were coming to do graduate work. The first Namibian, Abisai Shejavali, and his family stayed for about seven years. It was the Shejavalis who taught us where Namibia was and how to say the word "Namibia." Little by little, they—especially Dr. Shejavali's wife Selma—taught us about what was happening in their country. And little by little we learned and little by little their struggle became our struggle. So it was very personal—it wasn't that we set out looking for a cause. One moved in with us.

Abisai Shejavali's father was a retired Lutheran pastor living near the border of Angola. South African soldiers came and brutally beat him and raped and blinded his wife. And at that time Abisai wrote a letter of protest to Prime Minister Vorster. Selma is a Ndonga royal and her uncle, who had cooperated with South Africa, was assassinated while they were at Wartburg. The uncle, King Filemon Elifas, had allowed open, public flogging of SWAPO supporters, so he was really hated. Selma says her uncle was not a bad man, but he was not strong and therefore he was used by South Africa.

*Peter:* During the years Abisai was with us he became more and more politicized. When we first knew him, he [had] what I would now call a rather naïve belief that things were going to turn out quite well.

*Solveig:* They had full confidence that the United States was going to come down on their side. But in the 1970s, as he saw the U.S. repeatedly vetoing economic sanctions against South Africa at the U.N., he could see how the U.S. clearly sided with South Africa.

There was a little Namibia Concerns Committee at Wartburg—probably seven, eight people—and we began to study the issues and then we would accept invitations to speak at any little groups. Mainly it was women's church groups that Selma and I would speak to. And then Wartburg for the next 30 years always had Namibian pastors there, so with each succeeding year there was greater impact. Emma Mujoro was a Namibian pastor and she and I traveled hundreds and hundreds of miles on the back roads of Wisconsin and Iowa, talking about the situation in Namibia.

By 1990, the mailing list had grown to 11,000 and represented virtually every state, including Hawai'i and Alaska.

*Peter:* Dubuque is right at the corner of Wisconsin, Illinois, and Iowa, and not too far away from Minneapolis and that's the Midwest where Scandinavian Lutheran background is very influential.

*Solveig:* The other thing was that every year Wartburg would graduate probably 50 young pastors who went all over the U.S., and every single one of them knew Namibians. Not all of them were involved politically, but

Dubuque, Iowa, might seem an unlikely hotbed of Southern African organizing, but National Namibia Concerns based at Wartburg Theological Seminary mobilized more than 10,000 American Lutherans to support Namibian independence and impose sanctions on South Africa. Among the founders were two couples, Abisai and Selma Shejavali and Peter and Solveig Kjeseth. The Shejavalis, originally from Namibia, returned to their country at the end of the 1970s. They played prominent roles not only in the Evangelical Lutheran Church in Namibia, but also in the Namibian Council of Churches and in the struggle for liberation.

Peter and Solveig Kjeseth are both of Norwegian Lutheran immigrant stock, with family histories of commitment to social justice. Peter's great grandfather had left Norway as a poor farmer after being involved in peasant organizing. The couple met at the University of Chicago and spent the early 1960s in Geneva, where Peter worked with the Lutheran World Federation. When they met the Shejavalis at Wartburg, they already had been involved in organizing against the Vietnam War and had helped found the Dubuque County Democratic Club, a progressive alternative to the local established Democratic Party. It was Namibia, however, that became their life work.

Solveig and Peter Kjeseth spoke with Christopher Saunders, a historian at the University of Cape Town, on April 2, 2005 at the bed-and-breakfast that the Kjeseths now run near Cape Town.

they were aware of the story. They knew the issues and they would respond, you know, so over a period of a few years, the word spread. And they would have a captive audience where they were going: congregations.

In 1977 apartheid was declared to be an issue of *status confessionis* by the Lutheran World Federation, which meant that we were called by our faith to oppose it. So apartheid and Namibia's occupation was seen as a religious issue, and appropriate to be addressed from the pulpit, in sermons or in publications.

One of the things we did politically in those days—and I was so proud of how it worked—was that we asked people to put the question of Namibia on their local political [Democratic] "resolutions list." We have this tradition in Iowa that the candidates, the political candidates for U.S. president, come first to Iowa because Iowa's party caucuses are the earliest in the country. And I just loved it when *Time* magazine's reporter—it must have been in 1984—wrote that "the candidates were asked about such esoteric questions as U.N. resolution 435." When I read that, I knew "that's our network!"

It was very much a really grassroots movement. Just about everybody in the network had a passion for Namibia because it had become real for them; it was real people that they had gotten to know. It was the Shejavalis and the !Noabebs and the Mujoros and the Nambalas and the Uahengos and the Shivutes. It became much more than an abstract political issue.

One last story, which I have to tell to a South African. I was at a church conference in Wisconsin during the struggle, with probably 1,500 women. We went for lunch at the college cafeteria, and I noticed there were a couple of black African women students, and two older white women, and I sat down near them. And these women, the whites, were asking the African students, "Oh! Are you from Africa?" "Yes, we're from South Africa." The two women looked puzzled for a moment. Then one brightened and asked, "Oh, South Africa . . . is that next to Namibia?"

Solveig Kjeseth and Selma Shejavali. *Photo courtesy of Solveig Kjeseth.*

"South Africa Is Next to Namibia"

# Race and Anti-Apartheid Work in Chicago ✑

## Rachel Rubin

Rachel Rubin has been an anti-apartheid and Southern Africa solidarity activist for two decades. She lived and worked in Manica province in Mozambique from 1990 to 1992. She is currently an attending physician at Cook County Hospital in Chicago and a specialist in occupational and environmental medicine.

Excerpted from "The Anti-apartheid Struggle: Did It/Could It Challenge Racism in the U.S.?" In "African [Diaspora] Studies," edited by Lisa Brock, special issue, *Issue: A Journal of Opinion* 24, no. 2 (1996). Reprinted by permission of the African Studies Association.

Many whites, including myself, embraced anti-apartheid work, partly because we were outraged at the horror of South Africa but also because it gave us a way to fight racism here in the United States. I had always seen and disapproved of racism and from a very young age felt a need to fight against it. The anti-apartheid struggle gave me a solid way to do that.

In the mid-1970s, when I was in college, the campus I was on was so segregated and the institutional policies so paternalistic and racist that there were very few forums for blacks and whites to work together. The first full-fledged anti-apartheid group at my university, which I joined on its inception, was established by an African American who was a visiting artist on campus. However, as the organization developed, it became and remained an almost exclusively white organization. It worked in coalition with black groups and other more multiracial formations, but it never was able to make significant inroads into the African American community of the town or of the campus. Although this upset me and I was never totally sure why it was, it did not surprise me. Given the white power structure on campus and in society at large and some bitter experiences on both sides, there seemed to be little ground for working together. African American students feared white paternalism and insensitivity, while white students feared black anger, saying the wrong thing and then being rebuked. Unfortunately, I think most groups doing anti-apartheid work during that time were as segregated and separated as the communities their members came from.

Nonetheless, when I graduated and moved back to Chicago in the 1980s, I continued my determination to do anti-apartheid work. By this time there were more anti-apartheid organizations functioning in the country, and I joined, soon after its founding, the Coalition for Illinois Divestment in South Africa (CIDSA). It later became the Chicago Committee in Solidarity with Southern Africa (CCISSA). I served on the board and steering committees of this organization for nearly 12 years.

My experience with CCISSA was very different than my previous experience on the campus of the University of Illinois. CIDSA/CCISSA was conceived of and founded by a small group of African Americans and whites, and we maintained an equal number of African Americans and whites on our board. The group always had as many blacks as whites in its active leadership, and we were always careful to have black members or both white and black members together go to give talks or go to meetings as representatives of the group. CIDSA/CCISSA was a biracial collective. Our public as well as private faces were racially mixed.

In its first phase CIDSA successfully waged statewide divestment campaigns, working with primarily labor and church groups toward that end. As we reorganized ourselves into CCISSA we worked hard to place ourselves within both the white and African American communities, speaking at churches, synagogues, community centers, schools, etc. We also developed strong ties with resident South Africans. Our annual Soweto Day Walkathon was always a cooperative venture with black churches, community organizations, local politicians, and residents of the neighborhood we were to march through. Many of these links were forged by CCISSA members who had connections to those neighborhoods or communities. Slowly over the years this outreach garnered the organization a certain level of respect within segments of the black as well as certain white communities.

Problematically, though, to certain segments of the African American community in Chicago, we continued to be seen as a white group, albeit as the years went by, a well-meaning white group. This was because we were integrated and had an organization where blacks were willing to work with whites on an issue that some thought should remain in the African American community. In fact, it was felt by some, local black cultural nationalists in particular, that if anti-apartheid work was (merely) supporting black South Africans in their liberation struggle against the white apartheid regime then the solidarity movement was best seated within exclusively black organizations. It was believed that if whites wanted to help, then let them start their own organizations in their own communities. In other words, our very multiracial existence was seen as a problem.

This labeling as a white group was more fundamentally a consequence of the white power structure of this country. No matter what, when you have a group that is made up of whites and blacks that may on an internal basis function in a very equal way, the perception often is going to be that it is impossible to have equality on any level in a society where white racism has been so prevalent. This of course is not unique to the anti-apartheid movement. There were many feminist organizations in the 1970s who felt that no men should be allowed in women's organizations, given their natural inclination to dominate. Similarly, whites and blacks often have different understandings of integration. Recent housing surveys have shown that whites often think 10 percent black/90 percent white is the optimal formula of neighborhood integration, while blacks interviewed in these studies see 50 percent black/50 percent white as the only meaningful way to integrate. Our organization had always been about fifty-fifty. Nonetheless, some continued to think that we whites were the ones dominating the leadership and that we were trespassers on black turf. In other words, if a political organization had both black and white leadership and membership, then the blacks must be tokens or sellouts, or at the very least would be wasting their time trying to work with whites.

The development of CCISSA with all of its issues did, in fact, advance the struggle against racism in the United States in two small ways. First, the dismissals of the organization as white forced many of us to deal with black perceptions of the limitations of whites doing antiracist work. It made us have to check ourselves and make sure that we did not fit that category. This probably would not have happened if we had not maintained our multiracial membership. I think our determination to deal with the criticism made us better progressive organizers with African Americans as a whole.

Second, I think racial barriers were broken down in CCISSA and broken down through CCISSA. We did succeed in a small way as an anti-racist collective and not only as an anti-apartheid organization. We created an environment, a network of friends that was multiracial and multi-cultural—hopefully a network that will remain intact for the rest of our lives. What bound us together was our sense of being political comrades. We developed an analysis together. We learned, studied, and strategized together. We made connections between racism and colonialism here and in Southern Africa and reflected on these connections in the activities we planned. We also illustrated over time to a great number of members in the black community that there were whites willing to struggle against interna-tional racism and blacks willing to work with us. However, we still need to overcome the continued racial segregation within progressive, left political work and we need to continue to confront the difficulties of overcoming internalized white racism if we are really going to tackle racism in this country.

# From Local to National ✑
## Bay Area Connections

### Leo Robinson

Around 1974 or 1975 I happened to meet the girlfriend of my working partner. He was going to San Francisco State, and he brought her by the house one day. And right away I could tell she had an African accent. And she said that she was from South Africa and I said oh. And I said when you get back home, you're going to be in pretty good shape, huh? And she said I can't go back. And I said what do you mean, you can't go back? She said if I go back after I've finished my schooling, I'll be arrested the minute I step off the plane. And that was my first introduction to apartheid.

I had not yet made a genuine connection. I started to know about it because when you picked up a copy of *Jet* from time to time you would see something in there about what was going on in Africa. And it's in the back of your head, right? And then in 1976 when the student uprising occurred in Soweto, the massacre of innocent, unarmed people—it's a gut reaction that you act from then. But as you get to be knowledgeable about what it is that you're looking at, then it's a whole different focus. Because the gut reaction does not last long. [A massacre is] in the news one day and then it slowly dies out and it's forgotten about by people.

Until you actually start delving into things, you never know what's occurred prior to when you came along. William Bill Chester, who was a member of Local 10, who then moved to the International as a regional director for Northern California and beyond, who happened to be African American, had raised the question of apartheid back in the late fifties or early sixties.

Bill had raised the question, but it didn't go anywhere. In 1976 it was a different matter. It was a different matter entirely, because I guess you could say that by 1976 the African American population of this country had sort of arrived. We had started to be elected to various offices around the country and had gotten jobs, such as we could be a post person and get a job at the fire department if you really pressed—those kinds of things.

But the question of apartheid—once I looked into it, I found out that, number one, the government of the United States had been complicit. And so that upset me. I said as a result of that one of the aims of the anti-apartheid movement should be to expose the complicity of the United States government and to neutralize it insofar as the liberation movements are concerned.

In July of '76 the first of the anti-apartheid resolutions was introduced in Local 10 by myself and others. A little short resolution that simply said that due to the situation in South Africa, we were calling for a boycott of all goods to and from South Africa and Zimbabwe. Plus, the original resolution, when it left Local 10, it went to the International executive board. The International executive board changed the words from "demand" a boycott

In the San Francisco Bay Area, as elsewhere in the country, the anti-apartheid campaign of the 1980s and 1990s was closely tied to the local contours of progressive politics (see Walter Turner's chapter on the 1990s). At the same time, its impact was projected into the national arena through multiple organizational links and networks. As early as 1979, Berkeley, California, became the first U.S. city to opt for divestment through a public ballot initiative spearheaded by Mayor Gus Newport. In the 1980s Newport challenged the membership of the U.S. Conference of Mayors to follow Berkeley's example.

Another influential Bay Area figure with national connections was labor activist Leo Robinson, of Local 10 of the International Longshore and Warehouse Union. Robinson recalled the growth of the local's activism in an interview with Walter Turner in 2005.

of South African cargo to "urge," okay? Which means that we knew then that we had our work cut out for us in terms of educating the membership not only of Local 10 but of the entire international union.

We had become part of the labor-based anti-apartheid movement. At the time, we were the first anti-apartheid labor committee in the country. We raised the question of apartheid to the level of visibility within the trade union movement, because the AFL-CIO played its usual role when it came to foreign workers, particularly black workers in Africa. They gave it a one-line, half a paragraph blurb in their annual report.

And then committees started popping up all across the country. Starting here in the Bay Area, we started sending out resolutions to the state federation, to the national convention of CBTU [Coalition of Black Trade Unionists], even to the executive council of the AFL-CIO. This is over a period of years that this occurred. Then in 1977 or '78, we held the first anti-apartheid labor conference in the United States at Local 34 in San Francisco.

In April of 1977 we had a two-day shutdown. Myself and the committee had made arrangements with the chief dispatcher that the community people were going to come down to Pier 27 to protest that ship, the South African cargo. So we made sure that Local 10 members who were sympathetic took those jobs, knowing that they were not going to work. And so for two days we tied them up. We tied that ship up.

That was the first of many demonstrations at the docks. The one that got the most attention was in November 1984. By then we were better organized and the whole question of South Africa had become an issue nationally. They were calling for the release of Nelson Mandela. They were calling for entertainers, black entertainers, to boycott South Africa. Because by then Sun City was up and running in South Africa and they were inviting black entertainers from the U.S., offering them huge sums of money to come to Sun City to entertain. And we were saying to them, don't go. If you do go, demand to speak to Nelson Mandela. Otherwise, don't go.

U.S. trade unionist Leo Robinson and South African student Steve Nakana greet each other at an African Diaspora Dialogue meeting in Berkeley, California, 2006. Nakana told the gathering that when he was a student at the ANC school in exile in Tanzania, he had received packages from people in America, with clothing, books, and other items. Robinson told of packages that he and other union officials had put together to send, adding with a laugh that they had often slipped chewing gum, candy, or dollar bills into the pockets of clothes just before sealing them. Nakana, smiling broadly, stood up and said he was one of those who opened such packages. "It felt like Christmas," he added.
*Photo courtesy of Nunu Kidane.*

Ronald W. Dellums of California served in the U.S. House of Representatives from 1971 through 1999, representing the district that includes Berkeley and Oakland. He grew up in Oakland, the son of a longshoreman who was a member of the same union as Leo Robinson. His uncle was a protégé of national labor and civil rights leader A. Philip Randolph. Working as a social worker after a short stint in the Marine Corps, Dellums was urged by community activists to go into politics, and he gave up plans to pursue a PhD.

Elected to the Berkeley City Council in 1967 and then to the House in 1970, Dellums regarded himself as "a voice for the movements" in Congress (Dellums 2000, 2). He was one of a group of urban progressive legislators who, in his words, worked inside the system and learned its rules while relying on the "street heat" of activists to command the attention of those in power (5).

In his memoir, published in 2000, Dellums dedicated a chapter to the years of campaigning on apartheid. "The liberation of South Africa from the yoke of apartheid is one of the most important political and human rights events of my lifetime," he wrote, "and I consider having played some role in it to be my greatest legislative and personal achievement" (6).

The following excerpt is reprinted by permission from *Lying Down with the Lions: A Public Life from the Streets of Oakland to the Halls of Power* (Boston: Beacon, 2000), 121–40.

# Ronald Dellums

A group of workers from a Polaroid plant had come down from New England [in 1971] with the express purpose of meeting with members of Congress to discuss their concerns regarding their company's commercial engagement with South Africa. The [Congressional Black Caucus] chairman, Charles C. Diggs, Jr. (D-Michigan), asked me to meet with the Polaroid workers and report back on their concerns.

[John Conyers (D-Michigan) joined me, and] we agreed to receive their petition and to take up their cause within the Congress; we also promised to use our good offices to bring their case for sanctions against South Africa inside the system in any other way we could. . . . By February of 1972 we had introduced a disinvestment resolution for consideration by the House. . . . In fact, it would be more than a decade before the Congress was prepared to come to grips with ending U.S. complicity in the perpetuation of the apartheid regime. . . . But our resolution provided a vehicle for those on the outside to use to begin to build pressure on the Congress for legislative action.

In 1985 we were prepared to press for a vote on our bill—thirteen years in the making, and by now a rigorous and demanding bill. . . . Throughout the early 1980s, my office was in regular communication with the liberation forces in Southern Africa and with activists throughout the United States. Damu Smith of the Washington Office on Africa became one of our closest political supporters, in on the ground floor and working tirelessly on behalf of our effort to achieve a complete economic embargo of South Africa. . . .

At the same time, Representative Bill Gray sponsored an alternative approach, the focus of which was to prohibit new investment. The anti-apartheid movement was split on appropriate strategic next steps in the legislative arena. Some believed that they should strike to the center, support a more moderate bill and seek the "achievable" outcome; others wanted to press for maximum sanctions.

In addition to introducing a bill that reflected my own preference for the latter course, I had also co-sponsored the Gray bill, along with my CBC colleagues, in an effort to ensure that some action by the United States would be taken.

In 1985 neither bill became law, as President Reagan threatened a veto while issuing an executive order imposing very limited sanctions. The next year the Gray bill moved through the House of Representatives, as it had in 1985. At the end of the debate, the House voted on an amendment . . . substituting the stronger version.

At that moment there were more Democrats on the floor than there were Republicans. Those colleagues who surrounded me on the Democratic side wanted to voice strong support for our effort—and the ayes rang out loudly. They clearly overwhelmed the more tepid nay votes that arose mostly from the Republican side of the aisle.

184

From Local to National

The Republicans made a tactical error in failing to call for a recorded vote that would probably have defeated the amendment. Representative Mark Siljander (R-Michigan) [said] that they calculated that the vote would fail in the Senate, and would be seen as too radical.

But I sensed that in fact Siljander had loosed a tidal force by failing to call for a recorded vote. I had seen that no Democrat had the heart to oppose the disinvestment bill. It was also apparent that Republicans were reluctant to be seen as favoring apartheid. They were all caught in a conundrum.

The bill thus passed the House, but the Senate passed a weaker version, and the House Democratic Party leadership accepted a compromise to put forward the weaker Senate version to President Reagan for signature.

In the end, Reagan's veto made a Senate bill that I and other activists felt was a weak one far more significant than would otherwise have been. When the Republican Senate and the Democratic House both overrode the veto, a clear message was sent to South Africa—the people's representatives within the government of the United States had trumped the executive branch, and had taken control of the character of the sanctions that would be imposed.

Our three-pronged strategy had worked: first, consult with grassroots activists and provide them with the grounds from which to press in congressional districts for the most principled position possible—in this case, complete disinvestment and embargo; second, work with willing national organizations to generate a lobbying presence on behalf of bold government action—maximum sanctions, in the case of apartheid—always creating pressure to move the middle to the left; third, engage congressional colleagues and educate them about the issues and the pathways for change.

Congressman Ron Dellums of California protests in front of the South African embassy, December 1984. *Photo © Rick Reinhard.*

# Chapter 6

# The 1990s:
# Seeking New Directions

*Walter Turner*

For me, as for many other American activists, the historic April 1994 election in South Africa was the culmination of decades of political work and dreams. Personal connections had already made that country a part of my life. Now I was traveling to South Africa as part of a delegation from California's Bay Area with the mission to support the campaign of the African National Congress and its partners in a tripartite alliance, the South African Communist Party and the Congress of South African Trade Unions (COSATU). Our delegation included, among others, Fran Beal, Nesbit Crutchfield, Arla Ertz, Gerald Lenoir, and Essie Mormen. Linda Burnham, then and now director of the Women of Color Resource Center in Oakland, had coordinated planning for the group.

We arrived in South Africa a few days before the election to find the atmosphere charged with tension. I worked with COSATU-supported candidates in Germiston, just outside Johannesburg. Each day we drove between meetings in Johannesburg, voter training in the East Rand, and COSATU events throughout the Johannesburg region. Several days before the election a bomb exploded in the taxi rank near our offices. My first thoughts were whether any of my COSATU comrades—Disco Chigo, Joyce Kgoali, Elizabeth Thabete, or Godfrey Tsotetsi—had been killed.

But the election was held. Thabete, Kgoali, and Tsotetsi were elected to office, the ANC won an overwhelming victory, and our delegation celebrated along with millions of South Africans and supporters around the world.

Even as we were celebrating, however, it was already clear that we would face new questions about our work with South Africa and the African continent and how it related to our communities back home in California. Nesbit Crutchfield and I had known each other for 25 years, going back to our common involvement in the San Francisco State University student strike of 1968. Others in our delegation had come to the Bay Area later and had become part of the movement currents that brought together local and community issues of racism with internationalism built on antiracism, anti-imperialism, and Pan-Africanism. For all of us, South Africa was viscerally linked to our lived experience of racism at home. Personal contacts and common struggles had made the African continent and the trans-Atlantic connection part of our lives. By 1994, the connection between our work at home and our work abroad was not in question.

But would the spirit of activism that energized support for the Southern African liberation movements carry over to the

**Walter Turner**
*Photo courtesy of Walter Turner.*

new challenges of Africa in the 1990s? How should we set our personal priorities and strike a balance between coping with family and community issues at home, finding ways to connect to a new South Africa, and delving into areas and issues we were not familiar with—Rwanda, Nigeria, Liberia, Somalia, HIV/AIDS and more? How could we educate ourselves and help educate a new generation of activists for the period ahead?

The answers to these questions were not obvious. In the 1970s and 1980s, the liberation struggle in Southern Africa resonated with our own experiences and memories from the civil rights movement and with our continued experience of racial affronts at home. Now the issues required a different understanding and analysis of African history, and of political and economic realities. After 1994, we had no choice but to look for new directions.

As I talked to my fellow activists about the decade of the 1990s, everyone acknowledged that conditions had changed. There was no ready formula for what to do next, at home or abroad. There were, however, common convictions: that our consciousness of the trans-Atlantic connection should not be allowed to fade away; that new ways must be found to confront abuses to human dignity in Africa, at home, and around the world; and that the victories of the years of solidarity were real, however great the problems that remained to be confronted. The movement we were a part of, all were convinced, had made its own indispensable contribution to African freedom.

## Bay Area Activism in the 1970s and 1980s

The San Francisco State student strike in 1968 was the first major action demanding that Third World studies be offered at a large U.S. institution. It was also the first big leap in my consciousness about Africa. I was already a member of the Black Panther Party chapter in Marin City, north of San Francisco, and the Black Panther newspaper frequently carried stories on liberation struggles in Guinea-Bissau, Namibia, South Africa, and Mozambique, as well as in Asia and Latin America. At San Francisco State, the Third World Liberation Front, a political union of Asian Americans, Latin Americans, and African Americans, was at the forefront of the strike organizers. We were demanding changes in staff, curriculum, and recruitment policies.

The strike was a bitter one, and some of us went to jail for our participation in civil disobedience.

The strike made a clear connection between what was happening on our campus and what was happening in Africa. We knew of the visits to Africa by SNCC members and by Malcolm X. Malcolm's two historic visits to meet key leaders on the African continent in 1964 cemented our notion of a connection between our struggles. The film *The Battle of Algiers*, which first appeared in 1965, was shown repeatedly on campus, and we read *The Wretched of the Earth* by Frantz Fanon in study groups. It was a time of Black Power and of a new international consciousness.

For me, as for Nesbit Crutchfield, who later worked in community organizing and youth counseling in Marin County, international connections and local struggles became inseparable. In addition to his local work, Crutchfield visited Cuba with the Venceremos Brigade in 1979 and 1982. There he found Africa as well as Latin America to be high on the agenda for solidarity with world revolution.

For my part, I transferred to the University of California at Berkeley and was fortunate to participate in a summer study program in Ghana in 1971. This was another giant leap in my consciousness about Africa. By the end of that summer I was convinced that this would be the first of many trips to the continent; Africa would be central to my vision for the rest of my life. As I continued my studies and local community involvement after returning from Ghana, I worked on layout and editing for the Black Panther newspaper, with a strong emphasis on international affairs.

It was not only black community activists who were involved in support for African liberation. The Liberation Support Movement was based among white leftists in Oakland, Seattle, and Vancouver, Canada. Founded in 1968 by Don Barnett, an anthropologist from Iowa who had studied the Mau Mau in Kenya, it included Ole Gjerstad from Norway and Chantal Sarrazin from Quebec, as well as Americans. It played a key role in bringing information from the liberation movements to all of us.

The 1976 Soweto uprising in South Africa first brought Africa to the forefront for many in the United States, and the decade following Soweto was the high point of Africa solidarity work in the Bay Area, as else-

James Madhlope Phillips leads the multiracial choir Vukani Mawethu, based in Berkeley, California, in late 1980s. Phillips, a South African labor organizer and Communist Party member, was a founder of Mayibuye, the cultural unit of the African National Congress. He left the country in 1984 after a banning order curtailed his work. He began to train choirs in Europe and the United States to sing liberation songs in the indigenous languages of South Africa, using music as a vehicle to teach thousands about the freedom struggle. *Photo courtesy of Vukani Mawethu.*

The Vukani Mawethu choir visits South Africa in 1997. *Photo courtesy of Vukani Mawethu.*

where. Nesbit Crutchfield became intensely involved in support for the liberation struggle in Zimbabwe, working with a local group spurred on by the presence of Tirivafi Kangai, a Zimbabwean who studied at Berkeley and became the ZANU representative in the United States. Both Crutchfield and I were part of Bay Area coalitions on Southern Africa, which focused particularly on South Africa after the independence of Zimbabwe in 1980.

Ida Strickland and Belvie Rooks of the Third World Fund were among the leaders developing a support base for this work, often providing the resources to host liberation movement representatives. The Data Center in Oakland, an international research center that initially focused on Latin America, provided a home for the Africa Resource Center, which I helped found and directed from the late 1970s through the late 1980s. The resource center maintained a library and organized public events. California Newsreel in San Francisco became a key distribution point for films on the liberation struggle, serving schools, churches, and solidarity groups around the country.

The Bay Area became one of the pacesetters for action against apartheid, and we had a national impact through networks such as our trade union activists and public officials. We also hooked into national networks, using information, for example, from the national Stop Banking on Apartheid campaign. Miloanne Hecathorne, working out of the local offices of the American Friends Service Committee, spearheaded a campaign that targeted the California-based Bank of America.

The Vanguard Foundation, founded in 1972 in San Francisco, consistently made anti-apartheid work one of its priorities. Led by Hari Dillon and Danny Glover, it was one of the steady influences fostering a link between national and international issues around racism, social justice, gender equality, and human rights.

One of the key communications vehicles for the movement in the Bay Area was Pacifica radio station KPFA, where Faraha Hiyati started a regular radio program called *Africa Today* in 1977. I took over that slot two years later and have continued to host the program ever since. The program covered the African diaspora as well as events on the continent, allowing me to follow the ups and downs of Africa work in our community.

Nelson Mandela addresses the United Nations Special Committee Against Apartheid after his release from prison in 1990. *UN Photo.*

The year of the South African election, 1994, was the turning point, the culmination of decades of work and the beginning of a new period. Our trans-Atlantic African connections would begin to take different shape. This process had just barely begun as the decade, and the millennium, ended.

## New Ways of Connecting

Nelson Mandela's long-awaited release from prison in 1990 was an inspiration to some to remain involved with South Africa. For others it was a sign that priorities would now shift. One of those was Leo Robinson of the International Longshore and Warehouse Union. "We watched it on TV, when [Mandela] walked out and got in the car and drove away. When he drove away, my anti-apartheid work was over." Whatever might happen from that point on, Robinson felt, the South Africans would deal with it. Active in his local union, Robinson had also campaigned against police brutality and to raise awareness of the pressing economic situation facing workers at home. For him, these issues now became paramount.

Nesbit Crutchfield also turned his primary attention to local issues after 1994. But he still took every opportunity he could to travel to South Africa. Despite his years of solidarity work, his first such opportunity had only come in 1991, when he joined a trip to Zimbabwe and South Africa that I organized for the recently formed Global Exchange. The first time he set foot there, he immediately felt "more at home in South Africa than in the United States." He returned for the election in 1994 and later to visit his daughter, who had decided to spend her junior year of college studying in Cape Town. While he continued his professional career and engagement at home, Crutchfield told me that his community "had expanded tenfold." For his family and his wider social circle, Africa became not just a subject of interest but part of their lives.

Among groups maintaining close ties with South Africa was Vukani Mawethu, a multiracial choir of more than 60 people that was formed on the initiative of the great South African freedom singer James Madhlope Phillips during a visit to Berkeley in 1986.

During the anti-apartheid period this choir was a force for unity among activists of rival political tendencies, inspiring countless community audiences and raising funds for the liberation movements. The choir performed for Nelson Mandela's visit to the United States in 1990 and continued to sing at community events throughout the decade. In 1997 the singers toured South African cities and townships. A vibrant community institution for more than 20 years, Vukani Mawethu still performs concerts to support organizations working on HIV/AIDS in South African townships and other causes.

The Institute for a New South Africa, on whose board I served, began in the 1980s and continued in the 1990s to build links between communities and city officials in the United States and South Africa. Myesha Jenkins, a Bay Area activist, went to South Africa to head its office and was still living there in 2007. Although the institute itself did not survive the 1990s, many of the participants are still working in local governments in South Africa.

Global Exchange, a Bay Area organization founded in 1988 by Kevin Danaher, Kirsten Moller, and Medea Benjamin, continues today to make vital links between Southern African and U.S. activists. Danaher had become a leading researcher on Southern Africa after his initial engagement in the divestment movement at the University of California, Santa Cruz, while Benjamin had worked briefly in independent Mozambique. Global Exchange, for which I have been a tour leader and board member since 1989, has always included Southern Africa in its active program of "reality tours" intended to educate U.S. activists and engage them in dialogue with their counterparts in other countries.

Similarly, the Women of Color Resource Center, founded in 1990, treats dialogue with African women from the continent as an integral part of its work. Founder and director Linda Burnham carries on a family tradition of engagement with progressive causes. Her father, Louis Burnham, edited the magazine *Freedom* for Paul Robeson and was on the staff of the progressive *National Guardian* until his death in 1960. Linda Burnham made contacts with African liberation struggles through her participation in Venceremos Brigades to Cuba in 1971 and 1972. Cuba was actively involved in support for African liberation, hosting frequent visits by libera-

tion movement leaders and educating African students in Cuba. As part of the Third World Women's Alliance, Burnham helped organize annual South African Women's Day demonstrations in the Bay Area in the 1970s and 1980s. She also raised funds for an ANC child care center in Africa.

Burnham has led delegations of women of color from the United States to participate in U.N.-sponsored global interchanges, beginning with the World Conference on Women held in Nairobi in 1985 and continuing with the Beijing women's conference in 1995 and the World Conference against Racism in Durban in 2001. At these gatherings, which advanced global thinking on women's rights, African women were in the forefront. After Burnham returned from Beijing, I spoke with her on *Africa Today*. She had helped put together a delegation of more than 115 women of color from the United States to attend the conference. There were thousands of women from the African continent in attendance, she told our radio listeners. These women not only stressed familiar women's rights issues but also insisted that global economic policies—notably the cutbacks in public services imposed on African countries as part of "structural adjustment"—were at the heart of women's concerns. For Burnham, as for many others, African issues in the second half of the 1990s began to intertwine with issues of global policies and economic globalization.

Elsewhere in the United States, as in the Bay Area, veterans of the movement found new ways to engage with South Africa and the continent, often creatively bringing their connections into their ongoing professional work. In Washington, DC, for example, I talked to Sandra Rattley, who had been one of the coordinators of press coverage for Nelson Mandela's historic 1990 U.S. tour and for several subsequent visits by Winnie Mandela. Rattley began her career as a radio journalist at the Howard University station WHUR and worked closely with the local Southern Africa Support Project in the 1970s and 1980s. Her long career with public radio included directing the Satellite Program Development Fund that supported independent producers and public radio projects, and she has always been engaged with international as well as domestic issues.

In the 1990s much of Rattley's time in Africa was spent tracing the roots of her own Quander

National and local anti-apartheid activists at a reception at the South African embassy in Washington, 1997. Back row, from left: Joan Sonn, South African ambassador Franklin Sonn, Randall Robinson, Representative Ronald Dellums, Roger Wilkins, Coalition of Black Trade Unionists founder William Lucy, Dick Gregory, Chestivia Shoemaker. Front row, from left: a South African embassy official, Hazel Ross, Rev. Joseph Lowery, Gay McDougall, Cecelie Counts, Sylvia Hill, John Payton, Sandra Hill, A. C. Byrd. *Photo by Ron Lewis. Courtesy of Sylvia Hill.*

family, documenting ties to her ancestors in Cape Coast, Ghana. In 1999 she turned her radio expertise to launching the satellite-based Africa Learning Channel, now a part of First Voice International. The noncommercial channel works with more than 190 community broadcasting partners across Africa to distribute programs on HIV/AIDS and other health and development issues.

## Africa in the New Global Context

As I continued to question activists about the dilemmas that faced us after 1994, I found no common answers. But I did find common themes. For all of us, African Americans but also white activists, the parallels with our own country's history of racial oppression are fundamental. Our engagement with Africa is embedded in an understanding of the damage inflicted over the centuries on both sides of the Atlantic by slavery and colonialism—and by the new forms of economic exploitation and social inequality that followed. Although we came to the African connection at different times and in response to different events, that connection was rooted in the previous history of Pan-African connections.

Since the early Pan-African congresses that began in 1900, Africans of the diaspora have engaged with

anticolonial struggles in Africa. This engagement has responded to a consciousness of shared circumstances and intertwined histories and the felt need to speak out for the African continent within our home countries. Apartheid was not seen as merely an African issue; rather, the South African regime was the final embodiment of white minority rule that dominated almost the entire globe at the beginning of the twentieth century. For black activists, opposition to U.S. support for apartheid was also tied to our growing understanding of the history of U.S. imperial expansion and its toll in the Caribbean and Latin America. We placed our opposition to the Vietnam War and to Reagan-era interventions in the same historical framework.

After apartheid's fall, anti-apartheid activists in the United States were acutely aware from our own experience that the end of legal discrimination and the expansion of formal political rights would not mean the end of racial abuse or of the inequality and poverty left by generations of racial oppression. But on both sides of the Atlantic, it was clear that the issues ahead, as Sandra Rattley commented, would not lend themselves to "bumper sticker politics." The clearly visible enemy, the die-hard white racist leaders, had exited stage right.

Most activists understood that organizing around issues of debt, development, and corruption would require targeting both international economic institutions and corrupt and unaccountable African governments tied to these institutions. The Jubilee 2000 coalition focused on debt, while the 50 Years Is Enough campaign targeted the World Bank and governments that were accepting its right-wing economic prescriptions. These campaigns aimed to raise public consciousness about the World Bank and the International Monetary Fund and to link these issues with domestic policies that affected poor and minority communities in the United States. But while the issues were real and vital,

Walter Turner

they were not as dramatically visible as those that had characterized the anti-apartheid campaign.

Africa, we were discovering again, is immensely complex. More than three times the size of the United States, the continent by the mid-1990s included 54 countries and more than 800 million people. Few in the United States, even among activists, were familiar with more than a few chapters of the history. Fewer still understood the contemporary political landscape of the continent or had much knowledge of the countries that would feature in the headlines of the decade. African issues were still often perceived through long-standing stereotypes that had only partially been dislodged during the civil rights and anti-apartheid periods.

Meanwhile, at home, the televised beating of Rodney King by Los Angeles police officers in 1991 laid bare the continuing racial divide in the United States, as well as the unresolved issue of police brutality. The war on drugs particularly penalized minorities. That same year President George H. W. Bush chose right-wing ideologue Clarence Thomas to succeed civil rights pioneer Thurgood Marshall as the single African American on the Supreme Court. Although the Republican era of presidents Reagan and Bush was followed in 1993 by the two-term Democratic Clinton presidency, the rollback of social and economic rights for American workers and poor people continued. Large industries and unions were under the gun and the economic situation was difficult.

In terms of awareness of Africa, one problem was simply that, after Nelson Mandela's release from prison riveted worldwide attention for a brief instant, the U.S. gaze shifted elsewhere. Even South Africa's transition to freedom gained only minimal television time or policy attention in comparison to the Gulf War of 1990–91 or the conflicts in the

ANC deputy president Walter Sisulu and Imani Countess of the Washington Office on Africa greet each other in October 1991. Sisulu was released in October 1989 after serving 26 years in prison with Nelson Mandela and eight others convicted at the Rivonia Trial. The Africa Fund organized a tour of the United States for Sisulu and his wife Albertina Sisulu, deputy president of the ANC Women's League. *Photo © Rick Reinhard.*

former Yugoslavia. The rise of civil society and pro-democracy movements across the African continent in countries like Benin, Mali, and Kenya received almost no coverage in the U.S. media.

The violence in Somalia and then Rwanda gained momentary attention, long enough to reinforce stereotypes but not long enough to promote understanding or engagement. Even the wars in historically closer West Africa drew little attention. And only a few commentators and activists noted that a number of the countries experiencing the most intense conflict—Somalia, Liberia, Zaire—had been key Cold War clients of the United States.

Both Africa and the international community were still in denial about the spread of HIV/AIDS on the continent. From its initial area of concentration in East and Central Africa, the disease continued a steady march across the continent, hitting Southern Africa with particular force. In the United States, HIV/AIDS was also spreading rapidly in some African American communities. But the stigma associated with the disease closed off discussion about this new threat to Africans. Those living with HIV/AIDS feared public exposure. By the end of the decade more than 2 million Africans were dying of AIDS each year. In the

United States, antiretroviral drugs were increasingly in use by the 1990s, saving many lives. But even most medical experts assumed that the drugs were too expensive or too complicated for use in Africa. Until activists mobilized after the July 2000 AIDS conference in Durban, South Africa, few questioned that Africans with AIDS would just be left to die.

With the end of the Cold War and the end of political apartheid in South Africa, the context for mobilizing public pressure to change U.S. foreign policy in Africa was fundamentally altered. The U.S. government had little incentive to keep its former Cold War clients in power. And U.S. complicity with white minority regimes no longer provided a meaningful target. Indeed, the primary threat was no longer Washington's active involvement but rather its indifference—and growing economic imperialism in the guise of globalization.

The Rwandan genocide in 1994 was the most extreme example of this indifference. The United States played a decisive role in blocking U.N. action that could have saved hundreds of thousands of lives. But similar patterns played out elsewhere as well.

In Liberia, dictator Samuel Doe, who provided Washington with a covert base for operations against Libya's Qaddafi, was overthrown by rebels in 1990. Liberian pleas for the United States to take the lead in promoting peace were ignored. U.S. marines were deployed off the coast to evacuate U.S. citizens only— a pattern the United States and other Western powers would repeat both in Liberia and elsewhere in the following years. West African forces under Nigerian leadership intervened in Liberia late in 1990, but by that time the country was shattered. "What is certain is that failure to stop the fighting during 1990, before the entire country was demolished, erected barriers to a solution that still have not been overcome," noted Reed Kramer of Africa News Service (1995).

Meanwhile, other crises were erupting across the continent. Anarchy in Somalia followed the fall of Washington's Cold War client Siad Barre. In Angola, Jonas Savimbi lost internationally supervised elections in 1992 and promptly returned to war. The conflict raged for a decade while Washington stalled repeatedly on officially recognizing the newly elected Angola government and blocking the flow of arms to Savimbi's Unita. In Zaire, dictator Mobutu Sese Seko held on to power until 1997, but war continued at even higher levels after his fall. The complex conflict drew in almost all of Zaire's neighbors and allowed widespread looting of mineral resources. There were so many countries involved that the conflict was sometimes called "Africa's world war."

These conflicts and others caused hundreds of thousands, possibly millions of deaths—far more than the concurrent conflicts in the former Yugoslavia. Nevertheless, none of the African crises received a fraction of the media or policy attention given to the situation in southeastern Europe. A constructive U.S. role in resolving these African conflicts would have required American officials to work with multilateral African and international partners to mount coordinated pressures for peaceful solutions.

Africa advocacy groups in Washington—such as the Washington Office on Africa, TransAfrica, and the Africa Faith and Justice Network—could and did call for alternative policies. So did the church groups with personal ties to Liberia, Sierra Leone, and Zaire in particular. They were often joined by human rights groups, humanitarian agencies, and exiles from the affected African countries. But it was much more difficult to critique U.S. indifference and inaction than it had been to blast U.S. complicity with apartheid. Moreover, many activists were reluctant to call for U.S. action because they feared it might do more harm than good. In none of these cases was there a critical mass of activists around the country familiar with the issues and able to push them onto the public agenda.

## Starting Over with Public Education

Solidarity, we had learned, was impossible without a base of knowledge and networks of personal contacts. Many of us were already engaged in information and exchange projects that defined our tasks in continent-wide terms, and we were ready to continue even as the wave of intense interest in South Africa receded. In addition to maintaining and expanding our own contacts, we relied on publications such as *Africa News* for up-to-date information on what was happening in Africa. My weekly *Africa Today* program on KPFA was one of the longest-running local radio shows, along with Elombe Brath's *Afrikaleidoscope* in New York and Assumpta Oturu's *Spotlight Africa* on KPFK in Los Angeles. But there were also similar programs with loyal audiences on radio stations around the country.

In the 1990s, more Americans than ever before were traveling to Africa, or studying or working there. And more Africans were immigrating to the United States. Among African Americans, identification with Africa was still rising, with both cultural and political expressions.

Even so, I am not sure we realized how large was the public education task that lay ahead of us. Despite the natural parallels to our battles with racism at home, it had taken decades of political work to build up public understanding of South Africa. That work had benefited from a long-term emphasis by the African National Congress on educating Americans and others around the world. The pervasive involvement of U.S. companies in the apartheid system had given us political targets that captured local attention in communities throughout the United States. Now, although we had the advantages of easier communications and travel, and although we benefited from the new influx of African immigrants from a range of countries, we also faced new disadvantages. Most Americans did not even know the names of the countries where the burning issues of the decade were playing out, much less understand the complexity of these issues.

One group that quickly faced the issue of how to adapt to the changes was California Newsreel. Its Southern Africa work was directed by Cornelius Moore, who had grown up in Chester, Pennsylvania, and had become involved with the African Liberation Support Committee and other groups in Philadelphia in the 1970s. He had begun a career in film exhibition and distribution in Philadelphia before moving to California to work with Newsreel in 1981. Moore says that interest in their anti-apartheid films dropped significantly in the early 1990s, after Mandela's release. The films couldn't keep pace with events, he commented, while the momentum of activism was diminishing.

Nevertheless, in the 1990s, Newsreel, building on long-standing marketing connections to schools, churches, and community organizations, continued to grow. They maintained an emphasis on issues of racism and black history and culture in the United States, and they also launched a new "Library of African Cinema" that brought a wide variety of films to American audiences. Films from Senegal's Ousmane Sembène and other Francophone filmmakers featured prominently. As with the earlier

African liberation films, Newsreel offered background material and teaching aids to help students understand African realities.

Another movement veteran who focused on public education about African issues was Adwoa Dunn-Mouton, a fellow Berkeley student from the East Bay who was on the study tour to Ghana with me in 1971. Both of us stayed in Ghana after the tour, only returning to Berkeley to resume classes in the fall. Dunn-Mouton also made a lasting connection with Africa. After completing her master's degree in 1974, she left the doctoral history program at Berkeley and moved to the East Coast, thinking that the odds of finding Africa-related work would be greater there because at least it was closer to the continent. Working at Howard University's African studies program doing outreach to public schools, she also became an active member of the Southern Africa Support Project. In 1985 she joined the staff of the House Africa Subcommittee, and she became the lead staff person for the Senate Africa Subcommittee from 1990 to 1993.

"I never felt like I was just doing it for Africa," she told me when we talked in 2004. "I always felt that I was getting something from Africa. [I learned] that we

Adwoa Dunn-Mouton, then on the staff of the House Subcommittee on Africa, and Representative Howard Wolpe of Michigan, the subcommittee chair, on a congressional visit to Angola in 1985. *Photo courtesy of Adwoa Dunn-Mouton.*

did belong to a world that was larger than Richmond, California." From 1995 to 1999, Dunn-Mouton was involved with a large project to produce a two-hour documentary film on Africa in the 1990s called *Hopes on the Horizon*. The series was produced by Blackside, an African American company that had made its reputation with *Eyes on the Prize*, a history of the U.S. civil rights movement. *Hopes* was made in cooperation with African filmmakers and directed by Onyekachi Wambu, a London-based Nigerian filmmaker. Dunn-Mouton traveled between Washington, Boston, and Ghana, and around the African continent, ironing out problems and working with the team to ensure that the final product both reflected African realities and could communicate with American audiences. The film premiered on public television in 2001 with segments on the pro-democracy struggles in Benin and Nigeria, post-genocide Rwanda, women's rights in Morocco, and development challenges in Mozambique and South Africa.

Dunn-Mouton also served on the board of the Africa Policy Information Center (APIC), which evolved out of the Washington Office on Africa Educational Fund. In doing public education about African issues, APIC took advantage of the new possibilities for direct electronic communication with Africa and with activists around the world. In 1995 it began regular e-mail distribution of key information from sources that included organizations and activists on the African continent. Edited by William Minter, APIC's e-mail bulletin served to connect and amplify the efforts of APIC and other groups working on issues such as debt cancellation, the landmines treaty, and the struggle for democracy in Nigeria. It joined allAfrica.com, formerly Africa News Service, as one of the key sources for activists working on African issues, and continues today as *AfricaFocus Bulletin*.

## Campaigning for Democracy in Nigeria

The African issue that most engaged activists in the 1990s, paralleling in many ways the anti-apartheid cause, was the Nigeria pro-democracy movement. Nigeria had gained independence in October 1960 after a long but largely peaceful movement for independence led by figures such as Nnamdi Azikiwe and Chief Obafemi Awolowo. In the three decades preceding the 1990s, the country had alternated between short periods of intense civilian political competition and longer stretches of military rule. Between 1967 and 1970, the country fought a civil war over the secession of the eastern region, called Biafra. Despite intense ethnic polarization and perhaps as many as a million people killed during the brutal war, the central government, which won the conflict, followed a policy of nonretribution. Subsequent division of Nigeria into smaller states in a federal system produced larger representation for ethnic groups other than the big three (Yoruba in the west, Igbo in the east, and Hausa in the north).

But in spite of a vibrant civil society and world-renowned writers and intellectuals, Nigeria was caught in the trap of military rule. Corruption centered on competition for the revenue from an oil industry that began production just before independence and boomed in the 1970s and 1980s. In June 1993, elections for a return to civilian rule brought victory to Moshood Abiola. Although the military itself had approved both Abiola and his opponent Bashir Tofa, Abiola, a flamboyant media magnate and philanthropist, was seen as potentially more independent. The military regime annulled the election results. In November General Sani Abacha took over from a short-lived caretaker regime. Meanwhile, Ken Saro-Wiwa, a leading writer and social critic, was mobilizing support for his Ogoni people, one of the groups on oil-rich land whose chronic poverty had been made worse by devastation of their environment.

Abacha took military repression to new heights, despite a growing international movement to isolate the regime. In November 1995 his government executed Ken Saro-Wiwa and eight other leaders of the Movement for the Survival of the Ogoni People. The Clinton administration, as well as other Western governments, imposed limited sanctions, including a ban on arms sales and visa restrictions on Nigerian officials. After the execution of Saro-Wiwa, Nigeria was suspended from the Commonwealth. But the deep involvement of international oil companies, including Shell, Chevron, and Mobil, and Nigeria's role as a leading oil supplier to the United States meant that Washington and its allies held back from significant economic pressures.

In the United States as well as around the world, however, Nigeria's pro-democracy forces were able to launch a solidarity movement. Like the anti-apartheid movement, though on a shorter timeline and a

Demonstrators in front of a Shell station in Washington, DC, protest Shell Oil's ties to the Nigerian regime of dictator General Sani Abacha, 1994. Folabi Olagbaju of the Service Employees International Union leads the demonstration. Two people behind him is Stephen Mills of the Sierra Club. *Photo courtesy of Stephen Mills.*

smaller scale, the movement mobilized a broad coalition and added to the pressure that led to Nigeria's return to civilian rule in 1999. This organizing was of particular importance because it demonstrated that, at least in some cases, it was possible to be effective even when repression did not fall along racial lines.

In New York I talked with Mike Fleshman, who had taken on the Nigeria issue for The Africa Fund and the American Committee on Africa in the 1990s. Fleshman was a student at the University of California at Santa Cruz when the Soweto uprising broke out. "For me it was the culmination of all the things that I had been doing . . . antiracism and anti-imperialist stuff," he recalled. Fleshman had learned about racism, he says, from black classmates in a small high school in Roswell, Georgia. As the only Northerner, "I was a white student but the rednecks hated me." The black students "finally decided that the enemy of our enemy could conceivably be some sort of an ally," and ultimately they became friends. At Santa Cruz he was one of the leaders of the divestment campaign that mobilized students and professors and raised almost $40,000 on the campus to support Southern African liberation movements.

Fleshman was a member of The Africa Fund staff in the 1990s and recalls a planning meeting in June 1994, just after the South African election.

Should the organization declare victory and go out of business? Should it turn to development rather than political organizing? The decision was taken to continue the stress on organizing, but the question was how to focus. Three countries quickly presented themselves: Zaire, Liberia, and Nigeria.

Fleshman remembers that they discussed each case in turn. Although no national movement had arisen in the United States around Zaire, that country had been a focal point for activists because of the blatant corruption of the Mobutu regime and because of Zaire's intervention in Angola. Fleshman recalls:

> Mobutu was on his way out, but Mobutu was still there. But at that point the American [government] had pretty much cut him out, and there wasn't a particularly strong U.S. policy or economic connection anymore. And we always figured that basically what you needed to run an ACOA-style campaign was really to have [three elements]. Good guys so you could say, you have to support these folks. You need the bad guys to oppose. And you needed a strong U.S. economic and/or political connection to the bad guys.

They didn't really have a good idea of whom to support in Zaire, Fleshman explained, and language was another complication. It would be harder to find effective English-speaking spokespeople in French-speaking Zaire to bring a campaign to U.S. audiences.

Liberia was English-speaking, but the situation there by that time was even less clear. There was a strong historical U.S. connection, but Liberia was a country that had spiraled out of control. After the United States removed its citizens, the conflict in Liberia quickly dropped from visibility, the media moving on to other stories. The focus was on humanitarian rather than political issues. That left Nigeria under the Abacha regime.

Around the country, activists were turning to Nigeria, often at the initiative of pro-democracy advocates in the growing Nigerian diaspora. By the end of the 1990s the U.S. census counted 87,000 U.S. residents born in Nigeria. The actual numbers, including families, probably exceeded 200,000. In the Bay Area, Tunde Okorodudu of Oakland took the lead in getting the Oakland City Council and the Alameda County government to bar business ties with Nigeria. As he explained to me on *Africa Today* in July 1996, this comprehensive city action against Nigeria forced people to think about "blood money" for Nigeria. The Goldman Environmental Foundation awarded its 1995 prize in absentia to the imprisoned Ken Saro-Wiwa, only six months before his death. And the country's largest environmentalist group, the Sierra Club, with home offices in San Francisco, also joined in campaigning on Nigeria. After his brother's death, Dr. Owens Wiwa toured the United States, speaking on Pacifica's *Democracy Now* as well as on local shows such as *Africa Today*, and briefing members of Congress in Washington.

There were, of course, some voices in favor of Abacha in the United States, as the regime's lobbyists targeted black legislators and arranged visits by a host of less prominent figures. Ultimately, this attempt to sow confusion did not succeed. Activists maintained a concentrated focus on human rights and the role of the oil corporations in undermining democracy and accountable government in Nigeria.

Elombe Brath, the veteran Harlem Pan-Africanist, had hosted Ken Saro-Wiwa in 1990, before groups like The Africa Fund were ready to deal with Nigeria. Despite administration timidity, the Congressional Black Caucus called for sanctions. Significantly, when the only black member of the Senate, Carol Moseley-Braun of Illinois, took a "vacation" trip to Nigeria and defended the Nigerian regime, she was repudiated in the 1998 election. Nigerian immigrants mobilized against her stance on Abacha, and black voters helped usher her out of office by a scant 100,000-vote margin.

In 1994, The Africa Fund knew little about Nigeria. But the relationships it had established with U.S. unions during the anti-apartheid years now provided a natural network to turn to as they took on this new campaign. In particular, their union allies helped make contact with the Nigerian oil workers' union. Targeting the oil companies and focusing on local actions, U.S. activists hoped, might replicate some of the successful strategies used against South Africa.

As with the anti-apartheid movement, a diverse set of groups and networks made up the Nigeria pro-democracy movement. But with the advent of electronic communications, it was far easier than it had been to link their activities. Activists in the worldwide Nigerian diaspora were quick to take advantage of the Internet to mobilize coordinated action. New centers of activity emerged as exiled activists came together with local groups. In St. Louis, for example, a group including the vice president of the Movement for the Survival of the Ogoni People, Noble Obani-Nwibari, worked with the local office of the American Friends Service Committee to organize monthly protests against Shell Oil. In Washington, Ghanaian American human rights activist Adotei Akwei, who had worked in New York for the ACOA and moved to Washington to coordinate Africa issues for Amnesty International, was the guiding force for the International Roundtable on Nigeria. The roundtable's monthly meetings served as a key forum for communication and strategizing, drawing in the veteran anti-apartheid organizations, local and visiting Nigerian activists, trade union activists, environmentalists, and others.

In June 1998 General Sani Abacha died, and opposition leader Moshood Abiola died in prison a month later. The following year, chastened military leaders allowed new elections that brought Olusegun Obasanjo into office. Nigeria's problems—corruption, oil wealth, and more—remained to be solved. But the pro-democracy movement and its overseas supporters had at least contributed to the return to civilian rule.

## New Contexts for Solidarity

Other African immigrant groups in the United States were also mobilizing to support their homelands, but on a smaller scale. Eritreans in the Bay Area and around the country worked to assist their country's development after it gained independence in 1993. Refugees and other immigrants from Liberia and Sierra Leone called for greater U.S. efforts to support U.N. and West African peacekeeping efforts in their countries, and they also sought extended refugee status for those who had fled the fighting. That such efforts did not spark a wider movement is hardly surprising: in the mid-1990s the total populations of Liberia and Sierra Leone were only about 2 million and 4 million respectively, with proportionately small diasporas. By comparison, giant Nigeria had over 100 million people at home and perhaps as many as 15 million scattered around the world.

In these ways and others, a new wave of African immigration to the United States was adding an important dimension to the potential for new relationships with Africa. Although the immigrants' impact on policy and mobilization was still limited, that seemed likely to change. Between 1990 and 2000, according to census figures, the African immigrant population in the United States increased by 134 percent. The 2000 census reported more than 500,000 African-born residents, and estimates of the total community, including children born in the United States, were well in excess of 1 million. The census figures, it is generally recognized, represent a substantial undercount, although it is difficult to establish more accurate figures (Gordon 1988; Logan and Deane 2003).

The community of new African immigrants was also becoming more diverse than ever. They came from more countries and were moving to more communities around the United States. They included people at all levels of the U.S. class structure, with different experiences of assimilation into American life and of continuing ties with their home countries. And, as in every other immigrant group, different generations had contrasting experiences and divergent understandings of their identities.

Like members of other immigrant groups, most Africans were preoccupied with making a living for themselves and their families in a new country. But

when Amadou Diallo was shot and killed by four New York City policemen on February 4, 1999, it was an abrupt reminder that African immigrants in the United States shared the risks faced by all black communities across the country. Diallo, a quiet, hard-working street peddler from Guinea, was gunned down by 41 shots in the entrance to his own apartment building in the Bronx. The police said they thought he resembled a rape suspect, and they feared he was drawing a gun when he reached for his wallet. The murder provoked a mobilization not only in New York but across the country. The next year a jury acquitted the officers of misconduct. Finally, in 2004, Diallo's family received a $3 million civil settlement, and the block where he died was renamed Amadou Diallo Place.

The mobilization around Diallo's death involved African Americans, African immigrants, and supporters from other communities. Haitian American singer Wyclef Jean recorded a song about the death with Senegalese superstar Youssou N'Dour, with a line in the chorus: "Diallo, Diallo—similar to Steven Biko." "The murder of Amadou Diallo was not an aberration," wrote Elombe Brath (1999). "It was part of a tradition that has been going on far too long."

Brath is host of the radio program *Afrikaleidoscope* on radio station WBAI in New York. He has an intimate knowledge of the Pan-Africanist and black nationalist movement throughout the world, and he talks with ease and passion about Africa. Brath's involvement goes back over 50 years: growing up in the Bronx, he found his way to Harlem to join Dominican-born Carlos Cooks with the African Nationalist Pioneer Movement, a Garveyite group. Among its activities was strong support for the Namibian struggle. When Sam Nujoma of SWAPO first arrived in New York in June 1960 to petition the United Nations for Namibia's independence, the Harlem group raised $100,000 to support the Namibian movement (Nujoma 2004).

Brath never subscribed to the simplistic view that black African leaders should be exempt from criticism. He knew early on that skin color alone was hardly sufficient to guide political allegiance. His family was from Barbados, where his mother's cousin, Clennell Wickham, had been a radical newspaper editor who spoke up for the poor. In the Bronx Brath went to school with Colin Powell, who would become U.S. secretary of state (Brath 2004). In 1975, when some black nationalists were attracted to Jonas Savimbi's Unita, Brath founded the Patrice Lumumba Coalition to support Angola against U.S. and South African intervention. His group was also one of the most consistent in calling for opposition to Mobutu and to the military regime in Nigeria.

In the 1990s, even more than before, progressive forces relating to Africa often found themselves puzzled or on different sides when confronted with new conflicts and new issues. Brath, like many other longtime activists with a history of opposing U.S. intervention, was against calling for U.S. military involvement, even to support multilateral peacekeeping and humanitarian operations. Others of us, responding to calls from those directly caught up in disasters such as Liberia, denounced U.S. and international indifference and demanded that Washington "do the right thing" by providing resources for African-led initiatives to respond to crises.

The decade presented more opportunities than ever before for Americans to learn about African issues. African leaders were speaking up in international forums and traveling regularly to Washington and other U.S. cities. Progressive Americans could now travel to South Africa as well as elsewhere on the continent. E-mail connectivity was reaching almost all African capitals, even if not yet the countryside. Groups such as the Black Radical Congress, which emerged in 1998 as a national U.S. group, were well aware of the interconnections between domestic, global, and African issues, and outspoken on crises such as the war in the Congo, formerly Zaire.

Paradoxically, perhaps, the proliferation of voices and issues made it difficult to build consensus around any one course of action. And it was particularly difficult to see how activists could have a real impact. After the South African victory of 1994, the drumbeat of negative news elsewhere in Africa was almost unrelenting. There were seemingly endless wars in Angola, the Congo, Sudan, and West Africa. The HIV/AIDS pandemic was spreading across the continent, killing millions of people in the prime of their productive lives. No one could easily say how best to respond to these new crises; there were only questions.

It was a time of great discouragement. Many activists turned toward other less daunting issues or to purely personal matters. None of those I inter-

viewed for this project were giving up, however. And as I talked with veteran Bay Area activist Gerald Lenoir, who turned from anti-apartheid work to working on AIDS in the 1990s, I was reminded to take a longer-term perspective.

Lenoir had directed the American Friends Service Committee program on South Africa and Namibia in Seattle from 1976 to 1979, and he had played a key role in Seattle coalitions on Southern Africa. He came to the Bay Area in 1986. From 1989 to 1995 he directed the Black Coalition on AIDS in San Francisco, which in addition to its local work provided support for Haitian refugees and training and support for Africans from several countries. It was difficult working on AIDS then, Lenoir told me, "because at that point in the nineties, the black community was in denial about AIDS. . . . They didn't want to hear about AIDS for the most part, and there was an extreme amount of homophobia and fear of drug addicts, and just complete denial around HIV in the black community in America, let alone in Africa. . . . So we had a hard time." Still, they managed to mobilize significant additional resources for HIV/AIDS among African Americans and in Africa.

Today, he reflected,

> I don't think things are going that well, either in America or Africa. [But] I'm not necessarily that discouraged. I just liken it to the early days, when I first came into the anti-apartheid movement in the mid-seventies, when events in Africa sparked another level of activism in the U.S. Soweto slapped me in the face and got me to say, "OK, so what are you going to do?" We're back to some basic base-building and education around what's going on. We're back to those days when people were saying, "Africa? What about Africa?"

"It's still the same struggle, same fight," Lenoir summed up, quoting the often-cited words of Mozambique's Samora Machel. "International solidarity is not an act of charity. It is an act of unity between allies fighting on different terrains for the same objective."

---

*Oral sources for chapter 6 include interviews with Elombe Brath (2004), Linda Burnham (2005), Nesbit Crutchfield (2005), Adwoa Dunn-Mouton (2004), Michael Fleshman (2004), Gerald Lenoir (2005), Cornelius Moore (2004), Sandra Rattley (2004), and Leo Robinson (2005).*

# "Faces Filled with Joy" ✍ The 1994 South African Election

## Gail Hovey

As I stepped aboard the South African Airways plane, my thoughts drifted back to 1969. I had been one of a group of demonstrators picketing the airline to prevent it from landing in the United States as long as apartheid prevailed. That particular effort didn't succeed, but landing rights were finally blocked by the anti-apartheid act in 1986. Now, amazingly, I was boarding one of the airline's planes, flying to South Africa to observe the historic elections of April 26–28, 1994.

I got very little sleep on the long flight from New York. Almost all the passengers were on the same mission, had a history of anti-apartheid activism, and were as filled with anticipation as I was. All of us, in large and small ways, had been looking forward to this day for years if not decades. It was a kind of homecoming.

On arrival in South Africa, I was welcomed by my old friend Molly Bill, whom I had met along with her husband François in 1966 when we worked together in what was then the Northern Transvaal. The family's arena for action against apartheid was the ecumenical church. Their son Charles was forced into exile, and François spent 16 weeks in solitary confinement before being transferred to the white male section of the feared Diepkloof Prison outside Johannesburg in the mid-1980s. Already fluent in a local language, Tsonga, when I met her, Molly took up applied linguistics. Her specialty became training teachers, in what had been white schools, to teach Zulu and South Sotho, prominent languages of the newly named Gauteng province.

A resident of Johannesburg, Molly took me to St Paul's United Church where the preacher's text was from Micah, "beating swords into ploughshares." On the way home we stopped by the supermarket, where whites were frantically buying up canned goods and candles in fear that water and electricity would be cut off amid chaos and violence surrounding the election.

It was not unreasonable to anticipate a certain level of disorder. The Independent Election Commission had had just four months to organize the election. At the end of 1993, it had one employee; by the time the election was held, it had 200,000. There were 9,000 voting stations around the country, some of them still being selected as we arrived. National, regional, and district presiding officers had to be chosen, with two to 26 voting officials per district. Eighty percent of them had been appointed in the preceding week. Voters had to be educated: a substantial majority of the electorate was illiterate and 80 percent of them had never voted before.

As if these challenges were not enough, 18 parties had registered to participate in the election. The one dangerously missing was the Inkatha

Gail Hovey first went to South Africa in 1966 on the Frontier Internship Program of the United Presbyterian Church in the USA. While there, she continued her relationship with the Southern Africa Committee in New York and its publication, *Southern Africa* magazine. Hovey and Don Morlan, both recent graduates of Union Theological Seminary, were assigned to the Tsonga Presbyterian Church/Swiss Mission. Even at an isolated school, Lemana, located some 300 miles north of Johannesburg, they were watched. Finally the Department of Bantu Education called on the church to withdraw them from the school, saying the two were propagating "their own critical view of the generally accepted policies and established customs in this country."

Hovey was not able to return to South Africa until after Nelson Mandela's release in 1990. By this time she was living in Hawai'i, and she traveled halfway around the world to observe the 1994 elections.

Freedom Party (IFP) led by Mangosuthu Gatsha Buthelezi. The IFP and its supporters had been engaged in a long and bloody battle in KwaZulu-Natal against supporters of the United Democratic Front and the ANC. *The Sowetan* reported on April 20 that some 20,000 people had been killed in KwaZulu-Natal since 1985, including 172 in January 1994, 153 in February, and 331 in March. Extraordinary pressures were being exerted to persuade the IFP to participate in the election and end the violence.

The American Committee on Africa contingent of which I was a part included South Africans Jennifer Davis and Dumisani Kumalo, each of whom had spent decades in exile; Betsy Landis, a member of the board since the 1950s, who had become an expert on Namibia; and Prexy Nesbitt, who had played many roles in the solidarity movement over a quarter century. Aleah Bacquie, a member of ACOA's staff, had already been in South Africa for much of the year. At the request of President Frank Chikane of the South African Council of Churches, Bacquie had been seconded to that organization. She worked in communications, helping counter the minority government's continuing attempts to mislead the international community about progress in the country.

We were briefed first in Johannesburg. Davis, Nesbitt, and I had been assigned to KwaZulu-Natal. We drove to Durban for a second briefing and met colleagues from Oxfam Canada with whom we were paired. At last, we were briefed on site at our base in Empangeni.

The ACOA team was in South Africa as part of a larger observer presence organized by the Lawyers' Committee for Civil Rights Under Law. Concerned about our safety, the organizers had not wanted us to observe in KwaZulu-Natal. Jennifer Davis ended the heated discussion about this by saying simply, "If people are brave enough to vote, they deserve to have observers." At the eleventh hour, the Inkatha Freedom Party joined the election. New ballots were printed. The tension and fear in the region diminished quickly, and we were able to travel from one polling place to another without incident.

Our territory was rural: green rolling hills, potholed dirt roads, isolated schoolhouses, and tiny villages. Our job was to report immediately to an election official any incident that might compromise the standard of "free and fair" and to submit a daily record of our experiences.

Virtually everything that could go wrong, did go wrong. At Sundumbili Plaza, for example, an enormous tent was set up in the middle of a field for a double polling station, and the large, orderly crowd waited outside. But when we went inside, the presiding officer informed us that not a single person had voted. The generators had blown out the machines that could read the invisible ink on voters' hands that was intended to ensure that no one voted more than once. People got busy; the generator was repaired; new machines were brought. When the voting finally started, it went so fast that they ran out of ballots three times. The people waited, the wind rose, the tent shuddered and sighed, but the supply of ballots was replenished and the tent held.

Seemingly endless variations on this experience were repeated each day as we went out from Empangeni. What was at stake was in evidence again and again. We saw it in the ingenuity and perseverance of election officials. We saw it in the voters' faces. "We are going to vote," Mabungu, a waiting voter, said. "They can't kill all of us." "Thank God that before I died, I tasted voting." They queued up on sidewalks, stood in single lines that snaked like rivers or squared the corners of enormous fields. "I have waited for this day for all my life and I will wait for all the day if needs be," said another voter, Mashigo.

When eight white policemen burst into the polling place at Eshowe Town Hall, the fears and suspicion that had plagued the buildup to the election were suddenly manifest again. I felt the general panic. What was wrong? What had we failed to observe? And then I laughed out loud as the officers disarmed and stood in line to cast their ballots.

"It is good to get to vote while you are still alive," said Klaas.

Isithebe School ran short of ballots. Election officers and the police—both the South African police and the KwaZulu police—argued about what to do and someone was dispatched to bring more ballots. It was the first time that the South African police had been on what was KwaZulu police turf. The South African Defense Force was also present. Feared and hated until this moment, it was suddenly the welcome, neutral stabilizer.

"Now I can die with happiness in my heart," said 80-year-old Samuel Bhene. "Now I can walk like a real man."

The people came; the ballot boxes filled and were sealed with sealing wax. They switched to collecting ballots in mail bags. The people came, and the people in the great majority put Mandela in the box.

Every official observer's experience was different in the details. But all of us had participated in an event that marked both closure and conception, a rare moment that represented suffering and sacrifice beyond reckoning, courage and promise that only time would measure.

And so at last, after more than eight decades, with generations of petitioners, protestors, diplomacy, and armed struggle, the African National Congress won a resounding victory across the country. Nelson Mandela became the first president of all of South Africa's people. Some observers were able to stay on to hear Mandela's May 2 acceptance speech and attend the party that followed and the May 10 inauguration. I was among those who had to fly home before that. But my colleagues and indispensable friends Jennifer Davis and Dumisani Kumalo went to the party, which was the next best thing to being there myself, especially when Jen faxed me the news:

> As we waited the mood was wonderful—lots of our old friends—who hugged and kissed us and kept saying over and over, "Thank you." "We couldn't have done it without you." . . . [Zambia's Kenneth] Kaunda was there and asked where George [Houser] was, sent his greetings. . . . The ANC choir sang wonderful songs in the background. The mood kept building and the room filling. The walls

were lined . . . with TV sets, and with thousands of black, yellow and gold balloons.

Jennifer went on to say that President Mandela spoke with a strong but not a strident voice. He reached out to the other parties, saying that all leaders would be needed, were "worthy South Africans." He spoke of the legendary heroes across the generations and said that the people, with their courage, had won this night. He called on all South Africans to celebrate the birth of a new nation, but he asked them to do it in a peaceful and respectful way. "This is a joyous night for the human spirit."

Then it was party time, Jennifer wrote. "'We did it. We did it. Hundreds of people hugging and kissing, waving little ANC and SA flags. Dancing. It was beautiful. DK's and Bacquie's faces filled with joy."

Gail Hovey, left, and Jennifer Davis served as official observers at the historic April 1994 elections in Empangeni, KwaZulu-Natal, South Africa. They are shown here with a local pastor, Robert Mkhwanazi, who served with the Ecumenical Monitoring Programme organized by the South African Council of Churches. *Photo by James Knutson.*

"Faces Filled with Joy"

# Philippe Wamba *&*
# *New Pan-African Generation*

## Philippe Wamba

The lessons of my parents and the prevailing climate of 1970s black outspokenness and pride provided me with a strong sense of identification with Africa. But though my own father was from Africa, and though a celebration of Africa was part and parcel of the pro-black rhetoric that had shaped me, I really knew very little about the continent....

Africa was a place of my imagination, a mythical environment I constructed in my mind out of raw materials provided by my father, books I had read, and movies and TV shows I had seen. . . . Even my parents' ongoing critique of the stereotypical African images that appeared in the media and in books I read could not entirely shield me from the prevailing views of Africa that had long saturated the American psyche. . . . In the end, I knew more about Africa than my white classmates, but was still somewhat susceptible to the prevailing American popular wisdom, which held Africa to be a wild, untamed jungle plagued by famine and bereft of Western technology, infrastructure, and advanced social institutions. . . .

For me as a child in Boston, and for many other black Americans, despite Africa's new prominence as the inspiration for a revolution in African American culture, Africa remained a "dark" continent. . . . I venerated the glory of the African past in school projects on ancient Egypt, I expressed my cultural identification with Africa in my attire, and I eagerly absorbed my father's sentimental stories of his Congolese childhood. . . . For my brothers and me, a real understanding of Africa and what it meant to us only began when my family moved to Tanzania in 1980, an adventure that completely debunked our own myths of Africa and changed our lives forever.

*In Dar es Salaam, his father taught at the university and Philippe and his brothers attended school and learned KiSwahili. But in 1981, his father, an opponent of the Mobutu dictatorship, was arrested on a visit home to Zaire. He spent almost a year in prison.*

With the arrest of my father, an Africanist historian who had taught at several U.S. universities and at one of the most respected campuses in Africa, an international network of friends, family members, activists, academics, politicians, and students responded quickly to call for his release. My father had been a part of various political struggles while a student and professor in the United States, and many of those he had worked with in the 1960s and 1970s now moved to support him in his time of need. . . .

The campaign was truly international, and in many ways it was also pan-African, coordinated by his black American wife and his African, black American, and West Indian colleagues in Dar es Salaam. They alerted people all over Africa, Europe, the United States, and the Caribbean. . . . My mother

"This book is about my own journey along the fault lines of African–African American relations and the wider historical relationship between black Americans and their counterparts in the "motherland," writes Philippe Wamba in his acclaimed memoir, *Kinship*.

Born in Los Angeles, Philippe Wamba was the son of Elaine Brown of Cleveland and Ernest Wamba dia Wamba from rural Bas-Congo in the Democratic Republic of the Congo (formerly Zaire). He grew up in Boston and Dar es Salaam, finished high school in New Mexico, and graduated magna cum laude from Harvard University in 1993, going on to earn a master's degree from the Columbia School of Journalism. From 1999 through 2001 he was editor in chief of the Web site africana.com. Philippe Wamba died in 2002 in an automobile accident in Kenya, at the age of 31.

Reprinted by permission from *Kinship: A Family's Journey in Africa and America* (New York: Dutton, 1999). Additional information about Wamba is available on the Web site of the Harvard African Students Alumni Network at http://www.hasanweb.org/memphillipelife.asp.

shuttled between Dar, Kinshasa, and Boston, spreading the word and trying to generate political pressure on the Zairean government. Members of her family and activists in the American black community urged the U.S. government to intervene on my father's behalf, and a global coalition of Africa-oriented political groups launched letter-writing, petition, and speak-out campaigns, targeting the Zairean government from pan-African nerve centers all over the world.

But while my father survived a Zairean prison . . . we knew that the furor raised on his behalf would do little to change conditions in Zaire itself. . . . Some time after my father was released, my mother's sister in the United States told us how she had watched her TV with disgust while Mobutu was being warmly received at the White House. Reagan had smiled and embraced his African ally like an old friend. . . .

. . . I was thrilled and relieved to have my father safely back among us. . . . I resented the power of tyrants like Mobutu to imprison or even kill people seemingly on a whim . . . I began to wonder how I, too, could make a contribution to the struggle for freedom in Africa. Of course, at the time I had barely completed primary school, but in the years that followed I took an intense interest in African history and politics, and felt inspired by the courage and conviction of African freedom fighters who waged the continent's wars of liberation.

*Philippe Wamba finished his secondary education at United World College in New Mexico, where he and fellow black students raised funds for the ANC school in Tanzania. He enrolled at Harvard as an undergraduate in the fall of 1989.*

To my unhappy surprise, the African American students I met [at Harvard] were not necessarily any more interested in or informed about Africa than their white counterparts. I automatically gravitated toward the black students I met in those early weeks, and did establish some friendships that lasted. . . . But sometimes the cultural distance between my upbringing in Tanzania and that of African Americans from U.S. cities and suburbs seemed an obstacle to empathy. . . .

For myself and other African students, the examples of racism by the American media, as well as incidents we experienced every day, demonstrated the extent of the social obstacles that confronted us as blacks in America. . . . After the acquittal of Rodney King's torturers, some black students rallied in protest, angrily shouting our solidarity with those venting their frustrations in L.A. And we found plenty to complain about right at Harvard. We marched to protest the harassment of black students by white Harvard policemen, we demonstrated in support of the beleaguered Afro-American Studies Department, and we called for more faculty hiring of women and minorities.

Despite feeling encouraged by the black student solidarity that grew around such issues, I remained frustrated by my own perception of African American indifference to Africa and African affairs. . . . I became involved in local anti-apartheid initiatives, campaigning for Harvard's divestment from companies doing business in South Africa and raising money for

South African refugees, and I also worked on campaigns targeting other African countries where dictatorships held sway. But though the anti-apartheid movement in the United States was led by prominent black American leaders, I found less enthusiasm for the struggle among my black student peers. . . . Too often it seemed as though black Americans were mainly preoccupied with their lot in America and did not see events in Africa as relevant. More than anything else, it was ignorance and apathy that kept many students from greater participation in political activism on Africa.

The most memorable political campaign of my student activist career brought me up against the despotism that had imprisoned my father. If Harvard students seemed to pay little attention to events in South Africa, they cared even less what happened in less celebrated tyrannies like Zaire. But when President Mobutu Sese Seko was invited to speak at Harvard's John F. Kennedy School of Government in the spring of 1990, SASC, the local anti-apartheid group to which I belonged, and other political organizations mobilized to protest the visit.

A coalition of campus and community organizations joined together to denounce Mobutu and the college administrators who had invited him, arguing that by hosting Mobutu's speech Harvard was needlessly legitimizing his brutal politics. The coalition organized rallies at which I spoke of my experiences in Zaire and my father's detention; we canvassed the campus dormitories, informing students about Mobutu's speech and our protest against it; and we wrote letters expressing our disappointment that Mobutu had been invited, delivering them by hand to seemingly indifferent administrators at the Kennedy School.

. . . I told many African American acquaintances about our scheduled rally, but some admitted to me that they didn't know anything about Zaire and said they'd have to hear "the other side of the story" before they agreed to participate. We distributed as much information on Zaire as we could, but it was difficult to prove to a skeptical and completely uninformed audience that millions of people in a distant African country were suffering under the iron hand of a tyrant. I felt that the black students we spoke to were especially wary of accepting our indictments of Mobutu at face value, perhaps with good reason; black people are used to hearing criticism of black leaders and have learned to treat much of the fault-finding as hostile white propaganda. . . . But I knew it was probably more likely that in many cases ignorance would become an excuse for inaction. . . .

The day of Mobutu's speech found two groups of demonstrators positioned in front of the Kennedy School building: students and community activists who had come to denounce Mobutu, including some Boston-based Zairean dissidents, and a group of pro-Mobutu Zaireans from the Boston area who chanted their support for their president in French and Lingala. I picked out several faces that I recognized from the occasional Zairean parties at my uncle's home in Lynn. . . . I saw their actions as a traitorous insult to all of those who still languished under Zaire's repressive government. When I later told my uncle about the Zaireans' presence at the protest, he laughed bitterly and told me that some days previously one of Mobutu's aides had contacted members of the Zairean community in Boston and offered them money to show their support at his speech. My uncle had also been approached with the offer but had flatly refused to get involved.

At the protest scene, police barricades separated the hundreds of demonstrators from Mobutu's convoy as it entered the parking lot at the rear of the building. Men in suits stood behind the police lines, coolly eyeing the protestors, and a man within the cordoned-off area snapped pictures of us, perhaps with which to open classified files in some shadowy government department. I led students in the South African shuffling stomp of the "*toyi-toyi*," the protest dance of anti-apartheid youth, and some of the Zairean dissidents began a call-and-response chant in French: "Mobutu, Mobutu—Assassin!" Inside the building, the demonstrators who had managed to get inside interrupted Mobutu's speech by unfurling a large banner that read END THE OPPRESSION NOW and were promptly ejected.

The demonstration made the local television news and was covered in the city papers. Veteran Cambridge activists said that it was the largest protest in recent memory, and student activists returned to their dorms satisfied that they had helped to discredit a dictator. But I left the demonstration alone, feeling empty, plagued by the same sense of discouragement that burdened my political activism throughout my college years. Was this really the best I could do? . . . It was [hard to] keep the wider context in mind, to somehow link my activities in Cambridge with the suffering that continued in Zaire. But when I discussed the protest with my father I felt that he was proud of me and that maybe I had actually managed to emulate some of his courage and conviction.

**Philippe Wamba**
*Photo courtesy of Barbara Eisinger.*

# How I Learned African History from Reggae ✑

## Angela Walters

I was raised in northern New Mexico, a white girl in a predominantly Hispanic population. The public education I received in this small southwestern town was somewhat unusual, as it reflected the cultural diversity within at least our own community. So although I was subjected to the traditional Western canon, and plodded through Shakespeare, the American Revolution, and the diagramming of English sentences, the community made sure that I learned some Spanish and some aspects of Mexican culture as well. In elementary school I made skeletons from colored construction paper and paste to commemorate the Mexican Día de los Muertos, or Day of the Dead. Later, my classmates and I listened, enthralled, to stories of ancient Aztec warriors being sacrificed on altars to appease the feathered serpent god, Quetzalcoatl. By the time I graduated from high school I was nearly as familiar with the Treaty of Guadalupe Hidalgo as I was with the Declaration of Independence, and I celebrated Cinco de Mayo, Mexican Independence Day, as well as the Fourth of July.

While my background was unusual in one way, in that my education was largely bicultural, it was not unusual in another. Throughout my childhood I learned no in-depth history of Africa or African-descended people outside the occasional civil rights curriculum around Martin Luther King. While we were taught that he was a hero because he was a proud and non-violent man, we were also taught, perhaps inadvertently, that the struggle for civil rights for African Americans and the struggle for equitable relations between blacks and whites—which was a U.S. struggle alone—had reached its appropriate zenith with his life. I believed this, because after we were taught about Martin Luther King Jr.'s assassination some 15 years earlier, nothing more was said about African Americans today or about the peoples of Africa or the African diaspora.

If Mexican history was considered a strong river running alongside, and often intertwining with, the river of U.S. history, then African history was like a muddy stream one hardly noticed. And because there was not a single black family living in our little town, this muddy stream became my primary source of knowledge about Africa and the African diaspora. African history was diminished and made to fit into less than nine weeks of my tenth-grade U.S. history class. African history began with the Middle Passage and ended with the civil rights movement. Although we were taught that slavery was morally indefensible, the social and political foundations of the European colonization and exploitation of Africa were never discussed, and I consequently never considered what the profound ramifications of such a massive, protracted exploitation might be for Africa or the African diaspora.

Angela Marie Walters, a part-time student of Lisa Brock at the University of New Mexico in Albuquerque in 1995, chose this essay topic for a class assignment. Brock selected the essay as a contribution to a special journal issue she edited. A freelance writer and mother, Walters is interested in multicultural issues and how they affect contemporary American society.

Excerpted from "How I Learned African History from Reggae," in "African [Diaspora] Studies," edited by Lisa Brock, special issue, *Issue: A Journal of Opinion* 24, no. 2 (1996). Reprinted by permission of the African Studies Association. Lyrics are from Peter Tosh, "I Am That I Am," *Equal Rights* (Columbia Records, 1977), and Papa Levi, "Mi God, Mi King," *Reggae Greats: The DJ's* (Mango/Island Records, 1985).

I had a lot more to learn about Africa and her people, but it would not be taught to me in school.

> Don't belittle my authority
> It's time you recognized my quality
> I said I am that I am
> I am I am I am
> —Peter Tosh, "I Am That I Am"

While searching one day through my mother's rather eclectic music collection, I came across the album *Kayo* by Bob Marley and the Wailers. Intrigued by the long dreadlocks and open smile Marley wore on the cover photograph, I listened to the album and was immediately absorbed by the music's slow and sensual rhythm, its heavy bass tones, and Marley's melodic, amiable voice. Though *Kayo* is one of Marley's least political albums, the experience of listening to it served for me as initiation into a new community, a community consisting of individuals actively involved in the project of creating for themselves their own identity. Because this identity is a distinctly *black* identity, and is in part rooted in African history and culture, discovering reggae was for me tantamount to discovering a whole new world.

I had never conceived of precolonial Africa as anything other than a dry and expansive wasteland inhabited by either savages or idiots. These images were not my own; they were gleaned from many years of exposure to media portrayals of African people, from novels like Joseph Conrad's *Heart of Darkness* or movies like *The Gods Must Be Crazy*, in which native Africans possess a sort of endearing ignorance and little culture to speak of. By contrast, songs such as Mutabaruka's "Great Queens of Africa" furnished me with unprecedented images of African people as shrewd and resourceful, emanating from a culture and tradition that was vigorous, glorious, irrepressible.

Reggae also caused me to consider for the first time the phenomenon of slavery from an Afrocentric perspective, rather than the Eurocentric perspective, far more comfortable for whites, that I was accustomed to. I was shocked into a new, often afflicted, consciousness from songs such as "Mi God Mi King" by Papa Levi, who sings:

> They take 'way mi gold, they take mi silver.
> Them hang me up and rape mi muddah
> They take me from the wonderful land of Africa,
> To slave for the plantation owner. They take
> 'way mi name and call me "nigguh."
> The only word me know: "Aye's a comin, massuh."
> And then they say we ignorant and inferior
> And owe them intelligence and superior
> To the complexion of them skin color.

"Mi God Mi King" and other reggae songs like Third World's "96 Degrees in the Shade" or Burning Spear's "Do You Remember the Days of Slavery?" challenged me to look upon the raw actuality of our country's past with my eyes open. Slavery is ugly, it hurts me to look at it, but I suspect that the damage accrued from refusing to look is greater still.

The education I received from reggae was well-rounded. Apartheid was exposed as a virulent instrument of oppression and dehumanization in Alpha Blondy's "Apartheid Is Nazism," Peter Tosh's "Fight Apartheid," and countless other reggae songs. I first learned of Nelson Mandela's imprisonment in South Africa not in school but from Yellowman's song "Free Mandela." It was Bob Marley's *Survival* album that introduced me to the concept of Pan-Africanism. And Judy Mowatt's song "Black Woman" caused me to reflect upon the moral, physical, and psychological pain suffered by countless black women at the hands of white violators.

Though much of the information I have assimilated from reggae is undoubtedly painful, concerning a past that is rife with discrimination and disfranchisement, an equally significant impression I have received from reggae is that the African diaspora has not merely endured the atrocities of history but thrived despite them. Reggae musicians attribute a large part of their strength to Africa and a conception of African history that reaches far beyond the beginning of European colonization. Reggae musicians evoke a time when Africa existed solely for itself, for Africans, a continent rich with resources, tradition, science, art, and personalities free from shackles.

In school, African history is always taught only insofar as it relates to European history, and never *for itself*. And though we, as white people, may perceive that the treatment Africa received from our ancestors was clearly wrong, I believe there inevitably exists for many the remnant of thought that Africa and the African diaspora are inferior, and subordinate, to European history and people of European descent. This remnant of thought seems inevitable because of our collective Western persistence in refusing to perceive the world with anything other than a Eurocentric perspective, which, when not balanced with an Afrocentric perspective, presents a skewed conception of history and our place in it. Everywhere one looks, whether in school textbooks, the national news, or movies and television, one sees portrayals of the African diaspora that are distorted by the veil of racism.

Reggae musicians subvert the negative misrepresentations of the African diaspora in part by engaging in a *retelling* of African history that is at once more subjective, more complete, and more authentic. Reggae musicians are a few of the many who are actively involved in the project of disseminating the stories of African history: stories of history and culture, stories of slavery, racism, and struggle, stories of freedom, dignity, and victory. The sharing of these stories would seem to disarm racism of much of its power. And unlike many forums utilized for the retelling of African history, reggae is a part of popular culture and is primarily heard among youth, which is perhaps the ideal place to confront racism.

I thank God I found reggae music. For a long while it was reggae alone that injected living blood into what was for me the dead flesh of African history. It was reggae that led me to African American history and studies. And it was reggae that ultimately exposed the smug and elusive veil of racism

I viewed the world behind, the veil I wore without knowing or choosing. In exposing the veil, reggae *destroyed* the veil, and it is for this reason I hope that reggae musicians continue to, in the words of Bob Marley, "tell the children the truth," and I hope the children continue to listen.

## Bob Marley's Pan-African Consciousness

Jamaican reggae icon Robert Nesta Marley infused themes of African history and Pan-African solidarity and pride throughout his music. Bob Marley and the Wailers performed "Zimbabwe," from the album *Survival* (1979), at Zimbabwe's independence celebration in 1980.

> Every man got a right to decide his own destiny.
> And in this judgment there is no partiality.
> So arm in arms, with arms, we'll fight this little struggle,
> 'Cause that's the only way we can overcome our little trouble.
>
> Brother, you're right, you're right,
> You're right, you're right, you're so right!
> We gon' fight, we'll have to fight,
> We gonna fight, fight for our rights!
>
> Natty Dread it in-a Zimbabwe,
> Set it up in Zimbabwe,
> Mash it up-a in-a Zimbabwe,
> Africans a-liberate Zimbabwe. . . .

In "Africa Unite," on the same album, Marley proclaims Pan-African solidarity.

> Africa unite!
> 'Cause we're moving right out of Babylon,
> And we're going to our Father's land.
>
> Africa unite
> Africa unite
> Unite for the benefit for the benefit of your people!
> Unite for it's later than you think!
> Unite for the benefit of my children!
> Unite for it's later than you think!
> Africa awaits its creators!
> Africa awaiting its Creator!
> Africa, you're my forefather cornerstone!
> Unite for the Africans abroad
> Unite for the Africans a yard! [at home]

"Zion Train" is from *Uprising* (1980), the last album to be released before the singer's death from cancer in 1981. It pays homage to the history of African-descended peoples:

> Two thousand years of history
> Could not be wiped away so easily.
> Two thousand years of history (black history)
> Could not be wiped so easily.
>
> Oh, children, Zion train is comin' our way; get on board now!
> They said the Zion train is comin' our way.
> You got a ticket, so thank the Lord!

# In Motion ~
# The New African Immigration

## Sylviane A. Diouf

More Africans have come voluntarily to this country in the past thirty years than came during the entire era of the slave trade, which transported to these shores an estimated half million men, women, and children between the 1600s and 1860, the year the last known slave ship landed in Alabama. . . .

Sub-Saharan Africans are a very small percentage of a total population that has multiplied about ninety times since the first census in 1790, and they represent about 3 percent of the people who identify as blacks. Nevertheless, as small as it still is today, the African community has been steadily and rapidly increasing. Close-knit, attached to their cultures, and quick to seize the educational and professional opportunities of their host country, Africans have established themselves as one of the most dynamic, entrepreneurial, and upwardly mobile groups in the nation.

Voluntary immigration from sub-Saharan Africa dates back to the 1860s, when men from Cape Verde—then Portuguese-controlled islands off the coast of Senegal—made their way to Massachusetts. They were seamen, and most were employed as whalers. The movement accelerated at the turn of the century; between 1911 and 1920, about 10,000 Cape Verdeans made their way to New Bedford, Massachusetts. For several decades, Cape Verdeans were the largest African community—other than Egyptians and white South Africans—in the United States.

A small number of African students were also present at the end of the nineteenth century. They were sent by Christian missions to historically black colleges and universities. The trend continued in the early twentieth century. [But the community] residing permanently in the United States was kept small.

Starting in the early 1960s, with the independence of most African nations from colonial rule, students and by then newly appointed diplomats formed the bulk of the continental sub-Saharan African presence in the United States. However, the composition and size of the African community started to change in the 1970s. Between 1961 and 1970, 29,000 Africans (including North Africans) were admitted, but the numbers increased to almost 81,000 from 1971 to 1980.

In 1980, a new Refugee Act was passed: it placed less emphasis on the Cold War policies that had favored refugees from the Soviet Union and Eastern Europe, increased the ceilings of refugees by region, and offered them the option of permanent residence after one year. The Immigration Reform and Control Act of 1986 legalized eligible illegal aliens who resided in the country, and more than 31,000 Africans applied. This amnesty not only allowed many to regularize their situation, but also enabled their spouses and children to join them. Additionally, the Immigration Act of

"Migration has been central in the making of African American history and culture," declares the Schomburg Center for Research in Black Culture. The transatlantic slave trade is usually considered the defining element in the making of the African diaspora, "but it is centuries of additional movements that have given shape to the nation we know today. This is the story that has not been told."

The New York–based Schomburg Center has begun to document this history through an extensive research project, In Motion: The African-American Migration Experience. It traces 13 discrete migrations of African Americans, Caribbeans, and Africans, to, within, and out of the United States. The project Web site (http://www.inmotionaame.org/) presents more than 16,500 pages of texts, 8,300 illustrations, and 60 maps, as well as lesson plans.

The last of the migrations documented there is the new, voluntary immigration from Africa to the United States. Immigration and census statistics are inconsistent, and both are generally agreed to greatly underestimate the actual numbers of African immigrants. But even the lowest estimates point to close to a million African-born United States residents by the year 2000, with many more if the U.S.-born children of immigrants are included. This steadily increasing influx, all too often overlooked, has contributed to the growing diversity of the U.S. black population.

Reprinted by permission from Sylviane Diouf's "The New African Diaspora," in In Motion: The African-American Migration Experience (© Sylviane A. Diouf and The New York Public Library). The full article and an extensive bibliography are available on the In Motion Web site.

1990 established a lottery system that favors underrepresented nations, a category that includes all the African countries. In 2002, more than 50,000 sub-Saharan Africans entered the country as legal immigrants. . . .

Africans are highly urban: 95 percent reside in a metropolitan area, and like most immigrants, they tend to establish themselves where other countrymen have preceded them and established the basis of a community. West Africans are mostly found in New York (17 percent) and Maryland (11 percent), while 15 percent of East Africans have chosen California and 10 percent Minnesota. Sixteen percent of Central Africans live in Maryland and 9.5 percent in California. The largest number of Nigerians (21,000 or 15.5 percent of the community) reside in oil-rich Texas—their homeland is a major oil producer and they have experience in that industry. The Twin Cities, Minneapolis and St. Paul, have America's largest Somali population, estimated at between 15,000 and 30,000.

Besides their "migration experience," the most significant characteristic of the African immigrants is that they are the most educated group in the nation. Almost half (49 percent) have bachelor's or advanced degrees, compared to 23 percent of native-born Americans. Studies show that black Africans, on the whole, have a higher educational level than white Africans (from North Africa and South Africa).

According to the United Nations Economic Commission for Africa and to the International Organization for Migration, 27,000 [highly educated] Africans left the continent for industrialized nations between 1960 and 1975. While 40,000 followed them from 1975 to 1984, between 1985 and 1990 the number skyrocketed to 60,000, and has averaged 20,000 annually ever since. At least 60 percent of physicians trained in Ghana during the 1980s have left their country, and half of all Zimbabwe social workers trained in the past ten years are now working in Great Britain.

Sub-Saharan nations bear the great cost of educating students who will continue their education in the West and may not return home during their most productive years. As renowned Nigerian computer scientist Philippe Emeagwali puts it: "In essence, Africa is giving developmental assistance to the wealthier western nations which makes the rich nations richer and the poor nations poorer." This substantial brain drain is a significant obstacle to development, but African expatriates stress that it is economic and political conditions beyond their control, and human rights abuses, that are generally responsible for their leaving. They also point out that low salaries, lack of adequate equipment and research facilities, and the need to provide for their extended families are the reasons for their emigration, not individualistic motivations.

The African presence has become very visible on the streets of several U.S. cities. The prime example is Harlem. On and around 116th Street, in a neighborhood known as Little Africa, Africans—mostly from francophone West Africa—own several restaurants, a tax and computer center, grocery stores, a butcher shop, photocopy shops, a hardware store, tailor shops, wholesale stores, braiding salons, and telecommunication centers. Other businesses sell electronic equipment, cosmetics, household goods, and Islamic items. Little Africa is a microcosm of what African immigrants represent and create: they are attached to their cultural and religious values; are quick to take advantage of what modernity can offer; and play a major role in familial, communal, and national development at home.

Whatever their circumstances in America, [African immigrants] maintain a very high level of financial support for their extended families. "The main reason I came here was to support my family," stresses a Ghanaian nurse. "I send $250 every month, which is more than I used to make. I am nothing without my family and I would never think of not providing for them, even when it gets difficult here." Collectively, Africans in the United States send hundreds of millions of dollars home every year. In 1999, Nigerians abroad sent $1.3 billion home from all corners of the world. The sum was equivalent to 3.7 percent of their country's Gross Domestic Product, while the total development aid to Nigeria was only $152 million. Senegalese emigrants contributed close to 2 percent of their country's GDP. It is estimated that African émigrés the world over send more than $3 billion home every year through official channels and another $3 billion through informal channels, mostly person to person.

The number of African organizations and associations throughout the country is astonishing. Every nationality has national, regional, professional, gender, political, and sometimes ethnic organizations. In many areas, pan-African organizations, which bring together Africans from various nationalities, have also been established. People often belong to several organizations, and the multiplicity of groups shows the many layers of identity that Africans bring with them and are eager to maintain.

Like individual Africans, most associations are involved in development efforts in Africa. The Association of Nigerian Physicians in the Americas, which counts more than 2,000 members in the United States and Canada, sends doctors on medical missions to Nigeria to provide services and other support to people in underserved rural areas. Thousands of projects throughout the continent are being funded by the emigrants and are directly managed by the locals. The economic impact of the émigrés on their countries of origin, whether at the familial, local, regional, or national level, is extremely high.

Africans count on [the immigrants] and on information technology to counterbalance some of the effects of the brain drain. Nongovernmental organizations, international organizations, and African universities and associations are eager to capitalize on "the 'Diaspora option' which advocates making use of the resources of [African] nationals abroad, without necessarily having them relocate to their countries of origin." Thanks to the Internet, the expatriates' skills, expertise, and the networks they build in the United States and other countries of immigration are becoming increasingly available to colleagues and users in their countries of origin. This, they stress, transforms a problem into a potential asset. The digital divide is still enormous, but it is getting smaller. Major cities and many small towns on the Continent have telecommunication centers that provide telephone and fax services. Cyber cafes have sprung up at an amazingly rapid pace, and the Internet is thus available to a wide spectrum of urbanites, who can keep abreast of the expatriates' activities through their online magazines, or send e-mail to their kin and friends in the United States.

The flow of information also goes from Africa to America. Today, Africans from Los Angeles to Cincinnati can watch television programs and listen to radio broadcasts from their various countries of origin on their computers. They can read their national newspapers online, the same day they are published in Dakar, Nairobi, or Accra.

African expatriates are deeply conscious of the negative image of Africa projected in the United States. "Even in academia and the media Americans continue to use derogatory terms such as tribe for ethnic group and dialect instead of language," complains a Nigerian physician, "and even though in many countries more than half the population is urban, the only images you see on TV are national parks, which makes it look as if Africans lived in the forest!" Although they readily acknowledge the political, economic and social problems that mark the continent, most Africans do not recognize themselves or their countries in the stereotypical and pessimistic images with which Americans are presented. The often astonishing nature of the derogatory clichés coming from a wide spectrum of American society that is ignorant of African realities is a common subject of conversation and irritation.

Although there are many who wish to remain in America, Africans overwhelmingly express the desire to return to their home countries. As children are born or grow up in this country, issues of identity, continuity, change, and integration will become more pressing. Future developments, at home or in the United States, may change their plans; but for now their life strategies—savings, education, and strong links to home—are geared toward achieving the objective of returning to their home countries. In the meantime, they bring to the United States their robust work ethic, dynamism, and strong attachment to family, culture, and religion, just as other Africans did several centuries ago.

Liberians in Boston march in support of peace in their country, June 2003. *AP/World Wide Photos. Photo by Michael Dwyer.*

# VOICES

# Nunu Kidane

Nunu Kidane
*Photo by Cabral M. Mebratu.*

I grew up in Eritrea, in East Africa, and came to the United States in 1980. I arrived as a refugee, fleeing war between Eritrea and Ethiopia. For the first decade or so I focused my energies on my family, on going to school, and on my Eritrean community. My family and I sent support to the struggle for Eritrean independence, and we worked to keep our children grounded in Eritrean culture and identity. I was unengaged and unconnected to what was happening around me in the U.S.

This disengagement is common for many of us in immigrant communities when we first come here. We start out by focusing almost exclusively on issues concerning our own countries of origin. We do so because we're vulnerable and fearful of losing ourselves and our identities in the multicultural politics of this country. Our ethnic and national identities are an important grounding force. Whether Eritrean, Nigerian, Somali, or Ethiopian, we begin by viewing U.S. policy on Africa exclusively as it relates to our respective countries. We don't have much information, or any interest, in other African countries or the continent as a whole. And we rarely connect with the struggle for racial equality in the United States that preceded our arrival.

My children were the entryway through which I began to understand the history of race relations in this country. Raising three young black boys in America opened my eyes to the reality of structural racism. The personal became the political. Much has been said about the parallels between the civil rights movement in the U.S. in the sixties and the movement to end apartheid in South Africa. For me, as an African immigrant, it came as an astounding realization that the struggle for racial justice in the U.S. wasn't "completed" in the sixties. It's ongoing.

Over time my focus expanded beyond my immediate family and community. I no longer saw myself only as the "other," the outsider, but as an Eritrean, a black woman, an African American. And I saw that these identities didn't have to be mutually exclusive. I began to feel connected to struggles that included Eritrea but also went beyond it. At the University of California at Berkeley in the late 1980s, an active student movement was calling for divestment from the apartheid regime in South Africa. I got involved. Gradually I learned how this movement connected to others, both in the United States and internationally.

As we focused our efforts on nation building, Eritreans in this country started making connections with other organizations and individuals that had similar concerns. I read books and talked with people who were active in other African countries. I began to grasp the bigger picture. There were so many connections between what was happening in Eritrea and in other African countries, especially when you looked at the effects of U.S. foreign policy.

In the U.S., Africa is a concept beyond geography; it's embedded in a racial framework. The whole continent is misunderstood or viewed in very limited terms. Because of my heritage, it's important to me that Africa be appreciated in all its historic, political, and cultural complexity. I want to be part of a social justice movement that links the struggles against economic globalization in Africa with related struggles for global justice.

Here in the Bay Area, 26 of us, individuals and organizations, came together in April 2003 and founded the Priority Africa Network (PAN). The U.S. had just invaded Iraq and there was a sense of crisis in activist circles. We saw the Bush administration focusing on the "war against terrorism" but ignoring the real threats—the terror of poverty and HIV/AIDS, discrimination against people of color, and growing global economic inequalities.

Within PAN, diverse African immigrant individuals and groups are taking the lead. Our perspective is that the growing number of African immigrants in the U.S. opens up new opportunities for an Africa-focused movement in the U.S. This is a strategic demographic shift that requires all of us to adjust our outreach strategies.

We also have many members who are seasoned activists with decades of experience in fighting apartheid and other injustices. They brought their credibility gained in local communities and their understanding that work on different issues was connected and ongoing. Achieving political rights was not the end, but just the beginning.

Working for another Africa also means working for another America and another world. We can't afford not to learn from the past; we have to see history as a lens through which we plan for the future. In Africa we have the Sankofa, a mythical bird that flies forward while looking back. Like this bird, we need to look back in order to know where we are going.

# Neil Watkins

**Neil Watkins**
*Photo by Monet Cooper.*

Two pivotal events in my life drew me into Africa activism. One was a seminar on Africa I took in my sophomore year at Georgetown University, taught by Nii Akuetteh. We studied structural adjustment policies and their impact on Africa. The other was my junior year abroad at the University of Dakar in Senegal. That's where I saw the human impact of structural adjustment, up close.

These experiences set my direction. I've been working on economic justice issues, including structural adjustment and globalization, for more than a decade now. I'm the national coordinator of the Jubilee USA Network, the U.S. arm of the global debt campaign.

I grew up in Elk Grove, Illinois. My family wasn't really political, though my dad went to Vietnam and joined the antiwar movement when he came back. But I had a fascination for international issues, partly because my dad's job at an airline made it possible for our family to travel. My mom is a children's librarian, and she encouraged me to read. My first activist action was as a freshman in high school, opposing the Gulf War. I can't say it was a particularly principled act; it was more of a herd mentality, because people in the group I hung out with were involved.

Starting at Georgetown in 1994, I was in the School of Foreign Service. The first year you take a very prescribed curriculum. By the second year you can take one seminar, and I thought, let me get out of this focus on Europe and Western civilization. That was the overwhelming focus of year one, and I wasn't enjoying it. Once I got into the African seminar, it was by far my favorite class.

The seminar was co-taught by Nii Akuetteh, an activist originally from Ghana, and Herb Howe, an Africanist at Georgetown. Nii worked at TransAfrica in the 1980s, and in 2006 he succeeded Salih Booker as director of Africa Action, one of the partners of Jubilee USA. Back in 1997, though, I didn't know the activist connections. In the seminar we analyzed the structural adjustment policies of the World Bank and the International Monetary Fund, and we did role plays of the negotiations that had led to majority rule in South Africa.

That experience inspired me to do a minor in African studies and eventually to go to the University of Dakar. We took classes at the university, all in French, and also studied Wolof. Georgetown had a house that we lived in, and we spent weekends and holidays with African families.

Soon after classes started that fall, the students went on strike. As I made my way toward the campus, I walked into what felt like a war zone. A line of police were firing tear gas guns into a crowd of my fellow students, who were throwing rocks and running. It turned out that the World Bank had told the Senegalese government it had to spend less on education, and this forced the government to abandon scholarships for students from the rural areas. Of course, many couldn't afford the fees. It was an awakening for me.

During the year in Dakar, I learned more about the role of the IMF and the World Bank in imposing economic policies across the African continent. I returned to the United States determined to do something about it. I knew the U.S. government had the largest say in the international financial institutions. Couldn't U.S. citizens change our government's policy?

Since then, I've worked on campaigns to challenge the IMF, boycott World Bank bonds, and cancel Africa's debt. In my senior year I was involved in a Georgetown group campaigning against sweatshops. A couple of years later I went to Seattle with a Washington-based group called Preamble, helping organize discussion forums about trade and globalization. The next year, as the Washington organizer for a campaign to boycott World Bank bonds, I found myself on the streets of Washington along with 30,000 other demonstrators protesting the IMF and the World Bank. Our group brought 20 activists from Latin America, Africa, and Asia to the United States for that event. We wanted Americans to hear directly from them about the impact of World Bank policies in their countries.

The attacks of 9/11 brought the momentum of global justice work to a standstill. Suddenly the context changed. Talk of terrorism filled the airwaves, and many activists turned their priorities to opposing the war on Iraq. But the structural issues of global inequality have not gone away.

My interest and passion and focus is definitely on Africa. Globalization and trade are affecting Asia and Latin America too, but I think that IMF and World Bank policies hit Africa hardest, because the poverty is greater and it's very difficult for African nations to challenge those policies. So there's a particular need to challenge the role of the global institutions in Africa.

Africa's debt is relatively small compared to the debt of all developing countries, but the impact of that debt is much greater. There are so many resources flowing out in proportion to the size of the African economies and the resources they have. But we've won some victories. More than $100 billion of debt has been cancelled. Some of the most egregious IMF policies have been stopped.

It's only been 10 years, but in my limited experience as an activist, the anti-apartheid movement comes up in every context as an example of successful organizing. Experienced activists all talk about it, and it has always been very inspiring to me. But I've also realized that in some ways it was different, because it was focused on one country with a blatantly terrible political system. Trying to change worldwide economic structures is, if anything, even harder. Even so, when you feel down and you think that things aren't ever going to change, it's good to have an example to turn to and say, "Well, actually, it might take 30 or 40 years, but it can happen!"

# Anyango Reggy

My father is Kenyan, and my mother is African American. So I was raised in a Pan-African home. I was born in Washington, DC and I grew up in Kenya, where I finished elementary and high school.

My parents are educators, and they were actively involved in both the civil rights movement in the United States and the independence struggle in Africa. From the time I was very young, they instilled in me a sense of pride in being a woman of African descent. I was surrounded by the music, writing, and film of black artists and intellectuals, including Harry Belafonte, Hugh Masekela, Malcolm X, and Maya Angelou.

My heritage embraces the painful legacy of slavery and colonialism as well as the oppression and marginalization of the African diaspora. My parents challenged me to think critically about these complex realities, so my political education began at home. But my parents also believed in formal education; they saw it as a tool for social change. With their encouragement, I returned to the U.S. in 1993 to study. I received a BA in psychology from Eastern University and a master's in international affairs and development from Clark Atlanta University.

I wanted to find ways to use my education and my experience in Africa to focus on the pressing economic, political, and social issues affecting Africa and the world. Eventually I landed my dream job with the American Friends Service Committee. AFSC is a Quaker organization with a long tradition of international peace and justice work on every continent.

Today, after six years with AFSC, I'm coordinator of the Africa Youth Leadership Program. It's part of a broader effort to build a constituency that cares deeply about Africa and will become advocates for change. We work with young people 18 to 30, from the United States and Africa. The participants from the U.S. are mainly, though not exclusively, African Americans. Our vision of Africa promotes peace, African unity, and sustainable development. We're trying to create a cadre of empowered youth—to inspire the next generation of Africa activists.

I've worked with young people in training sessions in East, Central, and Southern Africa, and in the United States. In 2005 I helped organize a U.S. speaking tour of youths from six countries in Africa called "Life Over Debt: Africa in the Age of Global Apartheid." I traveled with three of the speakers, who came from Burundi, Zimbabwe, and South Africa. It was an intense 28 days on the road—we visited 11 cities and 36 college campuses! The African youths connected with audiences by telling of their firsthand experiences with economic justice and

Anyango Reggy, left, with Jean-Claude Nkundwa, John Bomba Briggs, and Nomsonto Mthimkulu, participants in the 2007 Africa Peace Tour, at Forest Park Community College in St. Louis, Missouri.
*Photo by Faheemah Thabit. Courtesy of American Friends Service Committee.*

peace-building struggles in Africa. For example, I remember Nomsonto Mthimkulu of South Africa, talking about how her brother died because the family didn't have enough money to buy the medicines that would have saved his life. People in Africa are dying because pharmaceutical companies and Western governments care more about profits than about saving lives.

Hearing these stories, people were energized to challenge U.S. government and corporate policies that are detrimental to Africa. The tour, I think, made especially strong connections between African youth and African Americans. There are deep historical and social connections— just as there are connections in my own family. That trip renewed my hope in the future of the continent I love so much and have dedicated my life to serving.

This work has been personally transformative for me. I'm now in a doctoral program in African studies at Howard University. My research focuses on the critical role that women have played in transforming post-genocide Rwanda.

Beginning in my home growing up, and now as a young activist, I know the importance of contributions made by seasoned activists. I honor their contributions to struggles for equality and justice for poor and marginalized people. The past informs the present and learning from the past will strengthen and guide the new generation of advocates for Africa as we carry on the work.

# Afterword

What can we say now from our vantage point well into the first decade of the new millennium? Much of the news from Africa is not good. Even as old conflicts are resolved, and Africans take initiatives to promote democracy and development, new crises emerge. Leaders heralded as bringing fresh hope turn out to fit the same authoritarian mold as their predecessors. Global trends continue to tip the balance against fundamental change: as with colonialism and apartheid, the internal causes of Africa's current condition are deeply intertwined with outside forces.

On virtually every global issue, with the sole exception of nuclear proliferation, Africa and Africans endure a horrendously disproportionate share of the damage. Poverty, war, the global AIDS pandemic, climate change, and the polarizing effects of economic globalization—in every case, Africa is particularly vulnerable.

Africa stands to gain significantly from efforts to confront these issues that threaten all of us. But that requires both fundamental changes in the international order and particular attention to Africa's concerns.

The HIV/AIDS pandemic illustrates the challenge, and it also shows that movements linking activists in Africa and around the world can have an enormous impact. In the 1990s the increased use of antiretroviral drugs against AIDS in developed countries began saving millions of lives. But in Africa, with some 2 million people a year dying of AIDS, the international medical establishment and even African governments assumed that treating Africans was just not feasible. Africans with AIDS would be left to die.

Activists believed otherwise. Beginning with the AIDS conference in Durban, South Africa, in July 2000, they challenged that assumption. Unprecedented mobilization by South Africa's Treatment Action Campaign and its allies around the world won support for new treatment and prevention programs. The Global Fund to Fight AIDS, Tuberculosis, and Malaria pioneered an international model for finding resources and allocating funds. It involves not only donor and recipient governments but also civil society and those directly affected by the diseases.

AIDS and other diseases are still taking their deadly toll. Even now, only a fraction of the millions who need AIDS treatment are receiving it. African health services are still starved of resources and personnel. But the belief that nothing can be done has been refuted, and the campaign is continuing. AIDS activists, addressing a summit of African health ministers in South Africa in April 2007, called for the governments to live up to their promises. "We will not be silent," they admonished. "We will hold you accountable."

Among Africa's conflicts, Darfur, in western Sudan, shows both the potential for activist mobilization and the obstacles to achieving real goals—in this case stopping the killing and building a framework for peace. In 2004 the slaughter in that region moved suddenly onto the media radar screen. Activists across the political spectrum demanded that the world act. In 2005 President George W. Bush and the U.S. Congress applied the term "genocide," evoking the earlier failure of the world to respond to the genocide in Rwanda.

It soon became clear, however, that naming an evil had served not as a commitment to act but as an excuse for inaction. As this is written in mid-2007, the United States and the world are providing only token support for the small African Union peacekeeping mission in Darfur. Washington has failed to provide resources or engage in the diplomacy required for effective multilateral action. And neither governments nor international activists have linked the Darfur crisis to the internal Sudanese debate on how to bring democracy and peace to the entire country.

## New Africa, New Issues

AIDS and Darfur are only two of the complex issues facing Africa in the new millennium. The details of these issues are beyond the scope of this afterword and this book. But it is important to recognize both that Africa is changing and that many of the patterns of the past persist. Trends that show the potential for a new Africa are real, and there is vast diversity within the continent. The worn stereotypes of a monolithic continent beset by traditional conflicts and age-old poverty are even more misleading than before. But the impact of the hopeful trends is still limited.

There are persistent economic and political problems, but there are also structural changes under way that create new opportunities for African initiatives to address these problems. The African Union replaced the Organization of African Unity in 2001, strengthened by the participation of the new South Africa. African states have taken the initiative in working for peace in places such as Liberia, the Democratic Republic of the Congo, Burundi, and southern Sudan. But Africa's rulers often still opt for ineffective "quiet diplomacy" in response to abuses by their fellow leaders, as in Zimbabwe and Darfur. And international support for diplomacy and peacekeeping is most often too little and too late. Resolving Africa's conflicts, almost everyone agrees, requires both African and international action. But governments will not act unless the pressure to do so grows overwhelming.

In the U.S. debate on foreign policy, the "war on terrorism" and the Iraq war have pushed African interests to the margins, much as the Cold War did in earlier decades. U.S. military attention to Africa is increasing. Rather than providing support for African peacemaking efforts, however, it is dominated by a single-minded focus on anti-terrorism that echoes the earlier preoccupation with anticommunism. As this is written, a disastrous U.S.-backed intervention in Somalia by Ethiopian troops risks repeating the Iraq adventure, but it is barely noticed by the media or by most activists. Few dissenting voices are heard in Washington, either on Somalia or on increased U.S. military involvement on the continent—at least not yet.

The basic structures of African marginalization in the world economy remain in place. Most African countries continue to be producers of commodities, whether agricultural products or oil. The most substantial outside economic interest in Africa is in its oil, a sector notorious for deals between corrupt elites and foreign interests rather than long-term benefits for development. But Africa's economic prospects include more than products like oil and coffee. South Africa is among the middle-income countries taking a more active role in the world economy. South African companies are investing in almost every country in Africa, both competing with and collaborating with investors from other continents. And there are new dynamics touching even the most devastated countries. For example, Africa is the region with the fastest growth in the market for cell phones. More generally, African telecommunications and provision of Internet access are attracting both African and overseas investment.

These technical changes are enabling Africans to take greater advantage of global links. While Africa is still the least-connected continent, business, government, media, civil society, and ordinary citizens are rapidly adopting and adapting the new technologies. Instant communications link groups in different African countries to each other, as well as to the African diaspora, which extends to every continent.

African civil society has continued to gain strength and is demanding to be heard on national, continental, and global issues. Activist groups in Africa are campaigning not only against AIDS but also for women's rights and on many other issues, targeting the African Union as well as their own governments and outside powers. While groups still lack the collective clout to force decision makers to act, they are calling attention to problems, and the impact is continuing to grow.

Africa has attracted new attention from world leaders in recent years. British prime minister Tony Blair declared 2005 the "Year of Africa," and President Bush joined in new promises to increase aid, relieve debt, and accept fairer rules for international trade. A parade of celebrities trekked to Africa, and news magazines declared the continent trendy. Yet modest increases in official aid have fallen far short of the promises. Debt cancellation has made new resources available to some African countries, but it is still embedded in a complex process tightly controlled by the international financial institutions.

Many activist groups, such as those campaigning for debt cancellation and fair trade, do see their engagement as solidarity in a common struggle against systemic global inequality. Still, some of the best-publicized efforts rely on more simplistic appeals to charity, effectively marginalizing Africans in campaigns for Africa.

Even sympathetic journalists covering African crises, or activists themselves, often reinforce stereotypes of "tribal" conflicts and helpless victims.

## Activist Responses

The outside world cannot and will not solve Africa's problems. The progress of Africa still depends, as before, on changes within the continent and on initiatives by the continent's people. But it will also be affected by the extent to which activists on other continents pay attention to new African realities and work to challenge indifference, cynical self-interest, and paternalism in the arenas of global power.

The obstacles are enormous. Nonetheless, activist groups and networks have been at work behind the scenes, much as they were in the formative decades before the anti-apartheid convergence of the 1980s.

Organizations from that period continue their work, although there have been some changes. The American Committee on Africa/The Africa Fund merged in 2001 with the Washington-based Africa Policy Information Center to form Africa Action, under the leadership of Salih Booker. Led by Nii Akuetteh since 2006, the organization currently focuses on global health, debt cancellation, and Darfur. The Washington Office on Africa, headed by Mhizha Edmund Chifamba, works to sustain cooperation among church groups and others concerned with Africa in the Washington policy debate. TransAfrica Forum, under the leadership of Bill Fletcher and now Nicole Lee, continues to speak out on African issues while also working on Haiti and on other issues concerning the African diaspora in the Americas. The American Friends Service Committee's Africa program, led by Imani Countess, has widened the campaign to cancel Africa's debts and also works to build connections with a new generation of young American and African activists.

The long-established groups, however, are only part of the picture. They have been joined by a host of others working on African issues. These include small groups focused on the continent or on a specific African region or country, as well as issue-oriented groups that are finding Africa to be increasingly central to their missions. Groups and networks working on human rights, debt cancellation, trade, the environment, conflict resolution, landmines, small arms, and many other issues are increasingly linking to counterparts in Africa.

In contrast to the 1980s, when activist influence on African issues was at its height, there are presently no strong institutional allies in the U.S. Congress. Only a handful of individual representatives consistently focus on Africa. This lack of reinforcement from Congress significantly reduces the scope for activist influence on policy. Paradoxically, the proliferation of groups on Africa has resulted in many different messages, with no clear consensus on priority demands.

There are, in short, no easy victories in sight.

## Taking a Long View

Yet it would be a mistake to judge the current activism solely by its public visibility and immediate impact. Africa continues to draw in new activists and groups. In sheer numbers, there are probably more Americans becoming involved with African issues than ever before. A core of American AIDS activists has taken the lead in demanding attention to the pandemic in Africa. This issue has also engaged students, including many medical students, as well as many others with direct experience of AIDS in Africa, such as African immigrants and religious workers across the spectrum of theological views. The mobilization around Darfur has also energized large coalitions of religious groups and human rights activists. Like the AIDS activist networks, they span the traditional divisions between right and left.

Mass media coverage remains sporadic, even on high-profile crises such as these. But detailed information on African issues is increasingly available over the Internet. Equally important, a steadily increasing number of Americans have personal knowledge of and ties to the continent. They include a small but growing number of second-generation immigrants with roots on both sides of the Atlantic. A literature of Africa and African immigration is growing, providing readers with deeper understandings of African realities and

American connections. Examples include works by Dinaw Mengestu, Uzodinma Iweala, Chimamanda Ngozi Adichie, Ishmael Beah, and the collaboration between Valentino Achak Deng and Dave Eggers.

It is impossible to predict how, when, or even whether these forces might converge to make an impact comparable to that achieved by the anti-apartheid movement. The lessons of the past cannot be applied mechanically to address the grotesque global inequality that penalizes Africa disproportionately and that some of us have called "global apartheid."

Nevertheless, there are continuities. As before, outcomes will depend not only on formal organizations but also on small local groups of activists and on personal networks that link them to national campaigns, to each other, and to specific African countries. Likewise, sustained engagement will require activists to challenge injustice inside the United States as well as in Africa and the global arena.

The systematic inequality of today's world order, which condemns millions of people to grinding poverty and untimely death, is as unacceptable as slavery, colonialism, and apartheid. In their time, these earlier systems appeared to be unshakeable. Yet they eventually fell, overcome by generations of resistance that crossed national and continental boundaries. Today we envision another world, one in which Africa and Africans enjoy full and equal rights. Such an outcome seems neither imminent nor predictable. We are convinced, nevertheless, that a more just and peaceful future will come in part from human connections of solidarity being built today, connecting activists across continents. *A luta continua.*

# References

ACOA (American Committee on Africa). 1970. "Apartheid and Imperialism: A Study of U.S. Corporate Involvement in South Africa." Special issue, *Africa Today* 17, no. 5.

Adjali, Mia. 2004. Interview by Mimi Edmunds, New York, NY, April 8.

Anderson, David. 2005. *Histories of the Hanged: The Dirty War in Kenya and the End of Empire.* New York: Norton.

Anthony, David Henry III. 2005. *Max Yergan: Race Man, Internationalist, Cold Warrior.* New York: New York University Press.

Atkins, Keletso E. 1996. "The 'Black Atlantic Communication Network': African American Sailors and the Cape of Good Hope Connection." In "African [Diaspora] Studies," ed. Lisa Brock, special issue, *Issue: A Journal of Opinion* (African Studies Association) 24, no. 2: 23–26.

Augusto, Geri. 2005. Interview by Charles Cobb Jr., Providence, RI, January 26.

Barr, Stringfellow. 1950. *Let's Join the Human Race.* Pamphlet. Chicago: University of Chicago Press.

Barrett, Laurence I. 1984. *Gambling with History: Reagan in the White House.* New York: Penguin.

Beeman, Frank. 2003. Interview by David Wiley and Peter Limb, East Lansing, MI, December 12.

Belafonte, Harry. 2000. Speech on occasion of International Freedom Conductor Award to Archbishop Desmond Tutu, Cincinnati, Ohio, August 5.

———. 2002. Interview by Ruth van Gelder. *Yes! Magazine*, Spring.

———. 2004a. Interview by Tavis Smiley. National Public Radio, February 4.

———. 2004b. Speech, Howard University, Washington, DC, April 4.

Bond, Julian. 1981. "Keynote Address to Conference on Public Investment and South Africa." New York, June 12. Reprinted in *ACOA Action News* 10 (Fall).

Booker, Salih, and William Minter. 2001. "Global Apartheid." *The Nation*, July 9.

Borstelmann, Thomas. 2001. *The Cold War and the Color Line: American Race Relations in the Global Arena.* Cambridge, MA: Harvard University Press.

Branch, Taylor. 1988. *Parting the Waters: America in the King Years, 1954–63.* New York: Simon and Schuster.

Brath, Elombe. 1999. "The Ritualistic Slaughter of Amadou Diallo." *New York Daily Challenge*, February 16.

———. 2004. Interview by Walter Turner, New York, NY, December 3.

Brock, Lisa. 1998. "Black America's Contradictory Politics of Inclusion: 1898–1998." *Peace Review: A Transnational Quarterly* 10, no. 3: 357–62.

Browne, Robert S. 1965. "The Freedom Movement and the War in Vietnam." In *Freedomways Reader: Prophets in Their Own Country*, ed. Esther Cooper Jackson, 152–66. Boulder, CO: Westview. Previously published in *Freedomways*, no. 4.

———. 1978. "Tribute to Paul Robeson." In *Paul Robeson: The Great Forerunner*, ed. Freedomways, 267–68. New York: Dodd, Mead.

———. 1995. "The U.S. and Africa's Trade: Prospects for Partnership." Background paper, Africa Policy Information Center, Washington, DC.

———. 2003. Interview by William Minter, Teaneck, NJ, June 4.

Browne, Robert S., and Robert J. Cummings. 1984. *The Lagos Plan of Action vs. the Berg Report*. Lawrenceville, VA: Brunswick Publishing.

Burnham, Linda. 2005. Interview by Walter Turner, Oakland, CA, March 16.

Cabral, Amilcar. 1965. "Our Solidarities: An Interview with Amilcar Cabral, October 1965." In *The African Liberation Reader*, vol. 2, *The National Liberation Movements*, ed. Aquino de Bragança and Immanuel Wallerstein, 110–11. London: Zed.

———. 1973a. "Connecting the Struggles: An Informal Talk With Black Americans." In Cabral 1973b, 71–92.

———. 1973b. *Return to the Source: Selected Speeches of Amilcar Cabral*. Ed. Africa Information Service. New York: Africa Information Service and the African Party for the Independence of Guinea and the Cape Verde Islands. Reprint, New York: Monthly Review Press, 1974.

Carmichael, Stokely, and Ekwueme Michael Thelwell. 2003. *Ready for Revolution: The Life and Struggle of Stokely Carmichael (Kwame Ture)*. New York: Scribner.

Carson, Clayborne, ed. 2001. *The Autobiography of Martin Luther King, Jr.* New York: IPM/Warner Books. http://www.stanford.edu/group/King/publications/autobiography.

———. 1981. *In Struggle: SNCC and the Black Awakening of the 1960s*. Cambridge, MA: Harvard University Press.

Cobb, Charles Jr. 1981. Interview by Julius Scott. In "Stayed on Freedom," special issue, *Southern Exposure* 9, no. 1: 84–88.

Corporate Campaign. 2004. "ACTWU vs. J. P. Stevens, 1976–1980." http://www.corporatecampaign.org/stevens.htm.

Corporate Information Center, Office of the General Secretary, National Council of Churches. 1972. *Church Investments, Corporations and Southern Africa*. New York: Friendship Press.

Countess, Imani, Loretta Hobbs, Doug McAdam, William Minter, and Lucinda Williams. 1997. *Making Connections for Africa: Report from a Constituency Builders' Dialogue*. Washington, DC: Africa Policy Information Center.

Counts-Blakey, Cecelie. 1995. "The FSAM Story." In "That Covenant Was Kept: Lessons of the Anti-Apartheid Movement," special issue, *CrossRoads* 50 (April): 11–14.

Crutchfield, Nesbit. 2005. Interview by Walter Turner, Richmond, CA, February 6.

Culverson, Donald R. 1999. *Contesting Apartheid: U.S. Activism, 1960–1987*. Boulder, CO: Westview.

Davis, Jennifer. 1986. "The Funeral: 'A People Cannot Bid Farewell to Its Own History.'" *Southern Africa Report* (Toronto), December, 10–12.

———. 1989. *ACOA Action News* 27 (Fall).

———. 2004. Interview by William Minter, Washington, DC, December 12.

———. 2005. Interview by William Minter, Washington, DC, August 6.

Dayall, Susan. 2004. "Documentary History of Hampshire College." Hampshire College Archives, vol. 2, chap. 6. http://library.hampshire.edu/archives.

Dellums, Ronald V. 2000. *Lying Down with the Lions: A Public Life from the Streets of Oakland to the Halls of Power*. Boston: Beacon.

des Forges, Alison. 2003. Interview in "Ghosts of Rwanda." Frontline, Public Broadcasting System. http://www.pbs.org/wgbh/pages/frontline/shows/ghosts/interviews/desforges.html.

Dodson, Howard, and Sylviane Diouf, eds. 2004. *In Motion: The African-American Migration Experience.* Washington, DC: National Geographic.

Du Bois, W. E. B. 1935. *Black Reconstruction in America.* Reprint, New York: Free Press, 1999.

DuBose, Carolyn P. 1998. *The Untold Story of Charles Diggs: The Public Figure, the Private Man.* Arlington, VA: Barton.

Dunn-Mouton, Adwoa. 2004. Interview by Walter Turner, Washington, DC, July 27.

Elkins, Caroline. 2005. *Imperial Reckoning: The Untold Story of Britain's Gulag in Kenya.* New York: Henry Holt.

Fanon, Frantz. 1961. *The Wretched of the Earth.* Reprint, New York: Grove, 2004.

Fleshman, Michael. 2004. Interview by Walter Turner, New York, NY, July 28.

Gastrow, Claudia. 2005. "Struggling for Freedom: The Divestment Movement at the University of Illinois at Urbana-Champaign, 1977–1987." *Safundi: The Journal of South African and American Studies* 20 (October).

Geiger, Susan. 1997. *TANU Women: Gender and Culture in the Making of Tanganyikan Nationalism 1955–1965.* Portsmouth, NH: Heinemann.

Gitlin, Todd. 1987. *The Sixties: Years of Hope, Days of Rage.* New York: Bantam.

Goodman, David. 2002. *Fault Lines: Journeys into the New South Africa.* Rev. ed. Berkeley: University of California Press.

Gordon, April. 1998. "The New Diaspora: African Immigration to the United States." *Journal of Third World Studies* 15, no. 1: 79–103.

Gunther, John. 1955. *Inside Africa.* New York: Harper and Brothers.

Hansberry, Lorraine. 1960. *The Drinking Gourd.* Reprinted in *Les Blancs: The Collected Last Plays.* New York: Vintage, 1994.

Harrison, Mark. 1995. "Churches at the Forefront." In "That Covenant Was Kept: Lessons of the Anti-Apartheid Movement," special issue, *CrossRoads* 50 (April): 22–24.

Harvard African Students Alumni Network. 2005. "Philippe's Life." http://www.hasanweb.org/memphillipelife.asp.

Hill, Sylvia. 1995. "Free South Africa! Notes from My Diary." In "That Covenant Was Kept: Lessons of the Anti-Apartheid Movement," special issue, *CrossRoads* 50 (April): 14–18.

———. 2003. Interview by William Minter, Washington, DC, September 23.

———. 2004. Interview by William Minter, Washington, DC, August 12.

Hochschild, Adam. 1998. *King Leopold's Ghost: A Story of Greed, Terror, and Heroism in Colonial Africa.* Boston: Houghton Mifflin.

Hostetter, David L. 2004. "Movement Matters: American Antiapartheid Activism and the Rise of Multicultural Politics." PhD diss., University of Maryland, College Park.

Houser, George. 1954. Letter to "Dear Friends," aboard the *Capetown Castle*, October 1. American Committee on Africa Records, Northwestern University Library, Evanston, IL.

———. 1988. Unpublished handwritten manuscript for *No One Can Stop the Rain*. Photocopied pages not included in the final manuscript made available by George Houser.

———. 1989. *No One Can Stop the Rain.* New York: Pilgrim Press.

———. 2004. Interview by Lisa Brock, Pomona, NY, July 19.

Hovey, Gail. 1991. "South Africa: The More Things Change. . ." In *Ethics in the Present Tense: Readings from Christianity and Crisis, 1966–1991*, ed. Leon Howell and Vivian Lindermayer. New York: Friendship Press. Previously published in *Christianity & Crisis* 49, no. 13 (1989).

Hultman, Tamela. 2003. "Tamela Hultman." In *Journeys that Opened Up the World: Women, Student Christian Movements, and Social Justice, 1955–1975*, ed. Sara M. Evans, 140–56. New Brunswick, NJ: Rutgers University Press.

Hunton, Dorothy. 1986. *Alphaeus Hunton: The Unsung Valiant*. Richmond Hill, NY: D. K. Hunton.

Johnson, Charles Denton. 2004. "African Americans and South Africans: The Anti-Apartheid Movement in the United States, 1921–1955." PhD diss., Howard University, Washington, DC.

Johnson, Willard R. 1999. "Getting Over by Reaching Out: Lessons from the Divestment and Krugerrand Campaigns." *Black Scholar* 29, no. 1: 2–19.

———. 2005. Telephone interview by David Goodman, April 28–29.

Kamau, Njoki. 1996. "From Kenya to North America: One Woman's Journey." In "African [Diaspora] Studies," ed. Lisa Brock, special issue, *Issue: A Journal of Opinion* (African Studies Association) 24, no. 2: 40–42.

Kennedy, Pagan. 2002. *Black Livingstone*. New York: Viking.

King, Martin Luther Jr. 1967. "Beyond Vietnam: A Time to Break Silence." Address to Clergy and Laity Concerned, Riverside Church, New York, NY, April 4. http://www.americanrhetoric.com/speeches/mlkatimetobreaksilence.htm.

King, Mel. 2004. Telephone interview by David Goodman, April 26.

Kjeseth, Peter, and Solveig Kjeseth. 2005. Interview by Christopher Saunders, Cape Town, South Africa, April 2.

Knight, Richard. 2004. "Documenting the U.S. Solidarity Movement, with Reflections on the Sanctions and Divestment Campaigns." Paper presented at conference, "International Anti-Apartheid Movements in South Africa's Freedom Struggle: Lessons for Today," University of KwaZulu-Natal, Durban, South Africa, October 10–13. African Activist Archive. http://www.africanactivist.msu.edu/remembrance.php?id=8.

Kramer, Reed. 1995. "Liberia: A Casualty of the Cold War's End." Africa News Service, Durham, NC. http://allafrica.com/stories/200101090216.html.

———. 2005. Interview by William Minter, Washington, DC, July 29.

Kumalo, Dumisani. 2005a. Interview by David Goodman, New York, NY, January 31.

———. 2005b. Telephone interview by Gail Hovey, August 23.

Layton, Azza Sadama. 2000. *International Politics and Civil Rights Policies in the United States, 1941–1960*. Cambridge: Cambridge University Press.

Lenoir, Gerald. 2005. Interview by Walter Turner, Berkeley, CA, June 29.

Linebaugh, Peter, and Marcus Rediker. 2000. *Many-Headed Hydra: Sailors, Slaves, Commoners, and the Hidden History of the Revolutionary Atlantic*. Boston: Beacon.

Lockwood, Edgar. 2004. Telephone interview by David Goodman, November 16.

———. 2005. Telephone interview by David Goodman, April 25.

Logan, John R., and Glenn Deane. 2003. "Black Diversity in Metropolitan America." Lewis Mumford Center for Comparative Urban and Regional Research, State University of New York, Albany. http://mumford.albany.edu/census/report.html.

Love, Janice. 1985. *The U.S. Anti-Apartheid Movement*. New York: Praeger.

Lutz, Christine. 2001. "The Dizzy Steep to Heaven: The Hunton Family, 1850–1970." PhD diss., Georgia State University, Atlanta.

Magubane, Bernard Makhosezwe. 1979. *The Political Economy of Race and Class in South Africa*. New York: Monthly Review.

———. 1987. *The Ties that Bind: African-American Consciousness of Africa*. Trenton, NJ: Africa World Press.

———. 2004. Interview by William Minter, Pretoria, South Africa, March 15.

Makeba, Miriam, with James Hall. 1987. *Makeba: My Story*. New York: Plume.

Manghezi, Nadja. 1999. *O meu coração está nas mãos de um negro: Uma história da vida de Janet Mondlane*. Maputo: Centro de Estudos Africanos/Livraria Universitária.

Masekela, Hugh, and D. Michael Cheers. 2004. *Still Grazing: The Musical Journey of Hugh Masekela*. New York: Crown.

Massie, Robert K. 1997. *Loosing the Bonds: The United States and South Africa in the Apartheid Years*. New York: Doubleday.

McDougall, Gay. 2005. Interview by Adwoa Dunn-Mouton, Washington, DC, July.

Meisenhelder, Tom. 1993. "Amilcar Cabral's Theory of Class Suicide and Revolutionary Socialism." *Monthly Review* 45, no. 6: 40–49.

Meriwether, James H. 2002. *Proudly We Can Be Africans: Black Americans and Africa, 1935–1961*. Chapel Hill: University of North Carolina Press.

Minter, William. 1986. *King Solomon's Mines Revisited: Western Interests and the Burdened History of Southern Africa*. New York: Basic Books.

Mitchell, Charlene. 2004. Interview by Lisa Brock, New York, NY, July 18.

Monhollon, Rusty. 2002. *This Is America? The Sixties in Lawrence, Kansas*. New York: Palgrave.

Moore, Cornelius. 2004. Interview by Walter Turner, San Francisco, CA, August 12.

Nesbitt, Francis Njubi. 2004. *Race for Sanctions: African Americans Against Apartheid, 1946–1994*. Bloomington: Indiana University Press.

Nesbitt, Prexy. 1998. Interview by William Minter, Chicago, IL, October 31.

———. 2003. Interview by the Alston/Bannerman Fellowship Program, Baltimore.

Nkrumah, Kwame. 1949. *What I Mean by Positive Action*. Pamphlet. Reprinted in *Revolutionary Path*. London: Panaf Books, 2002.

Nujoma, Sam. 2004. Address to the Harlem Community, New York, NY, September 24. http://www.un.int/namibia/other24-9-04.html.

Nwaubani, Ebere. 2001. *The United States and Decolonization in West Africa, 1950–1960*. Rochester, NY: University of Rochester Press.

Okoth, Pontian Godfrey. 1987. "United States Foreign Policy Toward Kenya, 1952–1969." PhD diss., University of California, Los Angeles.

Paton, Alan. 1948. *Cry the Beloved Country*. New York: Charles Scribner's Sons.

Patterson, Mary Jane. 2003. Interview by William Minter, Washington, DC, September 11.

———. 2004. Interview by Mimi Edmunds, Washington, DC, April 10.

Phipps, William E. 2002. *William Sheppard*. Louisville, KY: Geneva Press.

Plummer, Brenda Gayle. 1996. *Rising Wind: Black Americans and U.S. Foreign Affairs, 1935–1960*. Chapel Hill: University of North Carolina Press.

Rattley, Sandra. 2004. Interview by Walter Turner, Washington, DC, July 27.

Reddy, E. S. 2004. Interview by Lisa Brock, New York, NY, July 20.

Richards, Yvette. 2000. *Maida Springer: Pan Africanist and International Labor Leader*. Pittsburgh: University of Pittsburgh Press.

Robinson, Leo. 2005. Interview by Walter Turner, Berkeley, CA, March 3.

Robinson, Randall. 1999. *Defending the Spirit: A Black Life in America*. New York: Plume.

Rodney, Walter. 1972. *How Europe Underdeveloped Africa*. Dar es Salaam: Tanzania Publishing House; London: Bogle L'Ouverture.

———. 1976. "The Lessons of Angola." Address at Howard University, Washington, DC, April 22. Typescript with handwritten corrections. Prexy Nesbitt Papers, Wisconsin State Historical Society, Madison.

Ruark, Robert. 1955. *Something of Value*. New York: Doubleday.

Rubin, Rachel. 1996. "The Anti-apartheid Struggle: Did It/Could It Challenge Racism in the U.S.?" In "African [Diaspora] Studies," ed. Lisa Brock, special issue, *Issue: A Journal of Opinion* (African Studies Association) 24, no. 2: 46–47.

Shary, Tim. 2004. "A History of Student Activities & Achievements at Hampshire College." Hampshire College Archives. http://library.hampshire.edu/archives/index.html.

Shepherd, George. 1956. Memorandum on Project Fund to Board of Trustees, June 14. American Committee on Africa Records, Northwestern University Library, Evanston, IL.

Simons, Jack, and Ray Simons. 1969. *Class and Colour in South Africa, 1850–1950*. Baltimore: Penguin.

Sisulu, Walter Max. 2001. *I Will Go Singing: Walter Sisulu Speaks of His Life and the Struggle for Freedom in South Africa. In conversation with George M. Houser and Herbert Shore*. Cape Town: Robben Island Museum; New York: The Africa Fund.

Smith, J. Clay Jr. 2000. "United States Foreign Policy and Goler Teal Butcher." In *Critical Race Feminism: An International Reader*, ed. Adrien Katherine Wing, 192–203. New York: New York University Press.

Soule, Sarah Anne. 1995. "The Student Anti-Apartheid Movement in the United States: Diffusion of Protest Tactics and Policy Reform." PhD diss., Cornell University, Ithaca, NY.

*Spotlight on Africa*. 1952–55. Volumes 11–14. Council on African Affairs, New York, NY.

Sutherland, Bill. 2003. Interview by Prexy Nesbitt and Mimi Edmunds, Brooklyn, NY, July 19.

Sutherland, Bill, and Matt Meyer. 2000. *Guns and Gandhi in Africa: Pan African Insights and Nonviolence and Liberation in Africa*. Trenton, NJ: Africa World Press.

TransAfrica. 1981. *TransAfrica News Report*, August.

Urdang, Stephanie. 1979. *Fighting Two Colonialisms: Women in Guinea-Bissau*. New York: Monthly Review Press.

———. 1989. *And Still They Dance: Women, War, and the Struggle for Change in Mozambique*. New York: Monthly Review Press.

Van Lierop, Robert, ed. 1977. *Samora Machel Speaks, Mozambique Speaks*. New York: Black Liberation Press.

———. 2004. Interview by William Minter, New York, NY, April 16.

Von Eschen, Penny M. 1997. *Race against Empire: Black Americans and Anticolonialism, 1937–1957.* Ithaca, NY: Cornell University Press.

Waller, Signe. 2002. *Love and Revolution: A Political Memoir: People's History of the Greensboro Massacre, Its Setting and Aftermath.* Lanham, MD: Rowman and Littlefield.

Walters, Angela. 1996. "How I Learned African History from Reggae." In "African [Diaspora] Studies," ed. Lisa Brock, special issue, *Issue: A Journal of Opinion* (African Studies Association) 24, no. 2: 43–45.

Wamba, Philippe. 1999. *Kinship: A Family's Journey in Africa and America.* New York: Dutton.

Waters, Cherri. 2003. Interview by William Minter, Baltimore, MD, November 6.

Wechsler, George. 1959. Memo to George Houser, March 7. American Committee on Africa Records, Northwestern University Library, Evanston, IL.

Weiss, Cora. 1958. Memo to George Houser, Frank Montero, John Morsell, and Maurice Moss, September 15. American Committee on Africa Records, Northwestern University Library, Evanston, IL.

———. 2003. Interview by William Minter, New York, NY, June 5.

———. 2005. Interview by Gail Hovey, New York, NY, June 22.

Weiss, Peter. 2003. Interview by William Minter, New York, NY, June 4.

Williams, Canon Fred. 2003. Testimonial, October 11, 2003, New York, NY.

# Contributors

**Lisa Brock** is chair of the Liberal Education Department and professor of history and cultural studies at Columbia College Chicago. She has worked with activist groups on Africa for more than two decades. She was an observer at the Angolan election in 1992 and the South African election in 1994, where she helped coordinate participation of observers from Chicago. Brock holds a PhD in history from Northwestern University. Her books include *Between Race and Empire: African Americans and Cubans Before the Cuban Revolution* (Temple University Press, 1998) and the forthcoming *Black in Two Americas: Comparative Identity, History and Struggle in Cuba and in the United States*. She is a member of the editorial collective of *Radical History Review* and co-editor of *Thirty Years of Radical History: The Long March* (Duke University Press, 2001).

**Charles Cobb Jr.** is senior writer and diplomatic correspondent for allAfrica.com. In the 1960s he was a field secretary for the Student Nonviolent Coordinating Committee in Mississippi. Cobb moved to Tanzania in 1970. On his return, he served as a staff member of the U.S. House of Representatives Subcommittee on Africa in 1973. A founding member of the National Association of Black Journalists, Cobb began his journalism career in 1974 as a Capitol Hill reporter for WHUR radio. He has freelanced for National Public Radio, and during 1985–96 he was a senior staff writer for *National Geographic* magazine. His two-part series on Eritrea for Africa News Service in 1995 won the Harry Chapin Award for best radio broadcasting about a developing nation. Cobb is co-author (with activist and educator Robert Moses) of *Radical Equations: Math, Literacy, and Civil Rights* (Beacon Press, 2001). His most recent work is *On the Road to Freedom: A Guided Tour of the Civil Rights Trail*, forthcoming in January 2008 from Algonquin Books.

**Marianna (Mimi) Edmunds** has been a broadcast journalist and assistant professor of documentary journalism at the University of Southern California. Her work as a documentary journalist includes three years as an associate producer with *CBS Reports*, 10 years producing for *60 Minutes* (1981–91), and five years directing and writing for the Discovery Network's Learning Channel (1992–97). Her production *The Fall of the Maya* won the Cable Ace award for best documentary series for 1992–93. She served as a writer, reporter, and producer for the PBS program *Arizona Illustrated*. Edmunds was a Peace Corps volunteer in Kenya in the 1960s and was involved with several activist groups working on Southern Africa in the 1970s. She was associate editor of *Africa Report* and worked on *Southern Africa* magazine in New York during 1973–78.

**David Goodman** began as an anti-apartheid activist at Harvard University in the late 1970s and has been traveling to and writing about Southern Africa for two decades. He was Southern Africa correspondent for *In These Times* in the mid-1980s and is the author of *Fault Lines: Journeys into the New South Africa* (University of California Press, 1999; revised edition, 2002). Goodman is currently a contributing writer for *Mother Jones*, and his articles have also appeared in the *Washington Post*, *Outside*, the *Christian Science Monitor*, *The Nation*, *Newsday*, and numerous other publications. He is co-author (with Amy Goodman) of the bestseller *The Exception to the Rulers: Exposing Oily Politicians, War Profiteers, and the Media that Love Them* (Hyperion, 2004).

**Gail Hovey** was one of the founders of *Southern Africa* magazine in 1964 and continued as one of its editors until 1975. During that period she spent two years in South Africa, 1966–67. She has served as research director for the American Committee on Africa/The Africa Fund, managing editor of *Christianity and Crisis*, and executive director of Grassroots International. Her publications include *If You Want to Know Me: A New Collection of Poetry, Art and Photographs from Southern Africa* (with Peggy L. Halsey and Melba Smith, Friendship Press, 1976) and *Namibia's Stolen Wealth: North African Investment and South African Occupation* (The Africa Fund, 1982). She was an official observer for the 1994 South African elections.

Living in Hawai'i for 15 years, Hovey worked primarily with Native Hawaiian groups, helping to bring resources to community organizations. In 2006 she moved back to New York and continues to work as an editor and writer.

**Joseph F. Jordan** is director of the Sonja Haynes Stone Center for Black Culture and History at the University of North Carolina at Chapel Hill. He was previously head of the Auburn Avenue Research Library on African American Culture and History in Atlanta and a senior research analyst on Africa for the Library of Congress. Jordan has also taught at Xavier University of Louisiana and at Antioch College. He received his doctorate in African studies from Howard University in 1983. Jordan edited a special issue of *CrossRoads* magazine, "That Covenant Was Kept: Lessons of the U.S. Anti-Apartheid Movement," in 1995. As co-chair of the Southern Africa Support Project in Washington, DC, Jordan helped organize Nelson Mandela's first visit to the United States. He is curator of the widely acclaimed exhibit in Atlanta, "Without Sanctuary: Lynching Photography in America."

**William Minter** is the editor of *AfricaFocus Bulletin*, an independent e-mail and Web publication on current African issues (http://www.africafocus.org). He studied at the University of Ibadan in Nigeria in 1961–62 and taught in Tanzania and Mozambique at the Frelimo secondary school in 1966–68 and 1974–76. He holds a PhD in sociology and a certificate in African studies from the University of Wisconsin at Madison. A writer, researcher, and activist, he has worked with Africa News Service, the Washington Office on Africa, the Africa Policy Information Center, and Africa Action, among other organizations. Minter's books include *Portuguese Africa and the West* (Penguin Books, 1972); *Imperial Brain Trust* (with Laurence Shoup, Monthly Review Press, 1977); *King Solomon's Mines Revisited: Western Interests and the Burdened History of Southern Africa* (Basic Books, 1986); *Operation Timber: Pages from the Savimbi Dossier* (Africa World Press, 1988); and *Apartheid's Contras: An Inquiry into the Roots of War in Angola and Mozambique* (Zed Books, 1994). He is co-author, with Sylvia Hill, of "Anti-Apartheid Solidarity in U.S.-South African Relations: From the Margins to the Mainstream," in volume 3 of *The Road to Democracy in South Africa*, forthcoming from the South African Democracy Education Trust.

**Walter Turner** is a professor of contemporary African politics and chair of the Social Sciences Department in the Marin Community College District in Kentfield, California. He is president of the board of directors of Global Exchange, a San Francisco–based human rights organization, and was formerly the director of the Africa Resource Center in Oakland, California. Turner is host and producer of the weekly KPFA/Pacifica radio program *Africa Today*. As a journalist, he has traveled throughout the African continent, visiting and reporting from South Africa, Mozambique, and Nigeria. He is a co-author of *Oil for Nothing*, a report on multinational corporations and their impact on Nigerian society and environment (Global Exchange and Essential Action, 2000).

# Index

Bacquie, Aleah 49, 202

Bagamoyo, Tanzania 86

Baker, Ella 4, 59, 173

Baldwin, Roger 63

Baltimore, MD 42, 115

Bambatha Rebellion 90

Bandung Conference 61

Baptist Church 4, 41, 49, 60, 63, 122, 131, 161

Baraka, Amiri 32

Barnard College 111

Barnett, Don 188

Barr, Stringfellow 15, 79

*Battle of Algiers* 118, 188

Bay Area 52, 54, 90, 166, 182, 183, 187–189, 191, 198, 200, 219

Beal, Fran 187

Beeman, Frank and Patricia 115, 117, 128, 147–150, 159

Belafonte, Harry 26, 44–46, 60, 65, 98, 99, 101, 107, 222

Benjamin, Medea 191

Berkeley, CA 32, 83, 182–184, 188–190, 195, 218

Berry, Mary Frances 160

Bethany Presbyterian Church 85, 86

Bgoya, Walter 103–106

Biafra 196

Biko, Steven 9, 36, 120, 134, 199

Bill, Molly and François 201

Birmingham, AL 33, 36

Black Consciousness Movement 36, 41, 117, 120, 135

black nationalism 2, 6, 24, 27, 31, 32, 35, 60, 87, 114, 118, 120, 123, 199, 200

Black Panthers 87, 91, 114, 125, 188

Black Power 2, 32, 77, 102, 114, 123, 125, 153, 188

Boehm, Robert (Bob) 48

Boesak, Allan 44

Bogues, Anthony xii

Bok, Derek 116, 151

Bolling, Bruce 156

Bomani, Paul 31, 167

Bond, Julian 42, 84, 99, 175, 176

Booker, Salih 58, 220, 227

Booth, William 80, 170

Bophuthatswana, South Africa 45

Borinski, Ernst 94

Borstelmann, Thomas 14, 17

Boston Coalition for the Liberation of Southern Africa (BCLSA) 153, 154

Boston, MA 25, 26, 45, 68, 115, 124, 129, 152–156, 184, 196, 205–207, 216

Botswana 39, 162, 164

Boykins-Towns, Karen 53

Brand, Dollar (Abdullah Ibrahim) 26, 153

Brandon, Ruth 34

Brath, Elombe 194, 198–200

Briggs, John Bomba 222

Brock, Lisa 4, 12, 16, 59, 61, 144, 179, 209, 236

Bronx, NY 3, 199

Brooklyn, NY 158

Brooks, Angie 79

Brown, Elaine 205

Brown, Irene 92

Brown, Ted 125

Browne, Robert 48, 58, 77, 78, 169, 170

Brutus, Dennis 45, 46, 59, 170

Bullard, Perry 148

Bunche, Ralph 61, 69

Burnham, Linda 187, 191, 200

Bush, George W. 4, 50, 51, 132, 155, 193, 219, 225, 226

Butcher, Goler Teal 32, 131–133

Buthelezi, Gatsha 171, 202

Byrd Amendment 34, 163

Byrd, A. C. 192

## C

Cabo Delgado, Mozambique 171

Cabral, Amilcar i, viii, x, 9, 14, 27–29, 81, 93, 108, 117–119, 143

Cachalia, Yusuf 63, 64, 117

California 26, 28, 32, 43, 62, 83, 84, 87, 89, 131, 182–185, 187–189, 191, 195–197, 214, 218

California Newsreel 189, 195

Cambridge, MA 32, 115, 153, 208

Canaan Baptist Church 41, 161

Canada 25, 35, 56, 116, 126, 188, 202, 215

Cape Verde x, 10, 27, 28, 118, 119, 125, 213

Caribbean 11, 34, 41, 60, 126, 128, 213, 167, 192, 205

Carlson, Joel 80

Carmichael, Stokely (Kwame Ture) 26, 102, 107, 109, 125

Carpenter, George 63

Carstens, Ken 26, 110

Carter, Jimmy 35, 37, 132, 163, 175

Casey, William 38

Catalyst Project 37

Center for Black Education 9, 25, 31, 114

Center for Democratic Renewal xii

Champaign, IL 77, 91

Chaney, James 24

Chase Manhattan Bank 24, 28, 30, 110, 162

Checole, Kassahun xiii

Chemjor, Joseph 83

Chepterit, Kenya 85

Chester, William Bill 182

Chevron 196

Chicago, IL 2–4, 6, 10, 11, 19, 31, 39, 45, 47, 59, 61, 62, 68, 70, 77, 78, 87, 91–93, 95, 110, 115, 125, 143, 144, 177, 179, 180

Chicago Committee for the Liberation of Angola, Mozambique, and Guinea-Bissau 91

Chicago Committee in Solidarity with Southern Africa (CCISSA) 179

Chifamba, Mhizha Edmund 227

Chigo, Disco 187

Chikane, Frank 202

China 35, 47, 62, 104

Chipenda, José 135

Chisholm, Shirley 173

CIA (Central Intelligence Agency) 22, 24, 35, 38, 47, 66, 69, 104, 120, 135, 139

Cillie Commission 120

Cincinnati, OH 167, 216

Clark, Dick 161, 176

Clergy and Laity Concerned 37, 115, 123, 175

Cleveland, Roy and LeNoir 110

Clinton, Bill 50, 56, 193, 196

Clunie, Basil 174

Coalition for Illinois Divestment in South Africa (CIDSA) 179

Coalition of Black Trade Unionists (CBTU) 125, 183, 192

Cobb, Charles Jr. (Charlie) 9, 31, 77, 98, 100, 102, 105, 129, 135, 137, 236

Cobb, Charles Sr. 135

Cohen, Herman 171

Cold War 12–17, 24, 47, 55, 59–61, 66, 68, 74, 78, 84, 104, 115, 117, 119, 193, 194, 213, 226

Columbia University 93, 110

Columbus, OH 85, 86, 119

Committee to Oppose Bank Loans to South Africa 37, 93, 123

Communist Party (South Africa) 71, 170, 187, 189

Communist Party (USA) 16, 17, 61, 69–71, 91, 187, 189

Conakry, Guinea 26, 73

Congo (Zaire) 22, 24, 47, 52, 55, 69, 70, 84, 100, 110, 139, 165, 193, 194, 197, 200, 205–208, 226

Congregational Church 10, 35, 67, 91, 173

Congress of Racial Equality (CORE) 10, 16, 18, 62–64, 68, 83, 110, 114, 120, 125, 139

Congress of South African Trade Unions (COSATU) 187

Congressional Black Caucus (CBC) 26, 32, 34, 42, 43, 51, 56, 126, 128, 131, 137, 155, 184, 198

Connecticut 11, 43, 88, 90, 94, 175

Connell, Dan 48

Conyers, John 32, 147, 184

Cooks, Carlos 199

Cooper, Dara 6–7

Cooper, Monet 220

Cornell University 28

Corporate Information Center. *See* Interfaith Center on Corporate Responsibility

Council on African Affairs (CAA) 16, 17, 19, 60–62, 66, 67, 73, 74

Countess, Imani xii, 56, 193, 227

Counts, Cecelie (Cecelie Counts-Blakey) 12, 159–161, 192

Cox, Courtland 31, 105

Crain, Sadie 91, 93

Crane, Hank 110

Crocker, Chester 37, 38

Crofts, Marylee xii, 147

Crossland, Mills 137

Crutchfield, Nesbit 187–190, 200

Cuba ix, 4, 6, 35, 38, 47, 102, 104, 107, 139, 188, 191

Culverson, Donald 14, 122

Cummings, Robert 78

# D

Dadoo, Yusuf 70

Dakar, Senegal 220, 221

Danaher, Kevin 191

Dar es Salaam, Tanzania 9, 10, 31, 34, 71, 81, 91–93, 103–106, 130, 135, 140, 163, 167, 205

Darfur, Sudan 58, 225–227

Daughtry, Herbert 158

Davidson, Basil 27

Davis, Angela 71

Davis, Attieno 125

Davis, Ben 70

Davis, Jennifer 38, 41, 58, 70, 80, 112, 153, 155, 157, 161, 165, 166, 169, 170, 172, 202–204

Davis, Mike 169

Davis, Ossie 98

Day, Warren (Bud) 147, 162

De Klerk, F. W. 51, 165

De Rivera, Margaret xii

Deak Perera 156

Defiance Campaign 15, 16, 18, 62, 63, 68, 74, 88

Dellinger, David (Dave) 67, 68

Dellums, Ronald (Ron) 32, 131, 184, 185, 192

Derman, Bill 147

Des Forges, Alison 54, 55

Detroit, MI 26, 32, 115, 126, 131, 132, 140, 147, 148

Diallo, Amadou 199

Diggs, Charles Jr. 20, 21, 26, 28, 32, 126, 128, 131–133, 147, 184

DiGia, Ralph 68

Dillon, Hari 189

Dinkins, David 165

Diouf, Sylvianne 213

divestment 14, 36, 37, 41–45, 49–51, 115, 120–123, 135, 147, 150, 152–157, 163, 170, 179, 182, 191, 197, 206, 218

Doe, Samuel 47, 194

Douglass, Frederick 73, 87

Drake, St. Clair 59

Drum and Spear 25, 31, 105

Kidane, Nunu 125, 183, 218–219

King, Annie 42

King, Coretta 69

King, Edward 154

King, Martin Luther Jr. 9, 12, 13, 17, 19, 22, 24, 37, 41, 64, 69, 87, 90, 98, 109, 136, 149, 162, 209

King, Mel 153, 155, 156, 166

Kirobi, Mary 86

Kitange, Seth 137

Kjeseth, Solveig and Peter 177–178

Klein, Beate 157

Knight, Deborah xii

Knight, Richard xii, 30, 53, 121, 156, 165, 176

Koppel, Ted 43

KPFA 189, 194, 227

KPFK 194

Kramer, Reed 34, 58, 134–138, 194

Krugerrand 152, 156

Ku Klux Klan 85, 101, 103

Kumalo, Dumisani 41, 45, 48, 153, 154, 157–159, 161, 166, 169, 171, 202, 203

Kunene, Mazizi 88

Kuper, Leo 26, 88

KwaZulu 53, 202–204


**L**

Lagos, Nigeria 25

Lake, Anthony 54

Lambert, Rollins xiii

Landis, Betsy xii, 202

Lapchick, Richard 45

Lawrence, Ken 33, 116

Lawson, James 22

Lawson, Jennifer 105

Lawyers' Committee for Civil Rights Under Law 25, 44, 50, 132, 202

Lee, Canada 63

Lee, Jim 137

Lee, Nicole 227

Lee, Spike 51

Legassick, Martin 26, 89

LeMelle, Tilden 46

Lenoir, Gerald 54, 187, 200

Lesotho 162

Lester, Julius 102

Levin, Carl 40

Lewis, John 99

Lewis, Keith 2–3

Lewis, Ray 28

Lewis, Ron 192

Liberia 3, 47, 55, 79, 131, 188, 193, 194, 197–200, 216, 226

Limb, Peter 149

Lincoln University 19, 28, 69

Little Steven 46

Lockwood, Edgar (Ted) 39, 87, 153, 162–164, 166, 173, 174

Logan, Rayford 63

Logan, Willis 42

London, England 50, 62, 64, 68, 70, 71, 77, 78, 107, 143, 196

Los Angeles, CA 24, 70, 88–90, 107, 109, 147, 193, 205, 216

Louisiana 100, 115, 116

Louisville, KY 33

Love, Jan 14

Lowery, Joseph 192

Luanda, Angola 47, 139

Lubowski, Anton 166

Lucy, William 192

Lumumba, Patrice 9, 22, 24, 45, 69, 100, 117, 129, 200

Lusaka Manifesto 105

Lusaka, Zambia 23, 72, 90, 105, 135, 163

Lutheran Church 30, 44, 45, 172, 177, 178

Luthuli, Albert 42, 64, 90, 117

Luthuli-Gcabashe, Thandi 42

**M**

Mabuza, Lindiwe 51

Machel, Graça 172

Machel, Samora 9, 31, 34, 103, 143, 172, 200

Macmillan, Harold 22, 95

Madison, WI 28, 79, 147

Magubane, Bernard (Ben) 26, 58, 84, 88–90, 97

Makatini, Johnny 29, 38, 88, 117

Makeba, Miriam 26, 48, 99, 107–109

Makhuba, Mbuyisa 36

Malcolm X 9, 20, 21, 31, 85, 90, 92, 126, 142, 188, 222

Mandela, Nelson 4, 9, 11, 13, 24, 26, 45, 48, 49, 51–53, 55, 89, 99, 109, 117, 135, 150, 167–169, 183, 190, 191, 193, 195, 201, 203, 204, 211

Mandela, Winnie 38, 52, 191

Manica, Mozambique 179

Mansfield, Haaheo xii

Maputo, Mozambique 30, 37, 47, 164, 172

Marcum, John 65

Marley, Bob 153, 210–212

Marshall, Thurgood 59, 193

Maryland 83, 100, 214

Masekela, Hugh 26, 99, 107, 108, 222

Mashalaba, Vuye 134

Massachusetts 32, 36, 42, 43, 80, 100, 115, 124, 129, 153–156, 162, 213

MassDivest 154

Massie, Robert 14, 154

Matthews, Z. K. 18, 19, 63, 64, 117

Mau Mau 19, 64, 99, 100, 129, 188

Mbeki, Thabo 117

Mboya, Tom 19, 64–66, 80, 99, 117

McBride, Andrew xiii

McCarthy, Joseph 68

McCutcheon, Aubrey 39, 174

New York 43, 62, 73, 214

New York, NY i, 9, 11, 16, 17, 19, 20, 25–29, 31, 34, 38, 41, 43, 45, 48, 57, 60, 62, 64, 65, 68, 74, 77–80, 87, 93–96, 98, 107, 108, 110, 112, 115, 117, 123, 127, 135, 142, 152, 157, 158, 163, 165, 169, 170, 173, 175, 194, 197–199, 201, 213

New Zealand 28, 45

Newark, NJ 32, 67, 68

Newcomb, Eliot 66

Newport, Gus 182

Ngubo, Anthony 26

Nguyen, Huoi 48

Niassa, Mozambique 143

Nigeria 24, 25, 57, 60, 67, 79, 175, 188, 196–200, 215

Nixon, Richard 22–24, 30, 66, 69, 126, 131, 132, 175

Nkrumah, Kwame 19, 24, 26–28, 65, 69, 70, 80, 91, 108, 117, 129, 135

Nkundwa, Jean-Claude 222

Nkwinti, Gugile 53

Nokwe, Duma 163

Norfolk State University 113

Norfolk, VA 32, 113

North Carolina 26, 31, 34, 42, 90, 112, 126, 127, 134–138, 176

Northwestern University 19, 45, 59, 91, 144–146

Norton, Eleanor Holmes xiii

Ntarama, Rwanda 54

Nteta, Chris 26, 115, 116

Ntlabati, Gladstone 26, 90

Nujoma, Sam 25, 117, 165, 199

Nyerere, Julius 10, 17, 27, 31, 92, 104, 105, 108, 117, 129, 130, 167

Nzima, Sam 36, 121

## O

Oakland, CA 83, 159, 184, 187–189, 198

Obani-Nwibari, Noble 198

Obasanjo, Olusegun 198

Oberlin College 19, 22, 97

Odinga, Oginga 101

Offutt, Walter 64

Ogoni 57, 196, 198

Ohio 6, 18, 22, 42, 62, 67, 85, 86, 91, 113, 114, 117, 119, 121

Ohio State University (OSU) 6, 85, 113, 117, 119, 121

Okorodudu, Tunde 198

Olagbaju, Folabi 197

Oram, Harold 66

Organization of African Unity (OAU) 28, 31, 44, 67, 75, 104, 105, 226

Oshikati, Namibia 172

Oturu, Assumpta 194

*Our Choking Times* 113, 121

## P

Pacifica 189, 198

Padmore, George 68

PAIGC (African Party for the Independence of Guinea-Bissau and Cape Verde) 27, 87, 112, 118, 119, 139

Pan African Treatment Access Movement (PATAM) 6

Pan Africanist Congress (PAC) 26, 41, 88, 90, 116, 120, 128, 167

Pan-Africanism 2, 31, 53, 67–69, 91, 105, 106, 116, 120, 126, 128, 129, 167, 187, 192, 198, 199, 205, 206, 212, 215, 222

Parker, Jackie 40

Parker, Neville 105

Paton, Alan 63, 88

Patterson, Mary Jane 84–87, 97, 167

Payton, John 192

Peace Corps 13, 15, 29, 79, 84, 85, 87, 98, 99

Pennsylvania 19, 28, 195

Phelps Stokes Fund 20

Philadelphia, PA 34, 41, 115, 195

Phillips, James Madhlope 189, 190

Pieterson, Hector 36, 121

Pittsburgh, PA 45, 100

Plummer, Brenda Gayle 14

Poitier, Sidney 59, 64, 65, 98, 107

Polaroid Corporation 32, 115, 153, 184

Polley, Erin 4–5

Popular Movement for the Liberation of Angola (MPLA) 35, 47, 67, 87, 116, 118–120, 139–141

Portugal 27, 28, 32, 47, 117, 119, 132, 136, 143

Powell, Adam Clayton Jr. 64, 69

Powell, Colin 199

Presbyterian Church 85–87, 122, 142

Pretoria, South Africa 37, 38, 157

Princeton University 28, 110

Priority Africa Network (PAN) 219

## R

Randall, Tony 44

Randolph, A. Philip 69, 125, 184

Ranger, Terence (Terry) 92

Rattley, Sandra 191, 192, 200

Reagan, Ronald 13, 35, 37–39, 41, 45, 47, 87, 159, 184, 185, 192, 193, 206

Rebelo, Jorge 93

Reddy, E. S. 16, 17, 74–76

Reformed Church 44

Reggae 209–212

Reggy, Anyango 222–223

Reid, Harry 159

Reinhard, Rick v, xii, xiii, xviii, 12, 40, 49–51, 157, 160, 161, 185, 193

Renamo (Mozambican National Resistance) 37, 38, 46, 47

Resha, Robert 76

Reuther, Walter 65

Rhodesia. *See* Zimbabwe

Ribeira, Mario 112

Richardson, Judy 31

Rivonia Trial 193

Roberto, Holden 120

Robeson, Eslanda (Essie) 59, 69, 70

Robeson, Paul 12, 15, 16, 18, 45, 59, 60, 73, 74, 77, 91, 98, 191

Robinson, Cleveland 152

Robinson, Jackie 20, 64, 65

Robinson, Leo 182–184, 200

Robinson, Randall 34, 39, 40, 44, 52, 115, 128, 153, 155, 157, 159–161, 192

Rodney, Walter 105, 139–141

Rogers, Ray 157, 158

Rogosin, Lionel 107

Rooks, Belvie 189

Roosevelt, Eleanor 17

Roosevelt, Franklin 12

Root, Chris xii, 30

Rosenberg, Ethel and Julius 70

Ross, Hazel 192

Ruark, Robert 19

Rubin, Rachel 80, 171, 179

Rustin, Bayard 18, 62, 68

Rwanda x, 3, 13, 49, 54, 55, 99, 188, 193, 194, 196, 223, 225

# S

Sachs, Albie 4

Sadaukai, Owusu (Howard Fuller) 31, 126

Sampson, Edith 61

Samuel Rubin Foundation xii

San Francisco State University 187

San Francisco, CA 31, 114, 118, 125, 182, 183, 187–189, 200

Saro-Wiwa, Ken 57, 196, 198

Sarrazin, Chantal 188

Satterfield, John 94

Saunders, Christopher 177

Saverance, Sam xiii

Savimbi, Jonas 35, 47, 120, 161, 194

Savio, Mario 83, 90

Schechter, Danny 45

Scheinman, Bill 65

Schmidt, Betsy xiii

Schomburg Center for Research in Black Culture 213

Schultheis, Michael 162

Schwerner, Mickey 24

Scott, Julius 100

Seattle, WA 14, 42, 56, 58, 188, 200, 221

Selma, AL 23, 36, 162

Sembène, Ousmane 195

Senegal 3, 195, 199, 215, 220

Shakur, Assata 2, 6, 7

Shannon, Margaret 86

Shared Interest 38, 52

Sharp, Monroe 105

Sharpeville, South Africa 22, 24, 25, 46, 48, 88, 100, 107, 110, 129

Shaw University 90

Shearin, Morris 49

Shejavali, Abisai and Selma 177–178

Shell 6, 196–198

Shepherd, George 64

Sheppard, William 110

Shivji, Issa 103

Shoemaker, Chestivia 192

Shore, Herbert 15

Shriver, Eunice Kennedy 22

Shub, Ellen 36, 154, 156

Sibeko, David 26

Sierakowski, Stan 127, 158

Sierra Leone 194, 199

Simmons, Adele 80

Simons, Jack 90

Sindab, Jean 39, 41, 87, 163, 173–174

Sisulu, Albertina 15, 193

Sisulu, Walter 15, 16, 63, 64, 89, 117, 193

Sithole, Ndabaningi 35

Sixth Pan-African Congress (Six PAC) 106, 128, 167

Skinner, Richard 143

Smith, Damu 39, 40, 50, 87, 174, 184

Smith, Ian 35, 111

Smith, Tim 122, 158

Smith, Virgil 148

Somalia 55, 99, 188, 193, 194, 226

Somerville, Katherine 137

Sonn, Franklin and Joan 192

South Africa 3, 4, 6, 9–19, 22, 24–30, 32, 34–39, 41, 43–53, 55, 60, 62–64, 66, 71–76, 80, 84, 87–90, 93, 104, 107–111, 113–115, 117, 119–125, 132, 134–136, 139, 142, 143, 147–149, 151–163, 165–170, 172, 175–179, 182–185, 187–191, 194–196, 198, 200–202, 204, 206, 207, 211, 214, 218, 220, 222, 223, 225, 226

South African Indian Congress 61, 63, 117

South African Council of Churches 202–204

South African Institute of Race Relations 63

South African Nonracial Olympic Committee 45

South African Research and Archival Project 132

South African Students Organization (SASO) 134

South West Africa People's Organisation (SWAPO) 25, 29, 38, 41,